The Language of the Eyes

SUNY series in Feminist Criticism and Theory

Michelle A. Massé, editor

The Language of the Eyes

Science, Sexuality, and Female Vision in English Literature and Culture, 1690–1927

Daryl Ogden

State University of New York Press

Published by
State University of New York Press, Albany

Printed in the United States of America

For information, address State University of New York Press,
194 Washington Avenue, Suite 305, Albany, NY 12210-2384

Production by Marilyn P. Semerad
Marketing by Michael Campochiaro

Library of Congress Cataloging-in-Publication Data

Ogden, Daryl, 1965–
The language of the eyes : science, sexuality, and female vision in English literature and culture, 1690–1927 / Daryl Ogden.
p. cm — (SUNY series in feminist criticism and theory)
Includes bibliographical references and index.
ISBN 0-7914-6499-7 (alk. paper) — ISBN 0-7914-6500-4 (pbk. : alk. paper)
1. English literature—History and criticism. 2. Eye in literature. 3. Feminism and literature—Great Britain. 4. Literature and science—Great Britain. 5. Women and literature—Great Britain. 6. Visual perception in literature. 7. Sex role in literature. 8. Vision in literature. 9. Sex in literature. I. Title. II. Series.

PR408.E94O36 2005
820.9'3561—dc22

2004018789

10 9 8 7 6 5 4 3 2 1

This book is dedicated to Zoë and Benjamin,
who taught me how to see.

Contents

Illustrations

Acknowledgments

This book traces its origins to a short paper on voyeurism in Thomas Hardy's *Far from the Madding Crowd*, written for Joe Butwin's graduate seminar on the English 1870s at the University of Washington. The nascent ideas explored in that first essay subsequently grew into a seminar paper, a master's thesis, a dissertation, and, finally, this book. It would be difficult to acknowledge sufficiently the guidance, encouragement, and support that I received from my advisors, colleagues, family, and friends over the course of that multiyear metamorphosis.

In particular, I owe a tremendous debt of gratitude to the members of my dissertation committee at the University of Washington, who made this book possible. The talent, generosity, and collegiality of those individuals were gifts that I probably did not deserve but am thankful for nonetheless. Each committee member brought unique strengths and insights to the book and provided invaluable commentary on multiple drafts long after their committee responsibilities were past. As committee chair, Kathleen Blake provided an ideal combination of structure and freedom, allowing me the latitude to arrive at my own hypotheses and conclusions while providing sharp, on the mark comments from start to finish. Joe Butwin's astonishing knowledge of English cultural and literary history added a rich dimension to the book. Evan Watkins taught me how to think theoretically and to deploy theory in what I hope is a responsible and provocative way. And finally, Robert Markley inspired me to integrate scientific discourse more fully and to reach further back in English cultural history than I might otherwise have done. The particular methodology of this book owes more to Bob than perhaps to anyone else. At Washington, I was lucky to be part of Hazard Adams' faculty and graduate student colloquium in literary theory, where I had the opportunity to meet Teresa de Lauretis, whose work on film theory and female spectatorship became an important intellectual foundation.

While at Washington, I was surrounded by a wonderful group of fellow graduate students who helped make me a better critic. These include Suzy Anger, Kirk Branch, Dean Ferguson, Robin Kelson, Michelle Kendrick,

Desiree Hellegers, Kiki McMillan, David Moore, Dana Schiller, Jack Stewart, and in particular, Bill Christmas. Subsequent to our time together at Washington, Bill has proven to be an exceptional reader of my work, has corrected many of my errors, and has been my primary tutor in eighteenth-century literature and culture. Rebecca Merrens read this book, many times, from beginning to end. Not only did she dissuade me from proposing a disastrous title, she taught me how to read literary and cultural texts with respect, precision, and creativity.

In addition to the people of the University of Washington, I am indebted to the UW graduate school, which provided the Pembroke College dissertation fellowship, making possible two wonderful years at Cambridge University. At Cambridge, I was fortunate to work with Gillian Beer, who provided several helpful suggestions for deepening my research into areas of nineteenth-century science and philosophy that made this a better book. I also had the great good fortune to share work with Pembroke Fellow Mark Wormald, who serendipitously (for me) arrived in Cambridge the same year that I did. Now Senior Tutor of the college, Mark was (and is) a terrific reader of my work, and I am lucky to have forged such a close friendship with him. I am further thankful to Colin Wilcockson, longtime director of English studies at Pembroke, who did much to create an extremely supportive and collegial environment in the college and who helped to find me teaching at Cambridge during my second year. I learned much about historical methodology from three of my peers at Pembroke, Kathleen Quirk, James Cannon, and Fran Rosenfeld, all of whom were exceptional colleagues and friends.

The present shape of this book owes a great deal to my time in the School of Literature, Communication, and Culture at the Georgia Institute of Technology. I joined the faculty there at a particularly rich time in the life of the institute, as we were in the process of creating major and minor programs in the cultural studies of science and technology. The opportunity I had to be part of that moment played an important part in the composition of this book. In particular, I am grateful to Alan Rauch, Ken Knoespel, Richard Grusin, Sandra Corse, Terry Harpold, Kavita Philip, Paul Young, Blake Leland, Hugh Crawford, Phil Auslander, Larry Rubin, Carol Senf, Bob Wood, Andy McMurry, Alex Reid, and Tabitha Sparks for helping to create such a rich and dynamic intellectual environment at Georgia Tech. Special thanks go to my terrific colleague and collaborator Greg VanHoosier-Carey, who was a patient and careful reader of my book manuscript. I am thankful as well to Georgia Tech's Ivan Allen College and the Georgia Tech Research Foundation, which provided generous travel support for my research. I am also grateful to my students in the Science, Technology, and Culture (STAC) program at Georgia Tech. In several classes over several years, they helped me develop readings of specific texts that appear in this book.

Other colleagues who played a role in the making of this book include McKinsey and Company's Thom Shaw, Mark Ledden, and Cathy Boeckmann, who never stopped encouraging me to finish writing. Additional thanks go to my Business Operations Manager, Senyal Walton, who was instrumental in helping with permissions, research, and manuscript preparation.

Several libraries were indispensable to my research. At Washington, these included the Allen, Suzzallo, Odegaard, and Art History Libraries. In Cambridge, I made full use of the Pembroke College Library, the Fitzwilliam Museum, and the University Library; I owe an enormous debt to the librarians in the rare book room, who fetched countless volumes for me. In England, I am also grateful for the opportunity to have worked extensively in the British Library and the Bodleian Library, wonderfully stimulating environments. Another terrific and extraordinarily civilized venue for research was the Huntington Library in San Marino. I would also like to thank the librarians at Georgia Tech and Emory University who provided so much help and counsel in tracking down rare books and obscure articles.

I appreciate receiving permission to reprint paintings from the Museo de Arte de Ponce (*Flaming June*), the Art Gallery of New South Wales (*Cymon and Iphigenia*), Southampton City Art Gallery (*The Death of Medusa II*), and the National Galleries of Scotland (*Beads*). I am also grateful to *Literature and Psychology*, *Women's Studies: An Interdisciplinary Journal*, and *The Journal of Narrative Technique* for granting permission to republish revised versions of articles on, respectively, Samuel Richardson and *Clarissa* (chapter 1); George Eliot, Sarah Stickney Ellis, and *Adam Bede* (chapter 2); and Thomas Hardy and *Far from the Madding Crowd* (chapter 3). I am also thankful to several conferences, including the American Conference on Romanticism, the Society for Literature and Science, the Eighteenth and Nineteenth Century British Women's Studies Conference, the Northwest Conference of British Studies, and the Group for Early Modern Cultural Studies, all of which provided important venues for the extension of good ideas that appear in the pages that follow and the vetting of bad ideas that did not hold up to public scrutiny.

I would be remiss if I did not acknowledge three important mentors from my undergraduate days at Occidental College. Eric Newhall, Lewis Owen, and John Swift were all instrumental in exposing me to the richness and rewards of literary study; they were incomparable role models during my infancy as a critic and a scholar.

Introduction: A Feminine Language of the Eyes?

> *That's my last Duchess painted on the wall,*
> *Looking as if she were alive. I call*
> *That piece a wonder, now: Fra Pandolf's hands*
> *Worked busily a day, and there she stands.*
> *Will't please you sit and look at her?* (1–5)
>
> —Robert Browning, "My Last Duchess" (1842)

To possess empowered eyes has traditionally meant to occupy a male subject position, to engender oneself as masculine. Masculine visual power is the defining feature of "My Last Duchess": in putting the portrait of his dead duchess on view to another man—indeed, to any man whom he deems worthy—the duke sadistically controls the viewing of her image, circulating it within an exclusively patriarchal scopic economy. The Duke punishes what he perceives to be the Duchess' sexual indiscretions, indiscretions signaled by the fact that she used "to like whate'er/She looked on, and her looks went everywhere" (23–24). In the Duke's warped moral universe, the Duchess' wandering eyes, suggestive of overly active sexuality, justify murdering her.

Yet just how warped is Browning's Duke?

When one takes even a cursory look at the gendered representations and discourses of vision that have dominated Western culture at least from the early modern period forward, the Duke's representation might be regarded as only an exaggerated version of the pervasive visual power relations between women and men, with men dominating the field. Yet the question remains, why must the supremacy of male eyes and the accompanying suppression of female sexuality embodied by the Duke be assumed when men and women alike experience the world visually, each employing *a* look rather than *the* look? As a partial answer to this question, art historian and cultural critic John Berger, drawing from a decidedly patriarchal history of European oil painting, photography, and advertising, argues that there exists a sharply defined gender dichotomy within the field of heterosexual vision: the "masculine" direct visions of men and the "feminine" peripheral perceptions of women. The division of vision into these gendered realms leads Berger to conclude, "Men look at women. Women watch themselves being looked at."[1] The female look here functions as the unprivileged term in Berger's scopic binary because its very existence depends on the prior presence of male eyes. If Berger's conclusion reveals, as I believe it does, a widely held belief in Western culture, we are left to ask the following question: how did resistance to the free expression of female eyes, particularly in the cultural register of sexuality, become such a powerful and pervasive discourse?

Working out from these questions, the subject of this book takes as its starting point two fundamental propositions. First, I contend that the psychoanalytic discourse of vision, gender, and sexuality initiated by Sigmund Freud's theory of scopophilia/exhibitionism, and subsequently revised by Jacques Lacan's structuralist elaborations, has exerted among the most profound and long-lasting influences on the gendering of vision into masculine and feminine realms in the last century, particularly because it is precisely those theories that have been ambivalently taken up by an entire generation of feminist-psychoanalytic thinkers at once intent on deconstructing and deploying them, including Ann Kaplan, Laura Mulvey, Jacqueline Rose, Luce Irigary, Hélène Cixous, and Teresa de Lauretis.[2] Second, I aim to demonstrate that the psychoanalytic theory of vision in any of its permutations, feminist or otherwise, has a prehistory in specifically *English* scientific, cultural, and literary discourses that can be traced back at least to the eighteenth century. Several scholars have already provided historical contextualizations of psychoanalysis, variously placing it within the milieu of *fin de siécle* Vienna, examining it as the culmination of late nineteenth-century scientific culture, or providing biographical explanations based on Freud's life.[3] By contrast, my intention is to show how Freud's theory of sexuality and vision may be viewed within the context of a heterogeneous production of eighteenth- and nineteenth-century English discourses that preceded, and to a large degree shaped, his work in the scopic regime. In my view, the psychoanalytic account of sexuality and vision—a citadel attacked with only limited success by some of the most prominent feminist thinkers of the past century—can best be challenged when the historical discourses of vision at its foundation are brought to light.

To achieve that aim, this book recovers two neglected yet important critical narratives. The first narrative shows how vision, sexuality, and masculinity became conflated in the scientific works of Erasmus and Charles Darwin, underscoring the intimate yet repressed scopo-scientific influence between grandfather and grandson. This narrative focuses on how the writings of the younger Darwin—themselves shaped by the writings of Darwin *grand-pére*—profoundly influenced Freud's views on the sexuality of vision. The second narrative traces the discursive formation of an alternative women's tradition of visuality in English culture and its relationship to sexuality and domesticity in empirical philosophy, conduct books, the periodical press, poetry, and, most especially, the novel. My intention in illuminating these competing discursive histories—the former, which represses sexualized female vision, the latter, which represents the dynamic quality, sexual and otherwise, of female eyes—is motivated by a desire to recover from obscurity the female spectator as she has been widely depicted, yet strangely ignored, in modern English literature and culture. Oddly, however, the female spectator, a generalized term intended here to stand in for a broad rubric of female viewers and observers, has never received a history of her own written in what Catherine Trotter, the late-Restoration playwright, novelist, and philosopher, calls "the language of the eyes," a phrase that I have borrowed as the title of this book.[4]

Despite the attention devoted here to nonliterary discourses of vision, the novel stands out for me as the quintessential artifact in which to recover the female spectator and to call into question the so-called scopic dominance of her male counterpart. Although I am interested as well in the visual meanings of other literary genres, namely, poetry and drama, the novel occupies a privileged place in this book as a consequence of its status as that most flexible genre more capable than its rivals of enclosing multiple competing discourses into a single cultural space. In the subsequent chapters I am interested in how competing discourses (what Mikhail Bakhtin, like Trotter, might also call "languages") of vision exist within, and for that matter, between the novels of several English authors, including Samuel Richardson, Frances Burney, Jane Austen, Mary Shelley, George Eliot, Thomas Hardy, Olive Schreiner, and Virginia Woolf.

In Eliot's *Adam Bede*, for instance, it is difficult to ignore the self-conscious prominence of the omniscient narrator who wishes to see the English midlands with the clear-sighted eyes of a Dutch realist painter in the tradition of Van Eyck or Vermeer. Seeing with Vermeer-like eyes marks the narrator's status as the voice of *Adam Bede*'s dominant discourse of vision. As Audrey Jaffe has argued, however, while novel criticism such as W. J. Harvey's *Art of George Eliot* has traditionally conceived of omniscient narrators as representative of single personalities, more recent criticism, such as the Foucauldian interpretations of D. A. Miller, has tended to identify narrators less with individuals and more with institutions of surveillance.[5] I believe that Bakhtin's theoretical work can mediate between the generation gap and ideological chasm of narrative critics such as Harvey and Miller; Bakhtin would likely call the narrator's discourse in *Adam Bede* "authorial discourse" because it operates within Eliot's text, for all intents and purposes, as authorial intentionality. As Jaffe has shown, omniscient narrators such as *Adam Bede*'s "belong to a series of cultural phenomena through which the gaze—and, more generally, authoritative knowledge itself—is coded as white, male, and middle class."[6] Like Jaffe, Bakhtin argues that omniscient authorial discourse neither represents the wholesale views of the author nor is invulnerable to discursive analysis; rather, authorial discourse inevitably becomes enmeshed in what Bakhtin calls "alien languages" that contest the hegemony of authorial discourse, refracting that discourse through other meanings and other ideologies that operate in a novel. In the case of George Eliot's first novel, feminized visual possibilities—such as domestic, narcissistic, and theological visions—emerge to call into question the dominance of the narrator's Dutch (white, male, middle-class) vision. For Bakhtin, this is the "Tower-of-Babel mixing of languages that goes on around any object":

> As such they [novelistic languages] all may be juxtaposed to one another, contradict one another and be interrelated dialogically. As such they encounter one another and co-exist in the consciousness of real people—first and foremost in the creative consciousness of people who write novels.[7]

Adopting a Bakhtinian point of view, I argue that in the eighteenth and nineteenth centuries, various languages of vision derived from science, conduct books, art history, and illustrated periodicals became an important, indeed fundamental, aspect of novelistic discourse because those discourses prominently existed in a dynamic cultural matrix of linguistic exchange and multiplicity, or in Bakhtin's term, heteroglossia. Such a Bakhtinian dialogical approach to what is too often taken to be the monological given of male visual dominance goes far toward disassembling the foundations of that cultural given. More important for my argument, the visual heteroglossia found in the novel genre underlines the multiple versions of female vision (and their importance to cultural formations and practices) from the eighteenth century forward. As I will demonstrate in the following pages of this introduction, the critical discourse of vision at least from Freud forward has occluded this history and been dominated either by masculinist writings or feminist reinterpretations of those very same writings.

A History of Twentieth-Century Visual Theory

Aside from its discursive importance to the novel genre, vision as an object of study holds an important place in twentieth-century Western thought. *Vision* and its synonyms are, of course, linguistically imperialistic terms. As Ian Hacking and Richard Rorty have illustrated, metaphors of vision and their broader cultural, philosophical, and epistemological meanings are seemingly omnipresent in Western languages.[8] As such, the way I am employing 'vision' requires careful delineation. By 'vision' I mean to emphasize neither the actual physical operation of the human eye nor the abstraction of a political or aesthetic ideology, but rather something closer to what Hal Foster calls "visuality," sight as a social fact, sight as a culturally conceived reality and therefore a contested terrain with multiple permutations and possibilities.[9] As Martin Jay has demonstrated, a number of twentieth-century thinkers, particularly French theorists, have contributed to the critique of visuality with disparate and often conflicting goals leading to what Jay calls the "denigration of vision" from its former perch atop the human sensorium as the "noblest of the senses."[10] A brief survey of the most important twentieth-century theoretical, philosophical, and historical works on visuality is therefore appropriate to ascertain its relationship to such historical "eccentricities" as female observation, voyeurism, spectatorship, and surveillance.

Michel Foucault's dominant epistemological interest is in explaining how structures of surveillance, so pervasive in modern institutions, regulate individuals within the social body.[11] For Foucault, power is assumed by the observer through the invisible gaze of the Panopticon and other structures of institutional surveillance. In the Panopticon-like institution, a one-way screen variously precludes the prisoner, lunatic, and factory worker from returning the disciplinary looks of the prison guard, the doctor, and the industrial foreman. The effect of the half-opaque screen is to place the visual object under the threat of perennial surveillance. Just as important as the unperceived (but strongly experienced) gaze that emanates from the tower of the Panopticon is the self-regulating gaze the object of surveillance places over his own body and behavior.

A very different kind of power, the power to see with a roving eye cast over the city, is expressed in the eyes of Walter Benjamin's *flâneur*, a nineteenth-century metropolitan figure who emerged coincident with industrial capitalism and mass consumer culture. According to John Rignall, the *flâneur* "combines the casual eye of the stroller with the purposeful gaze of the detective."[12] Impressionistically drawn from Baudelaire's essays and poetry, Balzac's, Poe's, and Dickens' fiction, and Marx's theory of commodity fetishism, the *flâneur* is a bourgeois rambler who made the crowded labyrinths of London and Paris—with their promise of anonymity, ephemerality, and estrangement—his personal playground. In his promenades the *flâneur* expended cultural capital in such a way as to acquire and exploit the visual images of city life. The most attractive of those images were "fallen" women of the street, especially prostitutes, lesbians, and the seduced. He regarded women as a commodity; his interaction with them, predicated on superficiality and sexuality, amounted to a predatory version of window-shopping as he ran his eyes over his female social inferiors with no fear of recrimination or shame.[13]

Less historically inclined theorists than Foucault and Benjamin, including Jean-Paul Sartre and Jacques Lacan, have explored visuality from what Lacan calls the "field of the gaze."[14] Quite opposed to Foucault's account of the Panopticon, Lacan's and Sartre's gazes exist in a relational field between seen and seer. The recognition that the observer is, in fact, also observed disrupts the apparently stable boundaries between percipient and perceived, subject and object, thereby undermining the authority of the subject. For Lacan and Sartre, the voyeur, the spectator, the subject who appears from every angle to possess the look (*le regard*) and the power over the object that the look seems to bequeath, in fact exists in a much larger arena of vision, positioning the spectator in the paradoxical place of the one who sees and is seen. Upon recognition that the subject's look is returned by what Sartre views as a hostile and alienating world-as-spectator, the illusory unity of consciousness and uncontested wholeness the subject imagined its eyes to organize is dissolved. Lacan argues that when this realization occurs the subject ceases to conceive of himself as his own autonomous agent of scopic meaning, inaugurating profound and reverberating consequences for the ego.

Working out of and yet to some extent against Sartre and Lacan, feminist-psychoanalytic theorists have striven to demonstrate the political consequences that ensue from always assuming a Sartrean or Lacanian spectator, a spectator, they argue, who is overwhelmingly constructed as masculine and who, despite the disempowering aspects of the look that Sartre and Lacan underline, occupies a dominant subject position in relation to his female objects of vision. Lacan, for one, makes a claim for the libidinal pleasure experienced by women when they are made the self-conscious objects of a male spectator, arguing that "at the very level of the phenomenal experience of contemplation, this all-seeing aspect is to be found in the satisfaction of a woman who knows that she is being looked at, on condition that one does not show her that one knows that she knows."[15] Lacan's (and Western culture's) hypothetical spectator, these theorists contend, is dominantly constructed as a masculine-heterosexual subject whose object, a woman on display, revels in the field of the male look, perceiving that she is gazed upon but failing to perceive that the spectator is aware of her knowledge. The implication of Lacan's analysis is that women derive libidinal satisfaction from the self-conscious knowledge of their (scopic) desirability for men, not from their own direct vision(s). In Lacanian theory, therefore, the seeing-man (even though he himself is placed under indirect surveillance by the female object of vision) exerts a subtle yet tangible power over the seen woman because that man possesses (secret) knowledge of the woman's pleasure as his chosen visual object.

Those thinkers who have generated a critique of Sartre's and Lacan's masculine seeing subject share a sensibility with scholars such as Evelyn

Fox Keller, who paints a parallel picture of empiricism as an insistently "masculine" science.[16] In her research into Western scientific discourses, Keller demonstrates why vision has been constructed by a scientific culture as masculine. Keller shows that patriarchally conceived models of knowledge are communicated in pervasively visual terms that go far toward defining the metaphors of science as phallocentric. Ludmila Jordanova, complementing Keller's conclusions by chronicling the gender construction of science and medicine from the eighteenth century to the present, argues that Enlightenment science as theorized by Descartes and Bacon viewed nature as a personified woman, as a feminine object to be unveiled, unclothed, penetrated, and mastered by masculine science.[17] In the process of this unveiling, science places special emphasis on seeing, both intellectually and sensibly, further accentuating the masculine construction of scientific vision over and against feminized nature.

Similar to philosophy and science, the notion of a hegemonic, masculinized gaze occupies an important place in art history. Numerous art historians, including Berger, Griselda Pollock, Lynda Nead, Susan Casteras, and Joseph Kestner, to name a few, have shown how art in general, and paintings, sculptures, and photographs of women in particular, are constructed around the dual assumptions of a male artist and a male audience; this is especially true of the female nude tradition in art, a tradition of conventional, male-defined female beauty that continues to be exploited today in quasipornographic advertising and pornography.[18]

Taken as a body of complementary work, the writings of these various theorists, critics, and historians attempt to show how masculine-heterosexual eyes have come to dominate virtually every aspect of Western visual culture. As a strategy of resistance, then, de Lauretis, echoing other feminist thinkers, calls for the reconceptualization of vision outside the oppressive walls of a monolithic masculinist understanding, to imagine vision beyond dominant patriarchal ideologies, to liberate vision from masculine discourse, and most interesting for my work, "to reconstruct or organize vision from the 'impossible' place of female desire, the historical place of the female spectator."[19] To my knowledge, the only feminist scholar who has taken de Lauretis fully at her word is Deborah Epstein Nord, whose excellent book *Walking the Victorian Streets: Woman, Spectatorship, and the City* responds to de Lauretis' admonishment by proposing the historical existence of the *flâneuse*, a feminine version of Benjamin's *flâneur*.[20] For Epstein Nord, the *flâneur* is the stuff of authoritative cultural and literary criticism, a story told not just by Benjamin but also by his most important English comrade in the Marxist tradition, Raymond Williams. Echoing Williams' analysis of *flâneur*-like narrative technique in Victorian city novels, Epstein Nord argues that "the entire project of representing and understanding the exhilarating and distressing new phenomenon of urban life began, in some important sense, with this figure of the lone man who walked with impunity, aplomb and a penetrating gaze" (1). Far from an isolated phenomenon, she locates the "lone man" as a pervasive paradigm of nineteenth-century writing and narrating, including in her canon of *flâneur* authors romantics such as William Wordsworth, Charles Lamb, William Hazlitt, William Blake, Thomas De Quincey, and their most prominent Victorian descendent, Charles Dickens. With this feature of narrative spectatorship fully in mind, Epstein Nord poses a revisionist question: "[C]ould there have been a *female* spectator or a vision of the urban panorama crafted by a female imagination?" (3). In answering her question, Epstein Nord recovers several largely forgotten nineteenth-century women writers, including Flora Tristan, Margaret Harkness, Amy Levy, and Eleanor Marx, all of whom played a significant role in narrating as, and representing, a quasi *flâneuse*; Epstein Nord also conducts important research on the late-Victorian and Edwardian generation of New Women and social investigators who made their influence felt on the streets from the 1880s forward, including luminaries such as Beatrice Potter Webb as well as lesser lights such as Helen Bosquanet, Mary Higgs, Florence Bell, and Maud Pember Reeves.

Like de Lauretis, many feminist theorists have made the gendered gaze/look the principal object of their investigations. Contrary to recovering the historical female spectator, however, many of these scholars have, with the notable exception of Epstein Nord, generally insisted on employing either Freudian/Lacanian readings or anti-Freudian/Lacanian polemics on their chosen texts. This in no way diminishes the important work of the feminist theorists already cited or figures such as Linda Williams, Judith Mayne, and Mary Ann Doane, who offer sophisticated explorations of female visuality that often travel far afield from traditional psychoanalytic paradigms.[21] Yet there is also no question that the preponderance of feminist theorists investigating "gaze studies" have taken up the father of psychoanalysis as the seminal figure who must either be praised or slain. But interestingly, even a cursory perusal of Freud's prolific *oeuvre* demonstrates that his writings on sexuality and vision were tentative investigations at best. Indeed, Freud confined his most extended observations on the relationship between vision and psychoanalysis to a scant few paragraphs in *Three Essays on the Theory of Sexuality* (1905), only infrequently adding casual references to the problem of vision, gender, and sexuality for the rest of his career.[22] Because Freud wrote so little about vision, it is peculiar that his work on the subject has been taken up with such vigor by theorists who have unarguably surpassed him in sophistication, breadth, and depth. This is especially true of feminist theorists who otherwise reject Freud's phallocentric premises. Nevertheless, the generation of feminist and psychoanalytic film theorists contemporary with de Lauretis who have published, and still publish, their work in feminist- and psychoanalytically oriented journals like *Screen* and *Camera Obscura* continue to invoke Freud as an important initiator of sexual and gendered analyses, which inevitably overlap into the scopic regime.

The coupling of psychoanalysis and film studies is hardly surprising considering the near simultaneous appearance of psychoanalysis and cinema in or around 1900.[23] More than one critic has pointed to the congeniality between dream and film, and certainly no one can deny that Freud produces vivid film-like scenes in *The Interpretation of Dreams*. Nonetheless, Freud's actual analysis of dreams concentrates far more on the study of language (on, for instance, the analysand's narrative and linguistic choices in recounting dreams) than on any dream's specific visual qualities; indeed, all of Freud's references to vision throughout his writings appear only as part of larger works rather than as the primary subject of the works themselves.[24] Considering the influence Freud has had on film studies, it is surprising that he never focused a single study on the question of vision and sexuality.

One case in point of Freud including visual material in an otherwise unvisual paper proves especially illuminating. Describing the psychoanalytic situation in "Analysis of a Phobia in a Five-year Old Boy," Freud spells out his motivations for contriving the familiar analysand on the couch/analyst in the chair scenario:

> Since, while I am listening to the patient, I, too, give myself over to the currents of my unconscious thoughts, I do not wish my expressions of face to give the patient material for interpretations or to influence him in what he tells me. The patient usually regards being made to adopt this position as a hardship and rebels against it, especially if the instinct for looking (scopophilia) plays an important part in his neurosis. I insist on this procedure, however, for its purpose and result are to prevent the transference from mingling with the patient's associations imperceptibly, to isolate the transference, and to allow it to come forward in due course sharply defined as a resistance.[25]

An important effect of Freud's consulting-room choreography is to create an imbalance, tipped in the psychoanalyst's favor, in the visual relationship between patient and doctor: the analysand is made readily available to the analyst's gaze without being able to reciprocate. This physical arrangement fashions a situation where patients not only permit their discourse of sexuality to be placed under the institutional and discursive gaze of psychoanalysis, as Foucault argues in *The History of Sexuality*, but also place themselves under the literal, physical gaze of the analyst, in this case Freud. Freud's medical reasoning for such a seating arrangement—to ensure that the transference occurs in "due course"—provides only a partial, not a compelling justification for the specular arrangement of his analytical furniture.

A more intriguing justification, it would seem, was Freud's antipathy toward being made the object of the analysand's gaze. Indeed, in the same essay Freud confesses, "I cannot put up with being stared at by other people for eight hours a day (or more)."[26] Freud's decision to sit out of sight and to place the analysand under his own unreturnable gaze opens himself (and psychoanalysis) to accusations of a kind of analytic scopophilia. Cixous, for one, concurs with this analysis and has leveled charges emphasizing psychoanalysis' "strange emphasis on exteriority and the specular," concluding that it is the enactment of "a voyeur's theory of course."[27] It is ironic that Freud, whose work has been used with such zeal in explicating voyeurism, has been charged so damningly by Foucault and Cixous with intellectual voyeurism himself.

Of course, one of the central tenets of psychoanalysis is the explication by Freud of visual phenomena: the recognition by boys and girls that their genitalia are fundamentally different from one another, leading, in girls, to penis envy and in boys to the castration complex. Freud considers the discovery of genital difference to be a traumatic yet crucial psychic recognition, which makes possible the child's development into a gendered subject. With Freud's scopically-oriented explanation of gender difference in mind, Luce Irigary's work emerges as characteristic of the feminist extension and revision of psychoanalytic visual theory. Irigary concludes that a young girl's recognition of genital difference, of her lack of the biological fact of the penis, also robs her of the signifying power of the phallus.[28] So willing is Irigary to surrender possession of the gaze to an exclusively male ownership, that she concludes seeing and touching are *essentially* different from one another, are, in fact, masculine and feminine sensations: "Woman's desire does not speak the same language as man's desire. In this logic, the prevalence of the gaze is particularly foreign to female eroticism. Women find pleasure more in touch than in sight."[29] Unlike Irigary, I am not content to yield vision to a masculinist system of meanings. In apparent response to her surrender, Irigary has claimed a different sensory perception for women, which simply feminizes touch in the same way that vision has been masculinized, hardly a helpful suggestion because it inhibits men and women from experiencing the full range of their senses, keeping in rigid place the cultural hegemony of masculine vision. In contrast to these feminist critiques, this book traces a cultural history of vision preceding Freud that both acknowledges his important role as an initiator of twentieth-century visual discourses and at the same time traces the English scopo-scientific discourses that made his work on vision and sexuality possible; it also recovers a rich and varied discursive and representational history of female vision in English culture from the late seventeenth century forward that engages with the contemporaneous scopo-scientific discourses that I identify.

In addition to tracing the discursive origins of the psychoanalytic account of vision and sexuality and making visible the historical female spectator, another important goal of this book is to serve as a corrective to the uncritical and ahistorical deployment of Darwinian (visual) theory into the contemporary field of evolutionary psychology. Like so many of the discourses of vision described in the preceding pages, Charles Darwin's theory of sexual selection as articulated in *The Descent of Man* utterly privileges male eyes to the exclusion of their female counterparts and does so without recognizing the remarkable extent to which Victorian culture shaped and clouded his scientific observations. The uncritical embrace of Darwinian theory has profound implications for the scientific study of relations between the sexes because if it is true that the clinical and theoretical authority of psychoanalysis has been progressively called into question over the last several decades, it is also true that the status of Darwinism as a science, philosophy, and worldview has in the West perhaps never been more elevated. Indeed, it is generally assumed that Darwinism has largely superseded Freudianism as an explanatory model for human behavior (a fact that Freud would no doubt have found ironic since he self-consciously and proudly regarded psychoanalysis as an embellishment and extension of Darwinian theory).

For my purposes, the crucial dimension of Darwin's theory is that "civilized" men, in particular (as opposed to the specifically non-Westerners whom Darwin characterizes as "savages"), principally choose their mates on the basis of beauty. In the Darwinian system, women, by contrast, are preoccupied with self-ornamentation and adornment as they passively put themselves on display before sexually selective male eyes. In considering this admittedly simplified account of Darwin's theory, one need not be an overachieving student of Victorian culture to recognize the enormous degree to which Darwin's understanding of sexual selection was shaped by contemporary social mores that depicted ideal womanhood as inherently passive and domestic, in other words, in terms similar to Alfred, Lord Tennyson's *The Princess* (1847), Coventry Patmore's *The Angel in the House* (1858), John Ruskin's "Of Queens' Gardens" (1865), or any of the popular Victorian conduct book manuals written by Sarah Stickney Ellis.[30] Yet surprisingly, today's evolutionary psychologists utterly neglect the cultural dimensions of *The Descent of Man* by accepting its premises and conclusions virtually without dissent. In doing so, they betray extraordinary historical myopia in their headlong rush to canonize an uncritical version of Darwinism as the final word on scopo-sexual relations between men and women.

Armed with ever more elaborate and apparently compelling data, evolutionary psychologists such as David Buss—probably the most prominent figure in the field—seem intent on proving Darwin's contention that men sexually select women on the basis of their youth and beauty, and women, completely disregarding male appearances, discriminate among men principally on the basis of the financial and emotional resources they can bring to a relationship.[31] According to Buss and his colleagues, women have evolved psychological preferences for older, wealthier men endowed with elevated social prestige. The theory goes that because women are made vulnerable by pregnancy, childbirth, and childrearing, they sexually select mates who are able and willing to invest in a relationship in all the ways that "investment" suggests. From a woman's point of view, the best husbands and fathers must therefore be physically powerful, emotionally stable, and share the cultural values of the mother; blessed with these traits, evolutionarily successful men will be able, by turns, to protect their families, to exhibit good parenting skills, and to prove themselves compatible with their female counterparts.

In contrast to the long-term mating strategies of women, evolutionary psychologists and biologists argue that men above all privilege youth and beauty in their choice of a mate. To be sure, to read the chapters on sexual selection in Buss' textbook, *Evolutionary Psychology*, a distillation of the most widely admired research in the field, is to encounter a near absolute fetish of the evolutionary adaptiveness of the male eye to visually discern seemingly infinitesimal increments of physical desirability and fertility among women. Paraphrasing another researcher, Buss writes, for example, "Conventional wisdom dictates that beauty is in the eyes of the beholder, but those eyes and the minds behind those eyes have been shaped by millions of years of human evolution. Beauty is in the *adaptations* of the beholder."[32] Yet in reading the scholarship of contemporary evolutionary psychobiology, certainly one of the most influential new academic fields to emerge over the past several decades, one might conclude that only male eyes evolved sufficiently over the last several million years to make a difference in the processes of sexual selection.

As far as men are concerned, exclusively male-defined criteria of female beauty add up in the Darwinian arithmetic of evolutionary psychobiology. Nonfeminist evolutionary psychobiologists argue around the margins of the following givens: that standards of female beauty emerge early in life and are consistent across cultures and that "average" and symmetrical faces are more desirable to male eyes because of what these faces convey about female reproductive health. In one of the most famous recent research studies on sexual selection, Devendra Singh proposes that men virtually instinctively measure with their eyes the waist-to-hip ratios (WHR) of women they encounter in order to make judgments about desirable mates.[33] This research concludes that men possess a cross-cultural preference for women with a WHR of 0.70, finding women with this measurement more sexually desirable than those with higher and lower ratios. Singh claims that the attraction to this specific WHR has evolutionary advantages because, as it turns out, women endowed with it are likely to be more sexually fertile than women who deviate from the ideal. So thorough was research for this study that Singh voluntarily extended himself by recording the WHRs of *Playboy* centerfolds and Miss America contest winners—measurements that we all know (wink, wink) are never embellished or doctored. The implications of this research study, in which men were asked to evaluate the sexual attractiveness of drawn female figures endowed with varying WHRs, are clear: through evolutionary adaptation, the eyes of men have acquired the ability to measure instantly the ideal physical proportions of women.

In the canon of evolutionary psychology, women emphasize personal characteristics besides beauty in evaluating potential mates and either do not see with sexually selective eyes or, if they do, do not see with the same sexual intensity as men. This latter claim, especially, is supposedly borne out by a research study compiled over a fifty-seven-year period that demonstrates men, in Buss' words, "rate physical attractiveness and good looks as more important and desirable in a potential mate" than women. Buss readily acknowledges the extent to which twentieth-century culture, with its emphasis on advertising, and the nearly fetishistic celebration (and distortion) of the human body that so frequently accompanies advertising, plays a vital part in explaining the importance of physical beauty for both men and women. However, he underlines the "fact" that over the course of the research study, the "gap between men and women is no more nor less than it was in the late 1930s" (145). On a scale of 0 to 3, that gap remained more or less constant at approximately .5.

Presumably for the gap that Buss describes to have closed, media representations of the beautiful male figure would have had to proliferate over the six decades between 1930 and 1987 at a rate similar to the proliferation of beautiful female images, a phenomena that simply has not occurred, as anyone with even a cursory knowledge of popular culture in the West would assert. Instead, in our so-called postfeminist age of nonstop media representation, we continue to be inundated with frankly absurd images of ideal female beauty, emphasizing youth, slenderness, and vitality. The claim that advertising offers a value-free means by which to assess the importance of physical attractiveness for men and women because advertisers create mediated images for no purpose other than to sell their wares proposes a strangely circular reasoning, for it obviates the history of media and artistic representation in which advertising self-consciously participates. Buss contends, for example, that "advertisers are unlikely to have a special interest in inculcating a particular set of beauty standards. They are in the business of making money and seek to use whatever sells successfully" (154). Advertisers certainly care a great deal about the bottom line. However, we should also not discount the fact that advertisers, like anyone working in visual media, operate within a tradition that has, over many years, built up expectations of what that tradition in general, and advertising in particular, *should* do and be. Taking recourse to a research study begun in 1930 that demonstrates American men at the beginning of the Great Depression were more apt than women to privilege beauty in their selection of a mate presupposes that visual media culture in, say, the 1920s, was not already insistently patriarchal and masculinist in structure and ideology, something that simply does not jibe with the facts. As Natalie Angier has argued compellingly, the hurdle that evolutionary psychologists can never quite clear is the difficulty of finding reliable data about societies that are not organized patriarchally, as virtually every society in the world is, including all thirty-seven cultures that Buss proudly points to in his own research as evidence for the universality about his claims with respect to sexual selection and sex specific difference.[34] It is my hope that this book, in which women's scopo-sexuality is treated as historically situated and contingent, will serve as a counterbalance, however slight, to the overly influential, and often insufficiently critical, claims of evolutionary psychology.

Chapter 1 begins by examining the fictional, dramatic, and philosophical works of Catherine Trotter, an important yet almost forgotten late-Restoration woman of letters. Read in relation to one another, Trotter's novel, *Olinda's Adventures* (1693), the prefaces to her six plays, and her highly regarded *A Defence of Mr. Lock's [sic] Essay of Human Understanding* (1702) underline an important cultural nexus, namely between female spectatorship of the stage, then considered a highly immoral exercise, and Lockean empiricism. Exploring the intersections among female spectatorship, morality, and empiricism that Trotter's work points to is instrumental to my argument because they provide a meaningful point of departure for tracing the feminized discourses of visual conduct and domestic surveillance that played such an important function in England throughout the eighteenth century and beyond, especially as those discourses manifested themselves in the novel. Working from this set of premises, three major claims are made in the first chapter. First, the dominant discourse of female vision—epitomized by Samuel Richardson's *Pamela* (1740) and *Clarissa* (1747–48) as well as much post-Richardsonian fiction, such as the works of Eliza Haywood, Frances Burney, Maria Edgeworth, and Jane Austen—worked in two directions, at once valorizing empiricism's cultural authority to describe reality as well as authorizing women to become formidable observers of the domestic sphere. Second, discourses of visual conduct as articulated in eighteenth-century letters, particularly in domestic novels and conduct books, served the important didactic function of training young Englishwomen to see the world with empirically discerning, domestically oriented and sexually (self)regulating eyes. Third, these domestic discourses of vision, weighed down with middle-class notions of female virtue, prohibited girls and women from using their eyes in a manner that could be construed as either betraying sexual desire or inviting the sexual advances of men. An important outcome of the discourse of domestic vision's representational triumph within the eighteenth-century novel is that it became nearly impossible in the nineteenth and twentieth centuries to separate representations of seeing women from nonsexualized domestic settings without also casting aspersions on female morality. This chapter locates the English eighteenth century as a decisive moment in the pervasive Anglo-American representation of women either as sexual objects to be observed by men or as desexualized subjects who place the domestic sphere under observation and surveillance.

Here as elsewhere throughout the book, the chapter concludes with a case study in which a single novel is interpreted within the context of the previous chapter's visual discourses. The book's four case studies are intended to provide extended models of how, and to what effect, my critical approach can be fully deployed. These discussions are also intended to appropriate for my own quite different ends a method—the case study—employed so prolifically and persuasively by Freud.

The first case study brings to light the culturally repressed discourse of lesbian (what the English eighteenth century would have called "Sapphic") vision in *Clarissa.* By recovering lesbian vision from its history of repression, I show how Richardson's novel surprisingly resists the dominant discursive encoding of female visuality in the eighteenth century as nonsexual and preoccupied with domestic concerns and instead demonstrate how it represents the epistolary expressions of mutual scopo-sexual desire between Clarissa Harlowe and Anna Howe without appearing to violate the Richardsonian representation of ladylike-domestic vision. By identifying the lesbian dimensions of *Clarissa* (as well as the promiscuous heterosexual scopic possibilities for women in pre-Richardsonian fiction), I explore why "proper" ladylike vision became historically divorced from sexuality. This chapter therefore begins to answer within a historical framework a fundamental question: where and how can female sexual desire be found in the scopic register of human subjectivity, and why did it virtually disappear from mainstream representation in post-Richardsonian England? In my judgment this question has not been adequately explored because most cultural critics and theorists have neglected to look back to the eighteenth century and the early modern origins of the gendering of vision into male-sexual and female-domestic realms.

Chapter 2 takes up the medical philosophy of Erasmus Darwin, examining the ocular dimensions of his theory of sexual reproduction—what he calls "generation"—as put forward in the first volume of *Zoonomia* (1794). According to Erasmus Darwin's associationist understanding of human physiology, the testes and the retina function so similarly that male visual experience during sexual intercourse can conceive and constitute procreative outcomes by determining the physical characteristics of human offspring, especially their sex. This chapter proceeds by illustrating the close ideological relationship between Erasmus Darwin's theory of generation and Wordsworth's contribution to *Lyrical Ballads* (1798), particularly the masculine sublime masterpiece that concludes the collection, "Tintern Abbey." In that poem the poet implicitly contrasts the mature mind's eye of masculine vision that gives birth to his ideal species of romantic poetry with the "wild" material eyes of the mad, sexually active women that overpopulate the first half of *Lyrical Ballads*, women who are subsequently linked to Dorothy Wordsworth's "wild" eyes in "Tintern Abbey." Moving away from her brother's poetry, the chapter explores Dorothy's late poem, "Thoughts on My Sick-bed," a surprisingly neglected work that challenges William's understanding of the differences between male and female sight and creates a conceptual space that asserts the creative power of the female visual imagination. With Dorothy's revision of "Tintern Abbey" in mind, I turn to Mary Shelley's *Frankenstein* (1818, 1831), a novel that explicitly critiques Darwin's theory of generation and illustrates the folly of solipsistic procreation seemingly advocated by Darwin. In this novel the privileged status of the masculine romantic mind's eye put forward by "Tintern Abbey" is overturned by feminine discourses of vision, particularly by domestic vision.

The second chapter's case study argues that George Eliot's *Adam Bede* (1859), a novel set in the years just after publication of *Zoonomia* and *Lyrical Ballads*, more than merely parroting Erasmus Darwin's views on sexuality and vision, encloses several feminized discourses of vision that operate dialogically within its pages. As discussed earlier in this introduction, despite the visual heteroglossia at play in *Adam Bede*, Eliot stabilizes scopic meaning in the novel by moving from a dialogic to a monologic depiction of female vision confined to the domestic sphere. Eliot's deployment of domestic vision in *Adam Bede* has important consequences for the ways that we read, in particular, Erasmus Darwin's influence in that novel, especially as that influence is first mediated through Wordsworth and later mediated through Eliot's reading of Wordsworth. Domestic vision, represented in the end by Dinah Bede's calm, gray, overseeing eyes, is portrayed by Eliot as the antithesis of Hetty's "wild" eyes, eyes that were regarded by Wordsworth and many subsequent nineteenth-century writers as associated with illicit sexuality and illegitimate procreative power. In this respect, female domestic vision in *Adam Bede* emerges as culturally and ideologically triumphant over its sexualized counterpart.

Chapter 3 shows that while little attention has been paid to the relationship between Erasmus Darwin's theory of generation in *Zoonomia* and Charles Darwin's theory of sexual selection in *The Descent of Man* (1871), an important family resemblance connects the science of grandfather and grandson, demonstrating a hitherto neglected continuity of thinking between the two Darwins and their respective scopo-scientific languages of the eyes. Working through and beyond this connection, this chapter calls attention to important fissures in the theory of sexual selection, particularly by highlighting those facets of the theory that relegate women to the status of nonvisual agents in the selection of mates. In these pages I explore how Darwinian sexual selection in its visual dimensions was explicitly mediated in the illustrated pages of *Punch*, the Victorian Age's most popular periodical, and examine the relationship between the representation of vision and sexuality promulgated in *Punch* and Victorian classical-subject painting, the most prominent form of painting in the last third of the British nineteenth century. This chapter shows that the scoposexual depiction of women in both *Punch* and classical-subject painting shares representational strategies with sexual selection and, like Charles Darwin's theory, exerted often powerfully negative effects on the political agency of women at a time when Victorian women with progressive views were engaged in a fierce struggle to achieve electoral emancipation by winning the right to vote.

My critique of Charles Darwin, *Punch*, and classical-subject painting in chapter 3 is enriched with readings of Olive Schreiner's *Story of an African Farm* (1883), a novel that self-consciously responds to the Darwinian revolution. Schreiner's novel engages in a cultural dialogue not only with Darwin but also with the representation of women in *Punch*'s illustrations and classical subject painting; Schreiner complicates sexual selection by emphasizing the degree to which it is culturally, socially, and economically—rather than merely biologically—constituted. Far from the virtually timeless phenomenon that Charles Darwin imagined, sexual selection among humans is shown by Schreiner to be inextricably enmeshed within contemporary and lived cultures, something lost on many of today's most well regarded evolutionary psychologists who far too often accept Charles Darwin's account of sexual selection as a transhistorical reality despite the fact that its profound biases in favor of male activity, aggression, and spectatorship were steeped in the values of Victorian culture.

The third case study shows how Thomas Hardy draws from the biblical account of David and Bathsheba not, as we might expect, to reinforce male visual hegemony but rather to complicate and challenge the assumption of dominant, sexually selective male eyes. By christening his novel's protagonist "Bathsheba Everdene," Hardy invokes a correspondence with the biblical Bathsheba, depicting her as a passive target of male desire in the novel's opening chapters. Yet Hardy's subsequent characterization of his heroine reconstitutes the Bathsheba mythos in that it departs from II Samuel by portraying her not merely as a "feminized" spectator who perceives the visual attentions of male characters but also as a socially empowered, near "masculinized" spectator of those same male characters. Hardy, who as Gillian Beer, George Levine, and others have shown, was a scrupulous reader of Darwin, accomplishes this transformation of Bathsheba Everdene by employing a Darwinian discourse of sexual selection and performativity whereby men, especially Frank Troy and Farmer Boldwood, are likened to ornamental birds who perform before the discerning and critical eyes of Bathsheba.[35] In this respect, *Far from the Madding Crowd* (1873), published just two years after *The Descent of Man*, appears to resist Darwin's theory of human sexual selection, in which active, vigorous men compete for passive, beautiful women. Most crucial to Hardy's (re)constitution of Bathsheba Everdene as a sexually selective subject rather than a sexually selected object of vision is the transformation of her social position. By inheriting her wealthy uncle's farm, Bathsheba is transferred from the rural working class to the landowning class overnight. Hardy thereby intimates that ownership of a "masculine," Darwinian gaze of sexual selection is not confined to men alone. Instead, for Hardy, possession of sexually discriminating eyes seems determined by the social production of masculinely gendered subjects who are granted empowered status—status the great majority of Victorian countrywomen did not possess independent of their fathers or husbands. Bathsheba's inheritance, above and beyond her actual material gain, makes possible her new subject position as a nonfeminized female spectator in Hardy's Wessex.

Chapter 4 interrogates the section on masculine scopophilia and feminine exhibitionism in *Three Essays on the Theory of Sexuality* (1900), showing how Freud supports his argument by invoking Darwin's theory of sexual selection. In self-consciously relying on Darwin, Freud inherited an *English* understanding of scopo-sexual subjectivity consistent with the dominant bifurcation of vision into masculine-sexual/feminine-domestic regimes as those regimes became dominantly constructed in eighteenth- and nineteenth-century English culture. Working out of Darwin, Freud disregards the possibility of a sexualized female spectator largely because the historical female spectator, or at least her most common English representation, had long since been confined to a domestic, manifestly nonsexualized sphere where Darwin did not consider her to be important for his explanatory purposes. By contrast, in the fiction of Freud's great contemporary (and, ironically, his English publisher), Virginia Woolf, women enjoy a wide range of visual possibilities, especially as producers of their own scopic desires and subjectivities. The case study of this chapter examines *To the Lighthouse* (1927), a novel that explicitly conjures up the British empirical tradition by invoking the hallowed trinity of Locke, Berkeley, and Hume. In doing so, *To the Lighthouse* hinges not, as we might expect, on Mr. Ramsay's dominating and oppressive philosophical reflections but rather on Lily Briscoe's visual perceptions—perceptions that remind us of Catherine Trotter's philosophical investigations from the early eighteenth century. For Woolf, what Lily comes to represent is a specifically feminine response to the notorious conundrum that plagued British empiricism at least since Berkeley, namely, how to verify the reality of an object whose existence becomes doubtful once separated in time and place from an observer, an absolute separation of subject and object that has important consequences for the ways that we interpret Freud's theory of scopophilia and exhibitionism.

The Language of the Eyes closes with a brief but hopefully suggestive discussion of *Mrs. Dalloway* (1925). I take up this novel as a prism through which to view the discursive and representational history of female vision traced in the earlier chapters and in doing so demonstrate that Woolf believed women should not be circumscribed either to the Freudian position of woman-as-exhibitionist or the Victorian position of woman-as-domestic-supervisor. By looking through Clarissa Dalloway's multifaceted eyes, we see virtually every aspect of female visuality explored in the preceding chapters. In this respect, *Mrs. Dalloway* functions as a heuristic text that allows us to recover an eighteenth- and nineteenth-century tradition of female vision in English culture that not only resists the Darwinian and Freudian accounts but also brings together in a single volume the multiple visual possibilities produced from Richardson forward. The book therefore concludes not simply with a critique of Freud's theory of sexuality and vision but also offers, through Woolf's text, a contrasting and affirmative history of female visuality.

Throughout this book I have striven to demonstrate the prominence of female visuality in England from the eighteenth century forward. By returning the two Darwins and Freud to the cultural milieu in which their writings on sexuality and vision were actually conceived, it becomes possible at last to read the relative absence of female visuality in the sexual register of contemporary culture as part of a nineteenth- and early-twentieth-century phenomenon to which Anglo-America is still, remarkably, capitulating today. Rather than merely deconstruct the masculinist visual assumptions of Darwinian sexual selection and Freudian psychoanalysis, this book works to recover and synthesize the feminized discourses of vision neglected by literary, scientific, and cultural history. In undertaking this project, I have therefore attempted to represent female visuality in all of its fullness, complexity, and power.

1

The Conduct of the Eyes: Feminine Discourses of Vision in Eighteenth-Century England

Though [Mr. B] told Mrs. Jervis he had an eye upon me, in his mother's life-time; and that he intended to let me know as much by-the-bye.

—Samuel Richardson, *Pamela* (1740)

Let neither your Eyes nor your Thoughts wander.

—Wetenhall Wilkes, *A Letter of Genteel and Moral Advice to a Young Lady* (1744)

Late-seventeenth-century England was dominated by two seemingly unrelated cultural controversies. The first concerned the antitheatrical debate over the morality of the London stage waged most famously between the English divine, Jeremy Collier, author of the notorious *Short View of the English Stage* (1698), and several well-known Restoration playwrights, including William Congreve, William Wycherly, and John Dryden, among others.[1] The second challenged the materialist implications of John Locke's *Essay concerning Human Understanding* (1690) in which the philosopher's critics, including most prominently the Bishop of Worcester, John Toland, John Sergeant, Henry Lee, and John Broughton, maintained that if the tenets of Lockean empiricism were accepted then belief in an invisible, sensibly unknowable God would no longer be possible.[2] Although these controversies would seem at first glance to have little to do with one another, each was deeply implicated in questions about the cultural and epistemological authority of the senses to construct reality and influence human behavior.[3] Alone among her contemporaries, though invisibly to contemporary scholars, English dramatist Catherine Trotter engaged in both controversies—late-seventeenth- and early-eighteenth-century England's version of the culture wars—by bolstering Collier in support of reforming the stage and by defending Locke against his numerous philosophical detractors.

Beginning in 1698, with the production of *The Fatal Friendship* (performed two months after the appearance of Collier's *Short View*) and continuing throughout her dramatic career, Trotter responded to the theatrical debate in the lengthy dedications and prefaces to her plays. In these texts she argued in favor of reforming the stage by following the criteria for moral drama laid out by Collier. One need only read the prefaces and dedications to reflect on the insistently moralistic themes of Trotter's plays and their representation of strong, heroic women antithetical to the female characters of questionable morality that Collier lambasts in the *Short View* and finally to consider that Trotter's friends, Wycherly and Congreve, were among the most aggrieved figures in Collier's abundant criticism of the stage, to recognize that her dramatic works are clearly in dialogue—and, somewhat surprisingly given her amicable relationship to Wycherly and Congreve, largely in sympathy—with Collier's attacks.[4] Yet Trotter apparently played on both sides of the antitheatrical debate, preserving throughout her career as a dramatist alliances with the leading figures in English theater, in many cases forging friendships with the very men whom Collier excoriates in the *Short View* and elsewhere;[5] and yet as her dramatic works make clear, Trotter's tragedies are unmistakably Collieresque in their emphasis on representing public and private virtue for English playgoers.

Trotter even more obviously placed herself in Locke's camp than Collier's by publishing *A Defence of Mr. Lock's Essay of Human Understanding* (1702), one of only two book-length apologies to appear in the philosopher's lifetime. Trotter's first biographer, Thomas Birch, called attention to her bravery in the face of potential public censure in his observation that the *Defence* was "perhaps the only piece that had appeared in favour of [the] *Essay*, except one by Mr. *Samuel Bold*, Rector of *Steeple* in *Dorsetshire*, in 1699."[6] Unfortunately, Trotter scholars have remained content for three centuries to focus on her dramatic works at the expense of the *Defence*, neglecting to take it up in any serious or systematic way, never drawing a meaningful connection between it and her plays. To their mutual detriment, Trotter's drama and philosophy have been taken up as separate and discrete features of a long career in letters that began in the 1690s when an unmarried and youthful Trotter was making her living by writing for the London stage and ended with her death in 1749 at a moment when the married and elderly Catherine Cockburn, in anticipation of bringing out an edition of her published and unpublished writings, was putting the finishing touches on a body of late work in which she offers mostly theological views to an audience of largely women readers. Trotter scholarship has gone so far as to relegate the *Defence*, a work highly regarded by Locke himself, to the status of a footnote.[7]

By contrast to previous Trotter scholars, I consider it crucial to weave the hitherto disconnected strands of her oeuvre—the implicit dramatic alliance with Collier and the explicit apology for Locke—into a single critical tapestry. Doing so allows us not only to construct for the first time a critical narrative of Trotter's writings in the first decade of her public life, but also to make visible the important cultural nexus that Trotter brought together, namely, between female spectatorship of the stage and Lockean empiricism, both of which made their opponents apoplectic because of the identification with female sexual immodesty and drama on the one hand and the embrace of materialist philosophy on the other. Exploring the intersections among female spectatorship of the stage, empiricism, and morality that Trotter's work points to is instrumental to the argument of this book because it provides us with a meaningful point of departure for tracing the feminized discourses of visual conduct and domestic surveillance that played such an important function in England throughout the eighteenth century and beyond, especially as those discourses manifested themselves in the novel. We can begin to understand the importance of these discourses if we consider more fully Catherine Trotter's works and their wider relation to English culture.

Catherine Trotter, Female Spectatorship, and the Empirical Virtues of the English Stage

The antitheatrical culture to which Trotter was responding in the late seventeenth century was dominated both popularly and intellectually by the formidable English divine, Jeremy Collier. Collier regarded female spectators to be especially vulnerable to the immoral spectacle of the contemporary English theatre. He believed that women in particular were likely to identify with their "immodest" counterparts, whom, he contended, then overpopulated the stage:

> Obscenity in any Company is a rustick uncreditable Talent; but among Women 'tis particularly rude. Such talk would be very affrontive in Conversation, and not endur'd by any Lady of Reputation. Whence then comes it to Pass that those Liberties which disoblige so much in Conversation, should entertain upon the *Stage*? Do the Women leave all the regards to Decency and Conscience behind them when they come to the *Play-House*? Or does the Place transform their Inclinations, and turn their former Aversions into Pleasure? Or were their pretences to Sobriety elsewhere nothing but Hypocrisy and Grimace? Such Suppositions as these are all Satyr and Invective: They are rude Imputations upon the whole Sex. To

> treat the Ladys with such stuff is no better than taking their money to abuse them. It supposes their Imagination vitious, and their Memories ill furnish'd: That they are practised in the Language of the Stews, and pleas'd with the Scenes of Brutishness. When at the same time the Customs of Education, and the Laws of Decency, are so very cautious, and reserv'd in regard to Women: I say so very reserv'd, that 'tis almost a Fault for them to Understand they are ill Used. They can't discover their Disgust without disadvantage, nor Blush without disservice to their Modesty. . . . In a word, He that treats the Ladys with such Discourse, must conclude either that they like it, or they do not. To suppose the first, is a gross Reflection upon their Virtue. And as for the latter case, it entertains them with their own Aversion; which is ill Nature, and ill Manners enough in all Conscience. (14–15)

In this passage and elsewhere Collier reveals himself to be anxious about the weakness of female eyes and character to resist emulating the immodest actions of women on the stage. As Jean Marsden has cannily observed, in this section eight of the nine Restoration characters that Collier invokes to illustrate the gravity of his argument are female.[8] Throughout the section entitled "The Immodesty of the English Stage," Collier remains preoccupied with the threat to English womanhood posed by the theater. Once the witnesses of gross speech and debauchery, Collier implies, are not women more likely than men to imitate the censurable behavior that has taken place before their eyes? That Collier's critique with regard to the stage's deleterious effect on women resonated with many of his contemporaries is plain, as Josiah Woodward's *Some Thoughts concerning the Stage in a Letter to a Lady* (1704) reveals.[9] Woodward captures the sense of injury that antitheatrical enthusiasts claimed were perpetrated against women who attended the theater. He argues, for instance, that "*Ladies* (at least those who make any Pretensions to Virtue and Goodness) should never be seen at the last of these Places [the playhouse]," especially once they have been made aware of Collier's *Short View*. Exposed to Collier's argument, Woodward believes women "should never after be Tempted to appear in a Place where *Lewdness* and *Obscenity* (not to mention other Immoralities) are so great a part of the Entertainment; a Place that is now become the *Common Rendezvouz* of the most Lewd and Dissolute Persons" (4). Woodward proceeds by invoking and inverting the feminized language of childrearing to powerful rhetorical effect by showing how the perverted London stage functions as "the Nursery of all manner of *Wickedness*, where the Seeds of *Atheism* and *Irreligion* are sown, which Weak and Tender Minds too readily cultivate, and from thence are easily led into a *Contempt* of all that's Serious" (4). At the conclusion of his diatribe, Woodward asserts that it is "every one's Duty to run from a Place of such Infection, lest they contribute to the spreading of a Disease which may, in time, prove Fatal to the whole Nation" (13). Echoing Collier, Woodward contends that eighteenth-century dramatists glamorize sexual immorality, implicitly encourage highly impressionable female audiences to emulate the vice-ridden actions of actresses, and thereby poison English society by providing illicit training to otherwise virtuous women.[10]

Three decades later we see Collier's and Woodward's fears realized to an extreme in Eliza Haywood's novella, *Fantomina* (1725), in which "[a] Young Lady of distinguished Birth, Beauty, Wit and Spirit" (227) opens the work by attending a play and watching the wanton performance of prostitutes in the pit.[11] The convergence of the playhouse and prostitution was no mistake, given that Restoration actresses gained so much unfavorable notoriety when they first took the stage. Indeed, by the early eighteenth century the word *actress* had already become synonymous with prostitution.[12] Haywood's protagonist subsequently conflates the professions of actress and prostitute by masquerading in four distinct roles—Fantomina, a woman of pleasure; Celia, a rustic house servant; Mrs. Bloomer, a widow in mourning; and Incognita, a masked seductress—that allow her to deceive and enjoy prolific sexual relations with a single philanderer, Beauplasir, upon whom her wandering eyes fall at the theater. Predictably, Beauplasir grows tired of each role played by the protagonist; unpredictably, his ennui does not deter her from creating a new character every few weeks to perpetuate physical intimacy with him. The novella can easily be taken up as the unbridled expression of female desire on the part of an insatiable woman who cleverly fashions Beauplasir into her sexual plaything, but had Collier lived to read it he would have considered the work his nightmare come true: female spectatorship in the playhouse leading inexorably to a life of sexual vice.

Trotter's dramatic works, even the early *Agnes de Castro* (1696), which took as its source a novel by Aphra Behn, shows Trotter working to place virtue center stage.[13] For example, in the dedication to *The Fatal Friendship*, addressed to Princess Anne, Trotter echoes Collier's call for a reformation of the stage when she asserts that the play's "[e]nd is the most noble, to discourage Vice, and recommend a firm unshaken Virtue" (i), a theme substantiated by Mrs. Barry in the epilogue when she announced the purpose of the play: "Vice to discourage, Virtue recommend." The anonymously composed complimentary verses to *The Fatal Friendship* assert Trotter's unbesmirched reputation and her unique qualifications to provide especially female spectators with characters well worthy of emulation: "Chaste are your Thoughts, and your Expression clear . . . /Your Virgin Voice offends no Virgin Ear." Trotter's virtuous persona apparently was not manufactured in response to the antitheatrical controversy. Three years earlier, in the epilogue to *Agnes de Castro*, the well-known actress, Mrs. Verbruggen (whose husband played Alvaro in the play), anticipated Trotter's later claims to dramatic and personal virtue and, incidentally, confirmed Collier in his criticism of the debauched Restoration stage: "Our Poetess is Virtuous, Young, and

Fair;/But that first Epithet I must leave out,/'twill please but very few of you, I doubt."[14] Half a decade later, Trotter dedicated her third play, *The Unhappy Penitent* (1701), to Lord Hallifax, calling attention to her vulnerable status as a woman who has "ventur'd into the World to stand the Test of Publick Censure" (i). Yet even under the threat of such censure she did not shrink from criticizing the state of dramatic art in early eighteenth-century England in terms sympathetic to Collier's argument, terms that might very well have alienated Trotter from her fellow playwrights who had endured the full force of Collier's invective: "If the Drammatick rules were justly observ'd, the Stage would soon retrieve that Credit which the abuses of it has I fear with too great reason lost, and be again a Useful Entertainement" (ii). Trotter's explicit desire in the dedication of *The Unhappy Penitent* is to rehabilitate the English stage to the status of a "Useful Entertainement" (ii). Like Collier, she plainly aimed to reform the stage and return dramatic representation to the high heroic themes of the classical period.[15]

Aside from her one comedy, *Love at a Loss, or Most Votes Carry It* (1701), Trotter's dramatic works after *Agnes de Castro* feature none of the explicit sexuality or coarseness that Collier identified under the rubric of "immodesty"; for example, *The Fatal Friendship* sympathizes with two wronged women, Felicia and Lamira, and concerns itself with love, honor, and the dilemma of reconciling competing and incompatible loyalties, and *The Revolution of Sweden* (1706) represents the heroic and noble actions of Christina and Constantia, women loyal to Gustavus's revolution against the Danish viceroy of Sweden. In these and other plays Trotter consistently placed on the English stage women in roles that she considered well worthy of emulation by female spectators. In this respect, she actively resisted the dominant poetics of an era in the history of English drama that played fast and loose with the idea of public and private virtue for women, preferring a good laugh or a good scandal (or both) instead.

For her part, Trotter seems to have understood the cultural association between the stage and sexual vice as early as 1693 when, as a fourteen year old, she composed *Olinda's Adventures*, a loosely autobiographical novel that parallels much of its author's early life.[16] On two occasions Olinda attends the theater, and on both occasions she becomes unwillingly enmeshed in a romantic intrigue, the second of which nearly leads to her rape. The (often dangerous) sexual entanglements experienced by women who attend the theater became a common feature of eighteenth-century fiction, and although attending the theater does not appear to endanger Olinda's own moral principles, it plainly places her at great risk in two related ways: (1) by identifying her as a spectator of plays it suggests that Olinda condones what opponents of the stage would have regarded as the immodest dramatic behavior enacted for audiences, and (2) by sitting in the audience Olinda willingly makes herself the desired object of several male spectators who focus on her, not the play. As for the plays themselves, Olinda is silent, offering us no details as to their subject matter or moral effects. Elsewhere in the work, however, Olinda proves herself to be an acute observer of what she calls, knowingly, "the Language of the Eyes" (17).

Olinda's unspoken but articulate Language of the Eyes takes the form of two dichotomous, feminized discourses of vision, one identified with sexual desire and the other with domestic surveillance. Reflecting on her newly discovered love for Cloridon, a love that she had hitherto repressed under the guise of friendship, Olinda writes,

> In fine, I discovered, that what I had called Esteem and Gratitude was Love; and I was as much ashamed of the Discovery, as if it had been known to all the World. I fancyed every one that saw me, read it in my Eyes; And I hated my self, when Jealousie would give me leave to Reason, for my extravagant thoughts and wishes. (164)

Throughout *Olinda's Adventures*, we are constantly made aware of the narrator and title character's eyes and their status not as the windows to the soul but as the windows to desire. Although Olinda never falls into bed with a man, her various misadventures occur in large part as a consequence of eyes that all too frequently compromise her status as a lady; the expressive quality of her eyes, their "immodest" appearance before the English stage, and the young woman's inability to regulate their sexual eloquence cumulatively jeopardize her virtue. Quite differently, we are also confronted by a pair of watchful eyes in the person of Olinda's mother, who places her daughter under close surveillance. Olinda remarks that her mother "had observ'd, that [her confidante] Licydon often gave me, and I him, Letters in private" (139); suspicious that her daughter may be involved in an illicit relationship with Licydon, Olinda's mother obtains access to the gentleman's correspondence and mistakenly interprets a letter in Olinda's hand for an avowal of love and a surrender of sexual virtue. Far from themselves expressing sexual desire, these intruding, spying eyes attempt to discipline and regulate the sexual behavior of Olinda.

Olinda and her mother's eyes represent two extremes of feminine visual expression that form a striking dialectic in eighteenth-century English literature, particularly in the novel genre: one side of the dialectic, prevalent in the first half of the long eighteenth century, represented women as desiring subjects with sexually active eyes; the other side of the dialectic, dominant in the second half of the century, encodes ladylike vision as nonsexual and safely contained within the domestic sphere. Women who are represented in the latter half of the eighteenth century as wielding sexually charged eyes jeopardize their respectable standing within society while women who employ sexually deferential, ladylike eyes increase the likelihood that they will become wives and mothers who, like Olinda's mother, subsequently regulate the scopo-sexual activities of their own daughters.

Although Trotter apparently felt compelled to navigate delicately the war of words between Collier and her playwright friends, when she turned her sights on Locke's opponents she acquired a polemical voice, as illustrated in the following lines from the preface to *A Defence of Mr. Lock's Essay of Human Understanding*:

> [*The Essay*] came too late into the World to be receiv'd without Opposition, as it might have been in the first Ages of Philosophy, before Men's Heads were prepossest with Imaginary Science; at least, no doubt, if so Perfect a Work cou'd have been produc'd so Early, it wou'd have prevented a great deal of that unintelligible Jargon, and vain Pretence to Knowledge of things out of the reach of Human Understanding, which make a great part of the School-Learning, and disuse the Mind to Plain and solid Truth. (ii)

The particular object of Trotter's scorn in the *Defence* was Thomas Burnet—an English divine, master of the charterhouse and briefly clerk of the closet to King William—with whom she corresponded about Locke's philosophy.[17] A controversial figure in his own right, Burnet was no more charitable toward Locke than Collier was toward contemporary English dramatists. Burnet's criticisms of Locke, criticism characteristic of Locke's antagonists, motivated Trotter to compose in response a philosophical and theological treatise against the man whom she identifies throughout the volume only as "the Remarker." As Trotter observes, the scope of Burnet's critique is ambitious indeed, for he desires to ascertain how the "Principles of that ingenious Essay, taken together, will give us a sure Foundation for Morality, Reveal'd Religion, and a future Life, which he does not find that they do" (2–3). From Trotter's point of view, Burnet intends to undercut systematically Locke's philosophy, which he regards as a direct threat to the fundamental precepts of Christianity. For Burnet and Collier alike, the very survival of a virtuous and Christian England was at stake in the controversies whose flames they stoked. Reforming the stage and eradicating Lockean empiricism therefore emerged as moral and theological imperatives of the highest order.

A far more influential work than *Olinda's Adventures* where a feminized discourse of vision plainly emerges and with which the Trotter of the late 1690s would have been intimately familiar is Locke's *Essay.* As William Walker has shown, Locke's theory of the tabula rasa has for three centuries mistakenly been emphasized as his dominant metaphor of human understanding. In fact, Locke's controlling metaphor is *not* a two-dimensional "blank slate" but actually a three-dimensional spatial metaphor of a room (mind) and its furnishings (knowledge).[18] In a characteristic passage early in the *Essay* Locke writes, "First, I shall enquire into the Original of those Ideas, Notions, or whatever you please to call them, which a Man observes, and is conscious to himself he has in his Mind; and the ways whereby the Understanding comes to be furnished with them."[19] Walker argues that Locke's prevailing metaphor of understanding represents "the mind [as] some kind of space within which an idea may be had and observed, as a piece of furniture may be owned and observed in a room" (32). One important way of considering how Locke understands the negotiation of the respective "rooms" and their "furnishings" in the consciousness is by employing a kind of feminized *domestic* vision mediated through the mind's eye. With respect to the pervasiveness of Locke's domestic metaphor, we see that his epistemology—arguably the most influential that an English philosopher has ever produced—was profoundly shaped by his visualization of the kind of "furnished room" that would in his lifetime have been dominantly overseen by a woman. The tropes of space and furnishing that appear throughout so much of the *Essay* suggest that Locke's philosophy of empirical knowledge found its most resonant articulation in the profoundly feminized space of the domestic sphere which, as Peter Earle and Lawrence Stone have shown, had already become an intrinsic part of late seventeenth-century bourgeois England.[20]

Within the terms of my argument, the point of intersection between Trotter and Locke occurs in Locke's insistence that knowledge, even moral knowledge, is at its base made possible by Experience, a combination of Sensation and Reflection. As Locke distinguishes between these concepts in the *Essay*, he poses a question of central importance at the beginning of book II with respect to Knowledge or what we might call, extending Locke's metaphor, the "furnishings of the mind":

> Whence comes it by that vast store, which the busy and boundless Fancy of Man has painted on it, with an almost endless variety? Whence has it all the materials of Reason and Knowledge? To this I answer, in one word, From *Experience*: In that, all our Knowledge is founded; and from that it ultimately derives it self. Our Observation employ'd either about *external, sensible Objects; or about the internal Operations of our Minds, perceived and reflected on by our selves, is that which supplies our Understanding with all the materials of thinking.* (104)

Although Locke introduces the concepts of Sensation and Reflection as equal in terms of their importance for establishing Knowledge, he also privileges Sensation over Reflection because he regards Reflection as a metaphorical extension of the operations of Sensation within the human mind:

> The other Fountain, from which Experience furnisheth the Understanding with *Ideas*, is the *Perception of the Operations of our own Minds* within us, as it is employ'd about the *Ideas* it has got; which Operations, when the Soul comes to reflect on, and consider, do furnish the Understanding with another set of *Ideas*, which could not be had from things without: and such are *Perception, Thinking, Doubting, Believing, Reasoning, Knowing, Willing*, and all the different actings of our own Minds. . . . This Source of *Ideas*, every Man has wholly in himself: And though it be not Sense, as having nothing to do with external Objects; yet it is very like it, and might properly be call'd internal Sense. But I call the other *Sensation*, so I call this *REFLECTION*. (105)

In her *Defence*, Trotter demonstrates an acute understanding of the relationship between Lockean epistemology and morality. Her critique of Locke's theory of Reflection and Perception complements well her own writings, both dramatic and critical, in defense of a virtuous stage poetics. To illustrate this understanding, Trotter quotes at length a passage from Thomas Burnet:

> As to Morality, we think the great Foundation of it, is the distinction of Good and Evil, Virtue and Vice.______ And I do not find that my Eyes, Ears, Nostrils or any other outward Senses, make any distinction of these things, as they do of Colours, Sounds, &c.______ Nor from any Ideas taken in from them, or from their Reports, am I Conscious that I do, or can conclude that there is such a distinction in the Nature of things. (4)

Burnet, Trotter argues, misapprehends Locke by claiming that knowledge, moral and otherwise, that falls within the ken of Lockean epistemology must be Sensibly determined. Trotter's reply to Burnet shows her mastery of Locke's distinction between Sensation and Reflection:

> But this will not satisfie the Remarker, unless Mr. *Lock* tells us *what is to be understood by Perfection in his Way; how it is deriv'd from the Senses, and how it includes Veracity.* The Remarker is very apt to forget, that Mr. Lock has another principle of Knowledge, which he calls Reflection, or he thinks it insignificant; perhaps it may be so as to his purpose, but happening to be serviceable in the present Enquiry, I take leave to remind him of it, that we may consider how far it will help us to the Idea of Perfection. (19–20)

Trotter here issues a stinging rejoinder to Burnet, arguing in favor of what Locke calls the "internal sense" of Reflection. Locke makes clear that Reflection requires the employment of the mind's eye to navigate the rooms of one's mind for experiential models that, in this particular instance, approach if not quite attain perfection. For Trotter, models approaching perfection found in the crowded rooms of our consciousness are the closest things we have to conceiving perfection and along with it the idea of an omniscient, omnipotent, benevolent deity. According to Lockean epistemology, we are always limited by experience, yet nothing prevents us from conceiving something more perfect than what we have already sensibly experienced in the world. That Trotter relies on Locke's concept of Reflection to respond to a set of theological doubts then becoming increasingly widespread in the eighteenth century should compel us to consider the discursive parallels between Reflection and domestic vision as articulated in England from the late seventeenth century forward. Sensation in the form of seeing with domestically trained eyes and Reflection in the form of visually navigating a mind conceived as a domestic space rely on similar tropes of visual knowledge, each becoming a means for the percipient to validate experience as well as faith. Trotter's plays clearly participate in the logic of Sensation and Reflection, for they offer spectators, particularly the female spectators with whom Collier is so concerned, a powerful sensible experience that subsequently occupies interior space within the mind as a "furnishing" and becomes a subject of potential Reflection. If Trotter's dedications and prefaces can be accepted at face value, she clearly intended for her dramatic works to provide models of virtue, and as a Lockean thinker she could not help but see their continued efficacy beyond a dramatic performance as a consequence of the power of Reflection. If we read Trotter in terms of Locke we can understand how she would have been sympathetic to the antitheatrical arguments put forward by Collier because of what the often bawdy Restoration stage presented to the senses of playgoers, but we can also see how she would have conceived her own moral art as uniquely consonant with Collier's critique and Locke's philosophy.

One of the most intriguing features of Catherine Trotter's biography is that following publication of her *Defence*, she composed and saw performed only one more play in her lifetime, *The Revolution of Sweden*, a work that raises female virtue to a level of heroism that not even Trotter had hitherto achieved. Whether or not Trotter self-consciously composed the play as her last is difficult to ascertain, but *The Revolution of Sweden* does appear to be a fitting final salvo by Trotter to the antitheatrical debate then still raging in London, especially in terms of that debate's anxieties with respect to female spectatorship. Characteristically, Trotter put herself on both sides of the debate, seeking (and obtaining) dramatic advice from Congreve and writing a play populated by women whom Collier could not possibly criticize on moral grounds, thereby implicitly reconciling the two outspoken rivals. But after composing five plays for the London theater over the course of a decade and gaining a considerable reputation along the way, Trotter walked away from the stage for good, presumably because of her marriage to Patrick Cockburn, an Anglican minister who likely would not have approved of his wife's continued vocation as a playwright.[21] Permanently removed from the London stage and though an occasional poetry contributor to the periodical press, the now Catharine Cockburn turned her considerable energies to domestic and maternal duties, giving birth to and raising three daughters and a son.

Trotter's two lives—as a well-known dramatist and an ever more obscure wife and mother (and occasional writer on philosophical and theological themes)—represent in miniature the subject matter of this chapter. Trotter moved from theorizing and representing manifestations of female vision in the public arena that are concerned with issues of sexuality, desire, conduct, and epistemology to occupying a private domestic sphere that she inevitably supervised with her own disciplining, overseeing eyes. As the author of a novel, several plays, and an important philosophical defense of Locke, Trotter provides us with one of the earliest, fullest, and most diversified records of a woman deeply engaged in questioning the status of female vision at the discursive, representational, and epistemological levels. For the last four decades of her life, Trotter did not share with us nearly as much as during her first twenty-eight years, when so much of what she thought and reflected upon appeared in print and was performed for the play-going public. Yet although Trotter fell largely silent on the particulars of her domestic life as the eighteenth century proceeded, novelistic representations of domestic Englishwomen proliferated. These representations remind us of the cultural relationships among the empirical, sexual, and domestic discourses of female vision so important to Trotter's early career.

Domestic Surveillance and Scopic Sexuality in Eighteenth-Century Literature and Culture

Like Trotter's Olinda, the most prominent female protagonists of the eighteenth-century and early-nineteenth-century novel—including Samuel Richardson's Pamela and Clarissa, Eliza Haywood's Betsy, Frances Burney's Evelina and Cecilia, Maria Edgeworth's Belinda, and Jane Austen's Elizabeth and Emma—are so closely identified with visually oriented epistemology that empirical knowledge is to a great degree culturally authorized through their closely surveying eyes. In the history of the English novel, Richardson, in particular, has been credited with developing and extending psychological verisimilitude, and particularly the realistic representation of female characters such as Pamela Andrews who, according to Nancy Armstrong, came to represent the quintessence of the ideologically and representationally triumphant domestic woman in the eighteenth century. One of the distinctive characteristics that lends Pamela such powerful representational force is the detail-oriented quality of her eyes, eyes that are limited exclusively to the domestic sphere. Female characters such as Pamela are pervasively figured as the best interpreters of empirical reality because "reality" in the nonpicaresque English novel is overwhelmingly represented within the confines of the home, a cultural space that became subject to feminine (visual) mastery in the eighteenth century. As domestic women proliferated within the novel genre, which developed into the undisputed champion (in popular terms, at least) of literary expression in the eighteenth century, their quite specific form of observation and surveillance—consonant with Locke's and Trotter's philosophic tropes of domestic observation—acquired enormous cultural authority.

Beyond the philosophical and literary relationship between empiricism and the eighteenth-century novel that existed in their mutual use of domesticity as both a trope and literal manifestation of epistemological truth, the broader cultural significance of domestic surveillance is explicated by Armstrong's scholarship on the ideological construction of the modern bourgeois Englishwoman. In her reading of eighteenth-century conduct books and fiction, Armstrong underlines an important aspect of cultural agency that this new kind of woman exercised: "The domestic woman's capacity to supervise was clearly more important than any other factor in determining the victory of this ardently undazzling creature over all her cultural competitors. For this reason, the peculiar combination of invisibility and vigilance personified in the domestic woman came to represent the principle of domestic economy itself."[22] Like Armstrong's exploration of domestic subjectivity, my approach to female visuality does not dismiss domesticity as a patriarchal strategy for containing women in the home but rather treats it as a crucial political, economic, and representational force within English culture. As numerous scholars of the eighteenth century have argued, including Lawrence Stone, Peter Earle, Leonard Davidoff, and Catherine Hall, without domesticity's widespread advent, the transformation of England from an aristocratic, land-based to a bourgeois, capitalist political economy would not have occurred so comprehensively and in such a relatively short period. As we know, the sexual division of labor among the bourgeoisie that feminized the home and masculinized the marketplace occurred with dizzying swiftness in the eighteenth and early nineteenth centuries.[23] For capitalism to succeed, of course, the human senses—particularly a domesticated version of female vision—had to structure and record reality with Lockean confidence. In the early English novel, female visuality is dominantly articulated as both an ideological and epistemological justification of capitalist materialism.[24]

By emphasizing the domestic tradition in the English novel, I am exercising an implicit judgment about the relative obscurity of what we might consider to be an alternative novelistic "tradition," a tradition constituted by novelists such as Aphra Behn, Delariviere Manley, Daniel Defoe, and John Cleland, all of whom emphasize the sexuality, visual and otherwise, of their female characters. Richardson's attempt to negate his female protagonists' (scopic) sexuality—and, in fact, to have Pamela and Clarissa closely regulate the sexual behavior of others—marks an important departure from seventeenth- and early-eighteenth-century novelistic depictions of women, where female sexuality is often openly depicted and even encouraged. By having his female protagonists enact the virtues promulgated in conduct books, Richardson, and those who followed him in the domestic novel or novel of manners traditions, including the later Eliza Haywood, Frances Burney, Maria Edgeworth, and Jane Austen, among others, altered the course of the English novel and along with it constructed the discursive and representational possibilities of visual relations between the sexes. Male characters in these novels are overwhelmingly portrayed as sexual spectators, and their female counterparts are depicted either as domestic overseers or sexual spectacles.

In visual terms, conduct book admonishments called for young women to lower their eyes beyond the confines of the home. For instance, in Wetenhall Wilkes' contribution to the genre, *A Letter of Genteel and Moral Advice to a Young Lady* (1744), the author admonishes his niece to undertake a painstaking self-surveillance by "set[ting] a double Watch on all [her] Thoughts and Words" (9) and, complementarily, to regulate closely her eyes because of his conviction that "the very name of Virgin [which] imports a critical Niceness with respect to Virtue, Innocence, and decent Behaviour" is endangered by "immodest Glances" that "pollute the Eyes" (84).[25] Wilkes' justification for disciplining the conduct of his niece's vision relies on his understanding of men who, like Richardson's Lovelace, are careful observers of women's eyes:

> The double Temptation of Vanity and Desire is so prevalent in our Sex, that we are apt to interpret every obliging Look, Gesture, Smile or Sentence of a Female we like to the hopeful Side. Therefore let your Deportment forbid without Rudeness, and oblige without Invitation. We look upon a Woman's Eyes to be the Interpreters of her Heart; and we often gather more Encouragement from a pleasing Glance, than from her softest Words. The Language of the Eyes is very significant.[26]

In contrast to his warnings about the power of the female eye to elicit sexual impulses in men, Wilkes enjoins his niece to educate herself in watching over and tending the domestic sphere:

> It is a great Art in House-keeping, to have the Furniture always clean, and to lay by every thing in its proper Place, when out of Use. This Method will prevent Confusion, preserve the Things, and contribute greatly to your private Ease. A litter'd Room is a sure Sign of Indolence and Supineness in the Mistress, as it is of Sloth and Sluttishness in her Servants. (91)

Written in the Richardsonian 1740s, Wilkes' admonishments—particularly with respect to teaching his niece how to be regarded as the possessor of sexually irreproachable eyes—anticipate Lady Pennington's *An Unfortunate Mother's Advice to her Daughters* (1790), which appeared half a century later. In that volume the authoress enjoins her daughters to "[r]egard neither the actions nor the dress of others: let not your eyes rove in search of acquaintance."[27] Read within the tradition of female domestic vision in the eighteenth-century novel, *A Letter of Genteel and Moral Advice to a Young Lady and An Unfortunate Mother's Advice to her Daughters* suggests, at least from the 1740s forward, a wide-ranging cultural concern over the regulation of female eyes.

Volumes 1 and 2 of *Pamela*,[28] among the most popular of eighteenth-century novels, chronicle the interiorization of female vision within the domestic sphere. In these two novels Richardson explores the potential power that feminized "empirical" eyes can effect in the home. Once liberated in volume 1 from the threat of rape by becoming the new Mrs. B, Pamela, the former servant, principally focuses in volume 2 not on the otherwise pleasing figure of Mr. B, but rather on the interior of their home and her duties within it. Pamela's quick and perceptive domestic vision thereby enables her to oversee an efficient and well-regulated household, which was in the ensuing Richardsonian novel tradition widely established as the bourgeois Englishwoman's primary responsibility. The domestication of Pamela's vision in volume 2 is one of the principal discursive constructions of Richardson's sequel. Over the course of her two novels, Pamela moves from occupying a role as the sexualized object of Mr. B's scopic desire, to becoming the visual subject of domestic surveillance. Domestic vision in *Pamela*, with its insistent focus on cataloging the everyday objects, domestic duties, and subtle intrigues of the English home, and its relentless emphasis on ascertaining the truth about the workings of the domestic sphere, is methodologically constituted very much like empiricism, an unsurprising "coincidence" considering that both seventeenth- and eighteenth-century empiricism and the novel depend on tropes of domesticity to constitute their similar brands of epistemology.

In volume 2 of *Pamela* (1742), the now gentry-class Pamela B describes well her practice of domestic surveillance in a letter to Miss Darnford, her sexually and domestically inexperienced friend:

> [The countess and Lady Davers] told [Mr. B], how much they admired my family management: then they would have it that my genius was universal, for the employments and accomplishments of my sex, whether they considered it as employed in penmanship, in needlework, in paying or receiving visits, in music, and I can't tell how many other qualifications, which they were pleased to attribute to me, over and above the family management: saying, that I had

> an understanding which comprehended every thing, *and an eye that penetrated into the very bottom of matters in a moment*, and never was at a loss for the *should be*, the *why* or *wherefore*, and the *how*—these were their comprehensive words; that I did every thing with celerity, clearing all as I went, and left nothing, they observed, to come over again, that could be dispatched at once.[29] [emphasis mine]

Pamela's vision is marked in this and other instances by an extraordinarily particularized attention to physical detail, and her ability to infer an empirical version of reality on the basis of that detail even when it is not immediately present to her eyes. This points to her unequivocal confidence in an epistemology closely akin to Locke's theory of the double existence, what philosophers such as David Hume called a "continu'd" and "distinct" existence, that is, if objects have (1) an existence beyond their perception by our senses and (2) an autonomous existence independent of other objects.[30] In ways that are strikingly similar to those employed by empiricism, Pamela gets to the truth of her domestic sphere by employing eyes that penetrate through the rooms, chambers, and mundane mysteries of the household. Pamela uses an ocular language of "penetration" in her correspondence that causally explains everyday phenomena and pierces through the opacity of domestic organization.

The language of causality ("the *why*, or *wherefore*, and the *how*") Pamela employs to describe the workings of her eyes within the domestic sphere also corresponds in a number of respects to empiricism. The empirical tradition in English philosophy represented by Bacon, Locke, Berkeley, and Hume, among others, explains how the human senses, disciplined by induction, may explicate the mysteries of nature. Likewise, Pamela assumes her household to be full of mysteries that must be investigated by feminized eyes; Bacon, who exerted an enormous influence on Locke's epistemology, similarly regards nature as cloaked in secrecy that must be explicated by masculinized science. Seven decades before Locke, Bacon argued in *The Great Instauration* (1620) that nonempirical natural philosophers inevitably "fall to complaints of the subtlety of nature, the hiding-places of truth, the obscurity of things, the entanglements of causes."[31]

Whereas Bacon, who aspires to become a "true priest of the sense" (24), proposes to untangle the knots of cause and effect in nature, Pamela sets out to do just the same in the B household. Yet in comparing Bacon's dominantly masculine-empirical language to Locke's feminine tropes of domesticity, we begin to see how Locke reconfigured late-seventeenth-century empirical philosophy through a language of domesticity, a language that Pamela also invokes in her explanations of the domestic sphere's workings.

Whereas Bacon might hardly recognize the affinities between his masculinization of empirical inquiry and Pamela's femininization of domestic investigation, we retrospectively recognize the close relationship in methodology *and* language between Pamela and Locke's understanding of (domestic) knowledge-formation. As we discover in Pamela's letter to Miss Darnford, cited above, she describes in maddeningly minute detail the work of her domestic eyes as well as the surveillance she is subjected to by her husband's female relatives. This double articulation of the discourse of female vision functions as didactic instruction of Miss Darnford's uneducated eyes. Pamela brings Miss Darnford into being as a "modern" Englishwoman by teaching her how to see with empirically discerning domestic eyes that will—if I may be permitted to paraphrase Bacon's language—raise her to the status of a "true [domestic] priestess" of the senses. For us, Richardson's Pamela calls attention to how knowledge formation was feminized through the language of domesticity in the cultural sites of the novel and Lockean empiricism, respectively.

Writing yet again to Miss Darnford, Pamela describes how she spied through a key-hole to discover Polly and Mr. H's sexual indiscretions. Pamela's peeping-tom-like gaze confirms her earlier hypothesis about the sexual nature of Polly and Mr. H's relationship. By placing this improbable couple under domestic surveillance, Pamela checks her hypothesis against empirically gathered evidence and then double checks her physical evidence against interviews with both Polly and Mr. H to ensure that she witnessed what she believed she witnessed. Pamela's discoveries, and her confirmation of those discoveries, admirably illustrate how she employs a domesticated "empirical" methodology. I should emphasize that in highlighting the methodological similarities between the representation of female vision in the novel and the discourse of empirical vision in Locke, I am not making a case in favor of Pamela's domestic literalization of Lockean empiricism. Rather, what I am underscoring is the extent to which domesticity—and domestic observation—became in the eighteenth century a significant trope of knowledge formation, whether that knowledge formation was constituted in terms of empirical philosophy or in terms of the domestic novel.

Pamela's vision is not circumscribed to strictly household duties, for she also regulates sexual behavior in the household with her domestically discerning eyes. While the peeping-tom sequence detailed above conjures up familiar images of male voyeurism in the eighteenth-century novel, Pamela's vision does not elicit voyeuristic pleasure as accounts of male spectatorship so often do in, for instance, *Clarissa,* or in the work of Aphra Behn, Daniel Defoe, and John Cleland. Rather, Pamela's eyes, which once more have arrived at the "truth" of a previously inexplicable matter, permit the new mistress of the house to exercise her formidable domestic power. Her subsequent extraction of Polly's sexual history underscores the completeness of Pamela's visual mastery. Just as empirical observation and reasoning empowered English science over and against nature, Pamela's acute surveillance has granted her access to the power-knowledge apparati of the domestic sphere. In Pamela's case, ocular observation is not identified (as it is with Bacon) with masculine science's call to dominate feminine nature but rather with feminine surveillance's power to dominate the household.

Miss Darnford's domestic education by Pamela in volume 2 continues a generational passing-on of regulative surveillance from an older to a younger woman, for Richardson suggests that Pamela has learned her own skills of surveillance and investigation from Mr. B's mother. In volume 2, for instance, Mr. B informs Pamela that prior to her death Mrs. B often placed himself and Pamela under her "watchful" eyes, an attitude that too often stymied Mr. B's sexual designs. By watching over Polly and Mr. H—whose social positions as female servant and male landowner relative to Pamela in volume 2 mirror Pamela's and Mr. B's relative to Mrs. B in volume 1—Pamela duplicates Mrs. B's domestic role in the household. In both cases, the watchful lady of the house employs the evidence of her eyes to discover the reality of a socially unequal situation in order to prevent sexual advantage being taken against one of her female servants. This notion of an older woman educating the eyes of a younger woman focuses our attention on the didactic nature of representations of female vision in the English novel. The principal target of this (scopic) didacticism is, of course, not Pamela but the thousands of girls and young women who read Pamela's story.

In order to demonstrate the ideal principles of sexual conduct and ladylike vision that women were encouraged to embrace in the eighteenth century, one need look no farther than *Clarissa* (1747–48).[32] Stressing the importance of the language of the eyes to Clarissa's self-conception, the young woman's last will and testament stipulates that her corpse *not* be "unnecessarily exposed to the view of anybody" (1413). Clarissa bequeaths two portraits of herself—the first either to her aunt or mother and the second to her closest friend and confidante, Anna Howe. Clarissa posthumously controls both the viewing of her own body and its pictorial representations, distributing the latter within an exclusively scopic economy for the consumption of female spectators alone. Clarissa's instructions protect both body and image from Lovelace, under whose eyes she suffers almost from the moment of the couple's "elopement."

In the account of the events leading to her rape, Clarissa writes to Anna of Lovelace's "leering" gaze: "He terrified me with his looks and with his violent emotions as he gazed upon me. . . . Never I saw his abominable eyes look, as then they looked!—triumph in them!—fierce and wild" (1013). Lovelace acknowledges the sadistic quality of his eyes, proclaiming, "I love when I dig a pit, to have my prey tumble in with secure feet and open eyes; then a man can look down upon her, with an oh-ho charmer! how came you there?" (465). In this metaphor of domination, Lovelace makes two important rhetorical shifts: first, he moves from a specific reference to himself in the first person "I" to the general scopic sadist "man" and transitions from the generic "prey" to the gendered pronoun "her." The effect of Lovelace's two shifts not only universalizes the roles of an empowered male spectator looking down on a passive female object but also divests himself of responsibility for his reprehensible behavior. In making Clarissa the visual target of his exploitation, Lovelace simply does what "men" do: he engages in the "masculine" behavior of expressing his scopo-sexual desire.

According to Lovelace, women must strike an altogether different scopo-sexual attitude toward men if they are to be regarded as feminine and virtuous, an attitude that Clarissa exemplifies. Just prior to Clarissa's rape, Lovelace instructs two "fallen" women to pose as his aunt and cousin. In these guises he hopes they will appear to Clarissa as appropriate companions. Lovelace understands his plan to be fraught with complications, not least of which is teaching his "actresses" how to see and be seen as ladies, and he therefore instructs them to "be sure not to forget to look down, or aside, when looked at. When eyes meet eyes, be yours the retreating ones" (865), thereby suggesting a connection between deferential eyes and, in these women's case, the appearance of feminine virtue. Lovelace looks with disgust, for example, upon women who violate polite culture's injunction against the female transgression of looking about indiscriminately, and he calls the "staring" Miss Rawlins "a confident slut" (775), basing his judgment on what he considers to be her overly active eyes. Lovelace even more harshly condemns Anna: "Too much fire and spirit in her eye indeed, *for a girl*" [emphasis mine] (864). Further corroborating the active/passive vision-virtue connection, at Mrs. Sinclair's house, Clarissa remains under the constant surveillance of the prostitutes, all of whom wield active, sexualized eyes, and Sinclair and her protégés appear not merely to encourage and assist in Clarissa's rape; they also watch it, becoming, in Lovelace's understanding of scopo-sexual gender roles, "masculinized" spectators. Sinclair thereby conflates (and perverts) the masculine-sexual and feminine-domestic dichotomy of Richardsonian vision in that she watches over and controls Clarissa's behavior in the brothel (domestic surveillance) as well as views her rape (sexual spectatorship). Richardson's two popular novels thereby provide a culturally powerful discursive production of feminized and masculinized vision, telling in their pages what would become profoundly resonant narratives of proper and improper visual conduct. Clarissa's sexually deferential vision and Pamela's scrutinizing domestic vision capture the complementary characteristics of this newly constituted scopic ideology.

For women like Clarissa in the eighteenth-century novel, knowledge and the social power that accompanies knowledge derive principally from visually explicating the workings of the domestic sphere. Yet the domesticated knowledge of surveying women depended on how effectively they disciplined their visual behavior prior to marriage. In the novel, unmarried young women were depicted as placing their own and other women's (and men's) eyes under close surveillance in order to regulate their expressive power. Too much visual expressivity—especially of the "wrong," sexually oriented kind—became regarded as a double threat to feminine sexual and domestic virtue. To see with blatantly desiring eyes marked a woman as wanton and disqualified her from participating in the most desirable marriage markets. Possessing sexually charged eyes threatened young women with social decline and even ostracism; in addition, the articulation of sexually charged vision undermined the epistemological trope of domesticity that the novel and empirical philosophy came to rely upon to justify their cultural authority. In order to protect the sexual integrity of young women—as well as to protect the integrity of domesticity as a powerful epistemological trope—it became incumbent on novelists to emphasize the conduct of "proper" female vision and to produce visually didactic novels that disciplined English girls and young women to focus their eyes on the domestic sphere as well as to supervise the dangerously wandering eyes of other men and women.

The discourse of feminine visual conduct articulated in English conduct books and the Richardsonian novel differs drastically from pre-Richardsonian novelistic depictions of seeing women. One need only consider two of Richardson's popular predecessors, Daniel Defoe, and Aphra Behn, as well as a contemporary, John Cleland, to comprehend the radically different trajectory of the English novel following the publication of *Pamela*, especially with respect to representing female scopo-sexuality. In the following discussion of this trio of English novelists, what I hope to suggest is how different our understanding of female vision might look today had an alternative, frankly sexualized and feminized tradition in the English novel not been obscured by its domestic competition.

Neither Defoe nor Cleland hesitates to depict his Moll and Fanny as women in possession of scopo-sexual desires. In *Moll Flanders* (1722) Moll coldly laments the loss of her first husband, coldness that is the result of desire for her first lover, her husband's older brother. The intense sexuality of Moll's gaze becomes clear in the following passage:

> I confess I was not suitably affected with the loss of my husband, nor indeed can I say that I ever loved him as I ought to have done, or as was proportionable to the good usage I had from him, for he was a tender, kind, good-humoured man as any woman could desire; but his brother being so always *in my sight*, at least while we were in the country, was a continual snare to me, and I never was in bed with my husband but I

> wished myself in the arms of his brother; and though his brother never offered me the least kindness that way after our marriage, but carried it just as a brother ought to do, yet it was impossible to do so to him; in short, I committed adultery and incest with him every day in my desires, which, without doubt, was as effectually criminal in the nature of the guilt as if I had actually done it.[33]

The fact that it is the elder brother's habitual presence before Moll's eyes that compels her to fantasize sexual acts with him points to the conclusion that Moll, far from looking at men with Richardson's version of a deferential glance, sees with phallicly "penetrating" sexualized eyes. Moll's lusty gaze is one that Richardson would recognize as masculine.

Such a sexualized vision is even more a defining feature of Fanny Hill's depiction. Published just one year after *Clarissa*, Cleland's *Memoirs of a Woman of Pleasure* (1748) casts its heroine as almost all eyes and sex. Fanny's introduction to sex is the result of secretly watching with her friend, Phoebe, a "young *Genoese* merchant" and the beautiful prostitute, Polly, have sex, recalling (and inverting) Pamela's key-hole scene discussed in the first section in which Pamela *prevents* sex from occurring by secretly looking in on *her own* Polly and Mr. H. For Fanny, this first sight of sex does not compel her, like Pamela, to control her own or anyone else's physical desires, but rather awakens hitherto dormant urges:

> For my part, I will not pretend to describe what I felt all over me, during this scene; but from that instant, adieu all fears of what man could do unto me; they were now changed into such ardent desires, such ungovernable longings, that I could have pull'd the first of that sex that should present himself, by the sleeve, and offered him to the bauble, which I now imagin'd the loss of would be a gain I could not soon [enough] procure myself.[34]

What Fanny first procures after this scene is not erotic fulfillment with a man, but sexual play with a woman, Phoebe, who subsequently lifts Fanny's skirts and manually stimulates what turns out to be an unquenchable desire. Cleland's dalliance with lesbian sexuality, what Fanny calls "this foolery from woman to woman" (34), is short-lived as she quickly returns to, and remains within, patriarchal codes of heterosexuality and phallic desire. Rather than open up Fanny to the possibilities of sexual pleasure with women, her voyeurism in fact inaugurates a chain of promiscuous escapades that takes her from one man to another. The first of these is the virile Charles, with whom Fanny loses her virginity. The morning after this momentous event she looks upon her lover with what Richardson would no doubt have conceived as a masculine sexual gaze:

> [N]or could I refuse myself a pleasure that solicited me so irresistibly, as this fair occasion of feasting my sight with all those treasures of youthful beauty I had enjoy'd, and which lay now almost entirely naked, his shirt being trust up in a perfect wisp, which the warmth of the room and season made me easy about the consequence of. I hung over him enamour'd indeed! and devour'd all his naked charms with only two eyes, when I could have wish'd them at least a hundred, for the fuller enjoyment of the gaze.[35]

One objection to my exploration of the scopo-sexuality of Defoe's and Cleland's female protagonists might be that these characters' expressions of vision do not represent the "authentic" sexual longings of women, but rather qualify only as projections of masculine pornographic fantasy onto the feminine. Extending this line of reasoning, these characters are seen as products of the fictional imaginations of men, with subjectivities far more masculine than feminine. Such objections, though important to consider, cannot so easily be sustained against Aphra Behn and Delariviere Manley, who along with Eliza Haywood constitute two-thirds of the Restoration's "fair triumvirate of wits."[36]

Whereas Toni O'shaugnessy Bowers argues that women's amatory novels such as Behn's and Manley's "routinely connect sexuality to voyeurism, exploitation, and violence" and, as such, "the language of lust in amatory fiction follows codes of male arousal" (54), Ros Ballaster counters that "[t]he fiction of Aphra Behn, Delariviere Manley, and Eliza Haywood was perceived as distinctly different . . . from male pornography."[37] Ballaster contends that eighteenth-century amatory fiction was much closer in sensibility to didactic love fiction than male pornography and shares affinities with what Ann Barr Snitow calls "pornography for women."[38]

If Ballaster is right about amatory fiction's affinity with pornography for women, Aphra Behn was among the first female pornographers. Behn is just as inclined to depict female as male scopo-sexual desire in her *Love Letters Between a Nobleman and His Sister* (1684–87). In accounting for her illicit sexual attraction to Philander, Calista relies on her earlier viewing of him as a justification for what will shortly turn out to be adultery:

> I sat whole hours and days, and fixed my soul upon the lovely figure; I know its stature to an inch, tall and divinely made; I saw his hair, long, black, and curling to his waist, all loose and flowing; I saw his eyes, where all the *Cupids* played, black, large, and sparkling, piercing, loving, languishing; I saw his lips sweet, dimpled, red, and soft; a youth complete in all, like early *May*, that looks, and smells, and cheers above the rest: in fine, I saw him such as nothing but the nicest fancy can imagine, and nothing can describe; I saw him such as robs me of my rest, as gives me all the raging pains of love (love I believe it is) without the joy of any single hope.[39]

The intricate physical detail with which Calista has earlier looked upon and here envisions Philander points to the extreme scopo-sexual dimensions of her desire. The eyes of Behn's Calista, like Moll's and Fanny's—and unlike Pamela's and Clarissa's—express a strongly felt sexual cathexis.[40]

If the fictional space of female scopic sexuality inhabited by Calista, Moll, and Fanny was not obliterated by the Richardsonian domestic novel tradition after 1740, it was at least largely obscured by it, particularly with respect to what novels and novelists have been deemed canonical. By 1748, Cleland is not only attempting to extend the novelistic tradition of explicitly representing female sexuality inaugurated by Behn and Manley, among others, he is also explicitly working against the new and popular Richardsonian domestic tradition in an oppositional manner not unlike Henry Fielding in *Shamela* (1741) and *Joseph Andrews* (1742). Yet of the trio of authors and works I have cited to illustrate sexual possibilities for female vision, Defoe alone stands out as unreservedly "canonical"; it is only a relatively recent phenomenon that Behn and Cleland have come to be regarded as even potentially canonical. Richardson, by contrast, has been considered one of the "fathers" of the English novel for as long as there has been something we could recognizably call "novel criticism."[41] Consequently, Richardson's gender-determined discourse of vision is steeped in what were to become the culturally accepted, pervasive, and enduring assumptions of masculine-sexual vision and feminine-domestic vision that became an important cultural expression of knowledge formation in the eighteenth century.

Kathryn Shevelow has argued persuasively that one significant eighteenth-century cultural production that disseminated the lessons of conduct literature was the women's periodical. As editor and author of *The Female Spectator* (1744–46), what Shevelow calls "the first periodical for women written by a woman," Eliza Haywood therefore occupies an important place in the discursive history of female visuality in England.[42] *The Female Spectator* should be regarded as not simply a women's version of Addison and Steele's *Spectator* but rather as part of a much wider phenomenon of women expressing a kind of visual and domestic "will to power"; in the pages of *The Female Spectator* the visual surveillance and disciplinary power of Pamela are multiplied in the editorial and authorial figure of Eliza Haywood into something on the scale of a feminized Argos who places under surveillance the sexually threatened Ios of England.[43] Claiming to employ a network of spies who frequent London, the fashion centers of provincial England, "*Bath*, *Tunbridge* and *the Spaw*" as well as favored continental destinations such as "*France*, *Rome*, *Germany* so that nothing curious or worthy of Remark can escape me,"[44] Haywood basks in the glow of a formidable power of surveillance that enables her to see vicariously into the private domestic spaces of England and the continent:

> [T]his I look upon to be a more effectual way of penetrating into the Mysteries of the Alcove, the Cabinet, or Field, than if I had the Power of Invisibility, or could with a Wish transport myself wherever I pleased, since with the Aid of those supernatural Gifts, I could still be in no more than one Place at a Time; whereas now, by tumbling over a few Papers from my Emissaries, I have all the Secrets of Europe, at least such of them as are proper for my Purpose, laid open at one View. (8)

Of the numerous eighteenth-century women's periodicals, *The Female Spectator* was among the most important. Beyond its connection to "empirical" modes of domestic inquiry, the ideological purpose of the periodical is clear: to educate young bourgeois women (and in a roundabout way, young men) and their families about how to make and sustain domestically rewarding marriages and avoid disastrous sexual scandals. Shevelow observes that while the periodical "endorsed the domestic ideal," its "authority to pronounce upon conduct was represented as a particularly feminine one, authoritative within, and only within, a feminine province—the women's periodical and the specialized configuration of femininity it projected" (168–69). Shevelow contends that unlike *The Spectator* and other eighteenth-century periodicals principally written by and for men and that of necessity commented on issues important to women from a hierarchical position of superiority, *The Female Spectator* addressed women as equals, a shift in sensibility whose cultural importance should not be underestimated given that it represented a significant step in politically resituating women in relation to their reading material, even when that reading material's purpose was explicitly didactic.

Given the cultural importance of sexual and domestic conduct to women in the eighteenth century, it is significant that on the title page of *The Female Spectator*'s first number, Haywood explicitly casts her patron, the Duchess of Leeds, as a woman "of an unblemish'd Conduct, but also of an exalted Virtue, whose Example may enforce the Precepts they contain, and is Herself a shining Pattern for others to copy after, of all those Perfections I endeavour to recommend." As patron of the periodical, the Duchess of Leeds clearly parallels the role played by *Miss Betsy Thoughtless*' protective Lady Trusty and, for that matter, *Pamela*'s Mrs. B. Her goal in this case is to train young women in the methods of seeing with deferential eyes so that they may marry well, become domestic overseers, and, in turn, themselves interpellate a new generation of domestic women.

Haywood's *Miss Betsy Thoughtless* (1751), which appeared five years after the final number of the periodical, may be read as a continuation of the periodical's themes of female surveillance. The narrator of *Betsy Thoughtless* operates in a role analogous to Haywood-as-editor as Betsy gradually comes to embrace the lessons of domestic felicity *The Female Spectator* makes its principal aim. By highlighting the multiple threats to women's unsupervised sexual virtue through "empirical" observation of the private chambers and public ballrooms of England, Haywood strives in both the periodical and the novel to make possible women's ultimate domestic success. Early in the novel, Haywood suggests Betsy's own potentially sexually and domestically regulating powers as a spectator. In ways that evoke Pamela's observation of Polly and Mr. H, Betsy betrays a few symptoms of her ability to discipline the Goodman household with her own penetrating eyes. In her history's opening chapters, Betsy returns from an outside engagement and rushes upstairs to the room she shares with Miss Flora. Surprised to find the door locked, she gains access to the bedroom by spying from Lady Mellasin's dressing room door where "her eyes, as well as ears, contributed to a discovery she little expected. . . . [S]he plainly perceived Miss Flora and a man rise off the bed: she could not at first discern who he was, but, on his returning to go out of the room, knew him to be no other than Gayland" (38). Betsy's discovery of Flora's adolescent sexuality repulses and shocks her (not least because Gayland had been courting Betsy), in effect (self-)disciplining her code of virginal sexuality. From this point forward, Betsy remains vigilant about protecting her virginity, but she does not take the complementary steps of disciplining either her coquettish inclinations or the conduct of her eyes.

If the domestically rewarded virtues of Pamela Andrews' life may in part be attributed to her own observations of the domestic surveillance enacted by the watchful matriarch Mrs. B, the dangers and pitfalls of Betsy's career as a coquette are clearly the result of not having an older, domestically responsible woman to teach her how to see and be seen by the world. Orphaned at thirteen, Betsy removes to the household of her guardian, Mr. Goodman, his dissolute wife, Lady Mellasin, and her promiscuous daughter, Miss Flora. Almost immediately, Lady Trusty, an intimate friend of Betsy's deceased mother, recognizes what must be the grave deficiencies in the young woman's domestic education. Haywood is quick to spell out Lady Trusty's quite justified suspicions with regard to Lady Mellasin's qualifications as an appropriate domestic model:

> [Lady Trusty] was a woman of great prudence, piety, and virtue: she had heard many things relating to the conduct of Lady Mellasin, which made her think her a very unfit person to have the care of youth, especially those of her own sex. She had been extremely troubled when Sir Ralph told her that Miss Betsy was sent for from the country to live under such tuition. (11)

In lieu of creating discord between her own and Goodman's family, Lady Trusty resolves to "giv[e] Miss Betsy such instructions as she thought necessary for her behaviour in general, and especially towards the family in which it was her lot to be placed" (11). For Lady Trusty, whom the narrator calls, in the metaphorical language of eighteenth-century empirical-ocular observation, a "woman of penetration," clearly what is at stake is Miss Betsy's sexual and domestic virtue, and she thereafter makes a point of coming "more often to Mr. Goodman's than otherwise she would have done, on purpose to observe the behaviour of Miss Betsy" (32). Unfortunately for Betsy, circumstances make it impossible for her to accept Lady Trusty's invitation to spend a significant portion of her first summer as an orphan on the Trusty estate. Only at the end of the novel will Betsy have an opportunity to gain from "the benefits she might have received, by being under the eye of so excellent an instructress" (40). What follows Betsy's regrettable decision to join her brother in Oxford rather than Lady Trusty in the country are a series of misadventures—including two attempted rapes—that we are led to presume could have been avoided had Betsy allowed herself to be disciplined by Lady Trusty's eyes. Not until the visual conduct of Betsy's eyes is disciplined does she qualify as either a happy wife or an effective surveyor of the domestic realm. In the post-Richardsonian domestic novel, these two descriptions of womanhood (happy wife and domestic surveyor) increasingly came to depend on one another.

Betsy never benefits from the full-fledged visual education that would have been made available to her had she placed herself under the supervision of Lady Trusty, yet she shows herself early on to be quite skilled at reading the looks of potential suitors: "She had very penetrating eyes this way, and never made a conquest without knowing she did so" (70). Lacking as Betsy is in terms of domestic vision, she is something of a self-made woman, both in regard to making her own charms all-too scopically stimulating to men and herself recognizing signs of desire on the faces of the numerous men who pursue her. One of these men is the aptly named Trueworth, the favorite of Betsy's younger brother who has "regard[ed] her with glances . . . which she had interpreted as the certain indications of feeling something in his heart of the nature her brother had described [love]" (67).

Trueworth patiently pursues Betsy over the first third of the novel, but he eventually surrenders his suit, giving up on her principally because she insists on being seen at the theater with Miss Forward, an old friend who, unknown to her, has descended into prostitution.[45] Trueworth's rejection of Betsy on this basis recalls, of course, Jeremy Collier's contention that the English stage compromises the virtue of female spectators; it also reminds us of the scopo-sexual exploits engaged in by Haywood's own Fantomina from two decades earlier, a period when Haywood was writing amatory fiction that, unlike *Betsy Thoughtless*, was populated by women who are desiring sexual agents. Writing in a post-Richardsonian cultural milieu that she no longer dominated as she did the 1720s, Haywood highlights the shortcomings of Betsy's eyes in her relations with Miss Forward.[46] In her survey of Forward, Betsy notices nothing different from her preprostitution behavior, with the exception, perhaps, of an increase in gaiety. By contrast, Trueworth apprehends Miss Forward's lack of sexual virtue through close observation: "There was . . . a certain air of libertinism, both in her looks and gestures, which would have convinced Mr. Trueworth, if he had not been told before, that she was one of those unhappy creatures, who make traffick of their beauty" (198). Trueworth vainly implores Betsy not to attend a play with "a woman of [Forward's] class," not to appear "in a place where so many eyes will be upon you" and to refrain from "seeing yourself gazed and pointed at by those to whom she sells her favours!" (205). Betsy's indignant response is to assert her own agency as a spectatress rather than a spectacle: "Pish! . . . I want to see the play, not to be seen myself" (208). An urbane man of the world, Trueworth knows the difference, like Lovelace, between the looks of "fallen" and virtuous women. Trueworth concludes that for Betsy to be seen with Forward—indeed, for her to become the spectacle at the theater rather than the players themselves—must signify Betsy's own fall from sexual grace. Although Betsy dismisses Trueworth's grave suspicions, in the same instant that she defies his wishes (and in doing so delays their eventual marriage by 400 pages), she also promises herself to "'watch carefully [Miss Forward], not only the replies she makes to what I say, but also her very looks'" (206–07). The result of Betsy's observations leads to a definitive break in the friendship.

By separating Trueworth and Betsy on the basis of the latter's playgoing, Haywood establishes a contrast between the conduct of Betsy and that of Trueworth's first wife, the virtuous Miss Harriot. Unlike Betsy, Harriot shuns the role of spectatress, much preferring to read dramatic works and musical scores on her family's private country estate rather than attend public plays and concerts in London. Harriot's proclivity to focus her eyes on texts that never stray from the drawing room associates her with domestic virtues rather than coquettish faults, and it is hardly surprising on this account that she rapidly replaces Betsy as the object of Trueworth's matrimonial designs.

The public/private dichotomy that constitutes the principal difference between Betsy's and Harriot's visions is accentuated by the fact that Haywood repeatedly represents Betsy riding and walking on the streets of London where, on more than one occasion, she vainly seeks out Trueworth ("[S]he never went abroad without casting her eyes about, in search of him; nay, she sometimes even condescended to pass by the house where he was lodged, in hopes of seeing him either going in or going out, or from some one or other of the windows" [267]) and, later in the novel, encounters him on the street going about his business ("She was within three or four yards of the post-horse, when she saw Mr. Trueworth at some distance, on the other side of the street. Her heart fluttered at this unexpected sight of him—

she had no power to refrain from speaking to him" [417]). In these scenes, though Betsy's actions are more or less sexually neutral, as a woman who looks for and observes men on the street, she is implicitly identified with the class of streetwalkers that Miss Forward has joined as well as with the Parisian prostitutes that Charles Baudelaire would, a century later, make the focus of his *flâneur*'s gaze. Far from being enclosed within the domestic sphere, Betsy's eyes roam throughout London, a fact that contributes to her securing an unsatisfactory husband in the dissolute person of Mr. Munden.

In the absence of actually seeing Trueworth on favorable terms, Betsy adopts more extreme measures to place his face and body—or at least their representation—under her eyes. Having learned that a miniature of Trueworth has been completed for an unknown lady (Harriot), Betsy resolves to intercept and take possession of her former suitor's painted image. Though Haywood makes clear that Betsy remains unconscious of the degree to which she desires Trueworth ("It cannot be supposed that it was altogether owing to the regard she had for Mr. Trueworth, though in effect much more than she herself was yet sensible of, that she took all this [sic] pains" [412]), the portrait unquestionably becomes the object of Betsy's most fully articulated visual desire, and the act of stealing it functions as the most visible symptom of her concealed sexual feelings for Trueworth. In effect, Trueworth's portrait becomes the means by which Haywood allows her heroine to wield a sexualized vision, which, in opposition to Forward's libertine looks, remains ideologically acceptable within the strictures of feminine conduct.

Just as in *Pamela* and *Betsy Thoughtless*, in Frances Burney's *Cecilia* (1782) the domestic-empirical domination wielded by a matriarch figures prominently. Cecilia, another orphan, is largely attracted to the aristocratic Delvilles by Mrs. Delville, the only female character with whom she truly identifies. Cecilia's identification with Mrs. Delville lies in the initial visual relations between them. The two women regard each other as mirror images, separated only by a generation:

> The surprise and admiration with which Cecilia at the first glance was struck proved reciprocal: Mrs. Delville, though prepared for youth and beauty, expected not to see a countenance so intelligent, nor manners so well formed as those of Cecilia: thus mutually astonished and mutually pleased, their first salutations were accompanied by looks so flattering to both, that each saw in the other, an immediate prepossession in her favour, and from the moment that they met, they seemed instinctively impelled to admire. (155)

Mrs. Delville's warm affection for Cecilia has much to do with the latter's beauty and conduct, but Burney also makes clear that the "intelligence of [Cecilia's] eyes" attracts Mrs. Delville to her future daughter-in-law. Mrs. Delville's perceptive estimate of Cecilia's eyes corresponds well to the narrator's view of the young woman in the first chapter of the novel in which her eyes, "the heralds of her speech, now beamed with understanding and now glistened with sensibility" (6). Unlike the profligate Mrs. Harrel's and Miss Larolles' eyes, Cecilia's express both keen intelligence and sympathy; as such, they represent an ideal of empirical rationality and sympathetic feeling that Mrs. Delville apprehends immediately.

Mrs. Delville's unadulterated admiration of Cecilia endures only as long as she does not suspect her son and Cecilia of having fallen in love.[47] When Mrs. Delville, like Pamela before her, begins to recognize the possibility of undesirable romantic relations, she places Cecilia and the young Delville under surveillance. Cecilia is "shocked to find herself thus watchfully observed" (491) and "[t]he state of her mind seemed read by Mrs. Delville, who examined her with eyes of such penetrating keenness, that they rather made discoveries than enquiries" (501). So powerful is the behavior-regulating effect of Mrs. Delville on Cecilia that when the young woman reluctantly agrees to marry Delville against his parents' wishes she hardly considers the violent reaction that Lord Delville will inevitably betray, instead reflecting on how "she shrunk even in imagination from [Mrs. Delville's] wrath-darting eye" (577) and, once again, considering "how cruelly shall I sink before the severity of her eye!" (617). Cecilia's imagined response to Mrs. Delville's censuring eyes amounts to a Foucauldian internalization of enormous disciplinary power; Cecilia need not even fall under the gaze of Mrs. Delville for the latter's eyes to have their intended effect on Cecilia's behavior. The mere threat of (visual) punishment by Mrs. Delville, and all that it signifies to Cecilia's self-estimation, is enough to undermine her resolution to marry Delville. Burney's emphasis on Mrs. Delville's visual "discoveries" and "enquiries" clearly places the matriarch in a novelistic tradition of female domestic-empirical observation in the eighteenth century that culturally resonated because of the popularity across numerous cultural sites (including the periodical and the conduct book) of employing domesticity as a trope of knowledge, a trope that we see quite prominently played out both in "elite" cultural productions such as empirical philosophy and "popular" cultural productions such as the novel.[48]

Visual Conduct and the Novel of Manners

As I suggested in the previous section, one important antecedent of the Richardsonian novel lay in the female conduct book corpus of the late seventeenth and eighteenth centuries. The domestic novel and its cousin, the novel of manners, intersect with this body of popular work in a complicated crisscross fashion. Richardson is the exemplar of this intersection. Himself influenced by a tradition of advice literature, Richardson influenced a woman's tradition in fiction, which includes the likes of Frances Burney, Maria Edgeworth, Jane Austen, George Eliot, and even Virginia Woolf. In the hands of Jane Austen, the domestic novel climaxed into its most elegant and ideologically unproblematic form because, in the words of Ian Watt, Austen's novels were able "to combine into a harmonious unity the advantages both of realism of presentation and realism of assessment, of the internal and of the external approaches to character."[49] This section therefore begins with a discussion of the works of Frances Burney and Maria Edgeworth—writers who helped create the tradition in which Austen participated so brilliantly—before culminating in an analysis of Austen, whose novels form the chronological boundary of this chapter. In effect, my argument is that Austen's seemingly effortless aesthetic accomplishment naturalizes and consolidates the Richardsonian discourse of female vision, making it a standard by which subsequent nineteenth-century novelists—particularly women novelists—could be judged.

Frances Burney's *Evelina* (1778) contains none of the scopic extremes of domesticity or sexuality that are such important features of *Pamela*, *Clarissa,* and *Miss Betsy Thoughtless*. Nevertheless, the novel provides an unmistakable rendering of Richardson's gendered discourse of visual conduct. Nowhere is one element of this discourse, the appropriate visual behavior of men toward women, more apparent than in Evelina's account of a tea she attends at the Pantheon in London:

> At the same table with Lord Orville, sat a gentleman, —I call him so only because he *was* at the same table, —who, almost from the moment I was seated, fixed his eyes steadfastly on my face, and never once removed them to any other object during tea-time, notwithstanding my dislike of his staring must, I am sure, have been very evident. I was quite surprised, that a man whose boldness was so offensive, could have gained admission into a party of which Lord Orville made one; for I naturally concluded him to be some low-bred, and uneducated man; and I thought my idea was indubitably confirmed, when I heard him say to Sir Clement Willoughy, in an *audible whisper*, —which is a mode of speech very distressing and disagreeable to by-standers, —"For Heaven's sake, Willoughby, who is that lovely creature?"[50]

Evelina's distress before the sexualized gaze of this male spectator recalls Clarissa's more exaggerated fear of Lovelace's leering eyes. That Evelina's unknown admirer turns out to be, like Lovelace, an aristocrat, is even more astonishing to the young woman, for she believes such unseemly conduct beneath a gentleman. The unnamed lord contrasts with Lord Orville, whose own unimpeachable visual modesty Evelina notes admiringly when she observes during one of their conversations how "Lord Orville hardly spoke a word, and his countenance was grave and thoughtful; yet, whenever I raised my eyes, his, I perceived, were directed towards me, though instantly, upon meeting mine, he looked another way" (332–33). Such deferential behavior by Lord Orville constructs a gentlemanly code of vision that is contrasted in Richardson by the conduct of Mr. B and Lovelace—and that is paralleled, incidentally, in Sir Charles Grandison's extreme politeness.[51] When Evelina encounters or bids farewell to Lord Orville she either avoids his eyes altogether or meets them "accidentally." For Evelina and Orville, an intentional meeting of eyes and a prolongation of their mutual gaze would be indecorous.

Evelina's visual conduct concurs with a conversation during the same tea where she is looked upon by the anonymous lord. Commenting on the congregation of people who have gathered, ostensibly to see the Pantheon's collection of art, Captain Mirvan observes, "'[Y]ou all come here for no manner of purpose but to stare at one another's pretty faces'" (108). Objecting, Mr. Lovel interrupts to acknowledge the men's guilt with regard to the Captain's accusation but stalwartly defends the women: "'What the ladies may come hither for. . . . it would ill become *us* to determine; but as to we men, doubtless we can have no other view, than to admire them'" (108). In a significant absence of dissent, no one among the tea party bothers to contradict Mr. Lovel. Because of Mr. Lovel's universal unpopularity, had he issued a statement contrary to socially acceptable behavior he would no doubt have met with vociferous objections. His account of the appropriateness of men looking upon women and women neither returning these looks nor looking at men themselves must therefore be a popular, indeed unanimous, opinion.

Supporting this interpretation of Lovel's commentary on gendered visual relations are Lord Orville's aesthetic views:

> "O certainly," said Lord Orville, "the lifeless symmetry of architecture, however beautiful the design and proportion, no man would be so mad as to put in competition with the animated charms of nature: but when, as to-night, the eye may be regaled at the same time, and in one view, with all the excellence of art, and all the perfection of nature, I cannot think that either suffer by being seen together." (102)

Lord Orville's universalizing allusion to "the eye," in this context used as a reference to male eyes, erases the gendered specificity of his and the other men's visions. Like Lovelace, Lord Orville engages in accepted male behavior by looking on nature (or women figured as "the animated charms of nature") in conjunction with art, thereby conflating the aesthetic and sexual visions of men while eliminating women from activity in both domains.

For her part, Evelina goes far to censure her own eyes in language reminiscent of Jeremy Collier's criticism of the English stage. Having attended a performance of Congreve's *Love for Love*, Evelina enjoys the play because it is "fraught with wit and entertainment" but declares, "I hope I shall never see it represented again" because "it is extremely indelicate, —to use the softest word I can" (78). Here, Evelina concurs with Jeremy Collier's criticism of *Love for Love* as a play worthy of censure; accordingly, she regards her spectatorship of the performance to be a violation of proper female conduct, an indecorous experience not worth repeating because it jeopardizes her virtue. Yet aside from these few illuminating instances, in *Evelina* the representation of female vision is relatively marginalized, becoming visible only to a limited degree in Evelina's social interactions with men and her occasional observations on the dress and manners of women. Quite differently from *Clarissa*, *Evelina* constructs female vision not in Richardson's prescriptive ways but, possibly as a result of virtual wholesale English cultural acceptance of Richardson's discourse of vision, by simply providing an abbreviated account of Evelina's responses to proper and improper male visual behavior. By 1778, almost four decades after the publication of *Pamela* and three decades after the appearance of *Clarissa*, Richardson's discourse of proper male and female visualty had become so established that readers did not require Burney to elaborate upon it.

Whereas Evelina's visual education is limited to social situations, the eponymous heroine of Burney's *Cecilia* receives a far more comprehensive training in visual observation and conduct. *Cecilia* therefore proves far more ambitious in constructing a complete ideological portrait of proper female vision in the eighteenth century. Like Haywood's Betsy before her, and Edgeworth's Belinda after her, Cecilia begins her novel placed with questionable guardians, in this case the brazenly improvident Mr. and Mrs. Harrel. As the retiring, domestically inclined Cecilia is shocked to discover, at least a portion of the revenues the cash-strapped Harrel household generates results from Mr. Harrel's attempted trafficking in Cecilia's physical image; that is, Mr. Harrel quite intentionally places Cecilia, an heiress, on display to be surveyed by his coterie of wealthy acquaintances in the hope of selling her off as a wife to the highest bidder. Mr. Harrel's visual prostitution of Cecilia underlines the polarities of masculine/feminine scopic economies that Burney explores; those polarities are marked by the Harrels' economy of the social (female) spectacle and Cecilia's economy of domestic observation. The Harrels' practice is to place women on center stage of London life for all of high society to see. Quite differently, Cecilia's practice is to survey the household and to observe social interactions rather than be observed herself. When Cecilia perceives that it will prove more difficult in the London society she moves in to concentrate her efforts on seeing rather than being seen, she elects to remove herself from the public eye.

The irresolvable divide between these two scopic economies emerges most graphically early in the novel when Cecilia informs the Harrels of her wish to retire from the public spotlight and, in effect, no longer to be seen with or to be circulated by them in society:

> At first [Mr. Harrel] only laughed at her plan, gaily rallying her upon her love of solitude; but when he found it was serious, he very warmly opposed it, and called upon Mrs. Harrel to join in his expostulations. That lady complied, but in so faint a manner, that Cecilia soon saw she did not wish to prevail; and with a concern that cost her infinite pain, now finally perceived that not only all her former affection was subsided into indifference, but that, since she had endeavoured to abridge her amusements, she regarded her as a spy, and dreaded her as the censor of her conduct. (232)

Mrs. Harrel is correct to recognize how Cecilia—after closely surveying Mrs. Harrel's undisciplined social and domestic conduct—attempts to tame it. To some degree, Cecilia seems to have united Pamela and Harriot's scopic imperatives of domestic and social discipline: to observe the household closely and, whenever possible, to refrain from public display. When the Harrels shortly thereafter reach an economic crisis that threatens them with continental exile, Cecilia suggests Mrs. Harrel "study nothing while abroad but oeconomy, prudence and housewifry" (394), lessons that Pamela internalizes early on as Mrs. B and Betsy Thoughtless embraces at the end of her novel in time to enact domestic virtues as Mrs. Trueworth.

For those characters in *Cecilia* who participate in the scopic economy of the female spectacle, the closest they arrive at functioning as well-trained domestic observers occurs when an estate is announced for auction. Miss Larolles, a Mrs. Harrel in waiting, attempts to excite Cecilia at the prospect of attending the ruined Lord Belgrade's sale where "everything you can conceive" will be on display: "house, stables, china, laces, horses, caps, everything in the world" (31). When Cecilia inquires whether or not Miss Larolles "intend[s] to buy anything" the former's response reveals much about the inadequacies of her overly inquisitive and quasi-acquisitive vision: "'Lord, no; but one likes to see the people's things'" (31).[52] Short on cash, Miss Larolles trafficks in domestic images. By representing Lord Belgrade's estate auction in this light, Burney foreshadows the eventual fate of the Harrel household, a fate predestined by Mrs. Harrel's failure to exert any overseeing influence on Mr. Harrel's domestic improvidence. Mrs. Harrel's inability either to take seriously or enact Cecilia's admonishments eventually leads to bankruptcy and the melodramatic suicide of Mr. Harrel.

That Cecilia resolves quite early no longer to be seen in public with the Harrels is largely a consequence of having repeatedly been made the target of baldly sexual visual attentions while ostensibly in their care. In the opening chapters Cecilia makes clear her pleasure at being unknown in London where "neither my actions nor myself will be sufficiently known to attract public observation" (14). Yet Cecilia is surprised to find herself placed in one compromising pose after another and, distressingly, most often under the commodifying, sexualized eyes of Sir Robert Floyer, the Harrels' principal caller.[53] Sir Robert's objectifying gaze contrasts sharply with the eyes of Cecilia's eventual husband, young Delville, who "earnestly regarded her with eyes of speaking admiration, while the occasion of his notice rendered it too pleasant to distress her, and filled her with an inward satisfaction which brightened her whole countenance" (250). She is too rarely able to place herself in sight of Delville's gentlemanly eyes, for as long as she remains under the Harrels' roof she continually "find[s] herself almost constantly the object of [Sir Robert's] unrestrained examination" (53). Small wonder that Cecilia longs to escape from the Harrels, whose household violates every principle of scopo-domestic conduct she values.

Female visual conduct, which is such an important feature of *Pamela*, *Miss Betsy Thoughtless*, and *Cecilia*, largely initiates Maria Edgeworth's *Belinda* (1801). In the opening chapter of the novel, Belinda receives a cautionary letter from her Aunt Stanhope warning the young woman about the dangers of overly familiar, insincere flirtations. Mrs. Stanhope figures her words of advice through the trope of a censuring, disciplining female vision that she fancies as especially keen in its observations:

> I see—or at least when I went out more than my health will at present permit—I used to see multitudes of silly girls, seemingly all cut out upon the same pattern, who frequented public places day after day, and year after year, without any idea further than that of diverting themselves, or of obtaining transient admiration. How I have pitied and despised the giddy creatures, whilst I have observed them playing off their unmeaning airs, vying with one another in the most *obvious*, and consequently the most ridiculous manner, so as to expose themselves before the very men they would attract; chattering, tittering, and flirting; full of the present moment, never reflecting upon the future; quite satisfied if they got a partner at a ball, without ever thinking of a partner for life. I have often asked myself, what is to become of such girls, when they grow old or ugly, or when the public eye grows tired of them? (8)

Here and elsewhere in the novel's opening chapters, Mrs. Stanhope emerges as a version of the familiar matriarchal figure—such as the original Mrs. B, Lady Trusty, and Mrs. Delville—that populates so much eighteenth-century domestic fiction. Yet unlike the trio of matriarchs I have invoked above, Mrs. Stanhope is far more interested in training her nieces in the subtleties of finding rather than keeping a husband. According to Mrs. Stanhope, to find a husband one must adhere to a code of visual conduct by abhorring the public gaze; one must instead be seen in more controlled, socially acceptable conditions. On the question of what to do with one's eyes after marriage, Mrs. Stanhope is silent.

Aside from instructing Belinda and other young women how to read the actions and intentions of men, the foundation of Mrs. Stanhope's scopic pedagogy is to develop in her protégées the coquettish art of putting their eyes on display rather than seeing and disciplining the home, a fact unwittingly conveyed to the mortified Belinda Portman by an unnamed gentleman at a masquerade:

> "That Mrs. Stanhope must be a good clever dame, faith" said a third gentleman. "There's no less than six of her nieces, whom she has *got off* within these four winters. Not one of 'em now, that has not made a catch-match. There's the eldest of the set, Mrs. Tollemache, what had she, in the devil's name, to set up with in the world, but a pair of good eyes. Her aunt, to be sure, taught her the use of them early enough. They might have rolled to all eternity, before they would have rolled me out of my senses; but you see, they did Tollemache's business. However they are going to part now. I hear—Tollemache was tired of her, before the honey-moon was over, as I foretold." (24)

As an educator of female eyes Mrs. Stanhope focuses her efforts exclusively on the pursuit rather than its aftermath, on the sexual, seductive effect eyes will have on men in courtship instead of the regulating effect over conduct they might exert in the domestic sphere. Mrs. Stanhope's particular emphasis on eyes that are objects rather than subjects of vision precludes her success in teaching Belinda the techniques of the courtship trade, for the narrator informs us that Belinda is the least inclined of Mrs. Stanhope's nieces to embrace her aunt's teachings.[54]

Mrs. Stanhope hopes to alter the focus of her niece's eyes from domestic to coquettish ends by arranging for Belinda an extended stay with the fashionable Lady Delacour, a woman whom Stanhope believes will hasten her niece's training as a sought-after marriage prospect, particularly because "[t]o be seen in public with lady Delacour, to be a visitor at her house, were privileges of which numbers were vehemently ambitious" (10). Initially as enthusiastic as Mrs. Stanhope about her visit, Belinda soon recognizes the shortcomings of Lady Delacour's domestic life, a recognition that Edgeworth portrays with a metaphor of Belinda's visual perception: "A short time after her arrival at lady Delacour's, Belinda began to see through the thin veil, with which politeness covers domestic misery" (11). Indeed, Belinda emerges initially as a kind of domestic spy against Lady Delacour as she reports in a lengthy letter to Mrs. Stanhope the failings of the latter's domestic habits, an act of espionage that she soon regrets because it revealed "what she had seen in private" (16). In violating the sanctity of Lady Delacour's privacy, Belinda recognizes that she has fallen short of her own domestic ideal as someone wont to "conduct herself with prudence and integrity" (7).[55]

While Betsy Thoughtless never benefits from the advantages of coming under Lady Trusty's domestic tutelage, Belinda escapes for a time from the storm and stress of the Delacours. She retires to the domestic haven of the Percivals, where an altogether different paradigm of household management is embodied in the figure of Lady Anne. Even tempered, thoughtful, and altogether domestically oriented—in short, the foil of Lady Delacour—Lady Anne Percival is the very conduct-book quintessence of a wife and mother. Edgeworth underlines the distance between Lady Delacour and Lady Anne by placing Helena, Lady Delacour's adolescent daughter, under the maternal care of Lady Anne. Though Helena longs for a more intimate, affectionate relationship with her own mother, she comes to love Lady Anne as her de facto mother, and Lady Anne returns Helena's adoration. That Lady Anne has also married Lord Percival, Lady Delacour's first love, suggests the degree to which she has successfully outshone Lady Delacour in domestic conduct. Belinda is quick to recognize that while Lady Delacour continues to play the wit and coquette, utterly neglecting Helena along the way, Lady Anne has retired to full-time domestic supervision. And although Belinda expresses genuine affection for Lady Delacour, as far as she is concerned the choice between desiring Lady Anne and Lady Delacour's lifestyles is no contest, an observation supported by the principal subject of Belinda's art studies during her stay with the Percivals.

In the midst of "intently copying [a Mr.] Westal's sketch of Lady Anne Percival and her family" (236), Belinda seconds Mr. Vincent's observation that such a subject is superior to pastoral and mythical themes:[56]

> "Yes," said Belinda, "and how much more interesting this picture is to us, from our knowing that it is not a fancy-piece; that the happiness is real, not imaginary; that this is the natural expression of affection in the countenance of the mother; and that these children, who crowd round her, are what they seem to be, the pride and pleasure of her life!" (236)

Lady Anne supplants both Mrs. Stanhope and Lady Delacour as Belinda's principal instructress of how to see with eyes sensitive to domestic conduct; Lady Anne reinforces Belinda's strongly felt inclinations toward domestic life, and it is therefore not difficult to convince her—against the advice of Mrs. Stanhope—how preferable it is to focus one's eyes on children rather than feminine fashions, fallen women, or most dangerous of all, single men. In this section of the novel, the thrust of Edgeworth's work is beyond doubt: to educate budding domestic women such as Belinda how to reproduce themselves, visually and otherwise, into the mirror image of Lady Anne.

Perhaps the most intriguing aspect of *Belinda* from the point of view of the discourse of female vision and domesticity is not the fact that Belinda becomes the student of three very different teachers of femininity but that Belinda herself turns the tables on Lady Delacour, convincing the more experienced woman to reform her ways and adopt the scopo-domestic conduct of Lady Anne, the woman whom Lady Delacour has regarded as her principal rival.[57] On her return to the Delacour household, Belinda enjoins Lady Delacour to invite Helena back as well, something that Lady Delacour agrees, reluctantly, to do. Over the course of a few chapters, Lady Delacour's (visual) relations with Helena, formerly distant and chilly, are transformed:

> Belinda's bedchamber was next to Helena's; and after she had been in bed about an hour, she fancied that she heard some one walking softly in the next room. She rose, and found Lady Delacour standing beside her daughter's bed. She started at the sight of Belinda, but only said in a low voice, as she pointed to her child, "Don't waken her." She then looked at her for some moments in silence. The moon shone full upon her face. She stooped over Helena, parted her ringlets of hair upon her forehead, and kissed her gently. (306)

If many eighteenth-century domestic novels, such as *Pamela*, *Betsy Thoughtless*, and *Evelina*, are in fundamental ways bildungsromans whose young heroines learn to be domestic figures through the education of their eyes, *Belinda* is differentiated from them by the fact that the novel's title character teaches her teacher (Lady Delacour) how to see the workings of the home through domestic rather than coquettish eyes. In this respect, these novels function as plot-driven conduct manuals of vision.

In terms of gendered visual conduct, the depiction of women as the "natural" objects of the male gaze is perhaps most characteristic of the novels of Jane Austen, particularly *Pride and Prejudice* (1813) and *Emma* (1816). Austen portrays both Elizabeth Bennet and Emma Woodhouse as visually desirable. Mr. Knightley, for instance, tells Mrs. Weston of Emma, "I confess that I have seldom seen a face or figure more pleasing to me than hers," and, "I love to look at her."[58] For his part, Darcy, after initially dismissing Elizabeth's allure, makes her his particular object:

> Mr. Darcy had at first scarcely allowed her to be pretty; he had looked at her without admiration at the ball; and when they next met, he looked at her only to criticise. But no sooner had he made it clear to himself and his friends that she had hardly a good feature in her face, than he began to find it was rendered uncommonly intelligent by the beautiful expression of her dark eyes. To this discovery succeeded some others equally mortifying. Though he had detected with

> a critical eye more than one failure of perfect symmetry in her form, he was forced to acknowledge her figure to be light and pleasing.[59]

Examples like this of an active, sexually tinged male gaze abound in Austen. But what about female vision? On whom, what, and how do women focus in Austen's fictional world?

If Austen's men primarily look at women, Austen's women principally focus on three interrelated objects: first, they watch men looking at women; second, they focus critically on other women; third, they survey the domestic sphere. These apparently distinct visions are related insofar as they are all directed toward achieving or manipulating domestic success through marital matchmaking, either for the seeing woman herself or for her intimate friends and relations. They are also complementary manifestations of sight in that they go a long way toward constituting a multilayered version of empirical reality for Austen's heroines. The overall discursive effect of these representations of feminine visual conduct embellishes the novel's relationship to domestic tropes of knowledge formation and creates a far more complexly rendered account of domestic vision than Richardson's, thereby solidifying the novelistic foundations for Victorian domesticity that would occur in the ensuing decades.

Emma believes herself to possess a keen eye. Having decided that Mr. Elton and her friend, Harriet, must be married, Emma paints a portrait of the latter as Mr. Elton looks on. Emma's strategy is to assure herself of Mr. Elton's admiration of Harriet, and she "gave him credit for stationing himself where he might gaze and gaze again without offence" (74). The basis of Emma's matchmaking between Mr. Elton and Harriet is the result of her critical assessment of Robert Martin, Harriet's farmer admirer. Emma's is, as it turns out, a faulty evaluation:

> They met Mr. Martin the very next day, as they were walking on the Donwell Road. He was on foot, and after looking very respectfully at her, looked with most unfeigned satisfaction at her companion. Emma was not sorry to have an opportunity of survey; and walking a few yards forward, while they talked together, *soon made her quick eye sufficiently acquainted with Mr. Robert Martin.* His appearance was very neat and he looked like a sensible young man, but his person had no other advantage; and when he came to be contrasted with gentlemen, she thought he must lose all the ground he had gained in Harriet's inclination. [emphasis mine] (61)

In each case the motivation behind Emma's eyes, variously cast upon Harriet, Mr. Elton, and Mr. Martin, is to ascertain an economy of desire and then affect the best possible match for Harriet, thereby working toward her friend's domestic happiness. By focusing within the cultural and ideological boundaries of domesticity, reinforcing a collective notion of appropriate visual conduct for women, Emma brandishes an inordinate degree of social power as her neighborhood's principal assessor of personal worth, respectability, and attractiveness.

In this respect, Emma is not unlike *Pride and Prejudice*'s Elizabeth Bennet, who similarly (but with more perspicacity and detachment) observes Mr. Bingley's admiration of her sister Jane. Elizabeth's roving eye allows her to notice that Mr. Bingley "'could not help seeing that you [Jane] were about five times as pretty as every other woman in the room'" (62). Elizabeth's satisfaction in observing Jane's refined beauty contrasts with the agony at the spectacle of witnessing her younger sister Mary's bad singing: "Elizabeth's eyes were fixed on her with most painful sensations; and she watched her progress through the several stanzas with an impatience which was very ill rewarded at the close" (142). The fact that this unfortunate performance occurs at a dinner party is all the more painful for Elizabeth because it represents a kind of reverberating domestic dissonance incompatible with the goal of good marriage matches that Austen's female protagonists invariably have been taught to desire. Such, for example, is the domestic surveillance of Mrs. Collins, Elizabeth's friend, who watches Darcy's inscrutable focus upon Elizabeth:

> She watched him whenever they were at Rosings, and whenever he came to Hunsford; but without much success. He certainly looked at her friend a great deal, but the expression of that look was disputable. It was an earnest, steadfast gaze, but she often doubted whether there were much admiration in it, and sometimes it seemed nothing but absence of mind. (214)

Elizabeth's prejudice against Darcy only changes for good when she sees him as lord of his estate. Elizabeth's admiration for Pemberley's grounds, "where natural beauty had been so little counteracted by an awkward taste," functions as a substitute for her admiration of and desire for Darcy, and she recognizes "that to be mistress of Pemberley might be something!" (234). I do not mean to suggest that in finally accepting Darcy's marriage proposal Elizabeth merely succumbs to greedy or materialistic temptations—too much of the novel is devoted to a nuanced exploration of her growing love to sustain such an interpretation—but her enthusiasm toward being at the center of this grand setting and, by extension, exerting her eyes over Darcy's estate, places her within a novel tradition largely defined by domestic vision and its accompanying desires.

If Elizabeth is attracted by the exterior of Pemberley, she is even more fascinated by its interior, which increases her admiration of Darcy:

> As they [the Gardiners and Elizabeth] passed into other rooms, these objects were taking different positions; but from every window there were beauties to be seen. The rooms were lofty and handsome, and their furniture suitable

> to the fortune of their proprietor; but Elizabeth saw, with admiration of his taste, that it was neither gaudy nor uselessly fine; with less of splendor, and more real elegance, than the furniture of Rosings. (268)

After examining Darcy's furniture, Elizabeth sees Darcy, or at least his portrait. From this vantage point, Elizabeth's perception of what she had once regarded as his overly critical eyes alters irrevocably:

> She stood several minutes before the picture in earnest contemplation, and returned to it again before they quitted the gallery. . . . Every idea that had been brought forward by the housekeeper was favourable to his character, and as she stood before the canvas, on which he was represented, and fixed his eyes upon herself, she thought of his regard with a deeper sentiment of gratitude than it had ever raised before; she remembered its warmth, and softened its impropriety of expression. (272)

In the space of a few minutes, Elizabeth shortly encounters the real Darcy, and, standing before him, she mirrors almost exactly the conduct of Evelina before Lord Orville, for she "scarcely dared lift her eyes to his face" (272). This modest behavior is uncharacteristic for the socially confident and witty Elizabeth. One could perhaps argue that Austen has Elizabeth respond in this manner because she is, quite literally, on Darcy's territory or that her beginning feelings of affection elicit a shy response. Yet whereas prior to her Pemberley visit Elizabeth has always met Darcy's eyes directly on any social terms offered to her, and often to her own advantage, for the last third of the novel she increasingly defers to him visually, deference that coincides with her visit to Pemberley. For instance, when Bingley congratulates Elizabeth on her engagement to Darcy, she "dared not lift up her eyes" to see Darcy's reaction, thereby fulfilling Lovelace's instructions to his veiled harlots—"When eyes meet eyes, be yours the retreating ones"—from seven decades before. That looking up at one's acknowledged lover requires "daring" signals the extent to which polite female visuality was not permitted to be oversexualized in the domestic novel tradition. The cultural resonance of the discourse of domestic vision henceforth made such a feminized vision invisible to later masculinist discourses of vision unconcerned with domesticity, masculinist discourses, for example, like Charles Darwin's theory of sexual selection and Sigmund Freud's theory of scopo-exhibitionism.

What I have attempted to demonstrate in the previous two sections of this chapter is the degree to which the discourse and representation of eighteenth-century women's vision was constructed in ways compatible with domestic forms of knowledge formation. Accomplished wives such as Pamela B and Lady Delville are depicted as keen domestic observers and supervisors; closely related to these matriarchal overseers are virginal, potentially desirable wives and mothers, such as Cecilia and Belinda, who are depicted as the possessors of nonsexualized eyes. These virtuous young women may be readily trained to oversee the domestic realm with Pamela-like vigilance. Depicted as eminently marriageable on the basis of their numerous feminine virtues, one of Cecilia's and Belinda's most important physical manifestations of virtue is the possession of domestically oriented, sexually deferential eyes. By contrast to Burney's and Edgeworth's heroines, Betsy must undergo visual retraining under the tutelage of Lady Trusty. Only late in the novel—after she has begun to read conduct literature and to focus her eyes on the household—does Betsy qualify as an appropriate spouse for Mr. Trueworth.

In examining these novels the following pair of conclusions becomes apparent: (1) for the discourse of female vision to continue to function as an important trope of domestic knowledge formation in England it had first to be divorced from the kind of obvious sexuality expressed in the eyes of Behn's, Defoe's, and Cleland's women, and (2) after its divorce from female sexuality, women's scopic desire had to be permanently wedded to the domestic visions of Burney's, Edgeworth's, and Austen's novelistic tradition. Broadly speaking, the expression of domestic vision amounted to a significant degree of cultural power wielded by eighteenth-century women and their dominant representations, but it was also apparent that as a consequence of domestic vision's cultural resonance the opportunity was lost for women to express a fuller range of scopo-sexual subjectivity. As I will argue in my subsequent case study of *Clarissa*, genuine scopo-sexual desire for women in the eighteenth century may most clearly be seen only when it appears to work within the dominant discourse of Richardsonian vision, as Clarissa's eyes appear to do, when in fact Clarissa and Anna Howe's relationship may be read in complete opposition to that discourse.

Case Study 1. Lesbian Vision in *Clarissa*

My preliminary reading of Richardson's *Clarissa* was a useful way of examining a discourse of vision that Raymond Williams might label "emergent."[60] Nonsexual female vision emerged to such a degree in the eighteenth and nineteenth centuries that, paired with domestic vision, it became the dominant discourse of vision among Englishwomen. I will now turn to a very different kind of eighteenth-century discourse, far less pervasive than its domestic counterpart. To make this discourse visible it is useful once more to invoke Williams. During and following the period of Richardson's construction of feminine sexuality and domesticity in *Pamela* and *Clarissa*, what Williams calls "oppositional" ideologies would have been marginalized and "unnaturalized" to the point where today their vestiges have been obscured. We can best access this marginalized ideology of sexuality and vision by deploying a theoretical discourse that posits the representational and discursive possibility of sexual relations between women, a phenomenon in eighteenth-century Britain well documented by Emma Donoghue and Lisa Moore.[61] In this case, the discourse I have elected to deploy constitutes the most useful features of post-Freudian feminist theory. It is a discourse that reveals the gaps and fissures of the masculine-feminine ideology of vision explored in the previous two sections. My purpose here is not to apply convenient but ahistorical theories onto *Clarissa* but to use contemporary theory as a way of revealing historical possibilities within the novel. It is my intention that this case study of *Clarissa* will in fact bring into focus the sexual ideology of eighteenth-century Sapphism (or lesbianism), making clear the radical and subversive possibilities available to Clarissa Harlowe and Anna Howe (even in the midst of a novel that is pervasively about male scopo-sadism and rape) and to a minority of eighteenth-century women (even in the midst of a culture that pervasively valorized female domesticity and heterosexuality).

As we read Lovelace's prolongation of Clarissa's psychological, physical, and scopic torture, we can hardly imagine a crueler, more sadistic character in English literature. Seen in this light, Clarissa functions as the perfect Freudian match for Lovelace because if he is an accomplished sadist, she appears to be a consummate masochist; indeed, Clarissa regards suffering as a strategy of subjectivity and proudly proclaims herself "a proficient in the school of affliction" (1121). I am nonetheless obliged to complicate this account of *Clarissa* precisely because Freud's theory includes *passive-feminine exhibitionism* as a term of differentiation from *active-masculine scopophilia* within an exclusively heterosexual matrix governed by the phallus. As Luce Irigary has shown, Freud's conception of the gaze posits an irredeemable female lack, lack of the biological fact of the penis and, along with it, the significatory power of the phallus.[62] For women trapped within a Freudian paradigm, vision operates as a disarming function, which leads to their surrender of phallic/clitoral pretensions and to their eventual embrace of a passive vaginal femininity. In the ensuing pages I will demonstrate why classical psychoanalytic theory *can* indeed provide a descriptive model for scopo-sadistic relations as they are dominantly represented in *Clarissa*; but I will also show precisely why such a phallic explanation of vision is itself ultimately left lacking. Like Freud's reading of Dora's hysteria, Lovelace's (and most readers') reading of Clarissa's desire fails because Lovelace can only read Clarissa as a heterosexual subject, can only *see* Clarissa as the representation of a woman who wants the phallus and nothing but the phallus. I will argue instead that what have been characterized as Clarissa's seemingly inexplicable motivations are predicated not upon masochistic desire for a sadist such as Lovelace but rather on an identificatory desire with Anna Howe.

As I have suggested earlier, Clarissa's desire in her will is paradoxically written as a negation and an affirmation, a negation in that she requests her corpse *not* be shown to anyone and as an affirmation in that she leaves the two portraits of herself to Anna and either her mother or her aunt.[63] Clarissa's wish for her body not to be seen after death betrays a fear that Lovelace may return once more to gaze upon her, a continuation of her assertion to him that she wishes "to slide into some obscure corner, to hide myself from you" (933). Tormented psychologically and physically by Lovelace, even in death Clarissa resists the libertine's visual exploitation.

If the negation in Clarissa's will both repudiates her sexually violated physical body and literally shields it from Lovelace's gaze, the will's later affirmation symbolically positions Clarissa's body in full view of multiple female eyes. Although their differences are legion, what most distinguishes Clarissa's portraits from her corpse is that the portraits signify for her an ideal, virginal self, a prelapsarian representation of the female body free from male sexual degradation. While Clarissa laments after the rape that she has "sunk" in her own eyes, these idyllic representations capture, in her view, an image still worthy of selected female eyes.

The portrait given to Anna is particularly crucial because in it Clarissa affirms that the historical moment when the work was produced signifies for her the "time my dear Miss Howe and I began to know, to distinguish and to love one another—so dearly—I cannot express how dearly" (1415). Clarissa's inability to articulate the magnitude of this love points to a reciprocal affection that no other relationship in the novel—certainly neither Clarissa's and Lovelace's, nor Anna's and Hickman's—ever approaches. Having finally escaped from Lovelace, Clarissa implores Anna, "Love me still. But let it be with a weaning love. I am not what I was when we were *inseparable lovers*" [emphasis mine] (1088). This sensuous language is compatible with a tradition of romantic friendship between women that, according to Lillian Faderman, was still very much operative in the eighteenth century.[64] Yet the mutual affection between Clarissa and Anna suggests a female desire that is also, intriguingly, unrepresented within the same narrative frame.

Although *Clarissa* is an epistolary novel, it remains remarkable that Clarissa and Anna, these previously "inseparable lovers" are never seen together in the entire narrative. Though they are united during Clarissa's brief stay with Anna early on, that nearly month-long interval is only cursorily referred to, providing the single largest aporia in the text. Throughout the novel, we see Clarissa and Anna only separately. This spatial separation accomplishes one of Richardson's narrative goals—the double epistolary discourse between Clarissa/Anna and Lovelace/Belford, which Ian Watt and Phyllis Klotman, among others, have praised as an important narrative advance over the almost univocal *Pamela*.[65] Yet

Richardson keeps his two principal female characters safely apart from one another for what are more than merely formal concerns over narrative structure and voice; his refusal to represent Clarissa and Anna in the same time and place creates an ever-present narrative absence of female lack/desire that provokes the following question: would Richardson have been unable to contain Clarissa and Anna's mutual desire within the narrative frame he would have been obliged to create for them?

What I am proposing is that in his explicit depiction of female (hetero)sexuality and what became the dominant ideology of sexually deferential female eyes, Richardson unwittingly creates what de Lauretis calls the space-off, "spaces in the margins of hegemonic discourses, social spaces carved in the interstices of institutions and in the chinks and cracks of the power-knowledge apparati."[66] These resisting "chinks" exist concurrently and in opposition to culturally dominant spaces of discourse, which, in *Clarissa*, are represented by the heterosexual narratives of Clarissa/Lovelace and Anna/Hickman. To read *Clarissa* beyond this double heterosexual matrix, it becomes necessary to see the space-off of lesbian desire between Anna and Clarissa as a counternarrative to the phallic plots of Clarissa's rape and Anna's courtship. The visible plot of *Clarissa* represents what Laura Mulvey sees as a fundamental subject of hegemonic narratives: a sadomasochistic story that specularizes the image of Woman as the site of male desire and control.[67] The spaced-off plot of *Clarissa*, by contrast, resists the dominant narrative of Lovelace's exploitation by suggesting that lesbian desire between Anna and Clarissa is not predicated, like heterosexuality in the novel, upon their power relations with one another. In *Clarissa*, lesbianism (which most eighteenth-century observers called "Sapphism" for women of Clarissa and Anna's social class) is excluded or spaced-off from representation because such deviant, nonphallic desire fails to conform to the ideology of (hetero)sexuality in which the novel is steeped. In this sense, Sapphist vision in *Clarissa* functions dialectically with domestic vision in *Pamela* and other eighteenth-century novels. While the counternarrative of Sapphist desire does not exist as conscious, manifest material within the text, neither is it the unconscious, repressed material that much traditional psychoanalytic criticism has made its concern. Rather, to employ a Freudian heuristic, spaced-off Sapphism in *Clarissa* exists as preconscious material that can be retrieved and read in relation to the conscious narrative if the (heterosexual) reader chooses to see it.

Randolph Trumbach's scholarship on eighteenth-century Sapphism suggests one reason why Richardson might have quite unselfconsciously raised the specter of lesbian desire through his use of romantic rhetoric between Anna and Clarissa: Trumbach shows that as a well-articulated and viable sexuality, Sapphism did not emerge in England until midcentury (around the time of *Clarissa*'s publication) and did not become culturally visible until the last quarter of the century.[68] Thus the threat of Sapphist interpretations of Anna/Clarissa must have seemed remote indeed to Richardson. Even for John Cleland, a very different kind of author, explicit same-sex acts between women, such as those in which Fanny and Phoebe participate, are not threatening to the novel's phallic sexual regime because they are meant to appear as preparatory foreplay before women engage in mandatory heterosexual intercourse with men.

Nevertheless, Sapphist desire, which replaces the phallus and threatens the (re)production of male heirs, would no doubt have seemed subversive toward patrilineal authority. Not only would Sapphism as an alternative lifestyle have been unutterable for the likes of Richardson, but, more pointedly, Sapphism would have been, in Irigary's term, *unrepresentable* for the audience of "respectable" middle-class women readers Richardson courted. It is therefore through the will's portraiture gesture that Clarissa principally represents her desire for Anna.

Richardson casts Clarissa and Anna's relationship in terms of nonphysical intimacy. In her will, Clarissa prognosticates Anna and Clarissa's eventual heavenly union, an expression of physical desire sublimated into a spiritual state. Clarissa writes, "[O]ur love can only be exceeded in that state of perfection in which I hope to rejoice with her hereafter to all eternity," and she lends further credence to this prophecy of eternal union by bequeathing to Anna her "best diamond ring," clearly symbolic of a marriage bond (1416). Clarissa confines herself to envisioning a spiritual union with Anna because she cannot conceive of a physical union in the heterosexual milieu she has externally experienced and subsequently internalized. For Clarissa, no alternative social space exists in the symbolic order, and she must therefore relegate her scopo-sexual desire to the imaginary of her portrait.

That Clarissa and Anna's eventual union is the sublimated extension of an earthly bond that Richardson characterizes as nonphysical becomes clear late in the novel when Clarissa, writing to Anna, celebrates their "mundane" relationship: "If anything could give me a relish for life, after what I have suffered, it would be the hopes of a continuance of the *more than sisterly love* which has for years uninterruptedly bound us together as *one mind*" [emphasis mine] (1116). What is represented as near ideal female love precludes the possibility of *physical* female love; not only is the phallus/penis excluded, but so is the vagina. The two young women's union of minds coincides with Belford's judgment of Clarissa, in which he denies the presence of Clarissa's body and, by inference, her sexuality: "She is, in my eye, all mind" (555). Yet by having Clarissa bequeath her portrait to Anna, thereby making this image of Clarissa the object of Anna's gaze, Richardson disrupts his own fictional realm of nonphysical female desire, ironically calling into question the unchallenged dominance of heterosexual desire and of female sexual passivity by unveiling

Clarissa's and Anna's mutual visual desire. Through her portrait, Clarissa is able to make an image of her body available to Anna's gaze.

If Clarissa's will permits her to avoid the symbolic end of Robert Browning's Duchess—to appear forevermore in portrait form before the commanding gaze of a male aristocrat—she still shares the Duchess' ultimate physical fate (though not, like the Duchess, through the explicit death sentence of her adversary). The Duchess's transgression in the Duke's view is a wandering, indiscriminate eye, an eye that flits from man to man. Clarissa's opposite problem is an internalization of the gaze that the Duchess directs outward. Foucault demystifies this ideology of internalized vision in *The History of Sexuality* by demonstrating that through the proliferation of discourses on sex in the eighteenth century, the social apparati that had hitherto regulated human sexuality and reproduction began to be internalized by individual subjects on a grand scale. The result was a "modern" society that largely policed its own sexuality without the need for external controlling mechanisms.[69] While Clarissa can therefore be read "realistically" as a woman who has internalized sexual desire, she can also be seen as part of the discursive phenomena that Foucault locates in the eighteenth century, a representation of a woman who polices herself. The effect in *Clarissa* is a near absolute repression of manifest female desire, either heterosexual or homosexual, effectively fulfilling Richardson's preface to the novel in which he insists upon Clarissa's perfection as an "exemplar" to her sex.

Anna Howe expresses best the Richardsonian internalization of the female gaze. Warning Clarissa of the dangers female passion elicits, Anna enjoins her friend to "let us both, my dear, ponder well this thought; look into ourselves, and fear" (550). Clarissa follows Anna's Foucauldian analysis of sexual self-regulation, informing Lovelace that he has "ruined me in my own eyes and that is the same to me as if *all the world* knew it" (909), thereby redefining her own self-policing gaze in terms of society's. Still, Clarissa is defined not simply by the internalization of her own and society's gaze but also by an effort to veil herself from the many different eyes that focus on her, thus attempting to mitigate (hetero)sexual desire directed her way. Tragically, Anna's gaze, the gaze that Clarissa most desires (and that Richardson most represses), never rests upon Clarissa herself and only falls upon her portrait in a spaced-off future that the novel anticipates but does not represent. In this sense, the novel follows Terry Castle's compelling argument about the "specter" of lesbianism in English literature: "The literary history of lesbianism, I would like to argue, is first of all a history of derealization. . . . One woman or other must be a ghost, or on the way to becoming one. Passion is excited, only to be obscured, disembodied, decarnalized."[70]

It would appear that Richardson, with some important slippages, succeeds in repressing lesbian sexuality in *Clarissa*. Yet it is important to remember that de Lauretis' conception of the space-off is not limited to what occurs outside the narrative frame but also makes as the object of its study the contradiction between the seen and the unseen. De Lauretis contends that desire that appears "on-screen" paradoxically constructs desire concealed from direct view.[71] In *Clarissa*'s case, the desiring gazes Richardson represents form an oppositional fictional space with the gazes he represses. To formulate critically this dialectic of the on-screen and spaced-off gaze, it therefore becomes crucial to examine how various gazes in the novel are depicted and how they interact with the (non)representation of Sapphist vision.

Although Anna's look never actually falls upon Clarissa, other female eyes, the eyes of Sinclair's prostitutes, intrude on her throughout much of the novel. At Sinclair's, Clarissa remains under the constant surveillance of women, and she complains to Anna "[A]re these watchful ladies all eye?" (639), emphasizing both their intrusive, Panopticon-like gaze and what Lacan calls its "all-seeing aspect."[72] Similar to the scenario in Freud's "Medusa's Head," Sally, Polly, Dorcas, and Sinclair all perform as petrifying "castrating" women (they even intimidate Lovelace) who brazenly return and overwhelm any look directed upon them.[73] In her blurred rendering of the rape, Clarissa writes that she has some "visionary remembrances" of "female figures flitting, as I may say, before my sight: the wretched woman's particularly" (1061). As this example and others suggest, Richardson proposes a link between ownership of an empowered female gaze and the lack of feminine virtue, which manifests itself in the suggestion that Sinclair's women, like Cleland's Fanny and Phoebe, participate in lesbian acts that are only representable as a preface to heterosexual intercourse.

For Richardson, the cultural roots of this link between vision and virtue hearken back to a verse from *Ecclesiastes*, "The whoredom of a woman may be known in her haughty looks and eye-lids. Watch over an impudent eye, and marvel not if it trespasses against thee" (876)—that Lovelace asserts Clarissa has earlier invoked to him and that Richardson considers important enough to cite in one of his explanatory footnotes. As I have demonstrated in my initial reading of *Clarissa*, Lovelace's instructions to the two imposters who pose as his aunt and cousin and his condemnation of women who wield active gazes show him to be acutely aware of the female vision-virtue connection. His harsh judgment of Anna anticipates the malevolent looks she directs toward him later in the novel and, quite differently, suggests the gaze of unconsummated desire that she will eventually direct upon Clarissa's portrait. Of the Evil Eye, Anna writes to Clarissa: "Oh that I had the eye the basilisk is reported to have . . . and that his [Lovelace's] life were within the power of it—directly would I kill him" (1133). Anna's wish to wield visual power over Lovelace positions her gaze in competition with his over who will possess Clarissa.

In this regard, Lovelace's "rival" for Clarissa is far less the simian-like Solmes than Anna, and he is therefore obliged to figure Anna's vision as essentially unfeminine because the only active female eyes of which he can conceive, the eyes of his harlots in waiting, have of necessity to be defined within masculinist terms. In Lovelace's gendered understanding of vision, the active "masculine" gaze is marked as fundamentally different from Clarissa's more passive "feminine" look. He makes clear his definition of female vision: virtuous (heterosexual) women are to be looked upon rather than look themselves. Lovelace is not at all disposed to consider the possibility that when he encounters Anna's gaze, he in fact is witnessing a lesbian look that requires an entirely different interpretive apparatus from what his readings of "virtuous" women require. Similar to Lovelace's faulty interpretation of Clarissa is his misreading of Anna, because both women exist ambivalently at the periphery of the heterosexual matrix in which Lovelace thrives.

Implicit in Anna's active-masculine and Clarissa's passive-feminine gazes is an apparent reification of scopic roles into butch-femme realms. This reading of the two characters is further accentuated by the fact that, at novel's close, Anna is positioned to gaze upon Clarissa's portrait, thereby appearing to reinscribe a phallocentric mode of representation with what theorists such as Kaplan and Mulvey regard as the almost inevitable figures of the masculinized subject-spectator and feminized object-spectacle. I want, however, to resist this interpretation because it positions Anna and Clarissa once more within Freud's rigid scopic oppositions. Arguing that Anna possesses a masculinized desire for Clarissa merely transforms her into a kind of transvestite who, to paraphrase Mulvey, never achieves a scopic desire that is her "own," that is, is not phallocentric. What such a reading neglects is that, following Lacan, Anna, when looking at the portrait, is never able herself to exist outside the field of Clarissa's gaze as it is represented through the portrait. Rejecting traditional artistic paradigms, Lacan contends that the spectator-object dichotomy is an illusion because, even as the viewer gazes upon the picture, the spectator also becomes an object within *the picture's* field of vision.[74] In this sense, Anna's and Clarissa's portraits are never bound within rigid subject/object categories but rather achieve a more fluid interaction free from the hegemonic, heterosexual power struggles of which Lovelace is so enamored. Clarissa's portrait, bequeathed to Anna, makes possible a truly reciprocal female gaze for the first time in the novel.

A quite different interaction occurs between Lovelace and Clarissa. From the moment they meet, Lovelace's gaze centers on and revolves around the beautiful young woman, and Clarissa notes, "It was immediately observed that his attention was fixed on me" (45). Characteristically, Clarissa chronicles Lovelace's *active* gaze with her own *passive* voice, a stylistic construction she employs when writing about the heterosexual gaze, a rendering of vision that reproduces Freud's active-masculine/passive-feminine binary. Clarissa's surrender to Lovelace's gaze has foreboding consequences, for it eliminates the hope of achieving any relevant empowerment in her discourse and actions prior to the rape. Nowhere is Clarissa's passivity more apparent than at Lovelace's party, where she masochistically conceives of herself as a victimized spectacle:

> Mr. Belford looked at me, when he spoke: yes, my dear, he smilingly looked at me: . . . and all their *assenting*, and *affronting* eyes, both men's and women's, were turned upon your Clarissa: at least my self-reproaching heart made me think so; for that would hardly permit my eye to look up. [emphases mine] (546)

Clarissa here describes a variation of the Foucauldian gaze of self-surveillance. She cannot resist the multiple spectators not because, like the gaze that oversees the Panopticon, these looks are impossible to return but as a result of her own "self-reproaching heart," which causes her to believe that everyone *is* staring at her, a claim she can never verify because, as she writes herself, she refuses to "look up." Clarissa's description of events reproduces in miniature Foucault's narrative in *Discipline and Punish* of Western culture's move from a specular economy of spectacle-punishment to surveillance-discipline. For Clarissa the effect of this movement is a multiplication of self-regulating guilt, shame, and sexual policing that ends in her self-willed death, fulfilling Richardson's depiction of Clarissa as an "exemplar" no longer willing to live once her virtue has been besmirched.

If Clarissa suffers from a "self-reproaching" heart rather than from the actual gazes of the partygoers, it does not diminish the fact that she does become the victim of many different spectators who act as extensions and refractions of Lovelace's gaze. With the exception of Sinclair's harlots, Lovelace's most significant instrument is Joseph Leman, the disloyal Harlowe servant who spies into Clarissa's private domain. Lovelace boasts of Leman's voyeurism to Belford that he has "found out by my watchful spy almost as many of my charmer's notions as those of the rest of her relations" (362). Yet Lovelace's most useful spies remain Sinclair's harlots. These Medusa-like figures watch over Clarissa, reporting her every move to Lovelace. Unlike Leman, though, their voyeurism is not relegated to espial of Clarissa but extends to her letters as well, the folded, mysterious objects that Terry Eagleton regards (beyond his more materialist analysis) as representative of Clarissa's sexuality and thus the appropriate site of direct and vicarious male scopic desire: "The sex/text metaphor in Richardson is so insistent that it is difficult to believe it unconscious. The male's desire to view the female's letters is shamelessly voyeuristic."[75]

While Eagleton is correct in noting that Lovelace's manipulation and mastery of Clarissa's correspondence reflects voyeuristic desire, peeking into Clarissa's letters does not afford Lovelace the complete interior view of Clarissa's mind that he imagines. According to his specific instructions, the harlots transcribe Clarissa and Anna's letters verbatim with no textual corruptions. Consequently, he hopes to discover in the correspondence irrefutable evidence of Clarissa's desire for him: "I must," Lovelace says, "have the very words,"[76] an illusory wish for utter signification that post-structuralist theory deems unattainable. Even were Clarissa to express unequivocal desire for Lovelace, its meaning would slide away from the ever equivocating libertine, whom Eagleton calls a "post-structuralist precursor," because of his unquenchable need to seek out textual marginalia, coin neologisms, and call into question the very meaning of language itself *ad infinitum*. Lovelace's wish to possess Clarissa's and Anna's "very words" ironically perpetuates a *meconnaisance* of his own "post-structuralist" understanding of language because the material possession of signifiers can never capture for him the stable signification of Clarissa's desire.

Lovelace's inability to read Clarissa's desire goes far deeper than a misapplied critique of language. Clarissa remains, in Castle's term, a cipher for Lovelace precisely for the same reason that Dora eludes Freud's interpretive mastery: both Freud and Lovelace insist on imposing a phallic organization upon their female objects of study.[77] When Dora, subjected to Freud's own phallic/analytic gaze, describes her disgust at being forcibly kissed by Herr K (a less violent parallel to Clarissa's rape), Freud theorizes that her repugnance is provoked by the perception of Herr K's erect penis and her repressed desire to possess his penis through intercourse. Freud thus reads Dora's "No!" as a guilty "Yes" for the phallus. But what if Dora were not simply saying "No!" to Herr K but to *all* men?[78]

Like Lovelace after Clarissa's rape, Freud never considers that Dora desires women exclusively and men not at all. If Lovelace cannot fathom that Clarissa could desire anyone but him, Freud at least tips his cigar to the homosexual possibilities of Dora's desire for Frau K, but he never explores in depth this aspect of the psychoanalysis, attributing her lesbian desires instead to the homosexual tendencies that previous patients have experienced. Freud concludes, rather, that Dora's hysteria can be explicated by recognizing a transference of desire for her father to Herr K, and finally to Freud himself. In the end, Frau K is altogether excluded from Freud's analysis as a symptom of Dora's "real" desire for her father and Herr K. Because Dora terminated treatment prematurely, Freud never achieves a "satisfactory" conclusion to her family drama; Lovelace experiences a parallel lack of narrative closure in (what is for him) an abbreviated "analysis" of Clarissa. To employ Castle's terminology, Clarissa forever remains a cipher for Lovelace because he can only see her within a heterosexual relationship that positions him, the ultimate possessor of phallic signification, as the deserving recipient of a heterosexual desire that Clarissa cannot conceive.

Bequeathing her portrait to Anna remains Clarissa's most substantial expression of Sapphism. Yet Clarissa's pictorial affirmation of desire appears to be marred by her decision to will her locket, with its enclosed picture of Anna, to Hickman. Rather than take the locket to her grave, and thereby establish a reciprocal relationship of possession and union with Anna, Clarissa seems instead to assimilate to the novel's heterosexual matrix by conferring visual/marital approval onto Hickman. Nevertheless, while the representation of Clarissa's marriage endorsement must no doubt have pleased Richardson, it also ironically undermines his apparently intended effect. For if Clarissa's tiny locket symbolically seals Hickman's and Anna's marriage, Clarissa's life-size portrait dwarfs it, thus sealing a far more overwhelming affirmation of desire for Anna. Not only will Anna look upon Clarissa's portrait, but the portrait of Clarissa will also look back at Anna, finally establishing the mutual gaze that Clarissa has desired all along. By appearing to work within a hegemonic ideology of marriage, then, Richardson's Clarissa actually writes against Richardson himself, managing in her final words to construct a connection with the spaced-off lesbianism visible through the narrative "chinks" of *Clarissa*.

2

Ocular Reproduction, Sexual Difference, and Romantic Vision

Now it is probable, that the acting fibres of the ultimate terminations of the secreting apertures of the vessels of the testes, are as fine as those of the retina.

—Erasmus Darwin, *Zoonomia* (1794)

In the 1780s and 1790s, at the approximate historical moment when Frances Burney, Maria Edgeworth, and other women writers were putting the finishing touches on the representation of domestic vision in the eighteenth-century novel, the most famous and highly regarded physician of his day, Erasmus Darwin, was employing a discourse of biological reproduction that conflated the eyes of men with the male genitalia and, perhaps not surprisingly given the contemporary cultural milieu exemplified by the "respectable" English novel, excluded the eyes of women from the scopic regime of sexuality. *Zoonomia*[1] represents something of a culmination of eighteenth-century English ideas about vision, gender, and sexuality because it absolutely collapses the distance between male vision and sexual reproduction and completely disregards female vision from the sexual economy of reproduction. In this respect it is very much a work of its time and yet also anticipates Victorian and modernist scientific discourses of vision, like Charles Darwin's theory of sexual selection in *The Descent of Man* (1871) and Freud's theory of scopophilia and exhibitionism in *Three Essays on the Theory of Sexuality* (1900). Darwin and Freud, whose theories of evolution and psychoanalysis remain among our most culturally powerful discourses, can both, as I will demonstrate in the next two chapters, trace their masculinist ideas about vision and sexuality directly back to Erasmus Darwin's *Zoonomia*, but this genealogy of scientific descent occludes another culturally important discourse of vision, namely, the discourse and representation of female vision as synonymous with domesticity, a pervasive representation that women writers in particular inherited from their eighteenth-century predecessors and further contributed to in the nineteenth century. Rather than see these two genealogies as representing altogether different family trees, it is my purpose in this and the remaining chapters of this book to show how they share, and repress, a complementary cultural ancestry.

Zoonomia is today less important for its contributions to the scientific understanding of sexual reproduction than for how it was received and, in the years and decades followings its appearance, how it underwent a series of mediations by writers who reinterpreted Darwin's meaning, often with important (and unforeseen) consequences for the discourse and representation of female vision in English culture. The first and in some respects the most important nonscientific author to take up Darwin's *Zoonomia* and employ it substantially in his own writing was William Wordsworth. By poetically mediating *Zoonomia*, Wordsworth reshaped the meaning of Darwin's science, giving it new cultural significance and resonance. Though *Lyrical Ballads* (1798) represented the work of Samuel Taylor Coleridge and William Wordsworth, two young, relatively obscure poets, the collection proved to be among the most influential cultural productions of its time and, just as a handful of its poems mediated Darwin's theory of generation, it too was mediated by subsequent writers. This chapter investigates these mediations as they appear in the work of a trio of women writers—Dorothy Wordsworth, Mary Shelley, and George Eliot—all of whom, I will argue, provide implicit metacommentaries on Darwin's theory of generation via *Lyrical Ballads*.

Tracing these women's mediations of Darwin and Wordsworth allows us to see how one dominant strain of criticism reifies English romanticism's conception of male vision as primary, noumenal, and (pro)creative and marginalizes female vision as secondary, phenomenal, and imitative. Reexamining *Lyrical Ballads* in light of Darwin's reproductive optics shows how "Tintern Abbey," in particular, may be read in opposition to the critical tradition that has largely shaped our reading of it, an exemplary tradition stretching back to Robert Southey, John Keats, and Samuel Taylor Coleridge in the eighteenth and nineteenth centuries to M. H. Abrams, Harold Bloom, and Stephen Gill in the twentieth century.[2] As diversely as these critics have judged Wordsworth's poetry, "Tintern Abbey" is held in the highest esteem among them, in great measure because, as the poem which concludes perhaps the most famous collection of poetry in English romanticism, it has been seen as a culminating expression of masculine sublimity; in terms of its artistic relationship to *Zoonomia*, critics have argued that it formally and ideologically resolves the medical pathologies and psychological crises associated almost exclusively with women—in poems such as "The Mad Mother," "The Thorn," and "The Complaint of a Forsaken Indian Woman." The women of these works—desperate, abandoned, and forlorn—are utterly opposed in temperament and predicament from Dorothy's serene representation in "Tintern Abbey." Indeed, once we read the final verse paragraph of Wordsworth's poem, in which the silent Dorothy takes a pivotal role, it is difficult not to regard a woman so closely identified with Nature as her brother's ideal notion of femininity. If, however, we read Dorothy's appearance in the poem more broadly, in the context of Wordsworthian, Darwinian, and romantic visuality and in dialogue with the representations of women that come before her in *Lyrical Ballads*, a very different "Tintern Abbey" emerges, not only in the context of Dorothy and William but also in view of the later works by women that I have briefly mentioned, works that take up *Lyrical Ballads* in general and "Tintern Abbey" in particular. These include Dorothy's unpublished poem from 1831, "Thoughts on my sick-bed," as well as far more culturally prominent productions such as *Frankenstein* (1818, 1831) and *Adam Bede* (1859), best-selling novels in which serenity and confidence are replaced by anxiety and uncertainty, works in which the privileged status of romantic male vision is challenged and, to some degree, overturned by feminine discourses of vision.

Envisioning Progeny: Erasmus Darwin and the Theory of Generation

Dominated by the male visual imagination, Erasmus Darwin's theory of sexual reproduction appeared in "Generation," the final chapter of the first volume of *Zoonomia* (1794). Working out of the British empirical tradition of John Locke, David Hume, and Thomas Reid and applying David Hartley's associationist philosophy to sexual reproduction, Darwin links the workings of the retina and the testes, thereby explicitly identifying the physiology of vision with the sexual functions of the male genitalia:

> Our ideas are movements of the nerves of sense, as of the optic nerve in recollecting visible ideas, suppose of a triangle piece of ivory. The fine moving fibres of the retina act in a manner to which I give the name of white; and this action is confined to a defined part of it; to which figure I give the name of triangle. And it is a preceding pleasurable sensation existing in my mind, which occasions me to produce the particular motion of the retina, when no triangle is present. Now it is probable, that the acting fibres of the ultimate terminations of the secreting apertures of the vessels of the testes, are as fine

> as those of the retina; and that they are liable to be thrown into that particular action, which marks the sex of the secreted embryon, by sympathy with the pleasurable motions of the nerves of vision, or of touch; that is, with certain ideas of imagination. (520)

In the account that follows, the sex of the embryo is determined by what the copulating male pleasurably sees—or imaginatively envisions—at the moment of orgasm. Darwin is careful, of course, to stipulate that this does not mean an embryo will inevitably resemble its father, and he acknowledges the child may, in fact, turn out to be the mirror image of its mother if the idea of the mother, particularly the image of her face, is actively present in the father's imagination during intercourse, something he implies will more likely occur in certain sexual positions and less likely in others:

> It may again be objected, if a female child sometimes resembles the father, and a male child the mother, the ideas of the father, at the time of procreation, must suddenly change from himself to the mother, at the very instant, when the embryon is secreted or formed. This difficulty ceases when we consider, that it is as easy to form an idea of feminine features with male organs of reproduction, or of male features with female ones, as the contrary; as we conceive the idea of a sphinx or mermaid, as easily and as distinctly as of a woman. Add to this, that at the time of procreation the idea of the male organs, and of the female features, are often both excited at the same time, by contact, or by vision. (521)

In Darwin's economy of sexual reproduction the mother remains a wholly passive participant. She may be present at the moment of conception, may perform the enormous material labor of carrying the child through pregnancy, but whatever resemblance exists between her and her child has nothing, really, to do with her. She possesses no agency in the process of conception and only affects the fetus during gestation, something Darwin emphasizes as he discounts the power of the female imagination to exert any power over the procreative process: "In respect to the imagination of the mother, it is difficult to comprehend, how this can produce any alteration in the fetus, except by affecting the nutriment laid up for its first reception . . . or by affecting the nourishment or oxygenation with which she supplies it afterwards" (522).

Darwin's theory in many ways parallels one of the foundational arguments of Jean-Joseph Goux in *Symbolic Economies.*[3] Goux historicizes the asymmetrical power relations between the body's identification with femininity (*mater*iality) and the imagination's identification with masculinity (*pater*iality), showing these relations to be a dominant paradigm in the Western cultural tradition, particularly in terms of their connection to versions of philosophical idealism (Hegel) and historical materialism

(Engels). In his formulation, superficially unrelated cultural registers, from Judeo-Christian theology (which privileges the spirit over the body) to capitalist economics (which prefers symbolic exchange value to tangible use value) give precedence to the paterial imagination over the material body. As Goux writes, "[w]hat man brings to procreation is the *form* of the progeny; what woman brings is *matter*: so say all mythical discourses on procreations" (213). Despite Goux's claims to the contrary, not all scientific myths of procreation prior to Darwin told a tale of male reproductive domination. In fact, Darwin self-consciously regarded his ideas as a challenge to early modern theories of conception, theories such as William Harvey's in the midseventeenth century and the preformationist ovists of the late seveteenth century, in which the mother determines the outcome of sexual reproduction.[4] On what he regards to be the erroneous equation between the female imagination and procreation, Darwin writes, "From hence it would appear, that the world has long been mistaken in ascribing great power to the imagination of the female, whereas from this account of it, the real power of imagination, in the act of generation, belongs solely to the male" (520). In this respect, Darwin attempts to return the understanding of sexual reproduction to classical models of conception championed, for instance, by Aristotle and Galen.[5]

Reviled by many of his contemporaries as an atheistic Jacobin, Darwin's account of procreation nevertheless reenacts with great accuracy the two most important biblical births, Adam's and Christ's, from which Goux derives much of his theory.[6] In the births of Adam and Christ, Goux identifies a pattern whereby the paterial imagination in the forms of Jehovah and the Holy Spirit give shape and meaning to formless matter; the earth from which Jehovah molds Adam and the womb in which the Holy Spirit impregnates Mary tell the same story of pateriality's primacy and materiality's subservient status. Adam and Christ represent the quintessence of what Goux calls a "patrimony of meaning" passed on directly from father to child: "The legacy of a patrimony of signifiers is thus symbolized in the language of fertilization and sexual reproduction, in the belief that it is the father . . . who confers both visible and invisible form upon the offspring, while the maternal contribution, both physiologically and socially, has the neutrality of an excipient, the inert negativity of earth" (225). Likewise, in Darwin's rendering, men occupy an active Godlike role of imaginative creation, and women—similar to the clay in Genesis and Mary in the Gospels—remain passive partners lacking the ability to produce embodied meaning in the form of a child without the envisioning endowment of a male lover.

For all of the potential reproductive power that men wield in Darwin's theory, an alarming number of instances occur in the text of "Generation" that separate "healthy" procreation (in which a father begets a son) from what Darwin considers a kind of "infirm" procreation (in which the male reproductive imagination "fails" by producing a line of daughters). God's imagination in Genesis and the Gospels is the ultimate transcendental signifier, transforming spirit into matter without any slippage of signification. The male imagination that Darwin describes is, by contrast, fallen, ridden with flaws, which amount to medical pathologies that the physician attempts to treat by diagnosing and proposing remedies. One of these pathologies is the propensity of landowners to allow their sexual imaginations to dwell on the anxiety of producing male heirs.

Recounting the stories of two landowners, one with seven daughters, the other with nine—both of whom lived on entailed estates and therefore were desperate to father male heirs in order to ensure that their property remained in the immediate family—Darwin explains the undesired parade of female offspring as a consequence of the men focusing "more on their fear of generating a female, than on the pleasurable sensations or idea of his own male form or organs" (524). Darwin alludes to the therapeutic solutions to the landowners' troubles without detailing them, and, though he tips his hat in the direction of the desirability of being able to produce female offspring on demand, as a wealthy doctor himself who fathered six sons and five daughters, his patrilineal preferences in *Zoonomia* are clear:[7]

> [The] art . . . of procreating either males or females, may be taught by affecting the imagination of the male-parent; that is, by the fine extremities of the seminal glands imitating the actions of the organs of sense either of sight or touch. But the manner of accomplishing this cannot be unfolded with sufficient delicacy for the public eye; but may be worth the attention of those, who are seriously interested in the procreation of a male or female child. (524)

It stands out as one of the great disappointments of Darwin scholarship that the physician did not have sufficient boldness to place before the "public eye" a detailed rendering of his proposed sex therapy. He does recount, though, how the unhappy situations of the aforementioned landowners were eventually resolved because at "length in despair of generating a male these [anxious] ideas ceased, and those of the male character presided at the genial hour" (524). That profound anxiety surrounds the conception of female offspring while pleasurable ideas of the "male character" occur at the "genial hour" of male procreation should tell us everything we need to know about Darwin's core attitudes toward male and female children and the relative power of the male imagination to produce them.

Immediately after Darwin describes how sexual reproduction works, he leaves behind theory for anecdote and proceeds to tell a remarkable story, one of his characteristic case histories, that appears on first glance to illustrate the absolute power of the male ocular imagination in procreation:

> I am acquainted with a gentleman, who has one child with dark hair and eyes, though his lady and himself have light hair and eyes; and their other four children are like their parents. On observing this dissimilarity of one child to the others he assured me, that he believed it was his own imagination that produced the difference; and related to me the following story. He said, that when his lady lay in of her third child, he became attached to a daughter of one of his inferior tenants, and offered her a bribe for her favours in vain; and afterwards a greater bribe, and was equally unsuccessful; that the form of this girl dwelt much in his mind for some weeks, and that the next child, which was the dark-ey'd young lady above mentioned, was exceedingly like, in both features and colour, to the young woman who refused his addresses. (523–24)

The mother of the child is here not simply marginalized by the fact that she plays no part in her daughter's features—something that would have happened often in Darwin's reproductive system because a child (even a female child) would very often resemble its father rather than its mother—but in this case she does not even enjoy the pleasure of giving birth to a child that looks like her husband. Instead, she brings into the world the imaginatively conceived daughter of her husband, the "dark ey'd young lady" who looks nothing like the woman who begot her but resembles, rather, a woman whom her father desired but never possessed. In this respect, the female imagination is impotent, the landowner's wife's reproductive agency rendered even less consequential than in the elaboration of Darwin's theory. The tenant's daughter may be able to repel the landowner's unwanted advances, but she cannot prevent herself from being reproduced both paterially and materially by him. The landowner's version of events illustrates a paradigmatic wish fulfillment of masculine romanticism, a variant fantasy exposed by Margaret Homans and Anne Mellor among others, namely, that one of the characteristic (and unattainable) quests of the male romantic is to prevent any disruption of meaning between the imagined signifier and the embodied signified.[8] By acknowledging this imaginary power in the prosaic sexual fantasies of a common landowner, Darwin goes far to democratize an ideology that Wordsworth, as *The Prelude* (1805, 1850) makes clear, believed to be the exclusive province of male genius.[9]

Late in life, Darwin turned briefly from writing about natural history and medicine to female education. Having established his illegitimate daughters, Susan and Mary Parker (whose issue as the children of

Darwin and an obscure woman referred to in the historical record only as "Miss Parker" also perhaps played a role in his explanation of sexual reproduction), as the headmistresses of a girls' school at Ashborne in Derbyshire, Darwin describes in the apology to *A Plan for the Conduct of Female Education* (1797) how they "applied to me for any ideas I could furnish them with" (7). He responded to the request for a systematic treatise laying down the principles of an ideal education for young women by composing the influential book on female pedagogy, published a year before the *annus mirabilis* of Wordsworth and Coleridge's *Lyrical Ballads* (1798). That Susan and Mary Parker looked to Darwin for pedagogical advice is hardly surprising given the breadth and depth of his knowledge (Coleridge described Darwin in 1795 as possessing "perhaps, a greater range of knowledge than any other man in Europe"), but it also to a significant degree reinscribes the hierarchical relations between men and women implicitly proposed in *Zoonomia*.[10] While the Misses Parker performed the material labor of the institution, the ideas underlying the school's curriculum were given to them by their father.

Despite the objections that can be directed toward it from our historical vantage point, this slender volume is often justifiably credited with helping to usher female education in Britain into the modern age.[11] Its progressive provisions include, for example, the teaching of mathematics and natural philosophy at the expense of more conventional feminine training in music and dancing and encouraging girls to engage in strenuous physical exercise and outdoor activity. Although it emphasizes what we today might consider to be all too conventional notions of enhancing female beauty and grace, it also refreshingly deplores the use of stays and makeup to embellish the figure and face. Darwin is nevertheless careful not to step over an ideological boundary that separated the sexes. His reluctance to cross that boundary manifests itself, in particular, in his attempts to distinguish between appropriate intellectual activity for men and women in terms of relative degrees of mental abstraction. Like most of his contemporaries, for Darwin the less abstract an enterprise, the more culturally marked as feminine that enterprise is. Darwin's views on this question are philosophically consistent with *Zoonomia* in that intellectual abstraction corresponds to the dominance of the masculine imagination in sexual reproduction.

This correspondence can perhaps best be seen by considering what Darwin omits from his ideal education for girls and young women, omissions that, in effect, stand in for what his likely description of the ideal education for young men would be had he written a pedagogical treatise for them. Darwin, for instance, disregards philosophy altogether, only invoking figures like Locke and Rousseau in terms of their writings specifically directed at and for women. By neglecting to mention *An Essay Concerning Human Understanding* and *The Social Contract*, he reveals much about his attitudes toward women when we learn that he did not consider them intellectually advanced enough to encounter the most influential philosophical statements of eighteenth-century Europe. Furthermore, in the catalog of recommended books concluding the volume, Darwin declares (perhaps attempting to preempt detractors who regarded him as a dangerous atheist) that "[b]ooks of controversial divinity are not recommended to ladies" (188) and elsewhere in the catalog asserts that Bryant's *Mythology* and Abbé de Plache's *History of the Heavens* are "too difficult or too voluminous for young Ladies, who might learn heathen mythology more easily and more agreeably from a select collection of the impressions of antique gems and medallions or of prints of antient figures" (182); he also claims that Paley's *System of Morality* and Gisborne's *Answer to Paley* "are too scientific for young minds to encounter" (184). In many respects, *A Plan for the Conduct of Female Education* tells a story not unlike *Zoonomia* in that it implicitly privileges the ability of the active masculine intellect over its passive feminine counterpart.

Nowhere is feminine intellectual and artistic ability more undercut than in the first chapter, "The Female Character," where Darwin writes,

> The female character should possess the mild and retiring virtues rather than the bold and dazzling ones; great eminence in almost anything is sometimes injurious to a young lady; whose temper and disposition should appear to be pliant rather than robust; to be ready to take impressions rather than to be decidedly mark'd; as great apparent strength of character, however excellent, is liable to alarm her own and the other sex; and to create admiration rather than affection. (10–11)

What stands out in this passage is the ideal woman's ability to "take impressions" rather than imaginatively to create, or at least reconceive, those impressions herself. Certainly this resonates with Darwin's reproductive optics in which mothers passively accept the imaginative biological impressions thrust upon them by fathers; and certainly this is true of most recent critical accounts describing the relationship between William and Dorothy Wordsworth, accounts in which Dorothy—as her representation in "Tintern Abbey" suggests—so often stands in the background as the passive recipient and vehicle of William's creative and intellectual inner eye.[12]

"Tintern Abbey": Wordsworth Rewrites Darwin

When Erasmus Darwin is mentioned in connection with William Wordsworth, the influence of the physician's *Zoonomia* on the poet's *Lyrical Ballads* never lags far behind. Much has been made, for example, of Wordsworth's urgent letter to his publisher, Joseph Cottle, requesting "Darwin's *Zoonomia by the first carrier*."[13] Dorothy Wordsworth's reply to Cottle two weeks later that the books he sent "have already *completely* answered the purpose for which William wrote for them" (De Selincourt, 214–15, italics added) has been invoked by some scholars to suggest the scope of *Zoonomia*'s influence on *Lyrical Ballads* was limited, providing the source materials for "Goody Blake and Harry Gill" but perhaps little else.[14] Several critics, however, including James Averill, Richard Matlak, and Alan Bewell, have argued that Wordsworth's poetics were extensively influenced by his reading of *Zoonomia* in the early spring of 1798; they variously show how *Zoonomia*'s subject matter, organizational structure, and philosophical outlook are combined into the poetic form and content of *Lyrical Ballads*.[15]

If we agree with Richard Matlak that *Lyrical Ballads* mirrors the narrative organization of *Zoonomia,* then "Tintern Abbey," as the poem that completes the volume, should, according to this argument, express a vision of mental health, should to some degree heal the psychic wounds so prominently displayed earlier. Radically different in tone and philosophical scope from the works that precede it, "Tintern Abbey" is a triumph, as Theresa Kelley argues, of the masculine sublime.[16] Yet for all its apparent poetic and philosophic mastery, "Tintern Abbey" can also be seen as an attempt by Wordsworth to resolve a worrisome representational crisis that manifests itself elsewhere in the collection and that spills over into the meditative poem itself, namely, the proliferation of women who hold imaginative and material sway over their children. It might appear on first glance as though the women of poems such as "The Thorn" and "The Mad Mother" are entirely the victims of masculine power or neglect, but their voices and stories, particularly the Mad Mother's, ring out with such intensity that they impinge on Wordsworth's representation of Dorothy in "Tintern Abbey." Rarely considered in relation to "Tintern Abbey," "The Mad Mother" is often regarded as an indirect expression of guilt by Wordsworth over his separation from Annette Vallon shortly after the birth of their daughter, Caroline; read from another perspective, "The Mad Mother" also qualifies as a commentary on Darwin's reproductive optics in *Zoonomia* in its betrayal of Wordsworthian anxiety that sexual reproduction may not be, as articulated in Darwin's theory, dominated by the male visual imagination.[17]

In "The Mad Mother" we discover that the eponymous character's "wild" eyes seem to have been reproduced in the expressions of her infant son, thereby, if we can trust the first-person narration, relegating the child's father to material and paterial irrelevance. Near the end of the poem, when the mother looks at her son and says, "What wicked looks are those I see?/Alas! alas! that look so wild,/It never, never came from me/ (86–88), a rupture develops between Wordsworth's poetics and Darwin's science; despite the mother's disavowals to the contrary, this "wild" baby boy seems entirely to be under the visual spell of his mother, not his father. We know, of course, that according to Darwin the child's "wicked looks" and "look so wild" can be attributed to the mother's own "wild" eyes having been translated through the father's imaginative vision during sexual intercourse. If this is so, it still suggests that the infant's absent father was subject to the power of the wife's eyes to impose themselves on his generative imagination. In *Zoonomia* Darwin raises the specter of what an impotent or anxious male imagination is likely to engender—namely, daughters instead of sons—but he attributes a bevy of daughters in families without sons to paternal anxiety over inadequate sexual-reproductive performance within a patrilineal landed economy that demands male heirs. What we encounter in "The Mad Mother," quite differently, is an infant male who, as the child of vagrant parents, is clearly not the product of an anxious landowner's imagination and, as far as his eyes are concerned, resembles his mother. For Wordsworth, therefore, the poem tells a tale of sexual reproduction that, in its self-conscious emphasis on the eyes of the mother having been passed down to the son ascribes the optical power of generative imagination to the mother, not the father. These observations are further complicated by the fact that the child is a boy and therefore, according to Darwin, should have ideally been, but is not, the issue of his father's self-embodying imagination.[18]

As we consider "Tintern Abbey" in the context of the poems that precede it, it is worth noting the peculiarity that Wordsworth explicitly dated the composition of his poem on a particular day. While a number of critics have focused on the date, July 13, 1798, that Wordsworth claims for the composition of "Tintern Abbey," variously proposing its significance in terms of the Eve of Bastille Day, the anniversary of Marat's death, and the date of the Terror's inception, J. R. Watson is right to emphasize its importance as the eighth anniversary of Wordsworth's (and Robert Jones') first arrival on French soil in 1790.[19] This landing would take on profound significance for Wordsworth because first-time travel in France made possible a second journey eighteen months later; that second journey would signal for the idealistic English republican not only a political awakening by granting him the opportunity to witness some of the most important events of the French Revolution, but also a sexual awakening in the form of his relationship with Annette Vallon, a relationship that led to fatherhood and, only a few short days after the birth of Caroline, a more or less permanent separation from mother and daughter. That Wordsworth self-consciously alludes to July 13 in the poem concluding *Lyrical Ballads* can certainly be read as a dramatic gesture intended to close the period of his life identified with France and the French Revolution. Indeed, the political history of France in the 1790s does seem to be at least one of the foci of Wordsworth's dating; yet the sexual history of Wordsworth in France in the 1790s is also crucial here, particularly in a poem that is so self-reflective and, as Kenneth Johnston argues, that so insistently seeks to divest itself of overt political meanings.[20]

One of the many ways Wordsworth attempts to depoliticize "Tintern Abbey" is to describe the stages of his maturation from boyhood to manhood, an account that initially represents him as seeing literally and immaturely (when nature's "colour" and "forms" were "a feeling and a love,/That had no need for a remoter charm,/ By thought supplied, nor any interest/Unborrowed from the eye" [79–83]) to seeing figuratively and maturely (once he has "learned/To look on nature, not as in the hour/Of thoughtless youth" [88–90]). The period that Wordsworth identifies with his youth is demarcated by nature's substantiality, by its ability to overload the mind physically with sensory perceptions, especially by vision, what Wordsworth would later call in *The Prelude* "The most despotic of the senses" (XI, 173), but the period Wordsworth identifies with manhood is tangibly connected to a spiritual vision of the mind's eye.[21] To illustrate the evolution of Wordsworth's vision from materialist to idealist we need only turn to the conclusion of the second verse paragraph of "Tintern Abbey" where the poet describes "that serene and blessed mood" in which "we are laid asleep/In body, and become a living soul:/While with an eye made quiet by the power/Of harmony, and the deep power of joy,/We see into the life of things" (45–49). Certainly this passage is saturated with Wordsworth's youthful pantheism, but it also may be read as a translation of Darwin's "Generation" (and an anticipation of Goux's theory), retold from the point of view of a poet whose desire here is not to effect sexual reproduction triggered by actual or imagined ocular perceptions, but rather to generate within the inner eye a new imaginative reality. The epistemological and spiritual value of this reality—conceived as a potent offspring, namely, the most highly regarded poem Wordsworth had written to date—intrinsically outstrips anything empirical perceptions alone can offer. The action of Wordsworth's mature spiritual eye can be considered a paterial metaphor of sexual transmission, conception, and masculine birth leading to a poem of sublimity (rather than "mere" feminine beauty). From this point of view, "Tintern Abbey" attempts to assuage the masculine imaginative anxiety so powerfully elicited by "The Mad Mother"; Wordsworth's representation of Dorothy is intended to alleviate that anxiety further by casting her eyes in light of his own youthful vision, an immature stage of ocularity in which, as Harold Bloom observes, there is a correspondence between vision and emotion, between seeing nature and experiencing joy from it.[22] In possessing a type of vision that Wordsworth putatively admires and hopes to view in the future as a way of recapturing his own childlike joy of nature, Dorothy is also figured as someone who cannot, as Wordsworth writes elsewhere in the poem, "[h]alf-create" nature, but only sensibly experience it. That is, Dorothy, and by extension the Mad Mother who may function as her alter ego in *Lyrical Ballads*, cannot effect the kind of visuality necessary for the masculine (pro)creation Darwin describes in *Zoonomia*. In this way, William attempts to use Dorothy's representation to alleviate the procreative anxiety elicited by "The Mad Mother," and perhaps by the birth of his own female offspring, Caroline, anxiety that might have threatened what we have come for nearly two centuries to accept unquestioningly as the preeminence of the Wordsworthian visual imagination.

Although the question of biological generation is not at stake in "Tintern Abbey," the relationship between male and female eyes incontestably is. Arguably the most important moment in the poem occurs when the narrator, who seems to have been meditating in solitude, turns without warning to his sister in the last verse paragraph and declares that he may "read/My former pleasures in the shooting lights/Of thy wild eyes" (117–19). These lines have frequently been invoked by critics such as John Barrell intent on showing William's representation of Dorothy to be silent and docile, a cherished yet passive mirror image of the poet's earlier self with no discrete identity of her own, a kind of naturalized amanuensis, and certainly this interpretation rings true.[23] Yet Dorothy's "wild eyes," twice invoked by William in "Tintern Abbey," also link her to the Mad Mother, an abandoned woman whose wild eyes are her own most prominent and disturbing feature. In the latter poem's opening statement by a third-person narrator (who exits at the close of the first stanza, leaving the Mad Mother to tell her own story), those eyes take center stage in the first line: "Her eyes are wild." Unlike Dorothy, whom Wordsworth describes in nothing but laudatory terms, the Mad Mother appears to be a figure out of a Gothic nightmare, the kind of woman whom Wordsworth, similar to the mad woman's husband, apparently desired to abandon over the course of *Lyrical Ballads* in favor of a representation of ideal femininity embodied by his sister.

Wordsworth's use of the adjective *wild* to describe physical and psychological characteristics of both the Mad Mother and Dorothy of course begs the following question: does he intend for us to read this as the same wild? The *Oxford English Dictionary* supplies no fewer than fourteen definitions of "wild," most of them commonly in use at the time of "Tintern Abbey"'s composition. The most resonant of these historically situated meanings for the Mad Mother would seem to be a combination of two definitions: 6a "Not under, or not submitting to, control or restraint; taking, or disposed to take, one's own way; uncontrolled. Primarily of animals, and hence of persons and things, with various shades of meaning"; 12a "Not having control of one's mental faculties; demented, out of one's wits, distracted; hence in weakened sense; Extremely foolish or unreasonable; holding absurd or fantastic views." These meanings are quite different from those Wordsworth apparently intends for Dorothy, in all likelihood at least a combination of 3a and 14a: "produced naturally without cultivation" and "[a]rtless, free, unconventional, fanciful, or romantic in style; having a somewhat barbaric character (usually in good sense, as a pleasing quality)." But there is also a considerable overlap of "wild" meaning for both Dorothy and the Mad Mother, not least of which is the very specific definition focusing on ocular qualities in 12b and therefore a subsidiary and closely related definition of 12a above, a definition that I earlier identified with the Mad Mother: "Of the eyes or look; Having an expression of distraction." That 'wild' can have specific visual meanings even without the modifier *eyes* or *eye* is significant for my interpretation of Dorothy and the Mad Mother's poetic representations as being potentially shared or, at the very least, closely associated. Wordsworth employs 'wild' a total of twenty-four times in *Lyrical Ballads*, but in only three instances—once in "The Mad Mother" and twice in "Tintern Abbey"—does he appear to invoke 'wild''s meaning with specific reference to female eyes. If Wordsworth is given credit (and I think he should be) for understanding the differences, both subtle and substantial, between the various meanings of 'wild,' we can infer with some degree of certainty that he intended for the Mad Mother and Dorothy to be considered in relation to one another and not simply by their differences, which are manifest, but by similarities that have been seriously underrated by earlier critics. The wild eyes shared by the ranting Mad Mother and the silent Dorothy undeniably unite them.

Cast in this light, Dorothy appears not only as a clear reflection of a younger, immature William (even though, as several critics have noted, she was born just eighteen months after her brother) but also a distorted reflection of the unnamed mad mother, a woman whose generating imagination seems more powerful than her husband's; if Dorothy's association with the Mad Mother is not illusory, she also appears to be a distorted reflection of Annette Vallon, the real-life abandoned woman in Wordsworth's recent history, who seems to have been the most potent source material for the proliferation of abandoned women and single mothers in *Lyrical Ballads*. Reading "Tintern Abbey" as William's attempt to reconcile Dorothy's "wild eyes" with his reflections on the masculine sublime therefore does not so much heal as reopen the psychic wounds in the first half of the volume and, in terms of Wordsworth's biography, refocuses attention on the often conscience-stricken six years following the birth of Caroline in 1792. If we accept that "The Mad Mother" and "Tintern Abbey"—and for that matter other poems within *Lyrical Ballads*, such as "The Thorn" (a poem that describes an abandoned mother's state of mind, if not her eyes, to be "wild")—contain within them veiled narratives of Wordsworth's sexual history, obscurely exploring the relation of Annette and Dorothy (and Caroline) to that history, then we also must consider the very real possibility that the absent father and the ocular reproductive anxiety associated with him at the center of the Mad Mother's rambling monologue is at least partly a reference to Wordsworth himself, another man whose generating imagination apparently "failed" him in 1792 by issuing forth a daughter rather than a son. By reading the masculine "Tintern Abbey" in the context of the "mad" feminine poetry that precedes it in *Lyrical Ballads*, what we see for the first time is how the wild eyes of the Mad Mother and Dorothy Wordsworth expose a truth hitherto obscured in romantic studies, the truth that the masculine mind's eye of poetry and science embodied in the figures of Erasmus Darwin and William Wordsworth was not nearly as responsible for the conception and birth of its offspring, both artistic and biological, as they imagined it to be.

The Silent Sister Speaks: Dorothy's Re-Vision of "Tintern Abbey"

The principal objection of recent feminist criticism against "Tintern Abbey" is the perception that William's representation of Dorothy is patronizing and infantilizing. Cast forever in the role of William's (and the first generation of English romanticism's) little sister, Dorothy is prevented from seeing into the noumenal nature of things, as William does, with a mature mind's eye; instead, she is consigned by her brother to a future in which she must act, along with nature, as his muse, must make her mind accessible to him as "a mansion for all lovely forms," must revel in her phenomenal role as the living inspiration that enables

William to recall the emotions and experiences of youth once his childlike imagination fails him. Similar to the mother in Darwin's theory of generation, Dorothy is conceived by William as the raw material on which his imagination will work. A number of late-twentieth-century critics have interceded on Dorothy's behalf to defend her against the perception of William's benign misogyny, yet no one has adequately explored Dorothy's response to her representation in "Tintern Abbey," a representation that I see as ideologically and representationally enmeshed with the tenets of Darwinian generation. Although we have only an elliptical record of Dorothy's views of her relationship with William (or, for that matter, of her measure of Darwin's science), we can nevertheless infer a great deal by interpreting select entries in *The Grasmere Journal* as well as her late poem "Thoughts on my sick-bed" which seem actively to reply to "Tintern Abbey" and, by extension, partly to respond to Darwin's exclusion of female visuality from *Zoonomia*.

Writing in her journal on March 5, 1801, during a period in which her brother was away from the cottage, Dorothy reported her activities for the evening: "Wrote to William, read the *L.B.*, got into sad thoughts, tried at German, but could not go on. Read *L.B.* Blessings on that Brother of mine! Beautiful new moon over Silver How" (120). These few lines, which constitute the day's entire entry, capture well Dorothy's relations, both intellectual and personal, with William. Rarely apart from William during this period in their lives, when Dorothy is separated from her brother the journal is typically melancholy and filled with thoughts of him. In this particular entry, for example, Dorothy pens a letter to William, twice turns to *Lyrical Ballads*, and affectionately praises her brother in the strongest possible terms. Characteristically, William was at the center of Dorothy's thoughts during this period. We cannot be certain which poems Dorothy read on the occasion of this journal entry, but we do know from the previous day's entry that she had already devoted her precious reading time to "The Idiot Boy," and it is therefore unlikely that she reread that longish poem on consecutive days, despite her great affection for it. This, of course, leaves many other poems to consider as potential candidates, but several inferences point in the direction of "Tintern Abbey" as at least one of the works with which she chose to occupy herself during William's absence: (1) as the concluding poem of *Lyrical Ballads*, "Tintern Abbey" was a logical choice for inclusion in Dorothy's reading, particularly considering that she did not again seem to pick up the volume during William's absence or at least does not report doing so; (2) the fact that she turned her eyes to the moon over Silver How immediately after reading shows her to be responding to William's specific admonishment in "Tintern Abbey" to "let the moon/Shine on thee in thy solitary walk" (134–35); (3) finally, Dorothy's passionate benediction of William ("Blessings on that brother of mine!") suggests a sister's almost embarrassed response to the detailed fraternal affection of "Tintern Abbey"'s final verse paragraph in which William addresses Dorothy as "thou my dearest Friend/My dear, dear Friend" (116–17) and identifies her as, along with nature, his principal poetic inspiration. Without William's physical presence in the cottage, it seems more than plausible that she turned to some of the most intimate pages of poetry her brother ever wrote as a means of making his affectionate voice, directly addressed to her, present in Grasmere. If, indeed, Dorothy's brief entry from March 5 is intended as a response to "Tintern Abbey," there seems to be little question that she was flattered and honored by William's characterization of her as a mirror image of his youthful self, a rendering that remains so troubling for contemporary feminist critics. Although this entry may seem to implicate Dorothy in a decidedly antifeminist discourse, another more substantial entry written afterward and, significantly, in the same month shows her vision to be far more like William's than he is willing to admit in "Tintern Abbey."

Still alone in the cottage on the evening of March 8, Dorothy once again set her sights on Silver How where "the moon hung over the northern side of [its] highest point . . . , like a gold ring snapped in two and shaven off at the ends, it was so narrow. Within this ring lay the circle of the round moon, as distinctly to be seen as ever the enlightened moon is. William had observed the same appearance at Keswick, perhaps at the very same moment, hanging over the Newland Fells" (121). Although Dorothy Levin and Margaret Homans have rightly instructed us to read Dorothy as someone who refuses to project herself (as William does) into the natural objects she perceives, one cannot help but be tempted to read this entry symbolically, to see in the reference to the peak of Silver How something more than a metaphorical natural description but also a veiled allusion to the wedding bands that William and Mary Hutchinson would exchange with each other in October 1802, effectively marking the end of *The Grasmere Journal*. Whether or not we should read the perception of the "gold ring" as snapped in two because it is shared by two people or because it represents Dorothy's unconscious wish that the marriage not take place is open to question, but one thing remains certain, the moon, with which Dorothy is so often associated in William's poetry and in Dorothy's journal, is safely nestled within the snapped segments of the gold ring and not fading from view as a spinster sister might when her brother marries. It stands out as the most distinctly rendered object on her mental canvas precisely because it remains the most visible, the most illuminated entity in Dorothy's physical and mental landscape. The entry strongly suggests that, unlike Annette Vallon, Dorothy does not intend to disappear once her brother marries.

No matter what this passage reveals about Dorothy's potential feelings toward William and Mary, it indisputably attempts to establish a congruence of vision between Dorothy and William which, far from representing Dorothy's eyes as merely reflective of a youthful William's, shows them to be seeing precisely the same object at precisely the same moment. In this respect, Dorothy employs her eyes to connect with William but not, as William does in "Tintern Abbey," to distinguish what and how they see from one another. In short, Dorothy exploits the temporal moment of seeing Silver How simultaneously with William as an opportunity to illustrate their shared mature visions rather than underscore the dichotomy of masculine-paterial and feminine-material vision that William projects into "Tintern Abbey." To understand the significance of this reading in terms of Dorothy's sense of her own maturation, one needs to consider an early entry in the *Alfoxden Journal* where she describes how William "called me into the garden to observe a singular appearance about the moon. A perfect rainbow, within the bow one star, only of colours more vivid. The semi-circle soon became a complete circle, and in the course of three or four minutes the whole faded away" (5). Here, in late January of 1798, six months before the composition of "Tintern Abbey," when it comes to vision William plays tutor to Dorothy's student and the entry therefore functions in some respects as an appropriate and explanatory prelude to the asymmetrical visual relations of "Tintern Abbey."

Yet just three years later in *The Grasmere Journal*, Dorothy no longer seems as willing to defer to her brother's considerable talents to see with his mind's eye, instead representing their respective visions as a gift bestowed more or less on equals. In this regard, Dorothy's entry fulfills the expectations that Wordsworth lays out in "Tintern Abbey" when he impresses upon his sister the urgency with which he must observe her because he recognizes that only for "a little while/May I behold in thee what I was once" (119–20). Nevertheless, this disclaimer does not diminish the fact that, just a few lines later, he states a desire that for years to come Dorothy will be the repository for "all sweet sounds and harmonies" (142), an aural rather than visual metaphor in which he calls for her to function as a kind of family album displaying scenes from William's fading memory.

Although tracing entries from Dorothy's journals permits us to speculate on her changing (visual) relations with William, the most complete and direct response that she would ever offer to "Tintern Abbey" is found in her late poem "Thoughts on my sick-bed," recorded in her commonplace book in 1832. Written in thirteen quatrain stanzas, the poem contrasts Dorothy's late infirmity with her youthful vitality, employing self-conscious allusions not only to "Tintern Abbey" but also to "A Slumber Did My Spirit Seal" and "I Wandered Lonely as a Cloud" as it explores, just as "Tintern Abbey" does, the interplay of memory, vision, and the relationship between William and Dorothy. Looking back on her and William's life together, Dorothy contemplates the prophetic predictions of "Tintern Abbey"'s final verse paragraph in which William describes in great detail the life to come for Dorothy, a life full of feeling and natural wonder. Yet "Thoughts on my sick-bed" moves beyond "Tintern Abbey" in that it portrays the elderly Dorothy not with "wild" eyes sensitive alone to phenomenal nature but as someone possessing the same "evolved" mind's eye that William, the mature poet, had been representing himself as possessing for over three decades.[24]

Dorothy Wordsworth was without question the most dedicated reader of William's poetry. His more famous readers, Coleridge, Lamb, and De Quincey (as well as, for instance, the far less sympathetic Francis Jeffrey), may well have written some of the most authoritative and influential criticism about him during his lifetime, but none of these men was responsible for transcribing his poetry into fair copy, as Dorothy did so frequently and assiduously. In her perennial role as William's scribe, Dorothy was held to a rigid standard of literalization, often needing to respond at the last possible minute to one of her brother's seemingly innumerable revisions before a collection of poems was sent off to press. For these reasons "Thoughts on my sick-bed" emerges as an enormously important response by Dorothy to William's writing because in it she self-consciously underscores her own very different relationship to his poetry as she moves from scribe and proofreader to poet; the poem therefore arguably functions as Dorothy's single most important intervention in, and commentary on, her older brother's work.

"Thoughts on my sick-bed" insistently invokes the language and situation of "Tintern Abbey." From lines that parallel "Tintern Abbey" such as "No prisoner in this lonely room" ("But oft, in lonely rooms") "I felt a Power unfelt before" ("And I have felt/A presence that disturbs me" 93–94), to Dorothy's emphasis on her ability to conjure up the image of "the green Banks of the River Wye" and to recall "thy prophetic words,/Bard, Brother, Friend from infancy!", the strains of "Tintern Abbey" echo throughout. In at least one important way, however, the situation of the two poems is utterly reversed. Whereas in "Tintern Abbey" William (and the silent Dorothy) find themselves on the river Wye itself, triggering memories for William not only of his previous visit there five years before but also of his physical, if not imaginative alienation from it when, in the interval, he has found himself "mid the din/Of towns and cities" (26–27), Dorothy manages to evoke the Wye without any actual visual stimulation whatsoever, only with the power of her mind's eye and memory. In this respect, she repeats what William claims he had managed to do in years gone by when he, like the elderly Dorothy, was confined to "lonely rooms" (26) and was compelled to envision Tintern Abbey and its environs as a means of escape from the constraints of his claustrophobic and isolated existence when cut off from nature.

Beyond a self-conscious commentary on "Tintern Abbey," "Thoughts on my sick-bed" also echoes the strains of other important lyric poems from her brother's work, including the final stanza of "A Slumber Did My Spirit Seal":

> No motion has [Lucy] now, no force;
> She neither hears nor sees;
> Rolled round in earth's diurnal course,
> With rocks, and stones, and trees. (5–8)

Compare these lines with Dorothy's revision:

> No need of motion, or of strength,
> Or even the healing air:
> —I thought of Nature's loveliest scenes;
> And with Memory I was there. (49–52)

The invocation of "I Wandered Lonely as a Cloud" is somewhat less substantial but no less significant. Midway through the poem Dorothy writes "The daffodil dancing in the breeze" alluding to William's lines:

> When all at once I saw a crowd,
> A host, of golden daffodils;
> Beside the lake, beneath the trees,
> Fluttering and dancing in the breeze. (3–6)

Of course, William's lines themselves seem to be drawn at least in part from Dorothy's original journal entry:

> I never saw daffodils so beautiful they grew among the mossy stones about and about them, some rested their heads upon these stones as on a pillow for weariness and the rest tossed and reeled and danced and seemed as is they verily laughed with the wind that blew upon them over the lake, they looked so gay ever glancing ever changing.[25]

Several clues in "Thoughts on my sick-bed" suggest that Dorothy not only intended for the poem to be read in terms of "Tintern Abbey," "A Slumber Did My Spirit Seal" and "I Wandered Lonely as a Cloud," but also that it be read in *specific ways* in relation to them. Even in the few examples I have cited, the extreme intertextuality of Dorothy's and William's poems is manifest. One of the dimensions that especially unites them is their focus on specific forms of vision. The importance of those forms becomes clear when we consider that Dorothy draws her brother's poems into her own poem whose only two highlighted lines, "With busy eyes I pierced the lane/In quest of known and *un*known things" (13–14) and "No prisoner in this lonely room,/I *saw* the green Banks of the Wye" (45–46), emphasize the relationship between Dorothy's youthful and mature visions, her early physical experience of nature and her later imaginative perception and "half-creation" of it; significantly, the material vision here is associated with Dorothy's youth when she actually traversed the hills and lanes of Alfoxden and Grasmere, while her paterial vision is identified with her mature years of infirmity when confined to a domestic interior and relegated to bed and couch. In this respect the development of her vision matches William's prognostication that, over time, she will eventually become like him. References to vision in "Thoughts on my sick-bed" positively assert Dorothy's power to see objects unavailable to most spectators, and she interestingly employs two traditionally masculine tropes—"pierced" (usually connoting a parallel between perceptual unveiling and phallic penetration) in the first line and the insistent invocation of the mind's eye—"I *saw* the green banks of the River Wye" in the second. In this respect, Dorothy engages more directly with Darwin's representation of generation, a representation that depends on phallocentric masculine vision for sexual reproduction. As she addresses her brother, Dorothy wishes him to make no mistake: she does not simply remember the excursion to the Wye and the events surrounding "Tintern Abbey"'s composition; she envisions it, "half-creates" it, as vividly as William ever did. Where Dorothy's poem underscores the activity of her two visions, however, the three poems she draws into her text from William's works variously disregard a dead Lucy's vision altogether ("She neither hears nor sees"), celebrate the power of the masculine mind's eye ("For oft, when on my couch I lie/In vacant or in pensive mood,/[The daffodils] flash upon that inward eye/Which is the bliss of solitude"), or privilege the primacy of male vision over its female counterpart ("and read/My former pleasures in the shooting lights/Of thy wild eyes"). In effect, all of these poems occlude the female visual imagination and celebrate the primacy of male visuality in ways that recall Darwin's *Zoonomia*. Dorothy therefore appears to be calling attention to William's myopia. Among other things, her poem functions as a critique of William's poetic presumption that paterial vision, for him the highest form of visual expression, is exclusively the purview of naturally endowed men.

Elderly, bedridden, and long removed from the possibility of motherhood, in "Thoughts on my sick-bed" Dorothy rejects William's disregard of female vision but does so ambivalently. In one breath she positively asserts the power of her own mind's eye and in the next calls William's words "prophetic," labeling him "Bard, Brother, Friend from infancy!" (48). Dorothy's final written words on "Tintern Abbey" and its representation of her visual and imaginative powers is therefore characteristic of a life spent with William Wordsworth, an existence that in one sense enabled her to engage far more substantially in the life of the mind than the great majority of her female contemporaries and in another required so much material labor as aunt, sister-in-law, scribe, and secretary that it frustrated much of her own potential for creative and intellectual independence, independence that, as her biographers note, she arguably did not consciously desire. This lack of independence severely curtailed her own ability to generate creative work in keeping with the way the father generates children in *Zoonomia*. What Dorothy leaves us with in "Thoughts on my sick-bed" is an intriguing commingling of material-paterial visions in her own self-representation as well as a critique of William's various uses of vision in his poetry; Dorothy's poem calls attention to a well-developed understanding of how her "dear, dear Brother" visually represented her in "Tintern Abbey," and what possible ramifications ensue from that representation, ramifications that we see in their most extreme form in the extinguishing of Lucy's sight altogether in "A Slumber Did My Spirit Seal." By turning to poetry in lieu of prose to respond directly to her representation in "Tintern Abbey," and forcefully alluding to several of William's poems in the process, poems that themselves frequently draw on her prose, Dorothy Wordsworth shares in large part Mary Shelley's own critique in *Frankenstein* of masculine visuality, creativity, and sexuality as they are represented in "Tintern Abbey" and *Zoonomia*.

Darwinian Generation, Romantic Visuality, and Feminine Forms of Seeing in Frankenstein

As Anne Mellor has demonstrated, Mary Shelley was extremely familiar with the scientific work of Humphry Davy and Erasmus Darwin, both of whom she read carefully prior to writing *Frankenstein*. Mellor shows how the methodology of each natural philosopher emerges in the novel as an exemplar of "good" and "bad" science, and she interprets Shelley's great work as a multifaceted critique of Frankenstein's scientific practice, a practice that she considers to be shaped most substantially by Humphry Davy, with his emphasis on chemical experimentation and the manipulation of nature. By contrast to the negative depiction of Davyean chemistry, Mellor reads *Frankenstein* as a defense of Erasmus Darwin's natural philosophy, science consonant with William Wordsworth's and Percy Shelley's romantic embrace of nature, what Mellor calls "a careful observation and celebration of the operations of all-creating nature with no attempt radically to change . . . the way nature works."[26] Mellor argues that Mary Shelley employs Darwin in three important ways: (1) by privileging his theory of scientific observation over experimentation, (2) by concurring with Darwin's evolutionary argument that sexual reproduction between a male and female constitutes the highest form of procreation in the hierarchy of life, thereby undermining Frankenstein's circumvention of the female in the propagation of the monster, and (3) by calling attention to Frankenstein's feverish and diseased imagination at the time of the monster's generation, something Darwin would regard as a decisive causal factor in the birth of a monster rather than a normal child. Certainly Mellor makes a strong case for the importance of Darwin as an exemplary figure in the history of romantic science in general and for Mary Shelley in particular. Yet while Darwin may not have desired as ardently as Davy to change the workings of nature, the manner in which he describes sexual reproduction in "Generation" requires no scientific intervention because natural law props up Darwin's cultural biases regarding the inherent superiority of the procreative masculine imagination. When we consider more fully the intellectual and artistic relationship between Darwin and Wordsworth, particularly the ideological and representational similarities between *Zoonomia* and "Tintern Abbey," as I have done in the first section of this chapter, we are compelled to read the Wordsworthian and Darwinian themes of *Frankenstein* not simply, as Mellor does, as a celebration of the romantic experience of nature as against the philosophy of "murder[ing] to dissect," which Wordsworth condemns in "The Tables Turned," but also as a critique of Darwin's and Wordsworth's principles of imaginative vision, a critique based on their representation of essentially gendered and hierarchical forms of seeing.

What Shelley criticizes in particular is the degree to which Victor Frankenstein deploys the mind's eye in creating the monster that Darwin and Wordsworth each in their different ways privilege as the source of romantic inspiration and creation. The dominance in *Frankenstein* of this version of paterial vision obscures two alternative and complementary forms of seeing employed by Henry Clerval, Elizabeth Lavenza, and, early in his existence, the monster, namely, (1) sympathy predicated on domestic observation and (2) the celebration of natural beauty that Wordsworth identifies in "Tintern Abbey" with the vision of his boyhood (and, later, with Dorothy's visual perceptions of nature). If we read the monster's autobiography in the middle of the novel as a kind of bildungsroman of his intellectual, emotional, and moral development, we must pay attention to his sensible development, particularly to the education of his sense of sight because this education informs the monster's shifting identification from Henry Clerval and Elizabeth Lavenza in the first half of his life to his eventual identification with Victor Frankenstein thereafter. Prior to the monster's revealing himself to the DeLaceys, his eyes are feminized by Shelley not only because they are deployed to celebrate nature but also because in secretly surveying the DeLacey family they recall, with different intentions, the household surveillance of Pamela Andrews and her successors in the eighteenth-century domestic novel tradition. Whereas the strategy of Pamela is to regulate and discipline household economy and sexuality in the domestic sphere, the monster strives to achieve a sympathetic identification with his objects of vision. In this respect what emerges in *Frankenstein* is a noteworthy difference in emphasis between eighteenth- and nineteenth-century forms of domestic vision despite the fact that both are identified with feminine ways of seeing.

Perhaps the best theoretical articulation of this emerging representation of vision in the romantic period is Joanna Baillie's *Introductory Discourse of the Stage* (1798).[27] Influenced profoundly by Adam Smith's *Theory of Moral Sentiments* (1759) and published in the same year as *Lyrical Ballads*, the *Discourse* introduces a three-volume collection of drama predicated, Baillie argues, on sympathetic identification between spectators and actors, the kind of identification that Jeremy Collier feared so much in the Restoration when the English stage provided what he regarded to be far too few dramatic roles worth emulating, especially by women. Arguing that humanity is motivated, above all, by curiosity about humanity, Baillie makes a case for why the drama, and especially the tragedy, is better suited to eliciting a sympathetic response than other genres, such as poetry. For starters, the physical structure of the stage creates the illusion that we are peering unseen into the private passions of a collection of individuals. In this respect the stage is voyeuristic, but it is voyeurism with the pursuit of a moral in mind, a moral informed by Baillie's belief that the stage offers the playwright the ability to put forward the strongest moral and ethical lessons through embodied illustration. Baillie's school of drama simulates the kind of domestic voyeurism that the monster engages in so passionately. Indeed, the following passage, taken from Baillie's *Discourse*, seems as though it could be a blueprint of the monster's observations of the troubled DeLacey family:

> Let us understand, from observation or report, that any person harbours in his breast, concealed from the world's eye, some powerful rankling passion of what kind soever it may be, we will observe every word, every motion, every look, even the distant gait of such a man, with a constancy and attention bestowed upon no other. Nay, should we meet him unexpectedly on our way, a feeling will pass across our minds as though we found ourselves in the neighbourhood of some secret and fearful thing. If invisible, would we not follow him into his lonely haunts? There is, perhaps, no employment which the human mind will with so much avidity pursue, as the discovery of concealed passion, as the tracing the varieties and progress of a perturbed soul.[28]

At first the monster unwittingly pursues the DeLaceys to their "lonely haunts," but after a time his observations become calculated and insatiable. In spying on the DeLaceys the monster betrays an unshakeable belief in his moral and ethical improvement, edification that sounds remarkably like Baillie in her remarks on the salutary benefits of attending the right kind of plays: "[T]he Drama improves us by the knowledge we acquire of our own minds, from the natural desire we have to look into the thoughts, and observe the behaviour of others" (448). Like an ardent playgoer driven to improve his mind, virtually everything the monster knows he learns as a result of observing, and sympathizing with, the DeLaceys who, like him, are destitute of society. This sympathetic representation of vision, a decidedly feminine representation based not on creation but on identification, is opposed in every respect to Darwin and Frankenstein's masculine theory of generation.

Baillie's *Discourse* is not the only possible source for Shelley's representation of the monster's domestic vision. Having read closely *An Essay Concerning Human Understanding* in 1816, one year prior to the composition of *Frankenstein*, Shelley provides the monster with the most Lockean of educations in his observations of the DeLaceys, and, significantly, she calls attention to Locke's domestically oriented and insistently feminine metaphor of knowledge as a furnished room, explored in the previous chapter. The monster follows a Lockean trajectory of understanding as he moves progressively from a rudimentary education of the senses to a sophisticated education of the intellect, emotions, and morals. This Lockean education is described not simply in the two-dimensional metaphorical language of writing a sensibly oriented consciousness on the blank pages of the mind but also with a three-dimensional metaphor of furnishing the hitherto empty rooms of the monster's psyche. Running his eyes over the interior of the DeLacey cottage for the first time, the monster observes, "'On examining my dwelling, I found that one of the windows of the cottage had formerly occupied a part of it, but the panes had been filled up with wood. In one of these was a small and almost imperceptible chink, through which the eye could just penetrate. Through this crevice, a small room was visible, white-washed and clean, but very bare of furniture'" (85).[29] By emphasizing the clean, white-washed walls, Shelley seems to be responding to the eighteenth-century intellectual tradition of reading Locke's *Essay* in terms of tabula rasa, but her own emphasis on the sparse furnishings of the room suggests that she was a careful reader of the *Essay* itself rather than the critical tradition that subsequently informed it; it shows her, indeed, to be employing the trope of furnishing and (domestic) space that was Locke's prevailing metaphor of human knowledge. What the monster describes is not simply the physical state of the DeLacey cottage but also the mental stage of his own incipient knowledge. Having already learned a few of the rudimentary features of nature through observation and experimentation, and having been shunned from civil society because of his enormous size and grotesque appearance, the monster begins his observations of the DeLaceys with a mental room "very bare of furniture" (85). Throughout the course of the DeLaceys' time there, the cottage remains sparsely furnished; the monster's mind, by contrast, becomes furnished with the knowledge essential to a well-educated European of the eighteenth century as a result of the domestic vision he employs to survey the DeLaceys and their home and to gain access to the literature they read. Like Clerval and Elizabeth, the monster's gaze is here, without question, feminized.

In this respect, the monster's feminized, domesticated eyes reach back to eighteenth-century discourses of female vision and anticipate by two decades the work of Sarah Stickney Ellis, a publishing phenomenon in the early years of Queen Victoria's reign and by far the most popular author of female advice books in nineteenth-century Britain. In the preface to *The Daughters of England* (1842), the second in her series of four advice books, Ellis acknowledges the overwhelming popularity that her first title, *The Women of England*, elicited four years earlier in 1838: "There can be no more gratifying circumstance to a writer than to find that a subject which has occupied her thoughts and employed her pen, has also been occupying the thoughts of thousands of her fellow-beings" (1).[30]

In *The Daughters of England* (1842), Ellis admonishes young Englishwomen to acquire the ability to draw, for drawing is "of all other occupations the one most calculated to keep the mind from brooding upon self, and to maintain that general cheerfulness which is a part of social and domestic duty."[31] Yet before a woman can learn to draw, Ellis observes, she must first "learn to see" (108). Ellis proceeds to explain how women might best learn to see by offering a theory of feminine drawing: "[B]ut to such as have begun to practise the art, by first learning to *see*, each succeeding day unfolds some new scene in that vast picture, which the ever-varying aspect of nature presents . . . so the eye of the painter, from the habit of regarding every object with reference to its position and effect, beholds ten thousand points of interest, which the unpractised in this art never perceive" (110). For Ellis, visual appreciation of the mundane, satisfaction with viewing the most common of objects, proves to be invaluable preparation for the girl or young woman with a domestic life in front of her. To see the world from such a perspective prevents the dangerous "brooding upon self" that might obstruct the "social and domestic duty" incumbent upon Ellis's reading audience to embrace.[32]

Artistic training of the type Ellis envisions teaches young women how to become the ideal observers of domestic spheres, which they must oversee with special attention:

> If the sun is excluded when it would be more cheerful to let it shine in—if the cloth is not spread at the right time for the accustomed meal—if the fire is low, or the hearth unswept—if the chairs are not standing in the most inviting places, her quick eye detects in an instant what is wanting to complete the general air of comfort and order which it is woman's business to diffuse over her whole household. (156)

Once practiced in this domestic art of vision, able to recognize in a moment what her artistic training has taught her over many years, Ellis's ideal "daughter" translates the talent of managing the home into the ability "to perceive by an instantaneous glance of the eye, the peculiar temper of her husband's mind" (157). What Ellis is calling for in these pages and what emerged as a popular discourse in nineteenth-century England is a sympathetic domestic vision consonant with the monster's sympathetic identification with the Delaceys.

Shelley's conception of feminine vision and the association of the monster, Clerval, and Elizabeth as a consequence of their feminine eyes are further suggested in Frankenstein's interpretation of "Tintern Abbey." Traveling with Clerval through the Rhineland on their journey to Britain, Frankenstein calls upon "Tintern Abbey" to capture his friend's character:

> The sounding cataract
> Haunted him like a passion: the tall rock,
> The mountain, and the deep and gloomy wood,
> Their colours and their forms, were then to him

An appetite: a feeling, and a love,
That had no need of a remoter charm,
By thought supplied, or any interest
Unborrowed from the eye. (77–84)

These lines are employed by Frankenstein to mark the difference, in particular, between Clerval and Frankenstein's eyes and their experience of nature. Passionate about all that is visible in nature, Clerval, like Dorothy, sees phenomenally, with the eyes of the young William Wordsworth, while Frankenstein, like the mature William Wordsworth, creates his own natural reality, consequently "sees into the life" (and death) of things, because he has chosen the vocation of a natural philosopher who has "pursued nature to her hiding places" (36), and, in Davy's words "[i]nstead of slowly endeavouring to lift up the veil concealing the wonderful phenomena of living nature; full of ardent imaginations [he] vainly and presumptuously attempted to tear it asunder" (9). Reflecting on the months leading up to the creation of the monster, Frankenstein calls attention to his altered perceptual relations to nature, relations that have much to do with vision: "It was a most beautiful season; never did the fields bestow a more plentiful harvest, or the vines yield a more luxuriant vintage: but my eyes were insensible to the charms of nature" (37) and again "[w]inter, spring, and summer, passed away during my labours; but I did not watch the blossom or the expanding leaves—sights which before always yielded me supreme delight, so deeply was I engrossed in my occupation" (38). Contrast this neglect of nature with the monster, who describes the sensible experience of living through his first spring: "My senses were gratified and refreshed by a thousand scents of delight, and a thousand sights of beauty" (92).

If any doubts remain as to the self-conscious use of "Tintern Abbey" by Shelley, they should be dispelled in the second paragraph of the next chapter when Frankenstein observes that "in Clerval I saw the image of my former self" (131). Clerval is figured here in terms consonant with Wordsworth's representation of Dorothy in "Tintern Abbey" ("and in thy voice I catch/The language of my former heart, and read/My former pleasures in the shooting lights of thy wild eyes") with two exceptions: Clerval is a man and Frankenstein's, not Clerval's, eyes are depicted as wild. As Frankenstein admits that "when [Clerval] observed me more attentively, he saw a wildness in my eyes for which he could not account" (43), and in this respect Victor's eyes, whose wildness is shaped by the birth of a male progeny, are identified with the Mad Mother's far more concretely than they are with Dorothy's wild eyes, which return an image of the youthful Wordsworth back to the poet. The sexual discrepancy between Clerval and Dorothy is, strangely, a small point, for Clerval is depicted throughout the novel by Frankenstein as insistently feminine. Frankenstein most effectively feminizes Clerval by associating his friend with the domestic sphere, observing that his unexpected arrival in Ingolstadt "brought back to my thoughts my father, Elizabeth, and all those scenes of home so dear to my recollection" (41) and affirms Clerval's confidence in his qualifications to return Frankenstein back to health after his physical collapse: "[H]e knew that I could not have a more kind and attentive nurse than himself; and, firm in the hope he felt of my recovery, he did not doubt that, instead of doing harm, he performed the kindest action that he could towards them" (43). In this respect Clerval resembles Elizabeth, who, Frankenstein acknowledges, sacrifices whatever independent desires she possesses after the death of Caroline Frankenstein to nurse the male line of the Frankensteins back to emotional health:

> [She] determined to fulfill her duties with the greatest exactness; and she felt that that most imperious duty, of rendering her uncle and cousins happy, had devolved upon her. She consoled me, amused her uncle, instructed my brothers; and I never beheld her so enchanting as at this time, when she was continually endeavoring to contribute to the happiness of others, entirely forgetful of herself. (27)

Frankenstein further cements the similarities between Clerval and Elizabeth by paralleling their difference from him relative to nature. Frankenstein tells Walton that as a youth "[t]he world was to me a secret, which I desired to discover; to [Elizabeth] it was a vacancy, which she sought to people with imaginations of her own" (21). Elizabeth is here linked to Clerval who as a boy of nine, we learn, possessed "singular talent and fancy" and "wrote a fairy tale, which was the delight and amazement of all his companions (21). (Similar to Elizabeth, Clerval peoples the earth with his imaginations, but of course it is Frankenstein's masculine, scientific imagination that eventually increases the population of the earth with a creature that will, ironically, ultimately depopulate the Frankenstein family to the point of oblivion.) Finally, after abandoning the monster and experiencing a physical and mental collapse, Frankenstein praises Clerval, the most sympathetic of men, because he "called forth the better feelings of my heart; he again taught me to love the aspect of nature, and the cheerful faces of children" (50), and goes on to tell his friend that "'[a] selfish pursuit had cramped and narrowed me, until your gentleness and affection warmed and opened my senses'" (51). Here we clearly encounter Clerval as a male version of Elizabeth Lavenza (and, for that matter, of Dorothy Wordsworth), as the individual responsible for reminding Frankenstein *cum* Wordsworth of the manner in which his eyes and other senses formerly took in, and identified with, nature.

Although a great deal of critical attention has been devoted to the monster's gender and to the degree to which he is either feminized or masculinized, comparatively few connections have been made about the similarities between Clerval and the monster relative to Frankenstein, especially prior to the monster's rejection by the DeLacey family and his subsequent exploits of murder and deception. One important area of overlap for Clerval and the monster is their love of languages. When Clerval is at Ingolstadt Frankenstein observes that his friend "was no natural philosopher. . . . Languages were his principal study" (49), while arguably the most important discovery the monster makes during his observations of the DeLaceys are the mechanics of language, what he calls a "Godlike science." Without any formal training, the monster learns French fluently from his Parisian tutors. The other characteristic that Clerval and the monster (and, for that matter, Elizabeth) share, is the ability to sympathize to an enormous degree with the plight of others. Clerval's sympathy is never distracted from Frankenstein once he discovers the state of his friend's physical and mental health in Ingolstadt, and it only intensifies when the murdered body of William Frankenstein is discovered. Similarly, the monster learns the qualities of sympathy from observing the DeLaceys through the chink shared by their cottage and his hovel, and he thereby learns of their exile from France, their poverty, and Felix's frustrated love for Safie. All of this knowledge, obtained through domestic voyeurism, stimulates the monster to reflect sympathetically on the DeLaceys "whose story excited in me such various feelings of indignation, delight, and wonder, but which all terminated in additional love and reverence" (97) and in the language of sympathy consonant with Baillie's *Discourse*. The monster's education here is also, of course, sexual, and it is clearly by watching, and sympathetically identifying with, Felix and Safie that the first seeds are planted that Frankenstein might create a female companion.

If we reflect on the monster's early resemblance to Clerval it provides us with a way of understanding the monster's development as a move from a dominantly feminine identity early on to an insistently masculine identity at the time that he tells his story to Frankenstein in the ice cave on Mont Blanc, a story whose narrative form in great respect follows the pattern of autobiography laid down in "Tintern Abbey." The novel's overall narrative structure self-consciously mirrors *The Rime of the Ancient Mariner*, which draws on three levels of narration: the narrator's account of the wedding guest, the ancient mariner's story, and the marginal commentary (as it appeared in later editions of the poem). *Frankenstein* also relies on a trio of nested narratives: Walton's, Frankenstein's, and the Monster's. But the monster's autobiography patterns itself on "Tintern Abbey" far more substantially than it does on Coleridge's *Rime* in that it is a kind of elegy for the monster's former self, a prelapserian self that is innocent and virtuous as opposed to what that self has become, a Satanic murderer. We see these two selves most discretely drawn in the different experimental science that they pursue. Early on the monster practices nonviolent experiments on nature as he roasts nuts, roots, and vegetables and learns their different properties when introduced to fire. Quite differently, when the monster later encounters and strangles William Frankenstein (significantly, after he has discovered and read his father's Davyean-inspired scientific papers) he is "exultant" at the discovery that he can bring pain to the Frankenstein family. The first self practices what Mellor might see as a Darwinian science of gentle experimentalism, whereas the second self practices a Davyean science of violent intervention. As far as the monster is concerned, sympathy is left behind for good until the death of Frankenstein.

In "Tintern Abbey" Wordsworth's earlier self is identified strongly with the mature Dorothy. Similarly, through a series of identificatory substitutions that *Frankenstein* encourages almost ad infinitum (the numerous döppelgangers, including Walton and Frankenstein, Frankenstein and the Monster, Elizabeth and Caroline Frankenstein, the monster's identification with both Satan and Adam, Frankenstein's identification with Prometheus and the Judeo-Christian God, Clerval's identification with both Frankenstein and Elizabeth, etc.), the monster clearly comes to resemble not only Clerval, not only Wordsworth's boyhood self from "Tintern Abbey," but also, unexpectedly, Dorothy. In "Tintern Abbey," for example, Wordsworth enjoins Dorothy to "let the Moon/ Shine on Thee in thy solitary walk" (134–35). It would seem to be no coincidence that the monster is also identified with lunar wanderings. Frankenstein tells Walton that the monster was animated while "the moon gazed on my midnight labors" (36), and by the "dim and yellow light of the moon, as it forced its way through the window-shutters, I beheld the wretch—the miserable monster whom I had created" (39). The monster's personal associations with the moon are far more positive. Among his first memorable sensations, they are some of the few experiences that are for him genuinely steeped in pleasure:

> Soon a gentle light stole over the heavens, and gave me a sensation of pleasure. I started up, and beheld a radiant form rise from among the trees. I gazed with a kind of wonder. It moved slowly but it enlightened my path; and I again went out in search of berries. . . . [T]he only object that I could distinguish was the bright moon, and I fixed my eyes on that with pleasure. (80)

Later, after the monster's fall into murderous deceit, the moon ironically frustrates his pleasure because its reflected light allows Frankenstein to spot him just before the generation of the female monster. The sight of the monster motivates Frankenstein to destroy the female monster that would have been animated, as the monster had been, at the moment when a prominent moon lights up the night sky. Read in relation to "Tintern Abbey," the moonstruck monster's single-minded drive for a mate can be considered not simply as the wish fulfillment of long-frustrated sexual and emotional relations but also as the desire for the feminine embodiment of his former innocent self, of the very self that Dorothy represented for William in 1798.

Of course, as siblings William and Dorothy shared the same father in John Wordsworth, just as the monster and the half-conceived female monster would have shared the same father in Frankenstein had she been animated. This incestuous theme reminds us of the last verse stanza of "Tintern Abbey" in which the veiled language of incestuous desire is suffused in William's representation of his and Dorothy's relationship. The novel's recurring fear of sibling incest therefore perhaps drives Frankenstein to abort the female monster because the prospect of the two monsters' union too nearly parallels Frankenstein's own projected marriage to Elizabeth, the woman Frankenstein calls his "more than sister." In aborting the female monster Frankenstein unconsciously prevents a second incestuous union because the destruction of the female monster ensures Elizabeth's destruction as well by bringing the monster to her, as promised, on her wedding night. If preventing incest is indeed Frankenstein's motivation it remains unspoken, taboo, for to speak it would mean to bring his own desire for incest—well represented in his dream of Elizabeth transformed into the dead Caroline Frankenstein—out of the realm of the repressed and into conscious view. Conscious or unconscious, spoken or unspoken, what is revealed in the destruction of the female monster is an understanding of generation that echoes Darwin's because it is clear that Frankenstein regards patrimony to be the decisive factor in determining the identity of offspring. Frankenstein's sudden decision to destroy his female handiwork when she is on the verge of animation is odd (as is much of what Frankenstein does) because he has had months to contemplate, and reject, her creation. Yet when we consider Frankenstein's practice of generation as informed by Erasmus Darwin's theory of generation we recall the enormous paternal anxiety in *Zoonomia*, precipitated by the prospect of engendering female progeny. Frankenstein's destruction of the female monster is the most extreme and violent expression of that anxiety. Furthermore, what precipitates Frankenstein to react so violently is seeing the monster look with anticipatory desire at the unanimated female monster. It is as if at that moment Frankenstein sees in the monster's sexualized gaze the generative potential to create a "race of devils." Never mind that Frankenstein could likely have manufactured a female monster without the requisite reproductive organs, no matter what he can scientifically do to frustrate the biological birth of new monsters, the monster's paterial imagination continues to pose the threat of propagation in spite of material biological facts that state otherwise. The leer that the monster runs over the female monster is a gaze charged with sexuality, and in its lustful expressiveness the monster shows definitively that he has dropped the feminine vision of domestic sympathy that he employed so benevolently at the DeLacey cottage. When we therefore read *Frankenstein* in the multiple contexts of romantic sympathy, domesticity, and Darwinian sexuality that suffuse it, we recognize that the novel is both a critique of masculinist visuality, scientific and otherwise, and an apology for feminine forms of vision. Those forms are wholly eradicated in the deaths of Caroline Frankenstein, Clerval, Elizabeth, and, indeed, in the monster's childlike Wordsworthian self, which also experiences a kind of death that is never redeemed by the generation of a Dorothy-like companion. Perhaps, therefore, it is appropriate both for *Frankenstein* and the romantic representation of vision and gender put forward by Erasmus Darwin and William Wordsworth that the female monster is never once permitted to open her eyes.

Case Study 2. Domestic and Sexual Vision in *Adam Bede*

"'Talking of eyes,'" Arthur Donnithorne observes to Mr. Irwine in chapter 5 of *Adam Bede*, "'I know you are fond of queer, wizard like stories. It's a volume of poems, *Lyrical Ballads*. Most of them seem to be twaddling stuff, but the first is in a different style." The future squire is referring, of course, to *The Rime of the Ancient Mariner*, a work he calls a "strange, striking thing" (73). Arthur's observations on Coleridge's poem at once reveal a blind spot and an ironic insight: a blind spot because the story that follows in *Adam Bede* far more resembles one of Wordsworth's "twaddling" poems, especially "The Mad Mother" and "The Thorn," poems that take as their starting point the situation of women who have either been abandoned with a young child or seduced and made to bear a child out of wedlock. These are tragedies that call to mind Hetty Sorrel's experience in *Adam Bede*. The ironic insight is because the ultimate suffering experienced by Arthur for impregnating Hetty and holding himself responsible for the infanticide she commits resembles the permanent guilt endured by the Ancient Mariner for killing the albatross and surviving his crew. In focusing to the point of exclusion on the eyes of the Ancient Mariner, however, Arthur neglects at his peril other eyes in *Lyrical Ballads*, female eyes such as the Mad Mother's that gaze ahead with self-recognition to Hetty, a formerly respectable maiden who, as a consequence of her procreative sexual relationship with Arthur, comes to be identified as a "wild woman" with "[a] hard and even fierce look . . . in the eyes" (366).

Arthur's brief foray into literary criticism, the only such instance in the novel, follows upon an exchange between Mr. Irwine and his mother on the question of biological inheritance. Observing that visible appearances do not reveal everything about a creature's makeup, Mr. Irwine contends that one of his dogs may very well be the spitting image of its mother but reveals "two or three of its father's tricks notwithstanding" (72), a point that Mrs. Irwine refutes with all of the vehemence at her disposal:

> "Nonsense! Nature never makes a ferret in the shape of a mastiff. You'll never persuade me that I can't tell what men are by their outsides. If I don't like a man's looks, depend upon it I shall never like *him*. I don't want to know people that look ugly and disagreeable, any more than I want to taste dishes that look disagreeable. If they make me shudder at the first glance, I say, take them away. An ugly, piggish, or fishy eye, now, makes me feel quite ill; it's like a bad smell." (73)

The constellation of topics explored in these pages of the fifth chapter—biological inheritance, the importance of eyes as a marker of personality and character, and *Lyrical Ballads*—shows George Eliot to be covering discursive terrain that recalls the intellectual and aesthetic connections I have thus far highlighted among Erasmus Darwin, the Wordsworths, and Mary Shelley. When we consider *Adam Bede* as a neoromantic novel set for the most part in 1799 and 1800, an era in English literary and medical history closely identified with Wordsworth and Darwin, it is difficult to ignore how Eliot is here and elsewhere in *Adam Bede* intervening in those particular realms of romantic history by providing a self-consciously mid-Victorian commentary on them. The novels by Eliot that would follow *Adam Bede*—even those most obviously influenced by Wordsworth such as *The Mill on the Floss* (1860) and *Silas Marner* (1861)—dominantly engage not with the scientific work of Erasmus Darwin but rather with that of his more famous grandson, Charles, particularly in their fictional enactments of natural and sexual selection. But *Adam Bede*, published in 1859, the same year as *The Origin of Species*, is a genuinely pre-Darwinian novel (in the sense in which our culture has come to understand the term "Darwinian"). In terms of the relations between literature and science, *Adam Bede* is George Eliot's first and last romantic novel because the mediation of science that appears in its pages far more resembles that of Erasmus than Charles Darwin. Yet it is also true that in *Adam Bede* the medical theories of Erasmus Darwin are much less apparent, far more submerged than Charles Darwin's ideas are in Eliot's novels of the 1860s and 1870s. Indeed, Erasmus Darwin figures much less obviously in *Adam Bede* than he does either in *Lyrical Ballads* or *Frankenstein*, works in which, as I have argued above, *Zoonomia* is in fact instrumental. If Erasmus Darwin is anywhere to be seen in Hayslope village, he is not volunteering himself for house calls. Yet when we learn, for instance, that the sickly Misses Irwin, are considered by the villagers of Broxton to be "deep in the science of medicine" (74), we must remind ourselves that Darwin, like the Irwines and the young Eliot herself, made his home in the British midlands and it is therefore probable that the Irwine sisters would have been familiar with the diagnostic practices of the internationally famous Dr. Darwin. More substantial than this inference, however, are the repeated instances in the novel where characters of widely disparate stations engage in heated debates about the nature of biological inheritance and how parental traits are passed on to offspring. The characters of *Adam Bede* do not, of course, parrot Erasmus Darwin's views on the science of generation. This would be wildly unreasonable, especially given the fact that George Eliot's stalwart adherence to realism would have required her to have them actually read *Zoonomia*, something not even the intellectually wide-ranging Reverend Irwine would likely have done. Yet in the characters' preoccupation with the question of how physical and mental traits can be genealogically traced, they are clearly speculating on ground well trod by *Zoonomia*.

This is certainly true of Mr. Irwine and his mother, but it also holds for Mr. and Mrs. Poyser as well as the narrator himself, all three of whom ruminate on the unanticipated outcomes of generation. In the following exchange between the Poysers, for example, Mr. Poyser lights upon his daughter's eyes to explore their kinship with her immediate ancestors:

> "An' she's got such a long foot, she'll be her father's own child."
> "Aye, she'll be welly such a one as Hetty i' ten years' time, on'y she's got thy coloured eyes. I niver remember a blue eye i' my family; my mother had eyes as black as sloes, just like Hetty's." (187)

It bodes well for Totty, Eliot suggests, that her eyes do not resemble Hetty's, for it indicates that she will not eventually end up, as her cousin does, sporting the look of a wild woman and the title of child murderer. The narrator offers his own more subtle theory of generation and genealogy, once more invoking feminine eyes in his reflections:

> Family likeness has often a deep sadness in it. Nature, that great tragic dramatist, knits us together by bone and muscle, and divides us by the subtler web

> of our brains; blends yearning and repulsion; and ties us by our heart strings to the beings that jar us at every moment. We hear a voice with the very cadence of our own uttering the thoughts we despise; we see eyes—ah, so like our mother's!—averted from us in cold alienation; and our last darling child startles us with the air and gestures of the sister we parted from in bitterness long years ago. (49)

Even before the infanticide of Hetty's child, the elder Mr. Poyser recognizes the "tragic dramatist" at work in his granddaughter's lineage because "her mother's fortune had been spent by that good-for-nought Sorrel, and Hetty had Sorrel's blood in her veins" (323). What Eliot, a scrupulous historian, calls attention to in these passages is the uncertainty of cultural knowledge circulating around biological inheritance at the turn of the eighteenth century, despite Erasmus Darwin's best efforts to stabilize that knowledge by ascribing sole procreative power to the masculine visual imagination.

By discussing at such length Darwinian generation and Wordsworthian visuality in *Adam Bede*, I am in danger of repeating Arthur's error of focusing on a particular pair of eyes to the exclusion of all others. To be sure, other discourses of vision are important in the novel. As in *Zoonomia*, the masculine visual imagination also figures prominently in *Adam Bede*, but several complementary versions of male vision operate simultaneously in its pages, which skillfully weave together seventeenth-century Dutch painting and Wordsworthian poetics into a varied novelistic discourse of masculine vision. Certainly *Adam Bede* encloses several discourses of vision within its pages, and it is therefore worthwhile to consider how Eliot deploys within it a set of discourses—scientific, literary, aesthetic, and popular—that I have explored in earlier iterations, both in the previous and in the present chapters, especially those discourses located within the sexual and domestic regimes of visuality. Eliot's deployment of domestic vision in *Adam Bede* has important consequences for the ways that we read, in particular, Erasmus Darwin's influence in the novel—as it is initially mediated through Wordsworth and further mediated through Eliot's reading of Wordsworth—because domestic vision, represented in the end by Dinah Bede's calm, gray, overseeing eyes, is portrayed by Eliot as the antithesis to Hetty's "wild" eyes, eyes that in nineteenth-century England were associated with illicit sexuality and illegitimate procreative power. In this respect, female domestic vision in *Adam Bede* emerges as culturally and ideologically triumphant over its sexualized counterpart.

Adam Bede shares Sarah Ellis' version of female vision in the rendering of Mrs. Poyser's and, eventually, Dinah Bede's eyes. Quite different from the construction of ideal female vision in *The Daughters of England*, *Adam Bede* does not begin by confining itself to the domestic sphere alone. Instead, the novel offers three competing versions of female vision through the eyes of Mrs. Poyser and her two nieces, Dinah Morris and Hetty Sorel. In many ways, Mrs. Poyser embodies Ellis' ideal domestic observer. Dinah and Hetty, meanwhile, both deviate from their aunt's model. Dinah possesses the visionary, nondomestic eyes of a Methodist preacher, and Hetty performs the complementary visual roles of the narcissist and exhibitionist. Eliot thereby articulates two sharply defined alternatives to Ellis' domestic vision. Dinah and Hetty's disparate representations remind us, indeed, of the polarity of masculine and feminine vision as it is depicted in "Tintern Abbey." Dinah's Methodism, her Wordsworthian ability to envision reality through the mind's eye, allows her to call up images at will, to see what is not physically before her. By contrast, Hetty's narcissism and exhibitionism require physical presence rather than absence, and even when she imagines "an invisible spectator" (for Hetty, spectators are always men) to be gazing at her, her own embodied presence remains the key to the visual relations of male spectator and female performer. In Goux's terms, Dinah sees paterially, and Hetty sees materially.

Yet Hetty does not look upon the world with the modest eyes of a Dorothy Wordsworth. Indeed, Hetty's narcissism and exhibitionism before the eyes of Arthur Donnithorne and other men is partly what makes possible the eventual unveiling of her "wild" eyes at the end of the novel. When we encounter the Mad Mother in *Lyrical Ballads* we experience her only from the time of her madness and abandonment by the father of her child. What Eliot does in *Adam Bede*, quite differently, is provide us with a sexual and procreative history of how a woman comes to look wild. This is important because not only does it fill in what Wordsworth leaves out of "The Mad Mother," it also starkly reveals Eliot's understanding of the worst consequences wrought by narcissism and exhibitionism: the transformation of a vain, reckless maiden into what amounts to a wild animal. Eliot concludes *Adam Bede* by eliminating Hetty and representing female vision only through the domestically "converted" Dinah, who has given up her preaching. That is, Eliot only represents female vision within the rigid parameters enforced by domesticity, effectively valorizing Ellis' visual discourse. By the end of the novel we can no longer be sure if Dinah continues (in Wordsworth's words) to "half-create" the world with her visionary mind's eye, but we are definitively shown that she employs the eyes of a wife, sister, and mother to oversee Adam, Seth, and her two children.

My reading of the domestic theme in this novel is quite different from Nancy Armstrong's argument that domesticity in works such as *Pamela* and *Jane Eyre* empowers women politically by, in Pamela's case, signaling a triumph of Puritan bourgeois values of work and religion over Mr. B's aristocratic moral slackness, and in Jane Eyre's case by making the ex-governess the mistress and manager of a tamed (and, incidentally, a blind) Mr. Rochester. In *Adam Bede*, by contrast, I regard domesticity not as emancipatory or empowering but rather as denying women greater political agency. This is certainly true for a figure such as Dinah Morris. Dinah early on appears on the Hayslope scene as a radical Methodist preacher who challenges the authority of the patriarchal Church of England by preaching, for all to see, an evangelical theology implicitly opposed to the state religion. By the end of the novel, Dinah's political/public role is no longer hers to play, and she is largely contained, as Adam's wife, within the interior of the domestic sphere.[33]

Hetty flies in the face of Ellis' discourse of domesticity with her narcissistic vision, a vision that Eliot characterizes as incompatible with wifely duty. Whenever Mrs. Poyser's roving eye, which operates as domestic surveillance over her family, focuses elsewhere about the Hall Farm, Hetty takes the opportunity to turn her own gaze upon herself:

> Hetty Sorel often took the opportunity, when her aunt's back was turned, of looking at the pleasing reflection of herself in those polished surfaces, for the oak table was usually turned up like a screen, and was more for ornament than for use; and she could see herself sometimes in the great round pewter dishes that were ranged on the shelves above the long deal dinner table, or in the hobs of the grate, which always shone like jasper. (80)

Hetty's occasional views of her reflected image are overshadowed by nightly self-devotional services in her bedroom. She disdainfully regards her large mirror as "a queer old looking glass!" disfigured by "numerous dim blotches" and, most vexing, fixed in a stationery position, which affords only a single perspective from which to study her beauty; by contrast, Hetty's far more versatile hand-held mirror provides pleasing multiperspectives.

Hetty does not confine herself to private showings. Throughout the first half of the novel she translates her narcissism into performance, for she was "quite used to the thought that people liked to look at her" (102). By "people," the narrator really means men, for the only woman besides Dinah willing to watch Hetty closely is the ever watchful Mrs. Poyser who, true to Ellis' denunciations of female vanity, is perpetually on the alert for manifestations of Hetty's vanity:

> It is generally a feminine eye that first detects the moral deficiencies hidden under the "dear deceit" of beauty, so it is not surprising that Mrs. Poyser, with her keenness and abundant opportunity for observation, should have

> formed a tolerably fair estimate of what might be expected from Hetty in the way of feeling. (156)

Mrs. Poyser's "feminine eye," an eye of domestic surveillance consistent with the novelistic representation of female vision in England during the latter half of the eighteenth century, remains distinct from the male look, which, in Eliot's depiction, is presented as the norm, that of "people."

One of the "people" who looks most intently on Hetty is the narrator himself. His gaze, though focused after the Dutch fashion upon the social aspects of Hayslope life, often reveals a fascination with the female body. For instance, while the narrator minutely describes Mrs. Poyser's dairy, informing us that it "was certainly worth looking at," he acknowledges that "one gets only a confused notion of these details when they surround a distractingly pretty girl of seventeen, standing on a little pattens and rounding her dimpled arm to lift a pound of butter out of the scale" (89). Some objection might be made that here the narrator is simply narrating through Arthur's and not his own distracted gaze. Yet the sexualized tendency of the narrator's vision soon returns. Describing the vulnerability of men when exposed to female beauty in general and Arthur's vulnerability when exposed to Hetty in particular, the narrator rationalizes male behavior as a consequence of what Arthur sees in Hetty, "that Hetty's cheek was like a rose-petal, that dimples played about her pouting lips, that her large dark eyes hid a soft roguishness under their long lashes" (90). If Arthur's, Adam's, and the narrator's looks are normalized as the looks of genderless "people," then female vision in the novel, whether narcissistic, performative, visionary, or domestic, becomes marked as an unprivileged signifier of visual difference.[34]

In *Adam Bede*, the normalization of visual relations whereby a male spectator comes "naturally" to look at a female object, as in the case of Hetty and Arthur, operates as a dialectic by which all other visual relations are defined. It also suggests a fundamental difference in the ways the nineteenth century conceived how men and women were socially constructed to see. For Eliot, even the most sympathetic of men, such as Adam, "learn to see" not through a lens focused on domestic objects, like Ellis' students in *Daughters*, but rather through eyes drawn to female sexual objects, illustrating the nearly inseparable associations among masculinity, sexuality, and vision in the nineteenth century.

As a means of gaining a view of Hetty, Arthur feigns interest in the Poyser dairy, informing Mrs. Poyser that he "must see" it. For the flattered Mrs. Poyser, the dairy signifies an object worthy of Arthur's eyes because its efficient, high-quality production testifies to her domestic success; by contrast, the dairy functions for Arthur as little more than a place to catch Hetty in his sights. Once in the dairy, Arthur directs his eyes at the performative young woman: "Hetty tossed and patted her pound of butter with quite a self-possessed, coquettish air, slyly conscious that no turn of her head was lost [to Arthur]" (90). The masculinist discourse of vision here suggests that for Eliot and her contemporaries a gaze like Arthur's signified ownership, namely, in the late eighteenth century, possession of the kind of symbolic capital conferred on a landowning aristocrat, scopo-sexual privilege that Arthur shares with Lovelace, his fellow aristocrat. In this context, a socially privileged male spectator is empowered to gaze directly at his woman of choice with no regard for the potential consequences such an action forebodes. Conversely, that same woman must content herself with the knowledge that she is the preferred object of his eyes. In the visual regime of sexuality in which Arthur and Hetty participate, Eliot differentiates between the direct "masculinized" gaze of a male spectator and the peripheral "feminized" glance of a female performer who merely completes a dialectic of vision initiated by the spectator. Quite different from the domestic visual regime Ellis proposes, in which the woman possesses a significant, if still patriarchally constructed, degree of visual agency, Hetty possesses only the degree of agency granted by Arthur's eyes.

As Hetty gazes at herself in the mirror after she and Arthur first kiss, her own narcissistic vision triangulates with the fantasized perception of a masculine pair of eyes focused on her. Hetty's self-regard alone is no longer adequate: "And Hetty looked at herself to-night with quite a different sensation from what she had ever felt before; there was an invisible spectator whose eye rested on her like morning on the flowers" (151). Hetty's "invisible spectator" is, of course, an imagined Arthur, whose desiring gaze fulfills the young woman's Lacanian-like illusion of mirror-stage plenitude as only her narcissistic vision could do previously. To please the fantasized Arthur, Hetty imagines herself to be the "picture of a lady in Miss Lydia Donnithorne's dressing-room" (150), constructing herself into an upper-class female objet d'art for Arthur's continued viewing pleasure. Arthur also conceives of Hetty as a work of classical art, informing Reverend Irwine that "'she's a perfect Hebe; and if I were an artist, I would paint her'" (106). Arthur's invocation of the figure of Hebe does not at all resemble the solid, matronly women of seventeenth-century Dutch art. We are, rather, reminded of a classical-subject tradition in eighteenth and nineteenth-century painting that commonly depicted women as beautiful, idealized mythological figures. Arthur's artistic gaze, a gaze that would paint a Hebe if it could, betrays a patriarchal visual conservatism, and Arthur's eyes, whether they focus on Hetty at the dairy or see in her an image of Hebe, brings Hetty into full being, further suggesting the enormous degree of symbolic capital ascribed to Arthur in Hayslope as the district's largest landholder and patriarch.

Juxtaposed against the performativity of Hetty and the domesticity of Mrs. Poyser, Dinah's eyes are positively visionary. On the same evening that Hetty stares lovingly at herself in the mirror before the invisible Arthur, Dinah looks out her second-story window over the darkened landscape:

> And now the first thing she did on entering her room was to seat herself in this chair and look out on the peaceful fields beyond which the large moon was rising. . . . She closed her eyes that she might feel more intensely the presence of a Love and Sympathy deeper and more tender than was breathed from the earth and sky. (157)

Eschewing the landscape view of the Poyser fields, Dinah visualizes the abstract categories of Love and Sympathy instead. Dinah does not follow the Wordsworthian prescription to see nature mediated by the imagination; rather, Dinah's gaze is entirely imaginative. Minutes later, with Dinah's ideal Christian visions still motivating her, she quietly intrudes on Hetty's mirror exhibition before the imaginary Arthur. To Hetty's relief, Dinah does not for a moment suspect Hetty of self-indulgent behavior for she "seemed unobservent of all details" (160). In this encounter with Hetty, Dinah's gaze appears almost otherworldly and sharply contrasts with the detail-oriented eyes of Mrs. Poyser and the narrator. Dinah attempts to explain how her mind's eye works but only confuses Hetty in the process:

> It's a strange thing—sometimes when I'm quite alone, sitting in my room with my eyes closed, or walking over the hills, the people I've seen and known, if it's only been for a few days, are brought before me, and I hear their voices and see them look and move almost plainer than I ever did when they were really with me so as I could touch them. And then my heart is drawn out towards them, and I feel their lot as if it was my own, and I take comfort in spreading it before the Lord and resting in His love, on their behalf as well as my own. And so I am sure you will come before me. (143)

Dinah here foresees Hetty's eventual trouble, but Hetty will not, at novel's end, simply appear as a narcissist and performer before Dinah's mind's eye. She will, rather, present herself as a fearful, wild spectacle of a child murderer.

Paradoxically, Dinah's gaze is at once exteriorized toward ideal categories and interiorized toward constant examination of the soul. This reflects the two pulls of early Methodist theology: reception, as the narrator says, to "revelations by dreams and visions" (47) and reflection, as one of

Dinah's less enthusiastic spectators grumbles "'as a man must be doing nothing all's life but shutting's eyes and looking what's agoing on inside him'" (21). Dinah's utter lack of an exteriorized physical gaze is captured in our first view of her on the Green: "There was no keenness in the eyes; they seemed rather to be shedding love than making observations; they had the liquid look which tells that the mind is full of what it has to give out, rather than impressed by external objects" (34). These are not eyes either sensitive to the sexual attentions of men or interested in the prosaic details of domestic duty. Most important for my purposes, with respect to Dinah's role as a Methodist preacher is her position within English society as, literally, an antiestablishment figure. Not only is Dinah a member of a religious sect that subverts the authority of the established Church of England, but as a Methodist lay-preacher she speaks out publicly, an active role that Eliot makes clear could not be duplicated among Anglican women. Dinah functions as a political figure who resists the patriarchal domination of the state church. When the Reverend Irwine, the local rector of the Anglican church, inquires of Dinah whether she feels self-conscious about being "'a lovely young woman on whom men's eyes are fixed'" (97), Dinah rejects any notion of herself as a performer by responding, "'No, I've no room for such feelings'" (97).

Before Hetty's tragedy, Dinah also had no room for the feeling of domesticity, yet one apparent consequence for Dinah of returning to live in the Poyser household after Hetty's criminal transport to Australia is her own transformation from a Methodist lay-preacher into a domestic woman. Under the influence of the Hall Farm, the Poyser children "had managed to convert Dinah the preacher, before whom a circle of rough men had often trembled a little, into a convenient household slave" (461). As for Dinah's vision, it is also converted, and Adam observes of her increasingly domestic eyes, "'You're getting to be your aunt's own niece, I see, for particularness'" (464), household "particularness" that serves as a prelude to Dinah's concluding role as Adam's wife and the mother of his children, as well, in some sense, as the female domestic subject of Ellis' advice books, *The Women of England*, *The Daughters of England*, *The Mothers of England* (1843), and *The Wives of England* (1844). Yet Dinah's transformation is motivated not simply by her desire to capitulate to gendered cultural norms of household duty in the early nineteenth century but also by her strong sexual attraction for Adam. For that attraction to be realized, Dinah redirects her energies away from preaching the theology of John Wesley and toward executing the domesticity of Mrs. Poyser, a shift that, as Ellis would have informed her, greatly increases her chances of marriage. Ceasing to see with the romantic/Methodist mind's eye of a visionary, Dinah takes up the domestic vision of her aunt instead.

In this respect, Eliot shows female domesticity and sexuality to be complementary terms as long as female sexuality is made secondary to household and family responsibilities. Hetty's tragedy was wrought by reversing that hierarchy, and it leads her to be identified, like the Mad Mother, as a wild woman.

In *Adam Bede* the two alternatives to domestic vision—Hetty's narcissistic gaze and performative glance and Dinah's visionary mind's eye, the former sexualized and therefore domestically destructive and the latter idealized and therefore domestically impractical—altogether disappear from view. In this way Eliot achieves what Bakhtin calls "the general, deep-seated intentionality, the overarching ideological conceptualization of the work as a whole."[35] Domestic vision does not function in the novel as a means of political empowerment for women. Rather, the conversion to domesticity that Dinah embraces appears to rob the young woman of her political and spiritual efficacy. She ceases to stand visibly and vocally against the political and patriarchal hegemony of Anglicanism, and she submits instead to the patriarchy of marriage. Eliot concludes her novel by having Dinah, a woman who before did not pay heed to the particulars of the world, focus her eyes in the distance on Adam, her husband, and then redirect her eyes on the family home she is responsible for overseeing. Eliot describes Dinah at this moment with the clear-eyed, painterly gaze of the Dutch narrator:

> There is a figure we know well, just come out of the house, and shading her eyes with her hands as she looks for something in the distance, for the rays that fall on her white borderless cap and her pale auburn hair are very dazzling. But now she turns away from the sunlight and looks towards the door. (504)

What Dinah sees through the door is her brother-in-law, Seth, and children, Addy and Lisbeth, the namesakes of their father and grandmother respectively. In the arresting image that follows, Dinah walks hand in hand with Lisbeth, who has inherited Dinah's pale auburn hair and, most significantly, sees with her mother's gray eyes, four-year-old eyes that seem destined to follow a genealogical and cultural descent of domestic vision from grandmother to mother to daughter and oversee a house and family in the English midlands of the Victorian era.

3

The Descent of Sexual Selection: Evolution and the Politics of Female Vision in Victorian England

A pretty girl blushes when a young man gazes intently at her.
—Charles Darwin, *The Expression of the Emotions in Man and Animals* (1872)

Writing in his *Autobiography* in 1876, Charles Darwin reflects briefly on family connections in the making of his evolutionary theory. Recalling a conversation with a professor at Edinburgh's School of Medicine, he invokes the memory of his grandfather, famous in his day but since fallen into relative obscurity:

> [Dr. Grant] one day when we were walking together burst forth in high admiration of Lamarck and his views on evolution. I listened in silent astonishment, and as far as I can judge without any effect on my mind. I had previously read the *Zoonomia* of my grandfather, in which similar views are maintained, but without producing any effect on me. Nevertheless it is probable that the hearing rather early in life such views maintained and praised may have favoured my upholding them under a different form in my *Origin of Species*. At this time I admired greatly the *Zoonomia*; but on reading it a second time after an interval of 10 or 15 years, I was much disappointed, the proportion of speculation being so large to the facts given.[1]

In this passage Darwin has it both ways, crediting his grandfather for pointing him in the right direction while undercutting the value of Erasmus' nonempirical speculations. However pronounced Darwin's disappointment in *Zoonomia* may have been, numerous scholars have explored the extent to which Erasmus Darwin influenced his grandson.[2] The great majority of these accounts focus on the evolutionary similarities between Erasmus' poetry, especially *The Botanic Garden* (1789, 1791) and *The Temple of Nature* (1802) and *The Origin of Species* (1859).

Little attention, however, has been paid to the relationship between the theory of generation in *Zoonomia* and the theory of sexual selection in *The Descent of Man*.[3] In this chapter, therefore, I highlight the family resemblance between the science of grandfather and that of grandson, demonstrating a continuity of thinking between the two Darwins and their respective scientific-sexual languages of the eyes. Working through and beyond this connection my goals are threefold. First, I call attention to important fissures in the theory of sexual selection, particularly by exploring those facets of the theory that relegate women to the status of nonvisual agents in the selection of mates. Second, I explore how sexual selection in its visual dimensions was mediated in the illustrated pages of *Punch*, the Victorian Age's most popular periodical, and I examine the relationship between the representation of vision and sexuality promulgated in *Punch* and Victorian classical-subject painting, the most prominent form of painting in the last third of the British nineteenth century. The scopo-sexual depiction of women in both *Punch* and classical-subject painting shares representational strategies with sexual selection and, like Darwin's theory, exerted often powerfully negative effects on the political agency of women at a time when Victorian women with progressive views were engaged in a fierce struggle to achieve electoral emancipation by winning the right to vote. Third, the critique of Darwin, *Punch*, and classical-subject painting is enriched with readings of the fiction of two Victorian novelists who self-consciously respond to the Darwinian revolution, Olive Schreiner and Thomas Hardy, and who construct some of their most memorable female characters, in at least partial resistance to Darwin, as active scopo-sexual subjects.[4] The works of Schreiner and Hardy engage in a broad cultural dialogue not only with Darwin but also with the representation of women in *Punch*'s illustrations and classical-subject painting; these authors complicate sexual selection by emphasizing the degree to which it is culturally, socially, and economically—rather than merely biologically—constituted. Far from the virtually timeless phenomenon that Darwin imagined, sexual selection among humans is shown by these writers to be inextricably enmeshed within contemporary and lived cultures, something lost on many of today's most well regarded evolutionary psychologists who far too often accept Darwin's account of sexual selection as a transhistorical reality despite the fact that its profound biases in favor of male activity, aggression, and spectatorship were steeped in the values of Victorian culture.[5]

Charles Darwin's Scientific Inheritance and a Critique of Sexual Selection

The Descent of Man (1871) is really two volumes in one. Volume 1 focuses on humanity's place in the animal kingdom in which Darwin narrates a story only implied in *Origin*, namely, that humans are as much a part of natural selection as any other creature and can therefore trace their lineage to a common ancestor. Volume 2 explores in wide-ranging fashion how creatures from insects to humans choose their sexual partners.[6] Darwin regards sexual selection as distinct from, yet complementary to, natural selection, and it is via sexual selection that he imbues nature with the kind of agency that proves so elusive in natural selection. Whereas *Origin* proposes natural selection as a theory in which the evolutionary forces of competition, adaptation, and variation impersonally work to produce, and extinguish, the species of the earth over enormous periods of time, sexual selection in *Descent* allows individuals within species to choose their partners on the basis of conscious attraction, thereby incrementally altering the external appearance and equipage of animals and producing the sexual "taste" of species and subspecies.

According to Darwin, in species of all kinds sexual selection is pervasively dictated by females and, more particularly, by the erotic stimulation of female eyes in noticing the beauty, ornamentation, and performative abilities of their male counterparts. As Darwin moves systematically from one classification group to another, establishing a hierarchy of evolutionary sophistication along the way, he repeats again and again the same story with respect to sexually differentiated creatures, well summarized in the following lines: "Are we not justified in believing that the female exerts a choice, and that she receives the addresses of the male who pleases her most? It is not probable that she consciously deliberates; but she is most excited or attracted by the most beautiful, or melodious, or gallant males" (2: 123). Here, discussing the mating habits of birds, Darwin encapsulates the roles played by most species in sexual selection: females choose; males are chosen. In the Darwinian paradigm, virtually throughout nature female choice is driven by visual desire of physical attractions possessed or performed by the male. This scopo-sexual economy is demonstrated in the passage below, with its argument regarding the near universality of female choice: "From the ardour of the male throughout the animal kingdom, he is generally willing to accept any female; and it is the female which usually exerts a choice. Hence if sexual selection has here acted, the male, when the sexes differ, ought to be the most brilliantly coloured; and this undoubtedly is the ordinary rule" (1: 403).

By ascribing enormous agency to the discriminating powers of female eyes, sexual selection appears to break dramatically with Erasmus Darwin's theory of generation in which the male visual imagination determines procreative outcomes. However, when Charles Darwin explores sexual selection in humans he completely reverses himself, granting choice, and the power of vision, not to women but to men. Unlike the great majority of the animal kingdom in which females select the sire of their offspring, human sexual selection as articulated by Darwin upholds the dominance of patriarchy in mating. On the surface, Darwin's reversal provides an empirical basis for his grandfather's theory of generation: the male scopo-sexual imagination of Erasmus Darwin is transformed by Charles Darwin into the evolutionarily developed ability to recognize beauty and to differentiate between levels of beauty in potential female partners whose physical characteristics are then transferred through the laws of inheritance to offspring of the union. In this respect, Darwin explicates the long-term effects of sexual selection and sexual reproduction and, in his mind, corrects his grandfather's fanciful speculations with a totalizing theory, accounting for what he curiously regards as the great difference, in favor of women, in beauty between the sexes. What Darwin perceives as heightened female beauty in humans is the result, over thousands of generations, of males selecting and mating with the most attractive female partners possible. Sexual selection in humans therefore amounts to Erasmus Darwin's theory of generation by other means. In both theories male eyes determine the outcome of progeny. For Erasmus Darwin, paternally determined generation is responsible for the appearance of individuals within families and, cumulatively, the physical characteristics of families themselves; for Charles Darwin, sexual selection also has important consequences for the appearance of families but, more important, determines the appearance and variety of humanity itself, including racial differences. Once we understand the close resemblance between the two theories, we can begin to make sense of a declaration written by Charles Darwin in a letter to J. Jenner Weir three years prior to publication of *Descent*. Discussing the still nascent theory of sexual selection, the author writes, echoing *Zoonomia* (the book with which he claims in his *Autobiography* to have become disillusioned over time), "I cannot persuade myself of the truth of the common belief of the influence of the mother's imagination on the child."[7] Like his grandfather, who also denies the formative power of the maternal imagination over the fetus, Charles Darwin's theory greatly diminishes the agency of women in procreation with his theory. In this respect, grandfather and grandson in their own ways marginalized the importance of female eyes to human sexuality and reproduction. In place of the paterial theory of generation,

Charles Darwin offers a material account of how men control procreation and inheritance through the power of their eyes and that power's relationship to sexuality, a theory (as I will argue in chapter 4) subsequently embraced by Freud and psychoanalysis and still widely deployed today by the evolutionary scientific community.

According to the theory of sexual selection, the power of the eyes to discriminate among potential mates resides overwhelmingly in female creatures. For Darwin, this explains the pronounced differentiation in beauty and ornamentation between males and females of so many species. Unlike Darwin, his contemporary Alfred Russell Wallace believed that the relative plainness of females occurred exclusively through natural selection as a form of protection from predators; to Wallace's mind it would not have been evolutionarily advantageous for offspring to be made vulnerable by a highly decorated, and therefore visible, mother. Darwin, meanwhile, contends that male beauty had been accentuated as a consequence of females selecting mates with enhanced coloration or ornamentation; males thereby sacrificed the preservative quality of protective coloration for the advantage of heightened beauty and ornamentation and, consequently, the improved possibility of being chosen by more females, which of course would translate into more progeny. The discriminatory abilities of females to distinguish between the appearance of rival males and their preference for the more ornamental and colorful individuals would gradually eliminate less ornamented and colorful males. Only this understanding of sexual selection, Darwin argues, can explain the enormous external difference between males and females of so many species, difference that had to be selected over great periods of time. Ever so gradually, rudimentary colors and ornaments were embellished through inheritance and, as Darwin maintains, were often passed along to male progeny alone, explaining the widening gulf of external difference between males and females. Darwin's explanation accounts for virtually any species in which there is a pronounced discrepancy in color and ornamentation between mature males and females, discrepancies far more likely to favor male beauty and female aesthetic power. Darwin finds such a discrepancy in the secondary sexual differences of various insects:

> Sexual selection implies that the more attractive individuals are preferred by the opposite sex; and as with insects, when the sexes differ, it is the male which, with rare exceptions, is the most ornamented and departs most from the type to which the species belongs; —and as it is the male which searches eagerly for the female, we must suppose that the females habitually or occasionally prefer the more beautiful males, and that these have thus acquired their beauty. (1: 421)

Darwin anticipated critics (even among allies such as Wallace) in the great scientific debate of the nineteenth century whom it would strike as inconceivable that creatures so low on the evolutionary scale could possess a significantly heightened aesthetic sensibility. For insects or birds to recognize small gradations of color and ornamentation among males who, to the human eye, appeared nearly identical, seemed an impossibility. This criticism he heartily discounts, particularly as it relates to birds:

> Many will declare that it is utterly incredible that a female bird should be able to appreciate fine shading and exquisite patterns. It is undoubtedly a marvellous fact that she should possess this almost human degree of taste, though perhaps she admires the general effect rather than each separate detail. He who thinks that he can safely gauge the discrimination and taste of the lower animals, may deny that the female Argus pheasant can appreciate such refined beauty; but he will then be compelled to admit that the extraordinary attitudes assumed by the male during the act of courtship, by which the wonderful beauty of his plumage is fully displayed, are purposeless; and this is a conclusion which I for one will never admit. (2: 93)

The combination of enhanced male beauty, the instinctive drive of males to parade that beauty before female spectators, and the ability of females to discriminate between minute differences in the scale of beauty, are the bedrock principles on which sexual selection is based. Darwin repeatedly returns to this theme, particularly but not exclusively in his discussion of birds, and even on occasion in sexually charged language, as he does here in an evocative discourse of erection and engorgement: "The wild turkey-cock erects his glittering plumage, expands his finely-zoned tail and barred wing-feathers and altogether, with his gorged crimson and blue wattles, makes a superb, though, to our eyes, grotesque appearance" (2: 87). Here and elsewhere, Darwin is insistent: male display and performance are part and parcel of dynamic virility and successful procreation.

In moving from birds to mammals, Darwin observes "the male appears to win the female much more through the law of battle than through the display of his charms" (2: 239). Although alluding to the role that male strength and vitality play in battle, he emphasizes the importance of female beauty rather than choice as the motivating force behind human sexual selection.[8] Several important problems of consistency emerge, however, as he attempts to reconcile differences between humanity and the rest of the animal kingdom. Recalling the discussion of birds in which females almost invariably exert choice, Darwin points out that "it would be a strange anomaly if female quadrupeds, which stand higher in the scale of organization and have higher mental powers, did not generally, or at least often, exert some choice" (2: 268–69). If female quadrupeds are expected to wield the power of choice because, according to Darwin, they are more evolutionarily advanced than birds, then one would certainly expect it to be a glaring anomaly if women, far more (at least in Darwin's estimation) evolutionarily sophisticated than quadrupeds, did not also see with sexually selective eyes. But this, Darwin informs us, is not the case, at least as far as "existing semi-civilised and savage" (2: 338) women are concerned, the only women who may reliably be studied because they are closest to the natural state of humanity. He does not appear to recognize the anomaly in his own observations that, among primitive cultures, female choice is virtually nonexistent. Instead, he naturalizes the importance of female beauty, performing a complete reversal of sex roles from his earlier discussion of nonmammalian creatures:

> As I have heard it maintained that savages are quite indifferent about the beauty of their women, valuing them solely as slaves, it may be well to observe that this conclusion does not at all agree with the care which the women take in ornamenting themselves, or with their vanity. (2: 343)

Savage women are here "femininely" portrayed as performative, desiring to attract the eyes of men in ways parallel to gaudily ornamented male birds that perform for female spectators. While Darwin acknowledges the limited importance of male beauty in attracting women, he devotes a lengthy section to the differing ideas of female beauty in various cultures, underlining its special importance in the evolution of humanity. He conceives a nearly unbroken continuum between sexual selection in primitive and modern society, concluding that primitive men "at all times would prefer the handsomest slaves according to their standard of [female] beauty," while "in civilized life man is largely but by no means exclusively, influenced in the choice of his wife by external appearance" (2: 338). So important is the idea of the preservation of beauty for Darwin that it commonly drives primitive women to commit infanticide rather than risk the loss of beauty that motherhood threatens.

Yet on the question of sex, beauty, and perception in humans, Darwin's is a confused voice. He is careful to distinguish between the significance of beauty in women in primitive and civilized cultures but discounts the importance of this observation because "civilised" cultures are so far removed from the state of nature. Believing himself to be moving closer to the evolutionary development of humanity by studying primitive cultures, Darwin refutes the claim that male "savages" do not value female beauty in sexual selection and focuses on how primitive women ornament themselves to attract men. He seems to have forgotten however the words that appear just above this passage: "In most, but not all parts of the world, the men are more highly ornamented than the women, and often in a different manner; sometimes, though rarely, the women are hardly at all ornamented" (2: 343). This statement is extremely important because it establishes two facts that do not mesh with the dominant logic of sexual selection in humanity promulgated by Darwin: (1) that the majority of the world (and by world Darwin apparently means "existing semi-civilised and savage nations") is populated by cultures in which male, not female ornamentation is predominant and (2) that cultures exist, "though rarely," in which women shun ornamentation. What is noteworthy about this latter observation is that Darwin does not make a similar claim for diminished ornamentation in men, leading us to believe that everywhere, not "rarely," among the primitive cultures with which he came into contact firsthand on the Beagle voyage and with which he became aware secondhand from other travelers, men were ornamented in some noticeable fashion.

Comparing the participation of primitive and civilized women in sexual selection, he once more downplays the agency of female vision: "[A]lthough in civilised nations women have free or almost free choice, which is not the case with barbarous races, yet their choice is largely influenced by the social position and wealth of the men; and the success of the latter in life largely depends on their intellectual powers and energy, or on the fruits of these same powers in their forefathers" (2: 356). This passage contradicts an earlier pronouncement, written in a letter to Wallace, where he emphasizes the importance of male beauty to sexual selection by women: "In regard to sexual selection. A girl sees a handsome man, and without observing whether his nose or whiskers are the tenth of an inch longer or shorter than in some other man, admires his appearance and says she will marry him."[9] In *Descent*, however, the difference between the motivating drives of male and female choice are the consequence of a discrepancy in beauty between men and women analogous to the aesthetic divide separating peacocks and peahens, but in this case with women rather than peacocks having been blessed with more beauty than their sexual counterparts. Why, Darwin asks, would civilized women be motivated by male beauty when they are so much more beautiful than men? Other factors, such as wealth and social status, must compel women to choose one man over another. The enhanced beauty of women came about as a result of being, in effect, sexually enslaved by men because Darwin's understanding of anthropology stipulates that primitive women for the most part exerted no power in the process of sexual selection. In the Darwinian system primitive men dominantly selected, primitive women were dominantly selected. This explains how Darwin, recounting the evolutionary stages of the development of secondary sexual characteristics in women, describes the operations of selection that made women the fairer sex: "The females apparently were first denuded of hair in like manner as a sexual ornament. . . . It is not improbable that the females were modified in other respects for the same purpose and through the same means; so that women have acquired sweeter voices and become more beautiful than men" (2: 383). As women gradually lost more and more body hair and gained other secondary sexual attributes along the way, they were formed into the aesthetic image most desired by men. In this respect, sexual selection, second in importance in Darwin's theory only to natural selection, achieves the triumph of the primitive patriarchal eye.

But of course Darwin has a serious problem maintaining his claim that women are inherently more beautiful than men. Such a claim is predicated on his understanding of sexual beauty, an understanding shaped by his own experience as a man born and raised in nineteenth-century England who loved his wife passionately and who, like his grandfather, sired a large brood of offspring. Indeed, it would not be out of the question to argue that Darwin, whose nonscientific reading material was overpopulated by Victorian novels with female characters with whom he wished he could fall in love, was overdetermined by his own culturally constructed sexuality in the conclusion that women were more beautiful than men.[10] The evidence that he brings to bear on his claim of women's superior beauty is predicated not on their evolutionarily acquired secondary sexual characteristics but rather on their culturally specific ornamentation, such as elaborate hairstyles, fashion, and cosmetics, all of which cross the dividing line between nature and culture in a way that the biological ornamentation of peacocks, for instance, never does:

> Man is more powerful in body and mind than woman, and in the savage state he keeps her in a far more abject state of bondage than does the male of any other animal; therefore it is not surprising that he should have gained the power of selection. Women are everywhere conscious of the value of their beauty; and when they have the means, they take more delight in decorating themselves with all sorts of ornaments than do men. They borrow the plumes of male birds, with which nature decked this sex in order to charm the females. As women have long been selected for beauty, it is not surprising that some of the successive variations should not have been transmitted in a limited manner; and consequently that women should have transmitted their beauty in a somewhat higher degree to their female than their male offspring. Hence women have become more beautiful, as most persons will admit, than men. (2: 371–72)

For Darwin, the fact that women "both civilised and savage, [deck] their heads with borrowed plumes, and [use] gems which are hardly more brilliantly coloured than the naked skin and wattles of certain birds" (2: 39) speaks to the truth of his theory, but it negates the countervailing fact that these feminine ornamentations have not naturally evolved as a consequence of male selection but were acquired through the processes of culture.

Although he would not have acknowledged it, judging from the physical features of the species, humanity seems to have followed not a trajectory of sexual selection dominated by men but rather a process of double selection in which females and males wield more or less equal power in choosing a mate, a process that Darwin elaborates in great detail but ultimately discounts as unlikely:

> It may be suggested that in some cases a double process of selection has been carried on; the males having selected the more attractive females, and the latter the more attractive males. This process however, though it might lead to the modification of both sexes, would not make the one sex different from the other, unless indeed their taste for the beautiful differed; but this is a supposition too improbable in the case of any animal, excepting man, to be worth considering. There are, however, many animals, in which the sexes resemble each other, both being furnished with the same ornaments, which analogy would lead us to attribute to the agency of sexual selection. In such cases it may be suggested with more plausibility, that there has been a double or mutual process of sexual selection; the more vigorous and precocious females having selected the more attractive and vigorous males, the latter having rejected all except the more attractive females. (1: 276–77)

He does not wish to entertain the possibility that women and men resemble each other—"both being furnished with the same ornaments"—but this is indeed very much a possibility. When one sex of any species dominates sexual selection, a pronounced difference in external appearance should ensue, as with peacock and peahens. But perhaps with the exception of the ornamental feature of the male beard (an ornamental feature possessed exclusively by men and thereby, very possibly, selected by women), this is clearly not the case with men and women. Aside from size and stature (attributes that would seem to impact far more on what Darwin calls the "law of battle" than on sexual choice), those physical features that most significantly differentiate men and women—the shape of the hips and the presence of breasts—cannot be considered principally secondary sexual characteristics because they serve important biological functions, namely, making childbirth possible and providing milk to children. They are not, as in the case of the peacock and other ornamentally enhanced male species, features that have been evolutionarily developed strictly for beauty and to attract the notice of the opposite sex; they have gradually emerged, rather, for the development and preservation of the species and have evolved as objects of male sexual desire.

Another problematic position in Darwin's discussion of sexual selection among humans is the inverse relationship between perception and intelligence. He argues that possessing heightened perceptions (including the perception of beauty) signifies a concomitant lowering of intellectual ability: "Low powers of reasoning . . . are compatible as we see with mankind, with strong affections, acute perception, and a taste for the beautiful" (1: 108). This is a curious statement, given the fact that on one hand he makes a case through much of *Descent* for the superior intelligence of men over women and on the other contends that men have a more highly developed sense of the beautiful than women (and, presumably, than other intellectually inferior species) in sexual selection. These are claims difficult to reconcile. He would seem to be on more solid ground when he asserts that "[i]t is generally admitted that with woman the powers of intuition, of rapid perception, and perhaps of imitation, are more strongly marked than in man; but some, at least, of these faculties are characteristic of the lower races, and therefore of a past and lower state of civilisation" (2: 326–27). His belief that the intellectual attainments of women and the "lower races" were approximately equal was a well-worn theory in the nineteenth century, as Stephen Jay Gould and others have demonstrated.[11] Yet it is man, the sex that Darwin credits with having "[attained] to a higher eminence, in whatever he takes up, than woman . . . whether requiring deep thought, reason, or imagination, or merely the use of the senses and hands" (2: 327), who is most swayed in choosing a mate by the perception of beauty, something that is certainly compatible with possessing a "higher eminence . . . of the senses" but does not follow the claim of universal male superiority over women in virtually any field of intellectual pursuit because of what Darwin himself would have expected to be the relatively lower intelligence of anyone who wields higher perceptual ability.

Darwin regards the heightening of male sensory awareness as the evolutionary consequence of men having "to avoid enemies or to attack them with success, to capture wild animals, and to fashion weapons, which requires the aid of the higher mental faculties, namely observation, reason, invention, or imagination" (2: 327). Consistent with his understanding of biological inheritance, all of these attributes, including observation, "would at least tend to be transmitted chiefly to the male offspring at the corresponding period of manhood" (2: 328). Here, then, is the biological, essentialist foundation for his view of vision as the sense that most properly belongs to man- (as opposed to woman-) kind.

Darwin believed that through the processes of sexual selection men boast considerable perceptual superiority over women. Yet by his own reckoning this should translate into a lower intelligence relative to women, a possibility that Darwin, given his time and place in Victorian England, understandably refuses to entertain, even considering the fact that he was sympathetic to the women's suffrage movement and was convinced of the justice of John Stuart Mill's argument in *The Subjection of Women* (1867) that culture and society, not biology, are responsible for women's relative lack of accomplishment compared to men.[12] Ironically, the evolutionary narrative of sexual selection that Darwin puts forward in *Descent* does little to advance the cause of women's social, political, and sexual emancipation that progressive women (and some men) worked so hard to achieve in the Victorian era; on the contrary, the critique that I have unfolded in the preceding pages goes a long way toward impeding that progress.

Darwin's belief in the superiority of male eyes over their female counterparts was explicitly resisted by Eliza Gamble (1841–1920), an American who became one of the most important feminist evolutionary thinkers of the nineteenth century. Gamble rejects the Darwinian theory of sexual selection in her polemic, *The Evolution of Woman: An Inquiry into the Dogma of Her Inferiority to Man* (1893).[13] Unlike Darwin, who ascribes the power of sexual selection to men transhistorically and transculturally, Gamble argues that among humans, as is dominantly the case elsewhere in the animal kingdom, females, not males, were originally in charge of sexual selection. Gamble accomplishes her critique of Darwin through two principal means: (1) she reinterprets the results of human evolution by assuming that women rather than men have served in a role analogous to a vigilant domestic breeder by selecting the most desirable males; (2) she draws on contemporary ocular studies in the nineteenth century to show that men, far more than women, suffer from color blindness. The implications of this latter argument are profound because, if true, Gamble's analysis would demonstrate that because male vision is actually weaker and more susceptible to disorder than its female counterpart, then from a strictly evolutionary point of view men are far less likely than women to have served in the highly visually discriminating role as sexual selectors. Gamble proposes that in prehistory women operated as sexual selectors, which explains why humanity has evolved so successfully relative to nonhuman cohabitants of earth. While acknowledging that men function in a hegemonic role relative to women in virtually every known society, she contends that whatever perceived superiority men possess over women, especially in terms of physical strength, actually has resulted as the function of careful female choice. This is a point that Darwin himself seems to have granted in *Descent*, when he remarks that male beards are very likely the consequence of female sexual selection "for in utterly barbarous tribes the women have more power in choosing, rejecting, and tempting their lovers, of afterwards changing their husbands, than might have been expected" (2: 372).

For her part, Gamble refuses to regard women as physically inferior to men. In fact, she makes a strong claim for the physical *superiority* of women by challenging the scale on which men should be measured relative to women:

> Among the highest orders, the human species for instance, although man is larger than woman, he is still shorter lived, has less endurance, is more predisposed to organic diseases, and is more given to reversion to former types, facts which show that his greater size is not the result of higher development. We are assured that the liability to assume characters proper to lower orders belongs in a marked degree to males of all the higher species—man included. (37)

Gamble here exploits the then commonly invoked theory of evolutionary recapitulation—the belief that some humans manifest physical qualities of earlier evolutionary types, thereby betraying the degenerative direction of their development—to show that men far more often than women revert to animalistic identities. She cites a scientific study, for instance, that shows "fifty-three per cent of the males examined were possessed of muscles proper to lower orders" (38), but in "only about seventeen per cent of the females under observation, did this reversion appear" (39). She also points out that although "Mr. Darwin incautiously admits" that excessive hairiness is evidence of a "low stage of development," he refuses to use this observation as a way of "determining the comparative development of the female and male organizations" (41), a determination that Gamble explicitly makes in favor of the evolutionary development of women. In placing men closer to classifications inhabited by nonhumans, Gamble accomplishes two things: most obviously, she raises women above brutish men; more subtly, however, she challenges Darwin's gendered reversal of sexual selection among humans. If, from a biological perspective, men more closely resemble nonhumans than women, then sexual selection among humans is more likely ruled by females, as it is elsewhere in the animal kingdom.

Darwin's assumption of masculine control of sexual selection may have resulted from the perception, held by the majority of his contemporaries (including, for instance, Gamble's feminist predecessor, Antoinette Brown Blackwell), that men are far more sexually active and aggressive than women.[14] Gamble reinterprets this perceived superiority as a liability to the evolutionary development of men by arguing that men, as a result of biological necessity, are oversexed and therefore should be identified as closer in structure and organization to our primate relatives. Women, by contrast, eschew the violence, aggression, and animal sexuality characteristic of men and therefore qualify as the more rational, restrained, and evolved of the sexes. Implicitly, Gamble suggests that because of their restraint relative to men, women are the sex most qualified to make the considered judgment necessary for successful sexual selection.

If, as Darwin argues at length in *Origin*, natural selection is analogous to human breeding of domestic animals such as dogs, cattle, and sheep, then Gamble extends this logic to the theory of sexual selection in *Descent*. She shows that, far from occupying the position of the poor stepchild of evolutionary theory, sexual selection is actually on par with natural selection in terms of importance to the development of species: "Indeed, from the prominence given to Sexual Selection by Mr. Darwin, it would seem that it played a part in the development of males quite equal to that of Natural Selection itself" (13). Gamble reminds the Darwinians that virtually everywhere in the animal kingdom, including even among human "savages," females run the show when it comes to sexual selection, placing them in the role of the intelligent, detached breeder that is one of Darwin's favorite metaphors for evolution. Gamble implies that because men are so overly invested in gratifying their sexual urges they are not capable of making the same kinds of evolutionarily advantageous choices undertaken by women:

> Sexual selection, we are told, resembles artificial selection, save that the female takes the place of the human breeder. In other words, she represents the intelligent factor or cause in the operations involved. If this be true, if it is through her will, or through some agency or tendency latent in her constitution that Sexual Selection comes into play, then she is the primary cause of the very characters through which man's superiority over woman has been gained. As a stream may not rise higher than its source, or as the creature may not surpass its creator in excellence, it is difficult to understand the processes by which man, through Sexual Selection, has become superior to woman. (29)

Gamble here turns Darwin against himself, granting that men may rule domestic breeding practices but making a compelling case for why women in prehistory must dominantly have selected men, not vice versa. The implications of Gamble's argument suggest that the current dominance enjoyed by men in sexual selection will lead not to evolutionary advancement but rather to degeneration. For Gamble, the human species to a great degree owes its preeminence to women's agency in sexual selection. In modern society, with that evolutionary agency wrested from discriminating women, humanity becomes vulnerable to the animalistic urges of men, qualities that are far removed from the well-considered sexual judgments exhibited by women in prehistory.

Gamble goes on to provide empirical data justifying her argument that men cannot possibly be as visually discriminating as women. As she focuses on the greater incidence of color blindness in men, Gamble cites anecdotal evidence from well-known ocularists such as Dr. Andrew Wilson (who assures us that "Color-blindness is a condition which is certainly capable of transmission to the progeny. In one family the males alone were affected through seven generations"), a drawing teacher from a St. Paul school (who claims that "four per cent. of all male pupils were color-blind, while only one tenth of one per cent. of female pupils were so affected"), and an extensive study conducted in Boston (finding "that about one male in every twenty-five was color-blind, while the same defect among the girls and young women was extremely rare, only 0.066 per cent. of them being thus affected"). If the prevalence of color blindness among American men is not enough to convince Gamble's readers that women's sense of sight is superior, she proceeds by invoking more data to show that European studies confirm the thesis of color blindness: "We are informed that in Europe, investigations analogous to those instituted in America have been followed by the same or similar results" (49).

Whether or not these asymmetrical findings with regard to color blindness and sex would hold up under today's scientific scrutiny is irrelevant; what is important, rather, is determining Gamble's rhetorical intention for including this information in her polemic. Her explicit reason for doing so is that she, like so many nineteenth-century figures, equates the sense of sight with intelligence, calling it "far more than any other sense . . . the most intellectual" (41). Defective vision in men, then, is evidence of inferior intellect relative to women. A secondary reason, though, seems inescapably connected to sexual selection. Virtually across nature the female half of species judge the physical desirability of males by their bright colors and ornamentation. For females to be color blind would signify a serious detriment in their ability to make discriminating judgments on the suitability of their potential mates. The disparity in rates of color blindness among men and women therefore points in the direction of Gamble's general argument that formerly in human history, but as recently as when humans universally existed in a "savage" state (a state in which even Darwin admits that men commonly brightly ornament themselves to attract female attention), women who suffered from color blindness did not propagate at the same rates as their noncolor-blind competitors. By contrast, color blindness was not a significant negative check in the evolutionary development of men. Gamble's argument with respect to color blindness therefore not only emphasizes what she regards to be the intellectual superiority of women; it also points out the lack of ocular qualifications that men possess in selecting mates.

Despite the disparity to which she calls attention with regard to sex and sight, Gamble acknowledges the fact that men have dominated sexual selection for thousands of years. Yet she again and again distinguishes between the culturally informed sexual selection practiced by men and the naturally developed sexual selection that would be practiced by women if given the opportunity. This distinction finds its clearest expression in Gamble's critique of women's fashions in general and Victorian women's fashions in particular. Gamble asserts that "the style of dress adopted by women is not an expression of their natural ideas of taste and harmony" but rather reveals the extent to which "the controlling agency [of women] in courtship" has been surrendered. Now that "the female of the human species has so long been under subjection to the male . . . the styles of female dress and adornment . . . are largely the result of masculine taste" (70). This is evidence for Gamble that Western humanity at least still lives "under conditions peculiar to a sensual age" without having "outgrown the requirements which condemn women to a style of dress which hinders the free movement of the body and which checks all the activities of life" (70). She likens women to the male Argus pheasant, "whose decorations although they serve to please his mate, greatly hinder the power of motion and the free use of his body and limbs" (70).

In *The Evolution of Women* Eliza Gamble provides the most systematic and compelling feminist critique of Darwin in the "sensual age" of the Victorians, a period in which men's sexual appetites were whetted by their visual focus on women. Given the stature of Darwin's discourse in Western science, it is not surprising that Gamble's critique of sexual selection has for the most part fallen on deaf ears. Indeed, her position on Darwinism was virtually unique in a historical period during which the theory of sexual selection as articulated in *Descent* complemented several prominent antifeminist discourses of visuality that emerged in the last thirty years of the English nineteenth century. It is to these discourses that we will now turn.

Politics, Vision, and Performative Sexuality in Punch, *Darwin, and Classical-Subject Painting*

With publication of *The Origin of Species* in 1859, Darwinian science almost immediately became a source of histrionic and well-publicized debate, entering the layman's purview in newspapers, magazines, and various other public forums.[15] One site in popular culture where sexual selection was self-consciously put to work for the British middle classes was in the illustrated pages of *Punch*, by far the most popular of Victorian magazines.[16] The magazine's woodcut illustrations provide an important artifact for determining the Victorian public's understanding and reception of fashions, politics, art, gender roles, class difference, and science, as well as the relationships among these categories of representation. The trajectory through *Punch* that I will pursue in the pages that follow foregrounds the dialogues among Darwin, female visuality, and the political status of women in Victorian England, showing how Darwin was interpreted by the magazine's illustrators to achieve reactionary, antifeminist ends. An illustration from 1892, entitled "The Darwinian Theory—Variation from Environment," demonstrates the resonance of Darwin's discourse on sexual (and natural) selection. The illustration provides two distinct images of womanhood. The first frame, on the left, depicts a woman garbed in a dingy black dress standing on a London sidewalk. The caption reads, "Knocked 'em in the Old Kent Road!" Because of her attractiveness for East Enders, this woman is, in Darwinian terms, meant to be regarded as the feminine ideal for her environment, working-class London. The adjoining frame, meanwhile, realizes another Victorian ideal of femininity. Younger, thinner, and better attired than her Old Kent Road counterpart, this member of the affluent middle class appears in a sunny garden wearing a summer dress and carrying a parasol. She is clearly intended to be viewed as more physically and socially desirable to *Punch*'s readers than her working-class competitor. Her caption reads "Attracted All Eyes at Church Parade," thereby signaling her sexual desirability to men. Both frames of the illustration enact a version of scopic Darwinism. In each case, the most attractive woman in a specific social environment becomes the ideal candidate for sexual selection on the basis of physical charms that have been evolutionarily adapted over time. The beautiful female body becomes, indeed, the "natural" focus of male eyes (here represented as "all eyes" as if female eyes do not exist), which are themselves evolutionarily adapted for a particular London environment and a specific audience of men.

While this illustration invokes Darwinian science as the authority for such a varied depiction of womanhood, scientific observation in the Victorian *Punch* was often equated with a male gaze directed at female objects of desire—a relationship between science and observation that makes us consider Darwin's visual relations to the ornamented women he witnessed on the Beagle voyage as well as with Englishwomen he encountered in his day-to-day experience. As far back as 1860, just one year after Darwin's first tentative and incomplete remarks on sexual selection

Figure 1. "The Darwinian Theory—Variation from Environment" (1892). *Punch*.

appeared in *Origin* but more than a decade before the theory was fully elaborated in *Descent*, scientific language and observation were implicated within a discourse of male vision in another illustration, "Sea-Side Studies!" The illustration depicts a rocky beach where two men are standing with nets, each holding open a book. One of the men reads aloud from a passage about "beautiful zoophites" living on rock formations, which, one of the amateur scientists reads, "may be contemplated on a fine day to great advantage," because "few spectacles are calculated to afford more pleasure to a lover of Nature." The men are applying the lessons not to the natural marine formations that surround them but to two young women. In a common Victorian representation of female deference before male eyes, one of the women looks down while the other looks askance at the men. They both smile knowingly, as if to signal an understanding that they are the real objects of the men's interest. The second man's response to his friend's reading is illuminating: "H'm! Here are two lovely specimens, Fred! You take one, and I'll take the other!" One cannot imagine a more graphic prefiguration of the scopo-sexual privilege ascribed to men by Darwin in *Descent*. These men observe what they desire and effectively claim the women as their sexual property, inscribing an ideology of sexual domination by men that Darwin himself proposed as one of the bedrock principles of human evolution.

One species of visually discriminating female that Darwin focuses on in *Descent* is the peahen. Confronted with the spectacular plumage and exhibitionistic display of her male counterpart, Darwin argues that the peahen has developed such an active and discriminating eye in courtship that she is responsible for the unmatched beauty of the male: "Many female progenitors of the peacock must, during a long line of descent, have appreciated this superiority; for they have unconsciously, by the continued preference of the most beautiful males, rendered the peacock the most splendid of living birds" (2: 141). The secondary sexual characteristic of peacocks that Darwin particularly emphasizes is their highly evolved ocelli, or eye-like plumage markings. For peacocks, the possession of ocelli is one important key to finding a mate. In this way, the "eyes" of peacocks (and other species of bird) become an object of scopo-sexual desire for scrutinizing females. As far as ornithological society goes, males must defer to sexually selective female eyes.

Darwin's exploration of peahen and peacock mating habits became a popular subject for *Punch*'s illustrators, who translated the discourse more fully into a visual language for readers of the magazine. In fact, just a few weeks after *Descent* was published, "Mr. Punch's Designs after Nature" appeared, suggesting its artist was familiar with Darwin's recent work. The illustration appears side by side with "Most Natural Selection," a tongue-in-cheek commentary on Darwin and the evolutionary advantages of marriage between humans and apes. What Victorian readers encountered

Figure 2. "Sea-Side Studies!" (1860). *Punch*.

Figure 3. "Mr. Punch's Designs After Nature" (1871). *Punch*.

in the illustration is a rear view of an attractive young woman whose hair and parasol are adorned with the ocelli of the peacock. Similar to the visual attractions of peacocks, the fashionable ocelli adorning the young woman become the object of the implied (male) sexual spectator who resides beyond the frame of the illustration's—and the young woman's—point of view. While she looks out over the seaside scene, *Punch*'s male audience looks at her. By ascribing the physical characteristics of the peacock to a woman, the illustration constitutes a sophisticated interpretation of Darwinian science. Whereas Darwin attributes scopo-sexual selection to peahens, in Victorian society the explicit power of selection clearly belonged to men, not women. Far from a peahen, the woman adorned in the plumage of a peacock must clearly be intending to function in the male bird's role as a performer who desires to draw on herself the desiring eyes of the opposite sex. This interpretation speaks directly to Eliza Gamble's argument in *The Evolution of Women* with respect to women's ornamentation by male bird feathers. Reminding us that "Mr. Darwin calls attention to the fact that women 'all over the world' adorn themselves with the gay feathers of male birds," Gamble contends that "the beautiful plumage of male birds" has actually evolved "according to female standards of taste . . . in color and design" and it is therefore not surprising that women ornament themselves in such a way because "under present conditions of male supremacy, the female of the human species is obliged to captivate the male in order to secure her support" (72). Whereas Gamble provides a rationale for artificial female ornamentation, *Punch* never interrogates the cultural determinism of women's fashion, reading female ornithological display as natural.

The peacock illustration from 1871 was not the first occasion that ocelli figured prominently in *Punch*. In 1867 another "natural" illustration had taken up the same theme. In this woodcut male spectators, possibly deployed by the artist on the path in Hyde Park known as Rotten Row, are represented as important characters in the single-frame narrative. The plumage of a peacock trails behind "Miss Swellington" as she walks along a park path wielding a no less peacockish parasol. Such a sight attracts the ravenous eyes of at least two men, one nearby leaning on the path railing, the other from a distance, watching intently on horseback. In this illustration male spectators thrive within a discourse of masculine sexual selection that accurately prefigures Darwin, showing that sources for his discourse were in circulation well before publication in *Descent*.

Although the illustrated pages of *Punch* often provide an unproblematic format for the depiction of scopo-sexual masculinity, many of the magazine's illustrations make the gendering of vision a highly contested ideological issue where women vie with men, if not for dominance, then at least for something more akin to parity. To be sure, *Punch*'s illustra-

Figure 4. "As Birds' Feathers and Train Dresses Are All the Go, Miss Swellington Adopts One of Nature's Own Designs" (1867). *Punch*.

tions more commonly represent male rather than female observers; very often these male observers appear in conventional roles such as the artist, photographer, spectator, or voyeur, all granted considerable social, cultural, and sexual power over their chosen female objects. In these instances, women are nearly always represented in the equally conventional roles of the artist's model, the observed woman on the street, and the socially performative coquette, images that inform Darwin's rendering of women as the recipients rather than the possessors of a sexualized gaze. Nevertheless, *Punch*'s representations of female spectators and observers demonstrate that wielding powerful and discriminating eyes in the nineteenth century was not wholly encoded as masculine. Rather, there existed a quite substantial if still disproportionately small and patriarchally informed space for female spectators and viewers. Some of the more innovative illustrations of female observers in *Punch* convey a sense of just how much visual agency was ascribed to women and how they might challenge the masculinist Darwinian paradigm of sexual selection among humans. Even a brief investigation of a few illustrations will not simply afford a view of the conditions of possibility of seeing for women in nineteenth-century Britain but will also communicate a sense of male anxiety over the perceived (and feared) social progress of women in the midst of a predominantly conservative Victorian visual order in which Darwin very much participated.

The first illustration, from 1877, "Six of One, Half-a-Dozen of the Other," depicts three British women abroad, strolling on a boardwalk. They have just passed by three foreign soldiers (the uniforms and cut of beard suggest they are French). Both trios are peering over their shoulders, and, on discovering the men to be obtaining a second look, their response is utter shock: "Well, I never! To turn round, and stare at one like that!" Yet in looking back under the pretense of condemning the soldiers, the women have themselves violated a social taboo against women looking round at men on the street. Indeed, one of the markers of female prostitution in illustrations of the period was a woman's gaze cast directly at potential clients.[17] At the very end of the nineteenth century, for example, Mrs. Charlotte Eliza Humphry (an important figure in the English conduct-book tradition and an heiress to Sarah Stickney Ellis as the most popular Victorian author of conduct books for women and girls) would also participate in the cultural discourse of women's proper behavior on the street. Remarking on the decline in street etiquette among the generation of young women contemporary with the "New Woman" phenomenon of the 1890s, Humphry distinguishes between "well bred" and "florid" female manners; a well-bred girl is recognized "at the first glance, whether she is walking, shopping, in an omnibus, descending

SIX OF ONE, HALF-A-DOZEN OF THE OTHER.

Three of our Countrywomen Abroad. "WELL, I *NEVER!* TO TURN ROUND, AND STARE AT ONE LIKE THAT!"

Figure 5. "Six of One, Half-a-Dozen of the Other" (1877). *Punch*.

from a carriage or a cab, or sauntering up and down in the park," for there "is a quiet self-possession about the gentlewoman" as she remains "regardless of the rest of the world" (18). By contrast, a "florid" girl uses "lively gestures" and wields the "notice-attracting glance and the self-conscious air of the underbred" (18). In other words she performs in a manner consonant with the description of sexually performative peacocks in *Descent.* Humphry laments the new visual language spoken on the street and elsewhere, a language that earlier in the nineteenth century had been encoded as an explicit signifier of illicit female sexuality:[18]

> There was a good old rule of manners that forbade a lady to look back after any one in the street, or to turn and stare at any one in church, opera, theater, or concert room. These good old rules seem fast to be becoming obsolete; or so one might suppose from the frequency with which they are disregarded. (19)

Particularly captivating about the *Punch* illustration of the boardwalk is that not only does it disrupt the notion of an unchallenged male street spectator, but it also operates as a model of female agency in its deployment of an active, sexually interested regard, a more or less direct signifier of desire for the most part unavailable to "respectable" women in the mid-Victorian age.

According to *Punch*, one medium in which women's eyes could actively participate was in the world of art, and in the magazine's pages British art generally makes illustrated appearances in three forms: (1) at Royal Academy exhibits, (2) in a male artist's studio, and (3) at art tutorials taught by male teachers to female students. Depictions set in the Royal Academy are most commonly satirical commentaries on pretentious lay-critics, and they have little relevance for the ensuing analysis. In the case of both the artist's studio and the tutorials, however, the male artist is generally ascribed visual and aesthetic sovereignty: in the former case, he is empowered to look at his female model and to create any image of womanhood he desires or imagines; in the latter case, the male teacher instructs his female pupil how to draw, how to paint, and, in effect, how to see. Quite differently, the prolific illustrations of artist's studios and of art tutorials provide an important context for 1884's "Demoralising Effect of the Female Gaze on the Highly-Strung Artistic Temperament," which depicts a rural landscape with two artists ("Claude" and "Peter Paul," likely ironic references to Claude Lorraine, the French painter of idyllic landscapes and Peter Paul Rubens, the Dutch painter of unusually "receptive" women), one sitting and the other standing in front of their half-completed canvases, while a group of well-dressed young women walks by in a double line viewing the unfinished

DEMORALISING EFFECT OF THE FEMALE GAZE ON THE HIGHLY-STRUNG ARTISTIC TEMPERAMENT.

Figure 6. “Demoralising Effect of the Female Gaze on the Highly Strung Artistic Temperament” (1884). *Punch*.

works and, perhaps, the artists themselves. The illustration is important for several reasons. First, it reverses the usual relationship between the male artist and his female model; neither artist meets the looks of the women with his own eyes, yet each is clearly aware, as in the usual case with female models, of his status as a visual object. Second, women are here implicitly made the judges of artistic value as their eyes silently comment on the unfinished works. Finally, this illustration emphasizes the discomfiting, intimidating effects of the female gaze on the artists: the caption reads, "It will be observed that Claude and Peter Paul are looking at their canvases when their eyes ought to be intent on their palettes—and vice versa!" These are clearly not the sovereign male artists who otherwise overpopulate the pages of *Punch* in the Victorian years.

If "Demoralising Effect" confers critical powers on the female spectator in relation to the male artist, the following illustration from ten years earlier grants the discerning artist's eye to women. "Female School of Art" portrays a dandy working as a model in an all-female portraiture class. Leaning against a mantle with his head in his hand, his body posed in narcissistic self-confidence, and his eyes closed, he is surrounded by aspiring female artists, all of whom focus on him not with adoring eyes but with a scrutiny clearly more concerned with artistic technique. This illustration is a stark reversal from the usual studio scenes in *Punch* where women models almost always appear as passive figures before male artists, functioning as a *riposte* to the many scenes of male art instructors and female artists that appear elsewhere in *Punch*. The only man represented in the illustration is the vain model; no male master instructs this group of self-sufficient female students.

Such relatively isolated examples of female visual empowerment hardly threatened to overturn the masculine Victorian visual order. Yet these illustrations and others like them do, despite the fact that they occur in comic settings, reveal a kind of masculine anxiety over the changing social status of women, a changing status that was also a common subject of *Punch*'s illustrations. One illustration that combines women's social and visual progress appeared in 1876, seven years after the establishment of the all-women's Girton College, Cambridge. "Why Shouldn't Girton Rink, When Cambridge Rows?" explores the banning of women from university athletics. Although it changed the educational and social circumstances of only a small, relatively wealthy minority of Victorian women, the founding of Girton in 1869 provided *Punch* with abundant material for showing what it believed was the society to come once women attended Oxbridge, read classical poetry rather than lending library novels, and participated in athletic events rather than merely watched them. The illustration answers its own query with an imagined scene on the river Cam of a

Figure 7. "Female School of Art—(Useful Occupation for Idle and Ornamental Young Men)" (1874). *Punch*.

Figure 8. "Why Shouldn't Girton Rink When Cambridge Rows?" (1876). *Punch*.

group of Girton undergraduates roller-skating parallel to a crew team. Nearly all the female students glance across at the crew as they make their way along the bank, at once demonstrating their own athleticism and also positioning themselves in the role of active spectators in place of the reclining female observers usually depicted in *Punch* at cricket matches and other athletic events.

This instance of relatively unthreatening female athleticism (the women do not, after all, row themselves) appeared a few years after another far more radical and, as it turned out, prescient rendering of female rowing, entitled "Boat-race of the Future.—Drifting Down to the Starting Point," which depicts two women's crew teams preparing for their upcoming race.[19] We are here confronted with a larger common theme in *Punch* during the last half of the nineteenth century: the blurring of established gender roles. In the third quarter of the century, beginning about a decade after *Punch* was first launched in 1841, this blurring was depicted most often by women assuming roles like that of an Oxbridge undergraduate or crew member; in the last quarter of the century, once the idea of an Oxbridge women's college had lost some of its ability to provoke a socially or politically meaningful backlash, women assuming men's roles is portrayed in, for instance, the suffragette movement and especially in the New Woman theme of the 1890s, both "masculinized" roles that were viewed at best as unconventional and at worst as threatening to the established social order. These threats are made manifest by overstating the risk posed to a visual order that had formerly been stabilized along rigid masculine and feminine boundaries, boundaries quite familiar to someone like Darwin who regarded women, the more beautiful of the sexes, not men, as the appropriate objects of sexually selective eyes.

Yet ironically, coincident with an increased production of female spectators and observers of various types in *Punch*, the magazine's illustrations reveal a decided reaction against the trend in female visual agency. Between 1871 and 1901, the thirty-year period after publication of *Descent* often identified by literary and cultural historians as the late-Victorian age, a proliferation of images appeared that depict visual domination of women by men, most often in the form of male artists and their female models, as well as conventional narcissistic representations of women gazing at themselves in mirrors. We encounter in *Punch*, then, a near ideological double backing. While more women than ever before are portrayed in progressive roles that contest the masculine visual order, at the same time even more images of men and women appeared in ultra-conventional roles that reinforce the gendered bifurcation of vision the more progressive illustrations seem intended to undermine. One could argue the overriding message that this mass appeal, middle-class magazine

BOAT-RACE OF THE FUTURE.—DRIFTING DOWN TO THE STARTING-POINT.

Figure 9. "Boat-Race of the Future.—Drifting Down to the Starting-Point" (1866). *Punch*.

provides during these three decades is a suitably muddled picture, reflecting gender ambiguity between late-Victorian British men and women, as compared to the relative social stability represented by the High Victorian period from 1850 to about 1870, the period in which Darwin composed both *The Origin of Species* and *The Descent of Man*. Yet this *Punch*-as-a-mirror-of-society seems to be an oversimplified reading of what is, in fact, a far more complex ensemble of social and gender/visual relations. Although Victorian women did indeed make tangible gains in terms of their legal, educational, and political position during these years (such gains, for instance, as the founding of Girton and Newnham Colleges at Cambridge, passage of the 1857 Matrimonial Causes Act, and 1873 Married Women's Property Act), the extent to which women approached political, educational, and social equality with men was of a much smaller degree than the illustrated world of *Punch* acknowledges.

Many of *Punch*'s representations, for example, endow women with a social and political status out of all proportion to their actual power to transgress the constraints of Victorian society, let alone act as advocates on behalf of their legal and political rights. Had these illustrations been published in a different context they might possibly be regarded as radical, providing a promising vision of what women could attain in the near future. However, the biting, ironic captions often accompanying them preclude progressive readings. One such illustration from 1884, "'The Angel in the House'" Or, The Result of Female Suffrage." calls on the well-known Coventry Patmore poem of domesticity by depicting an androgynously dressed bluestocking orating in the House of Commons. Quite different from the sexually desirable female performers who often appear elsewhere in the magazine's pages—representations of women that would have resonated with Darwin's masculinist theory of sexual selection—this woman is the object of legislative rather than sexual spectacle as her reluctant colleagues look at her in general consternation. In a typical commentary, the caption reads "(A Troubled Dream of the Future)." The inevitable response to this and many similar illustrations is to regard them as part of a reactionary agenda intended to evoke not popular sentiment in favor of women's progress but a backlash against the kind of empowerment by women that would have leveled the playing field. Furthermore, *Punch*'s publication of a few progressive illustrations in the midst of a great sea of conservative woodcuts makes clear that the illustrations, taken as a whole, operate to recontain the social disruption depicted in progressive representations.

Given this analysis of trends of representation in *Punch*'s publishing history, it is no surprise that the high-art Royal Academy world so often lampooned by *Punch* was dominated by a form of classical-subject painting

Figure 10. "The Angel in 'the House'" Or, The Result of Female Suffrage. (A Troubled Dream of the Future.) (1884). *Punch.*

that, like *Punch*'s conservative illustrations, commonly represented women as the passive recipients of a male gaze. This tradition, in conjunction with the magazine's virtual deluge of women in conservative roles as the century drew to a close, confounded the very visual and political emancipation of women that *Punch* otherwise represents in its "feminist" illustrations. Two of the most noteworthy Victorian classical-subject painters were Frederic Leighton, President of the Royal Academy from 1878 until his death in 1896, and Albert Moore. Preceded in the British classical-subject tradition by William Etty, G. F. Watts, and, to a degree, Edward Burne-Jones, and succeeded by, among others, Edward John Poynter, and John William Waterhouse, Leighton and Moore stand out as among the most accomplished and well-received practitioners of this genre of Victorian painting.[20]

What unifies the canvases of Leighton, Moore, and other classical-subject painters is a proclivity to set their subjects, often nudes, in either a mythic or indeterminate classical past. In almost every case, the works are situated in idealized settings and adhere to a detached, elegant, highly stylized technique. Though male figures are depicted by classical-subject painters (this is particularly true of Leighton), female images, whether they are goddesses, nymphs, sirens, or "merely" women, dominate. In contrast to genre painting, which locates its subjects within specific historical contexts, mythological classical-subject painting universalizes the depicted gender roles. Thus, the Medusa-Perseus sequence of paintings that Burne-Jones produced from the 1870s to the 1890s associates heroic valor with the masculine and powerful demonism with the feminine.[21] Perseus' decapitation of Medusa amounts to a male triumph with implications that extend far beyond the painted canvas; Medusa's death functions as a symbolic representation whereby Victorian men saw enacted their own dominance over their female counterparts. That Perseus defeats the most dangerous female figure imaginable, a figure whom Freud was later to hypothesize signified the fear of castration, adds up to a persuasive patriarchal mythmaking for contemporary audiences: the woman with the powerful gaze cannot achieve victory over the male hero. Medusa will, in the end, be put down, her emasculating eyes extinguished by Perseus.

Joseph Kestner argues that by virtue of their prominence and their chosen subject matter, late-Victorian classical-subject painters played a crucial role in establishing the cultural discourse about women in the period.[22] By depicting women either as sexually dangerous, active subjects (such as Medusa), or sexually pleasing, passive objects (such as Venus), classical-subject painters represented the polarities of masculine sexual anxiety and fantasy. Similar to an earlier argument put forward by Nina Auerbach in *Woman and the Demon*, Kestner contends: "In Victorian

Figure 11. Sir Edward Burne-Jones, *The Death of Medusa II* (c. 1876). Gouache. 1365 × 1525 cm. Southampton City Art Gallery, Hampshire, UK/Bridgeman Art Library.

classical-subject canvases, women were continually represented in one or two ways: either as irresponsible, outcast, prostituted, vicious, sensuous . . . or as submissive, passive, forlorn, abject, somnolent."[23] Classical-subject painting thus reinforced popular stereotypes about women: it justified passage (and resisted the repeal) of misogynistic laws such as the Contagious Diseases Acts, intended to protect society from diseases transmitted by "fallen" women, the very same fallen women whose troublesome, direct gazes are encoded in Victorian illustrations as a signifier of prostitution. By contrast, classical-subject painting also helped *prevent* passage of progressive women's legislation, such as suffrage, by depicting women as objects of sexual spectacle. In the latter type of rendering especially, women were represented so as not to be taken seriously either in the intellectual or political realms. The collected works of these painters constituted a powerful conservative opposition to forward-thinking social reforms in late-Victorian England intended to liberalize the institutional restrictions against women's full participation in society.

One-half of the depiction of women in the classical-subject tradition—the image of woman as a sexually devouring demon selection—is, with notable exceptions such as Burne-Jones' Perseus-Medusa sequence, less important to my argument than her "companion piece," the woman as passive sleeper. This is so because although the image of demonic femininity perhaps betrays masculine anxiety over a sexually empowered female gaze, the production of demonic images of women diminished as the nineteenth century drew to a close, a somewhat surprising fact given a social milieu regarded by many as tumultuous. One might very well indeed have expected to see an increase in the demonization of women. The decline in the artistic production of such images coincides with the ascendancy of Leighton and Moore, neither of whom focuses on the demonic in women. Rather, their works more often display images of languorous or sleeping women and thus depict female subjects at their most visually, sexually, and politically passive. As such, they ideologically function to recontain the political disruptions then being orchestrated by women in the suffragist movement. Indeed, these paintings should be read as part of a more comprehensive narrative showing how women, at the very historical moment when their legal, political, and educational positions appeared to be improving, actually suffered from a backlash by illustrators and artists who declined to incorporate images of them with their own active, powerful gazes or did so, as in the case of *Punch*, on a limited basis. In the Victorian Age, the difference between a passive and an active look symbolically marked the difference between economic, political, and sexual mastery and servility. For male illustrators and painters to have represented women in nondemonic, noncastrating, visually active roles would therefore have signified a capitulation to increasing forms of female cultural agency. Leighton and Moore's common representation of women with their eyes closed therefore helped to prop up relatively diminishing male cultural authority.[24]

One of the greatest threats to British patriarchy in the late nineteenth and early twentieth centuries was the suffragist movement, which began in 1867 with John Stuart Mill's parliamentary reading of a petition calling for women's suffrage to be added to the Second Reform Bill, on the same terms of age and property ownership as men. Led by Emmeline Pankhurst's suffragettes, the cause of women's suffrage reached its most militant stage in the years leading up to World War I. Opposition among men (and among many antifeminist women) to granting women the vote was vast, for once women were allowed suffrage, it seemed, male political hegemony would disappear.

As an eminent artist and influential public figure, Leighton quite directly placed himself at the center of antisuffragist sentiment. In 1889 he wrote to the second wife of G. F. Watts inquiring whether she might be persuaded to add her name to a petition titled "An Appeal against Female Suffrage" destined for publication in the June 1889 edition of *The Nineteenth Century*.[25] Though Leighton's appeal to Mrs. Watts did not meet with success, the enormous prestige he possessed throughout his lifetime, not only as the most prolific and unsurpassed technician of the classical-subject style but also as one of the most able administrators the Royal Academy had ever seen, no doubt gained him a respectful following sympathetic to his conservative political views. Leighton's politics and aesthetics combined to create a formidable antifeminism as powerful as any antisuffragist declaration or rally.

Nowhere is Leighton's (visual) antifeminism more formidable than in his canvases of sleeping or reclining women. He was an undisputed master of the genre. Leighton's paintings of this type include *Idyll*, *Summer Slumber*, *Summer Moon*, and *Cymon and Iphigenia*. By far the most famous of these is *Flaming June*, an arresting canvas at once intense in color and delicate in form. June, clad in the sheerest of bedclothes, reclines on a small couch in a kind of fetal position that generously reveals, through the transparent red material of the gown, her right breast, buttock, and thigh. June's half-turned face shows her profile and rests on her folded left arm. Her eyes are, of course, closed. *Flaming June* quite simply exudes erotic sensuality but does so at the price of altogether excluding its female subject's look. The canvas thereby depicts an inviting, nonthreatening image of a woman who does not herself participate in any way with her audience. June does indeed "flame," but she burns for the pleasure of her

Figure 12. Lord Frederic Leighton, *Cymon and Iphigenia* (1884). Oil on canvas, 163 × 328 cm. Purchased 1976. Art Gallery of New South Wales. Sydney, Australia. Photograph Jenni Carter for AGNSW.

(male) viewers alone. As in Darwin's passive representation of female scopo-sexuality, June's desire remains a mystery.

Leighton's contemporary, Royal Academy colleague, and friend, Albert Moore, virtually made a career out of painting narcoleptic women. His canvases of this type, including *A Musician*, *Beads*, *Dreamers*, *Midsummer*, and *A Summer Night*, remain among his most famous works. *Beads*, for example, depicts two delicately featured young women, both dozing and dressed in loose fitting, nearly transparent, vaguely classical gowns, reclining on a sumptuous, rectangular couch. The woman on the left leans against one of the couch's pillowed arms, displaying her right profile, right leg crossed over left and feet resting on the couch itself. Her right arm, hanging limply over the front of the couch, attests to the depth of her sleep. Her companion is similarly somnolent. One is struck by the absolute enervation of both women, an enervation that puts the painting's audience at complacent ease. The work functions as a supreme male fantasy of contented female passivity. Indeed, these women are so content that even in their slumber they would never dream of demanding equality with men. It is difficult to imagine two images of women less threatening to the established Victorian political and sexual order. Difficult, that is, until one examines the rest of Moore's work. As the student of Moore soon discovers, *Beads* is only the preface to a prolific oeuvre of somnolent women that Darwin would have likely regarded as evidence for the prevalence of scopo-sexually passive women in sexual selection.

The political milieu in which the classical-subject tradition flourished is a paradoxical one in terms of Victorian and Edwardian feminism. Passage of progressive legislation for women, such as the Married Women's Property Act of 1873 (which occurred relatively soon after regressive legislation such as the Contagious Diseases Acts of 1864, 1866, and 1869), would have seemed to bode well for subsequent reformist, feminist legislation. But interestingly, coincident with the passage of new property legislation for married women, in the forty-year period following the Second Reform Bill of 1867, and along with it the beginnings of a formal suffragist organization selection, real progress toward achieving the vote for women virtually stood still until the concerted agitations of the suffragists gained momentum not long after the turn of the century. The emergence of a strong antifeminist movement in the last third of the nineteenth century in England corroborates Mary Poovey's thesis in *Uneven Developments*, a study of mid-Victorian England. Poovey shows that a similar push-and-pull narrative form women emerged, whereby a gain in one legal, political, social, or educational realm might be met by defeat or deferral in another.[26]

Figure 13. Lord Frederic Leighton, *Flaming June* (1895). Oil on canvas. 46 × 46 inches. Museo de Arte de Ponce. Ponce, Puerto Rico.

Figure 14. Albert Moore, *Beads* (1875). Oil on canvas. 28.9 × 50.1 cm. National Gallery of Scotland. Edinburgh, Scotland.

Such a paradox is captured exceedingly well in the account of Cambridge University's initial grudging acceptance of women with the establishment of Girton in 1869 and again with the founding of Newnham in 1873.[27] Doing away with the six-hundred-year tradition of all-male Cambridge would have seemed a harbinger of imminent feminist victories to come, such as the granting of suffrage. But the fight to prevent women from becoming official members of, and earning official degrees from, the university almost precisely mirrored the antisuffrage movement and the illustrated discourse surrounding women's scopo-social progress in *Punch* and, somewhat less obviously, in classical-subject painting. This microcosmic Cambridge narrative provides an insight into how to read the period's broader antifeminist backlash, a backlash in which I see Leighton and Moore and, indeed, Darwin, operating on various visual levels of "femininity."

At the time of women's *entrée* into the formerly monastic life of Cambridge, graduates of Oxbridge left their colleges behind but took with them a vote in the future administration of the university. Suffrage at Oxbridge looked very much like suffrage in England, with the alumni vote safely confined to men alone. Girton and Newnham Colleges, though looked upon with some suspicion, were deemed acceptable to the all-male administration of Cambridge because both colleges functioned as a kind of informal appendage and therefore did not directly participate in university governance. In order to participate in alumni votes, one had first to have been granted an official degree, a degree that neither Girton nor Newnham could provide as a consequence of their shadow status.[28] Consequently, Girton and Newnham students, so long as their exams were not marked with the end of a degree in mind, did not threaten the voting preeminence of their male contemporaries at Trinity, King's, Christ's (Darwin's college), or any of the other established colleges. Resistance to allowing women official status and granting them degrees had much to do with men's reluctance over sharing university political power with women.

Despite the chauvinistic objection to sharing administrative power, virulent male opposition toward the granting of degrees to women was not widespread as of 1896, a year when serious consideration of the idea was finally being given by the university. In 1896, a petition calling for the formal admission of women to the university was signed by two thousand Cambridge men, apparently making the vote that would take place in May of 1897 a mere formality, or so Girton and Newnham women thought. On May 21, 1897, as a result of prolonged rancorous debate and extended national media coverage, hundreds of Cambridge graduates flocked to their medieval university in order to cast votes against the proposal to allow women formal admission and, along with it, degrees and voting rights. As Rita Tulberg-Williams writes, "[t]he women lost by 1713 votes to 662, and the undergraduates celebrated the defeat with a night of riotous bonfires, fireworks and fun."[29] Presumably, Girton and Newnham students did not join in festivities where such blatantly misogynistic activities as hanging women in effigy took place.[30] While the pages of *Punch* had foreseen in the opening of Girton and Newnham the imminent dissolution of Oxbridge's male essence, the degree to which antifeminism pervaded Cambridge's undergraduate and alumni populations delayed progressive feminist educational reform by fifty years. Women were finally granted degrees at Cambridge only in 1947, once alumni voting had been relegated to mere tokenism.

A similar backlash against granting Englishwomen the vote occurred in Britain at the same time as the debate over granting women degrees at Cambridge. In 1896 and 1897, Faithfull Begg, a Conservative member of parliament, introduced two bills proposing the enfranchisement of women. The latter bill, provisionally voted on in February, enjoyed a majority of 71, but had been "talked out" by July 7 and, consequently, never reached committee.[31] Nevertheless, Begg's bills seemed to bode well for the immediate future of women's enfranchisement. But as we know, Englishwomen did not achieve even limited suffrage until 1918, and universal suffrage would not be won until 1928, more than thirty years after the introduction of Begg's initial bill. The enormous delay in granting women the vote had in the early years of the suffragist movement much to do with national apathy over the issue. But in 1908 the still nascent movement was opposed by the Women's National Anti-Suffrage League, the first organized antisuffragist organization in England. By 1910, the leadership of the Anti-Suffrage League had been assumed by prominent Tories, Lords Cromer and Curzon, both returned to England from their stints as the colonial leaders of Egypt and India respectively. The all-male leadership of the Anti-Suffrage League not only suggests the paradoxical difficulties that antisuffragist women encountered in politically agitating against women's further political involvement but also points to the deep-seated antifeminist assumptions that men such as Cromer and Curzon possessed about women's ability in the public sphere. The Anti-Suffrage League stands out as perhaps the most visible manifestation of the antifeminist backlash that existed from the last third of the nineteenth century forward and that participated in a discourse of vision, sexuality, and power that was very much part of Darwin's terrain in *Descent*.

One woman whose public ability Cromer and Curzon could never have underestimated was Mary Richardson. A suffragette of unquestioned zeal who did not flinch in the face of conservative politics,

Richardson slashed Velazquez's *Venus with a Mirror* on March 10, 1914, as a political protest against Emmeline Pankhurst's imprisonment.[32] Richardson brings our narrative about (anti)feminism, Victorian visual culture, and female vision to a cathartic pause, for in her destruction of this particular representation of the goddess of Love, Richardson set about to destroy symbolically a classical image of femininity that helped keep in place a host of antifeminist, Darwinian assumptions about women as the sexual object of male eyes and the narcissistic object of their own eyes.[33] Richardson implicitly makes a case for the quite different eyes of Pankhurst, eyes that envisioned political emancipation and equality for women and that, symbolically at least, looked Lords Curzon and Cromer straight in the eye.

Ostrich Feathers on the Karoo: Sexual Selection and The Story of an African Farm

Early in *The Story of an African Farm* (1883), the German overseer Otto graciously (and naively) donates his Sunday best to the vagrant Bonaparte Blenkins so that the newcomer, who turns out to be the worst kind of charlatan, can lead prayers in Otto's place. With Bonaparte fully outfitted for the service, Otto steps back and assesses the man he wrongly believes to be his friend: "The German looked at [Bonaparte] with profound admiration. It was wonderful what a difference feathers made in the bird."[34] Bonaparte's transformation by Otto's clothes begins his rehabilitation in the eyes of Tant' Sannie, who earlier inquires, "[W]as there ever such a red-rag-nosed thing with broken boots and crooked eyes before?" (53), but comes gradually to regard Bonaparte as the most likely candidate for her second husband. Ironically, it is simpleminded and faithful Otto—the very last character in the novel one would accuse of Darwinian infidelity to Christian dogma—who inaugurates a chain of references that unites Bonaparte with sexual desirability and bird imagery, recalling Darwin's discourse of sexual selection and the illustrated pages of *Punch* from a decade earlier. Later, having dispensed with Otto for good and spying at a distance Waldo, the old man's son, Bonaparte is once again paralleled to a bird as he adopts a watchful, semiaggressive pose: "[H]e chucked his coat-tails up and down in expectancy of a scene" (97). As it turns out, Bonaparte's fears are misdirected. Wrongly fearing violent repercussions by passive Waldo, Bonaparte neglects to pay attention to Lyndall, who shortly thereafter leads the ostrich, Hans, in a secret attack against him, thereby reversing the ornithological imagery that had before sexually and socially empowered Bonaparte. In a one-sided confrontation pitting a would-be ostrich cock against the genuine article, Hans pecks Bonaparte's crown four times and gives a "resolute tug at the grey curls at the back of his head" (100), an attack that Bonaparte, now in wholesale retreat, misinterprets as a visitation by the devil.

The pervasive bird imagery—laden with connotations of sexual selection—with reference to Bonaparte is no accident on the part of Olive Schreiner. *The Story of an African Farm* is suffused with Darwinian philosophy from start to finish, certainly not surprising for a novel written by an author who corresponded with Havelock Ellis over minutiae in *Descent*.[35] In some cases, Darwinism is used in the novel as a discourse of racist political reaction, as it is when Tant' Sannie concludes that because the Kaffir servants "were descended from apes" they required "no salvation" (2) or again when Lyndall, watching a Kaffir walk in the distance, speculates that "the men of the future" will "see his bones only in museums—a vestige of one link that spanned between the dog and the white man" (228). The fact that Schreiner connects Tant' Sannie, surely one of the most unsympathetic women in all of Victorian literature, with racist Darwinism is no surprise, but Lyndall's own association with this discourse is more problematic, especially given that she more regularly invokes and undercuts Darwinism to critique patriarchal Victorian social structures, especially courtship and marriage.[36]

Indeed, Lyndall's "New Woman" credentials as a feminist critic are on view in the same passage that she subscribes to a racist ideology of evolution.[37] Just prior to damning the Kaffir as an anthropological curiosity piece, she concludes that he is likely "to kick his wife with his beautiful legs when he gets home. He has a right to; he bought her for two oxen" (227). In these two lines Lyndall bridges the racial divide between Europeans and Africans for she has earlier equated herself (and all women) with the means of exchange by which she believes the Kaffir has acquired his wife: "I am so pressed in upon by new things that, lest they should trip one another up, I have to keep forcing them back. My head swings sometimes. But this one thought stands, never goes—if I might but be one of those born in the future; then, perhaps, to be born a woman will not be to be born branded" (188). Like oxen branded by their owner, Lyndall's sex condemns her to a life spent as an object of male possession. And whereas Darwin regards it as evolutionarily advantageous for women to possess youth and beauty (and for men to select such women), Lyndall considers these attributes a troubling inheritance at best, "with good looks and youth marriage is easy to attain. There are men enough; but a woman who has sold herself, ever for a ring and a new name, need hold her skirt aside for no creature in the street. They both earn their bread in the same way" (190). For Lyndall, married women are, in effect, the moral equivalent of streetwalkers.

As a feminist critic of the Darwinian ideology of courtship, sex, and marriage, Lyndall shares much with her two contemporaries, Antoinette Brown Blackwell and Eliza Gamble, women writers who challenged Darwinian orthodoxy on the subject of sexual selection.[38] Unlike Lyndall, who confines the scope of her critique to the scattered inhabitants of the South African Karoo, Blackwell and Gamble published important books that took Darwin to task among a much wider audience.

Although Lyndall is a creation of the 1880s, her Darwinian discourse alternates between that of a woman of the 1860s who might have read *Origin* alone or a woman of the 1870s who had read both *Origin* and *Descent*. (Lyndall's understanding of sexual selection is far more sophisticated than it would be had she been limited to the brief section on sexual selection in *Origin*.) In some respects, though, she is very much a character of the 1860s, and it is therefore not surprising that she never quite offers the positive feminist critique of Darwinism that Blackwell and Gamble made available to the Victorian reading public. The closest she comes to such a critique is when, as a girl, she declares, "When that day comes, and I am strong, I will hate everything that has power, and help everything that is weak" (93).[39] As an adult, Lyndall's is a liberal feminism reminiscent of John Stuart Mill. Like Mill, Lyndall contends that women should not be given any special favors in their social competition with men; they should simply be allowed the same opportunities as their male counterparts. Once equality of opportunity is achieved, Lyndall argues, Darwinian competition will ensue, thereby crowning a victor:

> Then they say, "If the women have the liberty you ask for, they will be found in positions for which they are not fitted!" If two men climb one ladder, did you ever see the weakest anywhere but at the foot? The surest sign of fitness is success. The weakest never wins but where there is handicapping. Nature left to herself will as beautifully apportion a man's work to his capacities as long ages ago she graduated the colors on the bird's breast. If we are not fit, you give us to no purpose the right to labour; the work will fall out of our hands into those that are wiser. (193)

Here, wonderfully synthesizing Mill's and Darwin's contemporaneous discourses, Schreiner parallels social competition with natural and sexual selection, once again conjuring up the evocative image of a beautiful male bird whose colors have gradually been enhanced over generations by careful and discriminating female sexual selection. In this case, however, Lyndall appropriates for her own purposes Darwin's discourse of ornithological beauty, arguing that either men or women should be (but are not) permitted to achieve social and cultural primacy reserved in nature for colorful male birds. In Lyndall's thinking, women are tyrannically reduced to the status of beautiful physical objects, a role that becomes, in effect, their career, as she laments to Waldo: "Professional duties always first, you know. It takes a great deal of time and thought always to look perfectly exquisite, even for a pretty woman" (199). For Lyndall, female beauty functions as a kind of imprisonment by the body that has its origins in the isolation and imprisonment of girls within the domestic sphere as against the freedom experienced by boys:

> We sit with our little feet drawn up under us in the window, and look out at the boys in their happy play. We want to go. Then a loving hand is laid on us: "Little one, you cannot go," they say; "your face will burn, and your nice white dress be spoiled." We feel it must be for our good, it is so lovingly said; but we cannot understand; and we kneel still with one little cheek wistfully pressed against the pane. Afterwards we go and thread blue beads, and make a string for our neck; and we go and stand before the glass. We see the complexion we were not to spoil, and the white frock, and we look into our own great eyes. Then the curse begins to act on us. It finishes its work when we are grown women, who no more look out wistfully at a more healthy life; we are contented. (189)

Lyndall regards the development of female visuality from girlhood to womanhood as a move from looking outward on the world to turning the gaze back critically on the self. Because of the cultural requirements of sexual selection, women are compelled to scrutinize their own beauty and to assess their chances of attracting male eyes. We are privy to the considerable anxieties surrounding the importance of female beauty in the novel when Em, describing Lyndall to her fiancé, Gregory Rose, declares, "When my cousin comes tomorrow you will see a beautiful woman. . . . You must come to see her tomorrow as soon as she comes" (181). Em at once defers to Lyndall by asserting to Gregory, "You could not help seeing that she is prettier [than Em]," and tries to reassure herself that Gregory will not be overly attracted to Lyndall as she nervously takes his hand. For Lyndall, preoccupation with female beauty, and the sexual rivalry that it engenders, functions as the "curse" of sexual selection experienced by all women at one level or another. While Gregory's unfavorable comparison of Em with Lyndall has tragic repercussions, we witness a comic version of female rivalry with respect to beauty in the "competition" for the affections of Bonaparte between the obese Tant' Sannie and her young niece, Trana. (As it turns out, this is in fact a one-woman competition as Trana remains completely unmoved by Bonaparte's attempts to seduce her.) Just as Gregory chooses to pursue Lyndall instead of Em once he sees Lyndall, Bonaparte attempts to sexually select Trana, more youthful and physically attractive than Tant' Sannie.

Lyndall critiques Darwin's ornithological discourse of sexual selection by contrasting the regressive mating habits of humans, which subjects women educationally, professionally, and sexually, with the progressive domestic arrangements of ostriches. Observing a pair of ostriches with Waldo, Lyndall looks on with the critical eye of a natural historian who, like Darwin (but for very different ideological ends), sees a desirable model for spousal relations between the sexes:

> "Let us wait at this camp and watch the birds," she said, as an ostrich hen came bounding towards them, with velvety wings outstretched, while far away over the bushes the head of the cock was visible as he sat brooding on the eggs. . . . "I like these birds," she said; "they share each other's work, and are companions." (187)

Whereas earlier in the novel we almost invariably encounter a discourse of male sexuality and aggression with respect to bird imagery, Lyndall here issues a challenge to the Darwinian paradigm of interpreting the behavior of birds. She accomplishes this by highlighting the mobility of the ostrich hen and the nesting impulse of the ostrich cock, division of labor that reverses Victorian conventions of gendered human behavior. Significantly, when Lyndall translates Waldo's frustrated intellectual experience into an ornithological metaphor, she likens him to "'an old hen that sits on its eggs month after month and they [his "few old thoughts"] never come out'" (188).

Concluding her observations on the mating pair of ostriches by inquiring of Waldo whether he "takes an interest in the position of women" (187) (to which he answers a simple "No"), Lyndall responds with disappointment: "'I'm sorry . . . I should have liked us to be friends'" (187). The young woman's disappointment is precipitated by the fact that Waldo, alone among the three men who claim to love her—the others being Gregory and the unnamed stranger who fathers her child—does not desire her principally for her beauty. Indeed, for Lyndall, Waldo is a disembodied spirit who therefore does not threaten her with his sexuality. Given Lyndall's critique of the ways the female body is sexually circulated among men, it should not be lost on us, however, that companionship with Waldo in turn makes her feel disembodied, emancipated from the prison of the flesh that causes women to pay too much attention to their physical charms in order to attract sexually selective male eyes:

> "I like you so much, I love you." She rested her cheek softly against his shoulder. "When I am with you I never know that I am a woman and you are a man; I only know that we are both things that think. Other men when I am with them, whether I love them or not, they are mere bodies to me; but you are a spirit; I like you." (210)

Lyndall's problem with men is not that they are mere bodies to her. Her problem, rather, is that she and all women are too frequently mere bodies to men. It is for this reason that she declares her love, albeit a Platonic version of love, for Waldo. If we were to deploy Eliza Gamble's critique of Darwin as a tool for reading Lyndall's attitude toward Waldo, we would see that Waldo's lack of sexual energy positively rather than negatively differentiates him from the great majority of men, making him, in some ways, the most appropriate love object for Lyndall because he seems, following Gamble's reasoning, to have evolutionarily advanced beyond the mere physicality and animality of men. On one hand, Waldo's ability to disaggregate the material from the spiritual merits Lyndall's love, yet on the other hand his capacity for removing his gaze from women's real-life struggle is exasperating. Lyndall berates Waldo for his earthly myopia: "'If women were the inhabitants of Jupiter, of whom you had happened to hear something, you would pore over us and our condition night and day; but because we are before your eyes you never look at us'" (187).

The asexual character of Waldo's eyes is utterly contrasted by the man whom we know only as "Lyndall's stranger." The single conversation between Lyndall and the stranger to which we are privy is suffused with anti-Darwinian discourse, revealing the extent to which Lyndall attempts to resist the theory of sexual selection as a paradigm for relations between the sexes. When the stranger asks Lyndall why she refuses to marry him, her reply is at once a direct paraphrase and a critique of Darwin's description in *Descent* of the special equipage given to some male animals ("[T]he male has special organs of prehension for holding her securely") to mate with females against their will: "'Because if once you have me you would hold me fast. I shall never be free again'" (236). Anticipating Gamble's explanation of the difference between men and women and sexuality, Lyndall describes to her suitor the two parts of her brain, one lower and sexually focused and one higher and culturally oriented. This higher part of Lyndall's brain clearly is intended to signify evolutionary progress over mere fleshly desire: "'You call into activity one part of my nature; there is a higher part that you know nothing of, that you never touch. If I married you, afterwards it would arise and assert itself, and I should hate you always, as I do now sometimes'" (237). The "sometimes" that Lyndall refers to has everything to do with female vision and sexual selection, for she tells the stranger, "'I love you when I see you; but when you are away from me I hate you'" (236). By contrast to Lyndall and Waldo, the stranger celebrates physical love that, like Darwin, values physical beauty in women above all else as the desirable signifier of sexuality:

> I love you. I do not pretend that it is in any high, superhuman sense; I do not say that I should like you as well if you were ugly and deformed, or that I should continue to prize you whatever your treatment of me might be, or to leave you though you were a spirit without any body at all. That is sentimentality for beardless boys. (237)

Whether self-consciously or not, the stranger here undercuts the ethereal quality of beardless Waldo's love for Lyndall, and also unwittingly anticipates the gesture of love that a soon-to-be beardless Gregory Rose will make to express his affection for Lyndall. Lyndall's resistance to the stranger appears to have everything to do with her sexual desire for him. That desire, which is considerable and that is predicated on the stranger's power—Lyndall herself accounts for her resistance of him "Because you are strong. You are the first man I ever was afraid of" (238)—threatens to abolish her anti-Darwinian philosophy of life to "hate everything that has power, and help everything that is weak" (93). The stranger's sexual power clearly aligns him with successful procreative males in *Descent*, a fact that, intellectually at least, Lyndall must abhor. For these reasons, Lyndall refuses to enter into a marriage that sexually, socially, and legally, stacks everything against her in terms of power differential.

The man who would never cease to look at Lyndall if he could is, of course, Gregory. But significantly, the only vantage point from which Gregory can gain a sustained and unobstructed view of Lyndall is as a female subject who, having raided a box of Em's mother's clothes, masquerades as a woman. Gregory's early strategy is to attract Lyndall's look of admiration by placing himself in what he believes to be hypermasculine performative poses before her eyes that invert what Darwin believes to be the dominant paradigm of human sexual selection in which female beauty and ornamentation are the keys to evolutionary success. In one such instance Schreiner portrays Gregory in the hybrid language of a failed rooster and ostrich cock "with shining spurs, an ostrich feather in his hat, and a silver-headed whip" (197). Despite, or perhaps because of, his ornamentation (even his overtly phallic whip), Lyndall immediately concludes that Gregory is a "'true woman—one born for the sphere that some women have to fill without being born for it. How happy he would be sewing frills into his little girls' frocks, and how pretty he would look sitting in a parlour, with a rough man making love to him!'" (197).

Lyndall rightly interprets Gregory's excessive pose of masculinity to be a fraud. Although the young farmer devotes a great proportion of the wall space of his one-room house to "prints cut from the *Illustrated London News* . . . in which there was a noticeable preponderance of female faces and figure" (174), he also adopts the closely surveying eye of the domestic

Englishwoman, a type of woman whose representation I have explored at length in the previous two chapters. This becomes clear when we learn that inside his house "all was scrupulously neat and clean, for Gregory kept a little duster folded in the corner of his table-drawer, just as he had seen his mother do, and every morning before he went out he said his prayers, and made his bed, and dusted the table and the legs of the chairs, and even the pictures on the wall and the gun-rack" (174). Schreiner's emphasis on "even" as Gregory moves, under the influence of his mother, from attending to "traditional" feminine domestic duties (making the bed and dusting the chairs) to untraditional and masculine chores (such as scrutinizing "girlie" pictures for dirt and cleaning the gun-rack), highlights the fact that Gregory is, at best, uneasy with his masculinity, an uneasiness that appears to disqualify him from being sexually selective, especially when his preferred love object, Lyndall, is a New Woman who resists the conventions of nineteenth-century gender codes. Lyndall looks perceptively beyond the facade of Gregory's public appearance and sees his desire to be a woman, desire that is literalized near the end of the novel when Gregory dons the disguise of a nurse and cares for Lyndall on her deathbed.

From the moment Gregory explicitly acts the part of a woman, Lyndall no longer sees past appearances. She simply regards him as a woman, as if he has found his natural identity. In surely one of the most bizarre sequences in all of English literature, Gregory inverts his gender identity by crossdressing as a nurse:

> He drew from his breast pocket a little sixpenny looking-glass, and hung it on one of the roots that struck out from the bank. Then he dressed himself in one of the old-fashioned gowns and a pinked-out collar. Then he took out a razor. Tuft by tuft the soft brown beard fell down into the sand, and the little ants took it to line their nests with. Then the glass showed a face surrounded by a frilled cap, white as a woman's, with a little mouth, a very short upper lip, and a receding chin. (270)

The degree to which Gregory is here feminized is accentuated by the fact that the tufts of his beard, formerly markers of virility and masculine power, become desirable material for an ant nest, among the most matriarchal of societies. Having finally caught up with Lyndall, his former fiancée, after she left the farm unannounced, Gregory does not adopt the conventional masculine role of the jealous lover. Rather, he surrenders any masculine pretensions (which Lyndall regards as fraudulent in any case) because he recognizes it to be his only chance of staying close to Lyndall. He trades in the possibility of marriage to Lyndall for the ability to sit "in the dark corner watching" (273). Gregory's love (or something like love) for Lyndall is so great that he makes himself erotically meaningless to her, once and for all diminishing the sexually selective power of his eyes. Although there are moments of genuine physical tenderness expressed between Lyndall and Gregory (whom Lyndall only knows to be a nurse), what ensues is not a domestic love story. Gregory is, indeed, the gentlest of nurses; Lyndall tells him "'other people hurt me when they touch me'" (273), and the attending physician concludes that Gregory is "'the most experienced nurse I ever came in contact with'" (268), a fact that rehabilitates the sometimes petty and almost always shallow Gregory in our eyes but only causes Lyndall to see him more as a woman than ever before.

At novel's end, Lyndall has utterly rejected the economy of sexual selection, an economy that specularizes women and forces them to play a passive role before further submitting to the subjection of marriage and motherhood. Schreiner's rejection of Darwinism on Lyndall's behalf may be read at the intersection of sexuality and visuality. Each of the three men with whom Lyndall has had meaningful (but not necessarily sexual) relationships is removed or radically altered from Lyndall's sight: the stranger, whom Lyndall is most vulnerable to in terms of scopo-sexuality, is pushed away and denied marriage by Lyndall, even as she finds herself deep into pregnancy with his child; as a nurse, Gregory is once more regarded by Lyndall as a true woman, this time actually dressed in women's clothes and therefore entirely out of the question as a Darwinian love object; and finally Waldo, the man who loved the higher nature in Lyndall but without any of the physical love fundamental to human relations, is ultimately compelled to envision an imaginative Lyndall who, in death, is now elevated to the status of a heavenly body (Lyndall might say Jupiter) genuinely worthy for the first time of serious philosophical investigation. Seeing no alternative but to reject wholesale sexual relations with men, Lyndall's interpretation and critique of Darwin's theory is pessimistic, perhaps betraying the sensibilities of the 1860s before the first feminist agitations of the nineteenth century had borne fruit. This conservative sensibility would have been even more true in unprogressive South Africa. For Lyndall, then, the most the scopic register of sexuality can offer to women is a bittersweet fruit that will turn, inevitably, to wormwood.

Case Study 3. Female Spectatorship and Sexual Selection in *Far from the Madding Crowd*

Few encounters are more enmeshed in the politics of vision than King David's first view of Bathsheba in II Samuel 11:2: "And it came to pass in an evening tide, that David arose from his bed, and walked upon the roof of the king's house; and from the roof of the king's house he saw a woman washing herself; and the woman was very beautiful to look upon." What follows for Bathsheba—her seduction and the effective sentencing to death of her husband by sending him to the front—testifies to the sexual and social power of David's voyeurism. Bathsheba remains an unwitting, utterly passive figure in the patriarchal scopic economy that exchanges her from one husband to another. In *Far from the Madding Crowd* Hardy draws from the biblical account of David and Bathsheba not, as we might expect, to reinforce male visual dominance, but rather to complicate and challenge the assumption of dominant, sexually selective male eyes. By christening his novel's protagonist "Bathsheba Everdene," Hardy invokes a correspondence with the biblical Bathsheba, depicting her as a passive target of male desire in the novel's opening chapters. Yet Hardy's subsequent characterization of his heroine reconstitutes the Bathsheba mythos in that it departs from II Samuel by portraying her not merely as a "feminized" recipient of the gaze who perceives the visual attentions of male characters but also as a socially empowered, near "masculinized" spectator of those same male characters. Hardy accomplishes this transformation of Bathsheba Everdene by employing a Darwinian discourse of sexual selection and performativity whereby men, especially Frank Troy and Farmer Boldwood, are likened to ornamental birds who perform before the discerning and critical eyes of Bathsheba. In this respect, *Far from the Madding Crowd*, published just three years after *Descent*, appears to resist Darwin's theory of sexual selection, in which active, vigorous men compete for passive, beautiful women.

Most crucial to Hardy's (re)constitution of Bathsheba Everdene as a sexually selective subject rather than a sexually selected object of vision is the transformation of her social position. By inheriting her wealthy uncle's farm, Bathsheba is transferred from the rural working class to the landowning class overnight. Hardy thereby intimates that ownership of a "masculine," Darwinian gaze of sexual selection is not confined to men alone. Instead, for Hardy, possession of sexually discriminating eyes seems determined by the social production of masculinely gendered subjects who are granted empowered status, status that the great majority of Victorian countrywomen did not possess independent of their fathers or husbands.[40] Bathsheba's inheritance, above and beyond her actual material gain, makes possible her new subject position as a nonfeminized female spectator in Hardy's Wessex.

Bathsheba begins her novel in possession of neither property nor sexually empowered eyes. Rather, similar to her fictional descendent, Tess Durbeyfield, Bathsheba is cast in the subordinate role of milkmaid. It is in this class position that Gabriel Oak first sees her as she drives in a wagon to her aunt's modest farm:

> Casually glancing over the hedge, Oak saw coming down the incline before him an ornamental spring wagon. . . . and on the apex of the whole sat a woman, young and attractive. Gabriel had not beheld the sight for more than half a minute when the vehicle was brought to a standstill just beneath his eyes.[41]

Gabriel and Bathsheba are here represented in terms reminiscent of David and Bathsheba: he as unseen spectator, she as unperceiving object. What follows in the next few chapters are two more scenes in which Gabriel surreptitiously watches Bathsheba, first from an advantageous rooftop during her late-night milking activities and second through a loophole as she rides a horse.[42] All three espials stimulate Gabriel's desire, and by the third encounter Gabriel actively embraces the role of male voyeur, a pervasive figure in Hardy's fiction that many critics, most notably J. Hillis Miller, have examined.[43]

Gabriel's mastery endures only as long as he withholds knowledge of his secret views from Bathsheba. When he bashfully admits to spying on her, advantage tips in Bathsheba's favor: "A perception caused him to withdraw his own eyes from hers as suddenly as if he had been caught in a theft" (68). Suggested in this trope of theft is the conflation of property ownership and possession of the gaze, raised above. Gabriel's confession functions as a return to Bathsheba of "stolen" property and a surrender of Gabriel's visual power position, as Bathsheba escapes from him unobserved. Gabriel's deferential eyes offer a stark reversal from the episode that opens the novel.

Moments after first being secretly watched by Gabriel as she sits in a wagon, Bathsheba refuses to pay the toll for the country road upon which she travels. At this literal impasse, Gabriel steps forward and pays the gatekeeper what is for him the insignificant sum of two pence. As he purchases the young maiden's passage, Gabriel engages in a visual exchange with Bathsheba: "He looked up at her then; she heard his words and looked down" (55). At the same time that Bathsheba's elevated position on the wagon suggests superiority over the foot-traveling Gabriel, her lowered gaze points to Gabriel's authority over her, an authority gained by his superior class standing as a tenant farmer, a socially empowered role relative to Bathsheba that he quite literally purchases. Yet when Gabriel confesses to seeing Bathsheba's performance on horseback, he effectively surrenders his symbolic capital. His earlier toll payment ceases to function as a version of what Goux might consider to be surplus social value, because the payment no longer confers upon Gabriel an excess amount of scopic, sexual, or economic power.[44] To this point, Hardy depicts Bathsheba Everdene, like her biblical prototype, as a mere visual object. Bathsheba's acute self-awareness of her physical desirability, coupled with the inheritance of her uncle's farm, prompts her transformation into a performative exhibitionist, and exhibitionism becomes Bathsheba's initial strategy of resistance against the objectifying eyes of the novel's male spectators.

After becoming the owner of Everdene farm, Bathsheba's exhibitionistic manipulation of male eyes first occurs at the corn market. Once there, Bathsheba, cast as the "queen of the corn market," walks alone among Wessex's male farmers, positioning herself as their unquestioned focus. In contrast to her earlier encounters with Gabriel, encounters defined by a lack of perception and economic independence, Bathsheba is quite aware of the desirable status she achieves. At the corn market she is characterized as far from the visually oppressed woman whom George Wotton argues is, in Hardy's fiction, "trapped and captured by the masculine gaze."[45] Bathsheba herself traps and captures the masculine gaze. Only later, when Bathsheba meets Sergeant Troy, her eventual first husband, does her power as an exhibitionist diminish. At the point of the market scene, then, Bathsheba has been captive to male eyes only as long as she remained unaware of Gabriel's focus on her and subject to the disadvantages of relative poverty.

While Bathsheba's debut at the corn market appears to be an unequivocal triumph, she regards her entrance onto the Wessex stage as a partial failure because of a perception that one farmer, Boldwood, expresses no interest in her whatsoever:

> The numerous evidences of her power to attract were only thrown into greater relief by a marked exception. Women seem to have eyes in their ribbons for such matters as these. Bathsheba, without looking within a right angle of him, was conscious of a black sheep among the flock. (141)

This passage illustrates Hardy's representation of gender-determined visual positions. Though Hardy depicts such characters as Eustacia Vye, Sue Bridehead, and of course, Bathsheba Everdene, in socially unorthodox, often emancipatory roles, he here generalizes all women to be perceivers both of the presence and absence of male eyes.[46] That Hardy describes Bathsheba's visual perception as more than merely pleasurable (and, in Boldwood's case, vexing), but also as a form of power, reveals the extent to which he valorizes traditional notions of how women achieve mastery: not as the consequence of active eyes but rather through the acquisition and "feminized" peripheral perception of visual attention from men. Hardy implies that in Bathsheba's role as exhibitionist, she must not disclose her desire to be looked upon. Such an indiscretion would constitute a disempowering confession of desire as damaging as Gabriel's earlier verbal confession, resulting in a similar loss of power.

On three separate occasions that mirror Gabriel's three earlier encounters with her, Bathsheba attempts and fails to attract Boldwood's eyes. Returning home by wagon from the corn market (following Boldwood's first demonstration of blindness in regard to Bathsheba), Boldwood, "with his eyes fixed on the most advanced point along the road, passes as unconsciously and abstractedly as if Bathsheba and her charms were thin air" (143). Boldwood's neglect culminates in church the next Sunday when Bathsheba's servant, Liddy, tells her mistress that he "'[d]idn't turn his head to look at you once all the service'" (145). Of particular interest here is Liddy's class-based observation of Boldwood's continued disregard: "But everybody else was noticing you; and it was odd he didn't. There, tis like him. *Rich and gentlemanly*, what does he care?" [emphasis mine] (145). Liddy concludes that his wealth and social status make him oblivious. Such an interpretation proves troubling to Bathsheba, who has grown accustomed to her conquests. She thus likens Boldwood not to the sensuous King David, but to another, quite different kind of Old Testament spectator, the visionary prophet, Daniel:

> Bathsheba paused to regard the idea at full length. Boldwood's had begun to be a troublesome image—a species of Daniel in her kingdom who persisted in kneeling eastward when reason and common sense said that he might just as well follow suit with the rest and afford her the official glance of admiration which cost nothing at all. (146–47)

To attract his "official glance of admiration," Bathsheba eschews performative display evocative of Darwin's theory. Instead, she sends the gentleman farmer a valentine with the words "Marry Me" written prominently on it. Oddly, the valentine achieves even more than its intended effect, not only drawing his attention but also functioning as what he believes to be a serious proposal. Shortly after receiving the correspondence, Boldwood scrutinizes the valentine in an evident metonymic substitution for Bathsheba: "Here the bachelor's gaze was continually fastening itself, till the large red seal became as a blot of blood on the retina of his eye" (149). The valentine profoundly affects Boldwood's view of Bathsheba, as well as his own self-perception. Looking at the valentine, he concurrently looks into the mirror, his face now "wan in expression and insubstantial in form" as opposed to the "distinctly outlined Roman features" of old (151). Boldwood ceases to be a self-possessed, independent farmer.

Given another opportunity at the corn market "Boldwood looked at [Bathsheba]—not slyly, critically, or understandingly, but blankly at gaze" (167). Unlike Gabriel, whose short-lived secret view of Bathsheba had at least temporarily empowered him, Bathsheba fully perceives Boldwood's transfixed gaze. According to Hardy's conception of power and "feminized" perception, she achieves a victory figured in military terms: "All this time Bathsheba was conscious of having broken into that dignified stronghold at last. His eyes, she knew, were following her everywhere" (168–69). Not long after this, Boldwood confesses his surrender: "'My life is not my own since I have beheld you clearly, Miss Everdene. . . . I may have been called a confirmed bachelor, and I was a confirmed bachelor. . . . But we all change, and my change, in this matter, came with seeing you'" (177–78). In spite of his rhetoric of self-surrender, he figures Bathsheba in terms of property acquisition, inquiring whether he can "hope to obtain" her. Later, he laments his loss of Bathsheba in language that further commodifies her, asking, "'Why did not Troy leave my treasure alone?'" (261). Although Bathsheba's rejection of Boldwood is partially due to his loss of an illusionary but nevertheless empowering selfhood, which gave him, paraphrasing Darwin's argument about female selection of male birds in *Descent*, "the sorry look of a grand bird without the feathers that make it grand" (211), it must also have been exacerbated by Boldwood's explicit desire to possess Bathsheba as a piece of property. Earlier, when the then milkmaid turns down Gabriel's marriage proposal, she rebuffs his conventional view of marriage on grounds that reject the notion of woman as mere male possession: "'I hate to be thought men's property in that way'" (78). Like Boldwood, Gabriel experiences a loss of autonomy after watching Bathsheba. He confesses to her, "'I shall do one thing in this life—one thing certain—that is, love you, and long for you and keep wanting you till I die'" (80).

That Hardy depicts both Boldwood's and Gabriel's desire for Bathsheba in terms of male crises of self, and the loss of property suggests a parallel. Certainly Boldwood and Gabriel's perception of Bathsheba as the only possession that can complete them is subject to a critique of the kind of sex/commodity fetish characteristic of capitalist economic formations.[47] Bathsheba becomes to the novel what Goux calls the "general equivalent" because she functions as the standard of ultimate exchange value in Wessex's sexual and economic registers.[48] By the time Boldwood finally regards Bathsheba, she is the mistress of an enormous farm bordering his own, suggesting that his desire is stimulated by the possibility of acquiring two conflated pieces of property: Bathsheba herself and Bathsheba's farm.

Hardy contrasts the permanent effect Bathsheba has on Boldwood and Gabriel with the transitory power her beauty exerts over Troy, who "simply feeling, considering and caring for what was before his eyes . . . was vulnerable only in the present" (219). Indeed, Bathsheba's beauty never makes a lasting impression on Troy. Consistent with this, Troy at first dominates Bathsheba with his direct, "masculine" gaze;

encountering Bathsheba by chance one evening and immediately shunning the idea of voyeuristic advantage, Troy instead forces Bathsheba to drop her eyes: "He looked hard into her eyes when she raised them for a moment; Bathsheba looked down again, for his gaze was too strong to be received point blank with her own" (215). Here Bathsheba, in what Hardy describes as a "position of captivity" because Troy's spur is entangled in her dress, admits that her face "'twas unwillingly shown'" (215). When Bathsheba meets Troy she no longer adopts the role of controlling exhibitionist but becomes the controlled target of Troy's gaze.

Later, in perhaps the novel's most critically examined episode, Troy embraces what had been Bathsheba's role as a performative exhibitionist, self-consciously manipulating Bathsheba's response during a demonstration of prodigious swordsmanship. Richard Carpenter has pointed out the vulgar Freudian interpretation of his lightning fast sword, which creates an optical illusion of sexual penetration, giving double significance to Troy's "performance," and, significantly, calling into question one half of the exhibitionist/scopophiliac binary with the apparent depiction of exhibitionism as a phallic visual subject position.[49] But what Carpenter and others have neglected about this scene are the Darwinian implications of Troy's performance, which casts him in the role not of a man who wins Bathsheba through what Darwin calls "the law of battle" against a rival suitor. Rather, outfitted in the red coat of the British army, Troy plays the role of a performative male bird that aims to impress the female with his colorful ornamentation and display of physical prowess. At this moment in her relationship with Troy, Bathsheba felt "powerless to withstand or deny him. He was altogether too much for her" (241). Troy's performance, far from granting the power of sexual selection to Bathsheba, overcomes the maiden.

Oddly, Hardy critics have almost completely neglected the crucial connection between Troy's potent, overwhelming sword demonstration and his later near impotent performance before Bathsheba at the Weatherbury circus. Having returned to Weatherbury ignominiously cast in the role of "Turpin," the legendary English bandit (and thus an ironically appropriate role for the roguish ex-sergeant), Troy is forced to perform in front of Bathsheba Troy, his estranged wife. Troy understands the effect of recognition. He will be diminished before Bathsheba's eyes: "Then he thought how the proud girl who had always looked down upon him even whilst it was to love him, would hate him on discovering him to be a strolling player" (407). Hardy emphasizes the couple's role reversal by highlighting their increasing class disparity: Bathsheba in steady command of her landowner status; Troy out of control as he slides down the social ladder.

Troy's spiral in Victorian England's rural class structure, though implied, is only obliquely referred to over the course of the novel. Legally born into a middle-class doctor's family, Troy is, according to Fanny, a "nobleman by blood" (160). Liddy later corroborates Fanny by asserting that Troy, though a "'doctor's son by name . . . [is] an earl's son by nature!'" and that Troy's relatively rapid progress in the army from enlisted man to sergeant was to be expected because "'nobility of blood will shine out even in the ranks and files'" (217). The evident conclusion: Troy is the bastard son of the Earl of Severn, whose watch Troy possesses and is, as he laments, his "'one poor patent of nobility'" (231). Nevertheless, Dr. Troy has provided his legal, if not biological, son with an education that surpasses Bathsheba's. Troy is multilingual; he speaks French, the English aristocracy's foreign language of preference, and a language Bathsheba does not know. Regardless of being able, as Gabriel observes, to "'speak like a lady'" (81), Bathsheba marries someone with a comparatively sophisticated education, nearly always an emblem of social superiority of one Hardy character over another.[50] But Troy has failed to use his Casterbridge School education to great advantage, squandering it by enlisting in the army as an uncommissioned common soldier. Gabriel, whom Bathsheba earlier dismisses as a suitor partly on the grounds of his lack of education, points to Troy's social decline during his attempt to dissuade her from entering into a disparate match with the sergeant: "'His being higher in learning and birth than the ruck o'soldiers is anything but a proof of his worth. It shows his course to be down'ard'" (246).

Precisely who is the master in Bathsheba and Troy's doomed marriage remains equivocal. Shortly after the wedding, Hardy indicates that Troy, "ruling now in the room of his wife," has assumed control of the farm's affairs by selecting the date of the harvest supper and dance. Yet Troy, who is never shown managing the farm in any way except to endanger the corn and wheat ricks on the night of the harvest supper, must continually request money from Bathsheba, either to sustain his reckless horse betting or to support his former lover, the impoverished Fanny, to whom he confesses, "'I have none but what my wife gives me, you know'" (320).[51]

As the owner of a large and prosperous farm, Bathsheba is accorded an elevated vantage point from which to view Troy's "Turpin" performance: "Troy, on peeping from his dressing-tent through a slit for a reconnoiter before entering, saw his unconscious wife on high before him as described, sitting as queen of the tournament" (403). Here, Troy is relegated to the role of peeping tom, no longer able to master his wife with the direct gaze of their previous encounters or able to generate the economic power Gabriel earlier exerts over her. This scene recalls Gabriel's prior view of Bathsheba on horseback, but now Bathsheba witnesses rather than performs the horse riding, a performance she has paid to see, casting Troy in the degrading position of hired performer. Yet because of Troy's hasty make-up job, "rendering him safe from the eyes of Bathsheba" (405), Bathsheba remains ignorant throughout the show of Turpin's identity. In spite of her socially unique position, Bathsheba fails to learn that Troy is still alive until he later elects to reveal himself. Hardy does not therefore use this scene to write his novel beyond patriarchal, Darwinian representations of vision but rather to emphasize Bathsheba's inability to translate her role as a masculinized spectator—as she translates her role as a feminized exhibitionist—into a controlling power position. For Hardy, empowered female spectatorship appears to be impossible.

As the novel concludes, Hardy steps definitively back from the unconventional, anti-Darwinian roles of male performer and female spectator he has written for Troy and Bathsheba. Neither Troy nor Bathsheba gains mastery over the other. When Troy once more attempts to play the role of male performer by his dramatic entrance and unveiling at Boldwood's Christmas party, his "transgression" is immediately and murderously punished by Boldwood, the party's deranged and visually conventional host. The deceased Troy is then replaced as Bathsheba's husband by Gabriel, another conventional male spectator, who has risen for a second time from dependent shepherd to independent farmer and who now, a far more established member of the rural hierarchy, assumes the utter visual and sexual power over Bathsheba he so desperately desires earlier. In recomposing both the Bathsheba myth and the Darwinian theory of sexual selection, Hardy only occasionally permits Bathsheba to possess anything beyond the role of the "feminized" performer. When Hardy *does* portray Bathsheba as a spectator, he approaches, but does not step beyond, a conventional representational and ideological boundary, because she only temporarily violates a patriarchal code along the single cultural register of property ownership. To conceive and represent a genuinely sexually selective female spectator requires a reformulation of gender roles and relations on numerous cultural registers, a step that Hardy, in spite of his profound criticism of his age's gender conventionality, was not prepared to take.

Like her biblical namesake, Bathsheba Everdene eventually marries the former shepherd who first spied on her. Once Gabriel acquires Bathsheba, he possesses not only the formerly subversive young woman herself, but also her property, thereby doubling his own land and reasserting patriarchal power in the social and economic spheres. Bathsheba's marriage to Gabriel functions as an ideological recontainment of female sexuality and the foreclosure of female property ownership. In terms of the sexual register of vision, it props up rather than undercuts Darwin's theory. The novel concludes by reifying a visual economy in which Bathsheba, ironically following both Darwin and the Old Testament (strange bedfellows, indeed), is made the visual, sexual, and material property of the male. In terms of visual representation, *Far from the Madding Crowd* looks forward to a Wessex (and an England) where one day sexually selective female eyes might no longer be unrepresentable. To locate such eyes we must ourselves look forward, to the mature works of Virginia Woolf that at once complicate and resist the Freudian discourse of scopophilia/exhibitionism and unite the feminine discourses of vision explored thus far.

4

Sigmund Freud, Virginia Woolf, and the Modernist Female Spectator

> *If you want to know more about femininity, enquire from your own experiences of life, or turn to the poets, or wait until science can give you deeper and more coherent information.*
>
> —Sigmund Freud, *New Introductory Lectures on Psychoanalysis* (1933)

Sigmund Freud's most important intellectual connection to Victorian England was with the work and figure of Charles Darwin. Darwin was Freud's intellectual hero. The father of psychoanalysis, never known for humility, regarded his intellectual offspring not simply as a continuation but an embellishment of the Darwinian scientific revolution. In *The Introductory Lectures* (1900) Freud celebrated Darwin, contending that the greatest scientist of the nineteenth century had toppled the foundations of human arrogance by "destroy[ing] man's supposedly privileged place in creation and prov[ing] his descent from the animal kingdom and his ineradicable animal nature."[1] Building upon Darwin's theories of natural and sexual selection, psychoanalysis had, according to Freud, dealt "human megalomania . . . its . . . most wounding blow" by showing "the ego that it is not even master in its own house."[2] On these grounds of monumental scientific progress, Freud concluded in the same passage that of all the great scientists in history, Copernicus alone should be granted entrance into that loftiest of Pantheons in which Darwin and, by implication, Freud himself resided. Most scholars who have chronicled Freud's debt to Darwin have emphasized either the influence of Darwinian biology on the Freudian theory of sexuality or have demonstrated how Darwin's observations on primitive cultures impacted Freud's anthropological writings, particularly *Totem and Taboo* (1912–1913) and *Civilization and Its*

Discontents (1930).[3] In this concluding chapter, I am interested in how Darwin's theory of sexual selection, a theory in large part predicated on visual relations between the male and female of each species, profoundly influenced Freud's theory of scopophilia and exhibitionism.

Yet this chapter aims to do more than trace the intellectual lineage between Darwin's and Freud's understanding of sexuality and vision. Following an explication of the theory of scopophilia and exhibitionism, I investigate how Virginia Woolf who, like Freud, inherited the intellectual and artistic currents of the eighteenth and nineteenth centuries, at once resisted the dominant scopo-sexual depictions of her day and drew from the representational traditions of female visuality in the English novel that Darwin's and Freud's theories strove, in effect, to obliterate. Woolf realizes this achievement most ambitiously in her two great novels of the 1920s, *Mrs. Dalloway* (1925) and *To the Lighthouse* (1927).

In considering the latter work, I am unaware of any novel in any language that more extensively and richly explores the meanings and motivations of female visual desire than *To the Lighthouse.* This chapter's case study shows how Woolf focuses on the ways in which Mrs. Ramsay and Lily Briscoe organize the world and themselves by traversing several visual categories, from painting to domestic vision to empirical sight to same-sex scopic desire. In representing the richly varied expressions of female visuality, Woolf at once fulfills and complicates the expressions of women's scopic subjectivity that she received from her predecessors in the novel tradition. In the discussion of *Mrs. Dalloway*, which functions as a conclusion both to this chapter and to the book, I show how Woolf, in her narrative of a day in the life of Clarissa Dalloway, brings into focus two centuries' worth of female spectators in English literature and culture.[4] By seeing through the eyes of Woolf's (as opposed to Richardson's) Clarissa, we encounter virtually every manifestation of female visuality explored in the preceding three chapters, including, most prominently, domestic, lesbian, *flâneuse*-like, and imperial representations of visual subjectivity. In this respect, Virginia Woolf encloses within the covers of *Mrs. Dalloway* a metahistorical survey of women and vision that reaches back, just as the argument of this book does, to the eighteenth and nineteenth centuries and the origins of modern female visuality.

Virginia Woolf, Bloomsbury, and Psychoanalysis

Throughout this chapter I make a case for the relevance of Woolf's stance in the scopic register of female desire relative to Freud. Given the orientation of my argument, it is important to underline the degree to which Woolf's relationship to Freudianism was ambivalent. Woolf remained largely aloof to the "truths" claimed by psychoanalysis for her entire life.[5] Certainly it is beyond doubt that Woolf much preferred her predecessors in the English novel tradition to the Viennese psychoanalyst. In distancing herself from Freud, Woolf aligned with the important Bloomsbury painters and critics, Roger Fry, and her sister Vanessa's husband, Clive Bell, the latter two of whom, as Elizabeth Abel has shown, also disdained psychoanalysis.[6] Yet the same Bloomsbury that psychoanalytic skeptics Woolf, Fry, and Bell did so much to create was, if not quite obsessed by Freud, certainly fascinated by and engaged with him.

In exploring the relationship between Woolf and psychoanalysis, Abel shows the myriad connections between Bloomsbury and Freud that had crystallized by the 1920s. Even a truncated summary of those connections is more than suggestive of the extent to which Woolf must have been exposed to psychoanalytic theory. Bloomsbury members and close Woolf friends James and Alix Strachey were practicing psychoanalysts who lived within blocks of Woolf in Tavistock Square. James Strachey was to become the standard English translator of Freud's works (pride of place he continues to occupy to this day). Remarkably, the Stracheys were not the only husband-wife team of practicing psychoanalytic therapists in Bloomsbury. Adrian and Karin Stephen, Virginia's brother and sister-in-law, themselves became certified psychoanalysts by mid-decade and would host a series of celebrated lectures in 1925 delivered by the formidable Freud disciple Melanie Klein, at 50 Gordon Square, just down the street from the Woolf residence. Even Lytton Strachey, Woolf's intimate friend and literary competitor (and brother of James), was taken by the psychoanalytic bug. He employed techniques borrowed from Freud to write the four psychobiographies that constitute *Eminent Victorians*, a book that created a sensation among the British reading public when it appeared in 1918. Woolf read it with great interest and, if we are to take her biographers' word for it, not a little envy.[7] Strachey's late biography, *Elizabeth and Essex* (1928), was even more explicitly psychoanalytic in orientation. For his part, Leonard Woolf, who contributed enormously to his wife's intellectual life, read *Interpretation of Dreams* in 1914 as a prelude to writing a review of *The Psychopathology of Everyday Life* for *The New Weekly*.[8] After officially becoming Freud's publishers in 1924, the Woolfs not only went on to produce all of his works in English (the Hogarth Press eventually became the publisher of Freud's comprehensive *Standard Edition*), but they also published seventy additional volumes of the International Psychoanalytic Library.

Virginia Woolf apparently preferred publishing Freud to reading him. Given the great psychoanalytic ferment experienced by Bloomsbury, it really is rather extraordinary that Woolf claimed never to have opened a volume of Freud for a thorough investigation until the late 1930s, just prior to meeting him in person in the last year of his life during his Nazi-enforced exile in London. Despite being Freud's English publisher and, by virtue of the imperial status of the English language, his global popularizer, Woolf rarely mentions Freud in her letters or journals. On the few occasions when she does so, the references are decidedly less than complimentary. For instance, in a letter dated October 2, 1924, approximately one year prior to publication of *Mrs. Dalloway*, Woolf is utterly contemptuous of the thinker whose work she and her husband would do so much, ironically, to spread:

> [W]e are publishing all Dr. Freud and I glance at the proof and read how Mr. A. B. threw a bottle of red ink on the sheets of his marriage bed to excuse his impotence to the housemaid, but threw it in the wrong place, which unhinged his wife's mind,—and to this day she pours claret on the dinner table. We could all go on like that for hours and yet these Germans think it proves something—besides their own gull-like imbecility.[9]

We have no real basis to disbelieve Virginia Woolf's claim of psychoanalytic ignorance, stated in a letter from March 19, 1932: "I have not studied Dr. Freud or any psychoanalyst—indeed I think I have never read any of their books; my knowledge is merely from superficial talk."[10] Of course, given the extent of Woolf's connections to Freudianism, it is not only possible but likely that her "superficial talk" would have betrayed considerably more knowledge of psychoanalysis than the average layperson's; yet it does seem clear, as she claimed, that Woolf never undertook systematic study of Freud until the close of the 1930s.[11] We are therefore left to conjecture whether, at the time of the composition of *Mrs. Dalloway* and *To the Lighthouse*, Woolf remained only cursorily aware from "superficial talk" of Freud's theory of scopophilia/exhibitionism and, if so, whether more substantial knowledge of the theory would have constituted for her further proof of his "gull-like imbecility."

Whatever Woolf knew or believed about psychoanalysis in the 1920s, and whatever we may know or believe today about psychoanalysis, one proposition cannot be cast in doubt: the psychoanalytic understanding of scopophilia and exhibitionism has reverberated through the twentieth century and beyond. Whether we like it or not, it is with the cultural and representational consequences of that theory that all subsequent writers, theorists, and critics of scopo-sexual subjectivity must grapple at some level, either implicitly or explicitly, myself and Woolf included. Over the course of this chapter and this book's conclusion, I will show both the relationship and the contrast between Freud's theory and the representation of visuality in *To the Lighthouse* and *Mrs. Dalloway*. Before undertaking those explorations, however, we must first turn directly to Freud.

Scopophilia, Exhibitionism, and Their Discontents

As I have demonstrated in the introduction, Freud significantly limited his writings on vision; unlike so many of his other major theoretical claims, he never significantly revised the discussion of scopophilia and exhibitionism that first appeared in print in 1905. Because so many subsequent and prominent writers on vision have made themselves subject to Freud's discourse it is worth examining in some detail what he actually wrote about vision, gender, and sexuality in his most thorough observations on the subject.

In the discussion of scopophilia and exhibitionism in *Three Essays*, Freud invokes Darwin by asserting that the human sexual act and subsequent procreation rely greatly on "visual impressions" that "remain the most frequent pathway along which libidinal excitation is aroused; indeed, natural selection counts upon the accessibility of this pathway—if such a teleological form of statement is permissable—when it encourages the development of beauty in the sexual object."[12] Although he invokes the theory of natural selection, Freud's understanding of the primeval quality of vision and sexual desire almost certainly emanates from Darwin's writings on beauty and sexual selection in *The Descent of Man*. By relying on Darwin's writings on sexual selection, Freud inherited a specifically *English* understanding of scopo-sexual subjectivity consistent with the dominant bifurcation of vision into masculine-sexual/feminine-domestic regimes as those regimes became dominantly constructed in eighteenth- and nineteenth-century English culture. Working out of Darwin, Freud disregards the possibility of a sexualized female spectator largely because the historical female spectator, or at least her most common English representation, had long since been confined to a domestic, manifestly nonsexualized sphere, where Darwin did not consider her to be important for his evolutionary purposes and Freud regarded her as a sexually repressed subject of modernity.

In *Three Essays* Freud sees a near direct correspondence between the perversions of sadomasochism and scopo-exhibitionism, with sadomasochism representing a parallel but more extreme version of sexual domination and humiliation than its scopic counterpart. For Freud, the perversion of finding sexual pleasure in giving and taking pain constituted an oscillation of masculine and feminine identity within the human subject.[13] In a section adjacent to the discussion of sadomasochism in the *First Essay*, Freud put forward his theory of scopophilia and exhibitionism, in which the subject derives pleasure from watching and performing sexual acts. The distancing effect that scopophilia makes possible between subject and object corresponds precisely to the objectification of the desired other that sadism requires; likewise, the surrender to the scopophiliac necessary for the exhibitionist takes a parallel if less drastic form in the relationship between the mastering sadist and the submissive masochist. For Freud, each pair of perversions is characterized by an active-masculine component and its passive-feminine counterpart. This binary theorizing is characteristic of Freud. As elsewhere in his work, whenever possible he stabilizes meaning by setting up similar dialectically oppositional terms. Freud regards sadomasochism and scopo-exhibitionism as reflecting essentially active/passive characteristics, and he assigns all too familiar gender orientations to them: active perversions are considered masculine, and their passive counterparts are feminine, "inversions" of their active-masculine opposites. In characteristic Freudian fashion, primacy is conferred upon the masculine side of the equation. What is feminine, then, must necessarily be viewed as a mere secondary mirror image of masculinity, not as feminine in and of itself but, rather, as a negative masculinity.

Freud's attempts to stabilize these perversions along a strict active/passive and masculine/feminine axis of difference meets with almost immediate difficulty, however, as the meanings of the terms slip into one another. This is especially true for Freud's account of active-masculine scopophilia as opposed to passive-feminine exhibitionism. In what seems at first to be an extraneous footnote during his brief remarks on exhibitionism, Freud fails to detect a fundamental contradiction between his theoretical articulation of exhibitionism and his illustration of it: he exclusively attributes exhibitionism to *males*. Freud writes, "The compulsion to exhibit, for instance, is also closely dependent on the castration complex: it is a means of constantly insisting upon the integrity of the subject's own (male) genitals and it reiterates his infantile satisfaction at the absence of a penis in those of women."[14] As presented in the context of Freudian theory, with its insistent privileging of the penis and the female's discovery of her fundamental biological lack, such an explanation may seem expected. Freud here conceives of exhibitionism in explicitly masculine terms, but, following his binary logic, he writes himself into the rather uncomfortable corner of implying that scopophilia, exhibitionism's opposite, must be feminine.

Before continuing, it seems important to consider whether Freud's use of a male example to illustrate a feminine perversion is actually contradictory. Of course, to label something either "masculine" or "feminine" does not necessarily imply that a woman cannot, in Freud's terminology, be "masculine" or that a man cannot be "feminine." Yet such terminology poses a serious problem for reversing sex-gender roles. For example, let us imagine a female exhibitionist displaying her genitals either to a man or to another woman. If, as Freud claims, one of the strategies of exhibitionism is to gain a return view of the spectator's genitals, what sexual pleasure could possibly be derived by a woman from such an action when, for Freud, such a response from the viewer, whether that viewer is male or female, would demonstrate to the female exhibitionist her fundamental lack, the absence of a penis through the negative comparison that any visual exchange of genitalia with a man would elicit or, by contrast, an identificatory comparison with any "castrated" female spectator/exhibitionist? Freud's footnote contrasts the "integrity" or presence of the male genitals against the "absence" represented by their female counterparts. It does not appear that Freud, within the "logic" of his own terminology, could have remotely hypothesized exhibitionism as "feminine." Indeed, in the example cited, exhibitionism takes on a tangibly active-masculine quality.

By the same token, it does not seem likely that scopophilia can possibly be conceived as a passive-feminine inversion of exhibitionism. Rather than qualifying as a passive perversion, as Freud's explanatory note for exhibitionism would seem to imply, scopophilia appears in almost all respects to fulfill Freud's conception of an active-masculine perversion. For one thing, Freud's scopophiliac reproduces the "male" role in the sexual act, utilizing a phallic gaze that attempts to penetrate and invade the sexual object. The fact that the "male" gaze is a dominant subject of so much feminist and psychoanalytic-inspired theory and criticism merely serves to corroborate the assertion that scopophilia and ownership of the gaze are culturally regarded as masculine.

In this sense, scopophilia parallels the version of sadism that Freud provides in *Three Essays*, for the scopophiliac and the sadist both derive libidinal pleasure from inflicting themselves "violently" upon the other. Quite differently, exhibitionism, like masochism, turns this sexual cruelty back on the ego, requiring the adoption of a passive role to achieve sexual satisfaction; in most cases (Freud's note on exhibitionism excepted, perhaps), the exhibitionist's passivity cannot fully be transformed into an active role because an exhibitionist most commonly remains a type of acted-upon object instead of an active subject. The exhibitionist, unlike the scopophiliac, requires a response from the target of his exhibitionism.

Freud's version of the exhibitionist/scopophiliac pair, ostensibly presented to establish a fundamental distinction between masculine/feminine perversions and, by implication, male/female sexuality, actually locates itself within a patriarchal discourse that defines both perversions (and subject positions) as masculine. In discussing vision, Freud neglects even to reduce femininity to a mirror image of masculinity; instead, he erases femininity altogether. As a scientist, Freud gazes on the masculine scopic regime alone, and his theory, disguised in a discourse that claims to explore feminine sexuality, rests entirely upon the phallic gaze.

Freud's theory, considered only in the context of *Three Essays*, appears far from satisfying. It neither permits a genuine discussion of feminine visuality, nor does its logic with respect to masculine sexuality and vision withstand close scrutiny. Despite the inadequacy of Freud's pairing of perversions, a more thorough examination of *Three Essays*, in conjunction with Freud's later work, which appears at first quite peripheral to scopophilia/exhibitionism, further undermines the authority of Freud's theory of vision. Pushing beyond my initial observations on the sadomasochist section of Freud's first essay proves useful, particularly in the ways that it informs and complicates a reading of *Beyond the Pleasure Principle* (1920), a text published fifteen years after *Three Essays*, which emerges as instrumental to my argument.[15]

Just as in the greater part of *Three Essays*, Freud is exploring the development of human sexuality when he writes in *Beyond the Pleasure Principle* that "the history of human civilization shows beyond any doubt that there is an intimate connection between cruelty and the sexual instinct."[16] Nowhere, Freud continues, is human sexual cruelty more compellingly or commonly manifested than in sadism and what at this point he regarded as sadism's inversion, masochism. According to Freud's masculine/feminine dichotomy (which I have shown collapses in his discussion of scopophilia/exhibitionism), one would be quite right in assuming that sadism and masochism, the former an active and the latter a passive perversion, should be categorized as masculine and feminine. This signifies, in Freud's apparent understanding of the terms, sadism's primacy over masochism. Following Freud's logic, if sadism is to be conceived as active and masculine, and therefore as the foundation for the masochistic inversion, it must necessarily appear *prior* to feminine masochism in terms of evolutionary origin. However, Freud's notions in *Three Essays* concerning the evident primacy of a masculine sadism are utterly dislocated in *Beyond the Pleasure Principle*, where he first articulates his theory of the death instinct, later known as *thanatos*. In *Beyond the Pleasure Principle* Freud breaks with all of his former work, discarding one of psychoanalysis' guiding precepts, the primacy of *eros*, the drive to seek pleasure and avoid pain. In *thanatos*, Freud believed he had located an even more primitive instinct, the ultimate conservative instinct that drives the subject to reattain the earliest form of existence, the inanimate state of stasis or death. According to Freud, *thanatos*, as the oldest human instinct, is also, by definition, the most essential instinct. Understanding *thanatos* therefore becomes important not only for a psychoanalytic theory of the human psyche, but also because it contributes to the explication of the gendered distinctions of the perversions in *Three Essays*. Through *thanatos*, Freud's theory of vision collapses on itself.

For Freud, the death instinct becomes visible to the analyst by manifesting itself in repetition and, most interestingly for my purposes, sadomasochism. Freud argues that *thanatos* was in its oldest form a masochistic drive toward stasis, internalized entirely within the subject. Only later did *thanatos* become a sadistic drive aiming toward domination of the other. Drawing on the premises of *Three Essays*, Freud proposes that in its origins *thanatos* was a passive and therefore feminine instinct. In this hypothetical paradigm, *thanatos'* masculine inversion outward only followed its initial feminine formation. Freud's reasoning leads to the contradictory position that humanity is essentially feminine in nature and only learns to *become* masculine, fundamentally different from the Freudian account of human development where children begin with an undifferentiated, polymorphous sexuality that, for both boys and girls, becomes in time a phallic/masculine sexuality, and for girls, only later and painfully, becomes a feminine sexuality. The ramifications for psychoanalysis that ensue from such a radically different narrative of human development are compelling, particularly for the active-masculine/passive-feminine dichotomy set up in *Three Essays*. These ramifications suggest that masculinity is in fact the inversion of femininity, not vice versa. Such a conclusion has profound implications for a psychoanalytic theory of vision because it supplies a means by which feminine rather than masculine visuality might be constructed as the primary term in Freud's scopic binary system.

To pursue such a manifest reversal, however, would be to ignore Freud's phallocentricity throughout the rest of his theoretical system, and, more important, would border precipitously on merely reversing privilege in favor of the feminine, privilege that, in Freud's thought, is relentlessly ascribed to the masculine realm. Such a project of simple reversal betrays a fundamental tenet of feminist theory, namely, not to replace the oppressive terms of patriarchy, in this case Freudian phallocentrism and the sadomasochistic drives of domination and subordination, with equally oppressive matriarchal meanings. As we shall see, Virginia Woolf avoided that error in *To the Lighthouse* by calling into question the very subject-object split upon which psychoanalysis in general and scopo-sadism in particular rely.

Case Study 4. Feminine Epistemology and Visual Desire in *To the Lighthouse*

Early in "The Window," the first section of *To the Lighthouse*, Lily Briscoe inquires of Andrew Ramsay about the nature of his father's philosophical investigations. Although the work of Mr. Ramsay, an Oxford philosopher in the British empirical tradition, is captured well by Andrew's pithily erudite reply, "Subject and object and the nature of reality," the young man is apparently dissatisfied by the lack of any concrete image attached to his abstract definition, and he therefore falls back on an everyday object to illustrate his point, "Think of a kitchen table then," he tells her "when you're not there."[17] On the face of things, Lily Briscoe seems an unlikely candidate for Andrew Ramsay's tutorial in empirical philosophy. An insecure artist infatuated with the domestic romance that she projects onto the Ramsay family, Lily proceeds to imagine a "scrubbed kitchen table" whenever she considers Mr. Ramsay's scholarship, on one occasion going so far as to lodge her table in "the fork of a pear tree" set against the front porch of the Ramsay summer home in the Hebrides as she paints an abstract rendering of Mrs. Ramsay and her youngest son, James. But if we delve more fully into Woolf's depiction of Lily, the young woman with "Chinese eyes" emerges as by far the most appropriate recipient of Andrew's philosophical reflections. Lily represents a specifically feminine response to the notorious conundrum of what eighteenth-century philosophers such as David Hume in *A Treatise of Human Nature* (1739) called the "double existence," which bedeviled British empiricism at least since George Berkeley, namely, how to verify the reality of an object whose existence becomes doubtful once separated in time and place from an observer.[18]

The novel grapples with the empirical problem of the double existence at the level of both narrative and character. Like the tradition of Richardsonian domestic women in the English novel from the eighteenth century forward, Mrs. Ramsay expresses faith in the double existence by her constant supervision and surveillance of home and family. We are repeatedly shown Mrs. Ramsay during moments of heightened domestic vision, as the nurturing mother, as the admiring wife, as the surveying mistress of the house, and these moments reaffirm the materiality and power that she exerts over others in her sphere of influence. The second section of the novel, "Time Passes," in which Mrs. Ramsay dies early on, describes, among other things, the physical decay of the family's summer home without the benefit of any Ramsay eyes falling on the house. In Mrs. Ramsay's absence it would appear that, to employ Humean terminology, the house's distinct and continued existence is only guaranteed by the visual perceptions of another woman, Mrs. McNabb, the housekeeper, who notes that if the house were sold and she not retained "it would want seeing to—it would" (135). While "Time Passes" underlines the nettlesome philosophical problem of objects in the absence of observers, the novel's third and final section, "The Lighthouse," explores how Lily addresses the problem. To comprehend Woolf's response to this philosophical riddle hinges in particular on understanding Lily's visual perceptions, whose meanings are exemplified in the painting begun in "The Window" and finished, years later, in "The Lighthouse." In completing her painting of the long dead Mrs. Ramsay at the conclusion of the novel, Lily imaginatively accomplishes an important intellectual and aesthetic task by putting a new twist on the central philosophical problem that the mournful Mr. Ramsay cannot himself solve: "Think of Mrs. Ramsay then, when she's not there."

In her representation of Lily, Woolf postulates a feminine visual epistemology that responds to the particular narrative uncertainties of this exemplary modernist novel. Woolf's rendering of Lily also self-consciously places the novel in historical dialogue with the domestic fictions of eighteenth-century England, fictions that, similar to *To the Lighthouse*, insistently engage with the representational problem of visual perception raised by empiricism and pervasively employ women as domestic observers of everyday life.[19] The domestic observers of the eighteenth-century novel—Pamela Andrews is their exemplar—dominantly employ their eyes in the interests of patriarchy and female subordination for the purposes of domestic surveillance, espial, and censure, thereby visually inscribing the definitive separation of the surveying and censuring subject and the surveyed or censured object. Mrs. Ramsay's and Lily Briscoe's eyes reply to this tradition as well as to the empirical problem of the subject-object split by merging their eyes with their objects of desire into a dynamic, fluid relationship predicated on mutuality and reciprocity rather than on a separation based on domination and subordination. What this means for Mrs. Ramsay and Lily is visual liberation from the cultural and representational constraints historically placed upon them and all women. In this respect, Woolf's novel also functions as a reply and rebuttal to Freud's theory of scopophilia/exhibitionism, which depends, as we have seen in the previous section of this chapter, on the most extreme possible separation of visual subject and object in the form of scopo-sadism.

The epistemological conundrum of the double existence has been a preoccupation of philosophers for several centuries. Although Immanuel Kant in *Critique of Pure Reason* (1781) largely circumvented the problem by proposing a distinction between phenomenal and noumenal realities, the challenge of the double existence continued to be handed down in British thought to the most admired philosophers of Bloomsbury, Bertrand Russell and G. E. Moore. Throughout his life Russell remained convinced that the problems initiated by Berkeley and explored most impressively by Hume had never satisfactorily been addressed, either by Kant or by himself.[20] For his part, Hume chose to engage with the problem of the double existence not by inventing an abstract Kantian category such as noumena, but simply by looking around his rooms. Hume counters the eighteenth century's commonly held Lockean opinion that the world is indeed sensibly verifiable by invoking his immediate domestic experience:

> I am here seated in my chamber with my face to the fire; and all the objects that strike my senses, are contain'd in a few yards around me. My memory, indeed, informs me of the existence of many objects; but then this information extends not beyond their past existence, nor do either my senses or memory give any testimony to the continuance of their being. When therefore I am thus seated, and revolve over these thoughts, I hear on a sudden a noise as of a door turning upon its hinges; and a little after see a porter who advances towards me. This gives occasion to many new reflexions and reasonings. (196)

In painting a picture of his bachelor's chamber and the objects within it, Hume's "new reflexions and reasonings" lead him to conclude that external to his interior space a vast world of subjects and objects exists that he must take for granted because they do not (indeed cannot) always present themselves to his senses. For Hume, the impossibility of simultaneously placing the entire world under our perceptions jeopardizes any reliable, literally "sensible" claim we can make about the world's continued existence.

Probing deeper into the problem of sensible skepticism, Hume calls once again on the image of his chamber to demonstrate why the eyes may not reliably record reality:

> I survey the furniture of my chamber; I shut my eyes, and afterwards open them; and find the new perceptions to resemble perfectly those, which formerly struck my senses. This resemblance is observ'd in a thousand instances, and naturally connects together our ideas of these interrupted perceptions by the strongest relation, and conveys the mind with an easy transition from one to another. An easy transition or passage of the imagination, along the ideas of these different and interrupted perceptions, is almost the same disposition of mind with that in which we consider one constant and uninterrupted perception. 'tis therefore very natural for us to mistake the one for the other. (204)

In alternately surveying and occluding his furniture (and presumably other domestic objects), Hume underlines the philosophic unreliability of sensible observation: "Think of a kitchen table, when you're not there." Judging from his extended references to domestic objects and their relevance to empirical skepticism, it would seem that Hume was a careful reader of Locke's *Essay*. While Hume repeatedly falls back on the representation of his chamber and the objects within it to illustrate his skepticism, Locke, as I have demonstrated in the first chapter, throughout the *Essay* invokes tropes of domesticity for precisely the opposite purpose: to impress upon his reader a new and reliable brand of sensible realism.[21] Yet Woolf in *To the Lighthouse* does not respond to Hume's skepticism by suggesting that we merely return to Locke against Hume. If this were the solution to the epistemological problems raised by Hume, Mr. Ramsay would have long since picked up Locke and fashioned a convincing apology for the *Essay* against Hume's *Treatise*, a course of philosophical action he never takes. As far as Mr. Ramsay is concerned, Humean skepticism hangs as ominously over Woolf's novel as the stormy weather that threatens the Ramsays' excursion to the lighthouse on the first page of "The Window"; that skepticism will not be blown away by any innovative reading of Locke's *Essay*.

Hume argues that empirical philosophers such as Locke confuse past perceptions, their memories, and present perceptions, in the process constructing an elaborate fictional reality that wrongly assumes the continued and distinct existence of objects beyond our sensible perceptions of them. And since, according to Hume, perceptions do not in any case correlate absolutely to their objects we can never know the world on the basis of our senses; even if we could know such a world, we would have no good reason for believing in our perceptions beyond the present moment because our perceptions do not construct a trustworthy bridge between the past and the present. Looking back on his explorations, Hume pessimistically concludes the chapter entitled "Of Scepticism with Regard to the Senses" by musing on the epistemological hopelessness of dwelling on the problem:

> I begun this subject with premising, that we ought to have an implicit faith in our senses, and that this wou'd be the conclusion I shou'd draw from the whole of my reasoning. But to be ingenuous, I feel myself at present of a quite contrary sentiment and am more inclin'd to repose no faith at all in my senses, or rather imagination, than to place in it such an implicit confidence. (217)

Hume seems so chastened by the implications of his reasoning that he admits to wishing he could believe in what he calls a "vulgar" understanding of the world, an understanding that, as against his critique of the double existence, would take for granted the correlation between perceptions and objects.

To the Lighthouse has been convincingly interpreted by Gillian Beer as a meditation on the problems of Humean philosophy as raised by Virginia Woolf's father, Leslie Stephen (whom Mr. Ramsay is clearly based upon), the author of the definitive Victorian study of eighteenth-century letters and philosophy, *The History of English Thought in the Eighteenth Century* (1876).[22] Hume is among the most admired figures in that work of Stephen's (Stephen claims that "Hume's skepticism . . . . marks one of the great turning points in the history of thought") and it is therefore no surprise that he also plays an important role in Woolf's novel.[23] As Beer and others have underlined, the specter of Hume makes repeated appearances in Mr. Ramsay's consciousness. We learn, for example, that six weeks following the period covered in "The Window" he is scheduled "to talk 'some nonsense' to the young men of Cardiff about Locke, Hume, Berkeley and the causes of the French Revolution" (44–45); and on three separate occasions he silently returns to a well-known anecdote from Hume's life in which the corpulent philosopher, having fallen into a bog, requires assistance from an old woman who compels Hume, a notorious atheist, to recite the Lord's prayer before helping to extricate him. This footnote from Hume's biography appears to be Mr. Ramsay's one solace in confronting the great Scottish philosopher because it required Hume, over and against his skepticism, to admit to the insistent materiality of reality. On another score, however, Ramsay's minor consolation relies upon ridicule rather than a serious philosophical critique. As a respondent to the epistemological problems initiated by Hume, Ramsay is reduced to invoking lines from Tennyson's "Charge of the Light Brigade" (he shows particular fondness for the phrase "someone has blundered"), a poem that takes as its subject matter the overwhelming of the British cavalry during the Crimean War by a larger and more strategically placed Russian army, an apt metaphor for the overmatched Ramsay's clashes with Hume's genius.

As Laura Hinton has shown, eighteenth-century British philosophy, especially the moral philosophy of Locke, Hume, and Adam Smith, was preoccupied with questions of spectatorship and sympathy.[24] For Hinton, sympathy, far from the virtuous emotion that brings individuals into closer connection with one another, requires the objectified distancing of one human subject from another that functions, in effect, like Freudian scopo-sadism. Hinton explores the neglected conceptual relationship between Freud, on one hand, and Locke, Hume, and Smith, on the other. Embedded in the philosophical writings of the latter triumvirate is a preoccupation with sympathy and what sympathy means for human relationships. Hume, rejecting the Lockean theory of natural law in which right reason asserts the integrity of the self against oppressive authority, argues that human passions, not rationality, take precedence in human behavior. For Hume, then, his moral spectator possesses an unfixed identity without a well-defined ontological shape. According to Hinton, the Humean spectator is, in fact, perverse and "exists representationally as a kind of mirror through which moral images are reflected and received."[25] In this view, morality is a representation, not a fact.

What amounts to Hume's amoral theory of spectatorship provides a perspective on the characterization of Mr. Ramsay as a man with an insatiable, unhealthy hunger for sympathy. Given Hume's interest in sympathy, and given Mr. Ramsay's preoccupation with Hume, it is not surprising that Mr. Ramsay is obsessed with extracting sympathy from the novel's principal female characters, Mrs. Ramsay and, after his wife's death, Lily. Mr. Ramsay's perverse desire for sympathy, his insatiable demand to be regarded sympathetically by women, is clearly aligned with Freud's theories of sadomasochism and scopo-exhibitionism. In Freudian-Humean terms, the economy of Mr. Ramsay's desire for sympathy would appear to be passive and masochistic, but it functions instead as active and sadistic. Relative to Lily, in particular, Woolf depicts Mr. Ramsay as punishing in his drive for sympathy. For example, before setting off on the long delayed voyage to the lighthouse, Mr. Ramsay seeks out Lily and does everything in his power to extract sympathy from her. Mr. Ramsay's actions are consistently depicted in violent language: Lily sees him coming and concludes, almost like a hunted animal, that "he'll be down on me in a moment" (149); unfortunately for Lily, it is "one of those moments when an enormous need urged him, without being conscious what it was, to approach any woman, to force them, he did not care how, his need was so great, to give him what he wanted: sympathy" (150–51). Certainly it is not going too far to say that Mr. Ramsay's habitual drive for sympathy is described here in the metaphorical discourse of rape. To be sure, Lily experiences this and other interactions with Mr. Ramsay as pain, yet she masochistically refuses to release the pain by being coerced into seeing him with sympathetic eyes. Even in his immediate absence, the pain of refusing him sympathy lingers, disrupting her ability to finish the canvas: "The sympathy she had not given him weighed her down. It made it difficult for her to paint" (170).

The presence of Mr. Ramsay in "The Lighthouse" initially stymies Lily's efforts to revisit, with any success, her painting. If, by taking up her paints again, Lily wants to recreate the scene from ten years earlier when she was painting Mrs. Ramsay and James, it seems to her that Mr. Ramsay will do anything in his power to stop her and, by doing so, prevent the completion of an imaginative connection between herself and his dead wife that she wants so desperately: "You shan't touch your canvas, he seemed to say, bearing down on her, till you've given me what I want of you" (150). Were Lily to surrender and give Mr. Ramsay what he wants, she recognizes that she would be figured very much in terms of Mrs. Ramsay, who made a virtue of providing Mr. Ramsay with the sympathy he craved. Lily tries in vain to convince herself to act the part of the sympathetic spouse: "Surely, she could imitate from recollection the glow, the rhapsody of self-surrender, she had seen on so many women's faces (on Mrs. Ramsay's, for instance) when on some occasion like this they blazed up—she could remember the look on Mrs. Ramsay's face—into a rapture of sympathy, of delight in the reward they had" (150). For his part, Mr. Ramsay is willing at least to entertain the possibility of Lily in the role of poor substitute for Mrs. Ramsay: "She looked a little skimpy, wispy; but not unattractive. He liked her. There had been some talk of marrying William Bankes once, but nothing had come of it. His wife had been fond of her" (150). Although Mr. Ramsay does not pursue anything like a courtship with Lily, in this passage he clearly desires from Lily that she see him with the sympathetic eyes that his wife habitually directed at him. Try as she might, however, Lily is incapable of functioning as a heterosexually compliant version of herself, and she therefore leaves Mr. Ramsay to ponder why "she should look at the sea when I am here?" (151).

Mr. Ramsay's are not the only male eyes that elicit exquisite pain in Lily. Indeed, Lily's experience of the male gaze in *To the Lighthouse*, especially relative to her painting, is consistently aligned with sadomasochism. The most obvious scopo-sadist is Charles Tansley, who asserts matter-of-factly, "women can't paint." (Tansley also claims in the same sentence that "women can't write," and so his simplistic damnation of female creativity applies to the talented Stephen sisters, the painter Vanessa Bell, and the writer Virginia Woolf.)[26] Tansley, of course, is a student and disciple of Mr. Ramsay; like his mentor, he demands sympathy from women and offers them nothing in return. At the Ramsay family dinner in "The Window," the perceptive Lily observes Tansley with X-ray eyes and recognizes a lack in the student of philosophy that needs to be filled by female sympathy, something she relishes withholding from him:

> Sitting opposite him, could she not see, as in an X-ray photograph, the ribs and thigh bones of the young man's desire to impress himself, lying dark in the mist of his flesh—that thin mist which convention had laid over his burning desire to break into the conversation? But, she thought, screwing up her Chinese eyes, and remembering how he sneered at women, "can't paint, can't write," why should I help him to relieve himself? (90–91)

Lily's experience of Mr. Bankes's eyes is even more painful than her exchanges with Mr. Tansley. In fact, even though Mr. Bankes is, aside from

Mrs. Ramsay, the character with whom Lily shares herself most fully, she still shudders at the prospect of his seeing her canvas. When Bankes dons his spectacles and first considers the unfinished painting, Lily "winced like a dog who sees a hand raised to strike it" (52) and "braced herself to stand the awful trial of some one looking at her picture" (52). Remarkably, the only characters who bother to look at Lily's picture in the entire novel are men, and the most considerate among them is Bankes who, pointing with his phallic, bone-handled pen knife, finds the "triangular purple shape" that represents Mrs. Ramsay to be intriguing, a declaration of genuine interest that accomplishes little to allay Lily's fears. And yet for all of Lily's agony, she finds Bankes' viewing "immensely exciting" (52). Later, however, Lily's sense of physical and emotional violation returns with a vengeance: "But [the painting] had been seen; it had been taken from her. This man had shared with her something profoundly intimate" (53). Whatever Woolf thought of Freud, she certainly portrays in striking masochistic terms Lily's experience of having her picture looked at by Bankes. Lily may find stimulating Bankes' viewing of her painting, but only when she manages altogether to escape the penetrating eyes of men, eyes even as different as Tansley's and Bankes', is she capable of completing her canvas and imaginatively envisioning a connection with Mrs. Ramsay, a connection that is clearly more than about merely the fruition of artistic desire. Indeed, Lily's longing for Mrs. Ramsay, both in life and in death, involves learning to see with eyes that, like the Ramsay matriarch, merge subject and object together into a coherent unity.

Quite different from Mr. Ramsay, who suffers debilitating philosophical and existential doubts from beginning to end, Mrs. Ramsay experiences no such epistemological or personal crisis, and this is due, in large part, to her imaginative perceptual sophistication. Mrs. Ramsay does not insist upon stabilizing the subject-object split as a strategy for establishing reliable claims of reality. Instead, she habitually merges subjects and objects into a new relational category of unity. Frequent instances of the "short-sighted" Mrs. Ramsay's manipulation of the subject-object split occur in *To the Lighthouse*. Among the first of her successful navigations between the poles of subject and object occurs early in "The Window" as she looks over the lawn, sees Lily, and remembers that she is posing for a painting: ". . . [T]he sight of the girl standing on the edge of the lawn painting reminded her; she was supposed to be keeping her head as much in the same position as possible for Lily's picture. Lily's picture!" (17). Here, Mrs. Ramsay's active sight triggers the realization that she is herself under Lily's view and must remain more or less stationery. Mrs. Ramsay functions in this passage as visual object and subject, at once being perceived by, and perceiving, Lily. In this regard, Mrs. Ramsay differentiates herself from the "sleeping" models that sat for Victorian classical-subject artists such as Fredric Leighton and Albert Moore, languorous models who, with closed eyes, made themselves exclusively the passive objects of the male artistic gaze. Later in "The Window," after nightfall has overtaken the ability of Lily to continue her painting, Mrs. Ramsay considers the significance of her dynamic visual relations with the objects she sees in general and with the lighthouse beam in particular:

> Often she found herself sitting and looking, sitting and looking, with her work in her hands until she became the thing she looked at—that light, for example. . . . She looked up over her knitting and met the third stroke [of light] and it seemed to her like her own eyes meeting her own eyes, searching as she alone could search into her mind and her heart, purifying out of existence that lie, any lie. She praised herself in praising the light, without vanity, for she was stern, she was searching, she was beautiful like that light. (63)

Where before, in her perceptual relations with Lily, Mrs. Ramsay is able to function both as subject and object of vision in relation to another observer, here she self-consciously transforms herself into the object she sees, projecting her subjective identity literally into an external object and thereby even more comprehensively collapsing the subject-object division between them.

Mrs. Ramsay's interior account of how she breaks down subject-object relations is in fact a metaphor for the novel's narrative form. Continually shifting back and forth and back again between the consciousnesses of her characters, the technique Woolf deploys is predicated on so radically breaking down the subject-object split that it becomes nearly impossible on a first reading of the novel to follow for certain which character's consciousness you are privy to at any particular time, a version of mimesis that does not rely on the stability of separation (or, rather, the illusion of separation) between the subject and object.[27] Yet Woolf attributes this action of merging identities exclusively to women. As Mrs. Ramsay wearily observes to herself at the beginning of dinner, "They all sat separate. And the whole of the effort of merging and flowing and creating rested on her. Again she felt, as a fact without hostility, the sterility of men" (83).

The most important "merging and flowing and creating" that occurs in the novel takes place in Lily's ponderings on Mrs. Ramsay's character and, later, her successful painterly rendering of the older woman. Certainly Lily rather than Mrs. Ramsay generates the energy of this creative merging. Indeed, Mrs. Ramsay's affection for Lily is more condescension than admiration. She considers, for example, Lily to be "an independent little creature" (17), and yet her fundamental belief in female beauty, marriage, and motherhood as the source of women's significance causes her to dismiss Lily's prospects: "With her little Chinese eyes and her puckered-up face, she would never marry" (17). Mrs. Ramsay is, however, very clearly an object of unequivocal desire for Lily. At first, that desire seems to manifest itself very much like Tansley's desire for Mr. Ramsay, namely, as the attainment and transfer of knowledge from an older and wiser parental figure to a youthful disciple. Just as Mr. Ramsay, the man who has reached "R" in the intellectual alphabet, possesses the keys to the philosophical citadel of knowledge, Lily considers that Mrs. Ramsay must harbor parallel secrets of enormous value:

> Sitting on the floor with her arms round Mrs. Ramsay's knees, close as she could get, smiling to think that Mrs. Ramsay would never know the reason of that pressure, she imagined how in the chambers of the mind and heart of the woman who was, physically, touching her, were stood, like the treasures in the tombs of kings, tablets bearing sacred inscriptions which, if one could spell them out, would teach one everything, but they would never be offered openly, never made public. (51)

Having considered a linguistic metaphor of fully inscribed tablets (a metaphor that appears to build off of Locke's notion of tabula rasa), of worldly knowledge being passed from an older to a younger woman, thereby preserving the subjective integrity of each and, with it, the subject-object split, Lily rejects that outcome and replaces it with another quite different metaphor of physical and emotional intimacy:

> What device for becoming like waters poured into one jar, inextricably the same, one with the object one adored? Could the body achieve, or the mind, subtly mingling in the intricate passages of the brain? or the heart? Could loving, as people called it, make her and Mrs. Ramsay one? for it was not knowledge but unity that she desired, not inscriptions on tablets, nothing that could be written in any language known to men, but intimacy itself, which is knowledge, she had thought, leaning her head on Mrs. Ramsay's knee. (51)

Whereas Charles Tansley decidedly wants Mr. Ramsay to pass down to him the inscribed tablets of empirical philosophy, Lily wants no such thing from Mrs. Ramsay. And while it is tempting to read Lily's wish to identify absolutely with Mrs. Ramsay in Lacanian terms as a classic fantasy of mirror-stage connection with the mother and an accompanying rejection of the law of the father signified by the Symbolic of the inscribed tablets, the unity that Lily desires is less a collapse of her own identity into that of a vicarious mother and more of a synthesis of the two identities of "Mrs. Ramsay" and "Lily Briscoe" that would recognize the individuation of each.

Mrs. Ramsay's further reflections on her relations to the lighthouse light reveal the intense pleasure associated with the realization of her desire for unity with it:

> She saw the light again. With some irony in her interrogation, for when one woke at all, one's relations changed, she looked at the steady light, the pitiless, the remorseless, which was so much her, yet so little her, which had her at its beck and call . . . but for all that she thought, watching it with fascination, hypnotized, as if it were stroking with its silver fingers some sealed vessel in her brain whose bursting would flood her with delight, she had known happiness, exquisite happiness, intense happiness, and it silvered the rough waves a little more brightly, as daylight faded, and the blue went out of the sea and it rolled in waves of pure lemon which curved and swelled and broke upon the beach and the ecstasy burst in her eyes and waves of pure delight raced over the floor of her mind and she felt, It is enough! It is enough! (64–65)

This passage, laden with latent yet intense sexual language, captures Mrs. Ramsay's most expressive emotional and visual experience in the novel. By sublimating her erotic energy onto these observations of the lighthouse and their effect on her, Mrs. Ramsay at once contains her scopo-sexuality within the confines of a safe external object and reveals the degree of sexual intensity that can be expressed in her—and presumably other women's—eyes. It goes without saying that Mrs. Ramsay looks on her family, particularly James and Mr. Ramsay, with enormous tenderness, but she never before or again approaches the intensity of this transcendent passage. In the case of her husband, Mrs. Ramsay may elect not to share with him the expressive quality of her eyes because he is himself incapable of seeing things. Following her ecstatic experience of connecting with the lighthouse light, Mrs. Ramsay "saw above the thin trees the first pulse of the full-throbbing star, and wanted to make her husband look at it; for the sight gave her such keen pleasure. But she stopped herself. He never looked at things" (71). Moments earlier, Mrs. Ramsay observes that Mr. Ramsay was "born blind, deaf, and dumb, to the ordinary things, but to the extraordinary things with an eye like an eagle's" (70). One of the "ordinary things" that Mr. Ramsay clearly neglects are the eyes of his wife, eyes that Lily Briscoe, by contrast, finds extraordinary.

Although Mrs. Ramsay manages to establish a profoundly intimate unity with nonhuman objects, "that light, for example," Lily desires the same degree of unity not with inanimate objects but with Mrs. Ramsay herself. This difference perhaps indicates a recognition on Mrs. Ramsay's part of the limitations that she, a married woman and mother of eight, must place on her intimate relations. Whatever the reason for the distinction between Lily and Mrs. Ramsay in the register of same-sex desire, their drive to connect and unify with objects outside themselves, and the language Woolf employs to describe their unification, are remarkably similar. That Lily at least unconsciously recognizes the forbidden quality of her desire for Mrs. Ramsay is driven home when, in the midst of her panic-stricken anxiety over sharing her painting with Bankes, she concludes, "But that any other eyes should see the residue of her thirty-three years, the deposit of each day's living mixed with something more secret than she had ever spoken or shown in the course of all those days was an agony" (52).[28] Lily's tortured reflections on the secrets to be found in her painting following immediately on her musings of connection with Mrs. Ramsay point to the high probability that her longing for Mrs. Ramsay is indeed on display there. Lily's longing persists even years after Mrs. Ramsay's death, and she manages to express that longing by again picking up her paintbrushes and recreating the canvas that Bankes had once before figuratively taken from her.

In "The Lighthouse" Bankes is now absent, but Mr. Ramsay, who had formerly been blind to Lily's painting in "The Window," takes his place. Lily soon discovers that to render her painting successfully she must put distance between herself and the oppressive eyes of Mr. Ramsay. Through an act of supreme will, Lily repels Mr. Ramsay's remorseless demands for sympathy and sees him off on his voyage to the lighthouse with James and Cam. Over the course of "The Lighthouse," Lily observes Mr. Ramsay's boat (and his eyes) move further and further from her canvas, and, along with that movement, she experiences a sense of artistic liberation that permits her to recall, in her mind's eye, the image of Mrs. Ramsay from a decade before that had once frustrated, her so profoundly. By self-consciously underlining the importance of separation between Mr. Ramsay and Lily, Woolf reminds us once more of Berkeley, who famously argued in his *Essay Towards a New Theory of Vision* (1709) that distance cannot be measured or known directly by the eyes but only through custom and relative to other objects whose size and distance is, at least approximately, known.[29] Woolf underlines the influence of Berkeley in "The Lighthouse" by making constant references to the importance of distance and, taking Berkeley's point of view on the matter, showing how the lighthouse appears, by turns, closer and farther—"the lighthouse looked this morning at an immense distance" (156)—depending on the swirling seascape that surrounds it. As she makes progress on her canvas, Lily periodically checks on the parallel progress of what she believes to be the Ramsay boat; significantly, Woolf emphasizes the narrative uncertainty of this observation because Lily possesses no independent confirmation that it is in fact the Ramsay boat, for she has, arbitrarily perhaps, merely "decided that there in that very distant and entirely silent little boat Mr. Ramsay was sitting with Cam and James" (162); on each occasion that Lily focuses on the boat (which may or may not be the Ramsay boat), Woolf drives home the importance for the novel of the concept of distance. Contrary to Berkeley, who was fascinated with the idea of distance as an abstraction independent of social interpretation, Woolf gives concrete meaning to the concept by linking it to issues of gender and vision that are at the heart of her novel. In the following passage, Woolf emphasizes the importance of distance between Lily's canvas and Mr. Ramsay, what Lily considers to be "two opposite forces" (193):

> So much depends then, thought Lily Briscoe, looking at the sea which had scarcely a stain on it, which was so soft that the sails and the clouds seemed set in its blue, so much depends, she thought, upon distance; whether people are near us or far from us; for her feeling for Mr. Ramsay changed as he sailed further and further across the bay. It seemed to be elongated, stretched out; he seemed to become more and more remote. He and his children seemed to be swallowed up in that blue, that distance. (191)

The "so much" that Lily is depending upon has everything to do with her as yet unfinished canvas and her ability to paint in solitude, with no fear of curious male criticism (Mr. Carmichael, who does not join the voyage to the lighthouse, never bothers to raise his opium-addled eyes to Lily's painting) to disturb her from making an imaginative and long-delayed connection with Mrs. Ramsay. Indeed, as the Ramsay boat rises and falls on the waves, receding ever further from Lily's consciousness and drawing closer and closer to the lighthouse, Mrs. Ramsay becomes more and more vivid in the aritist's mind's eye, "It was strange how clearly she saw her, stepping with her usual quickness across fields among whose folds, purplish and soft, among whose flowers, hyacinths or lilies, she vanished" (182). And yet, even as Mrs. Ramsay comes into sharper focus, Lily acknowledges how far her eyes fall short of capturing the dead woman in all of her fullness and complexity. In marking the visual disjunction between what she is and is not capable of vis-à-vis Mrs. Ramsay, Lily reveals the depths of her desire for the dead woman:

> One wanted fifty pairs of eyes to see with, she reflected. Fifty pairs of eyes were not enough to get round that one woman with, she thought. Among them, must be one that is stone blind to her beauty. One wanted most some secret sense, fine as air, with which to steal through keyholes and surround her where she sat knitting, talking, sitting silent in the window alone, which took to herself and treasured up like the air which held the smoke of the steamer, her thoughts, her imaginations, her desires. (198)

On two occasions Lily's imagination explicitly calls out for Mrs. Ramsay, marking her inability to create the kind of unity she longs for: "And then to want and not to have—to want and want—how that wrung the heart, and wrung it again and again!" (178); and again, later, near the end of the novel, "'Mrs. Ramsay! Mrs. Ramsay!' she cried, feeling the old horror come back—to want and want and not to have" (202). For Lily to be satisfied, however, she must have more than an imaginative, Lovelacian 360-degree view of the dead woman. She must instead achieve a genuine unity with Mrs. Ramsay that moves beyond subject-object relations.

From the moment that Lily takes up her paintbrushes in "The Window" she struggles with accurately representing the relationship between masses on her canvas, what we might consider to be, echoing Andrew Ramsay, another version of the problem of "subject and object and the nature of reality." In both "The Window" and "The Lighthouse," Lily comes to believe that she can solve the problem by placing "the tree further in the middle" so as "to avoid that awkward space" (84). Yet in recreating her canvas in "The Lighthouse," Lily's artistic ambitions continue to be thwarted by the problem of masses that cannot be solved except through a fortuitous chain of events such as the ghostly presence of Mrs. Ramsay making a surprise appearance in the frame of her painting and, almost simultaneously, Mr. Ramsay's boat reaching the tiny island on which the lighthouse stands, thus achieving the greatest possible physical and imaginative distance between Mr. Ramsay's eyes and Lily's canvas. The "sympathetic" battle that Lily and Mr. Ramsay earlier engaged in is a vivid representation of the kind of subject-object power struggle that Sigmund Freud would have been able to explicate all too well, as Mr. Ramsay, wrapped in self-pity, sadistically demands that "[Lily] should surrender herself up to him entirely" (151). In *The History of English Thought in the Eighteenth Century*, Leslie Stephen argues that "the whole history of philosophical thought is but a history of attempts to separate the object and the subject, and each new attempt implies that the previous line of separation was erroneously drawn or partly 'fictitious'" (40). To be sure, Hume and Freud certainly achieved their own particular forms of notoriety by demonstrating the fictitiousness of earlier attempts to stabilize the separation of subject and object.

What was Woolf's reply to Hume and Freud and all other thinkers intent on separating the subject and object in some new way? At the conclusion of *To the Lighthouse*, Lily Briscoe appears to challenge what Stephen calls "the whole history of philosophical thought" by completing her painting with an apparently simple brush stroke: "With a sudden intensity, as if she saw it clear for a second, she drew a line there, in the center. It was done; it was finished. Yes, she thought, laying down her brush in extreme fatigue, I have had my vision" (208). Far from creating yet another line of separation between subject and object that will be proven by a subsequent artist to have been "erroneously drawn," Lily's line at the center of her painting eliminates the awkward space that has haunted her from "The Window" and, more than simply bringing together the masses of her painting, creates a unity between herself and Mrs. Ramsay that transcends the subject-object epistemologies of empirical philosophy and the subject-object vicissitudes of psychoanalysis.

Conclusion: Clarissa Dalloway and Modern Female Visuality in England

The first chapter of this book concluded by considering the Sapphist quality of Clarissa Harlowe's desiring eyes. We close here by reflecting on the multifaceted eyes of that tragic character's modern namesake, Clarissa Dalloway. What the English would call Clarissa Dalloway's "Christian name" certainly appears to be a self-conscious reference on Woolf's part to Richardson's great heroine, especially given the fact that Woolf was contemplating reading *Clarissa* at the same time that she was writing *Mrs. Dalloway*.[1] Certainly Woolf possessed ample ambition to conjoin symbolically her novel with Richardson's, one of the acknowledged masterpieces in the rich history of the English novel. Woolf's novel, another masterpiece, may be taken as a prism through which the discursive and representational history of female visual subjectivity can be viewed. Though conventional to norms of feminine behavior in ways that Virginia Woolf never was, Clarissa Dalloway enjoys a wide range of visual subjectivities. In this respect, she is the antithesis of Clarissa Harlowe, who, shut away and imprisoned by Lovelace and a passive, masochistic object of his rapacious eyes, can only express in writing her visual desire for Anna. In *Mrs. Dalloway*, therefore, Woolf symbolically removes the blinders from Richardson's Clarissa as well as, crucially, the eyes of all subsequent "Clarissas."

Superficial as her knowledge of psychoanalysis may have been in 1925, in *Mrs. Dalloway* Woolf proves herself to be an expert at complicating Freud's understanding of female eyes. In her rendering of Clarissa Dalloway, Woolf, an accomplished student, critic, and practitioner of the English novel, presents her readers with a complex female observer who looks far beyond Freud's monolithic rendering of woman-as-exhibitionist. I have adopted this particular critical stance toward *Mrs. Dalloway* not so that it may be seen as simply another work in a tradition of female visual subjectivity in the English novel; rather, I am arguing that in its exploration of female visuality, *Mrs. Dalloway* provides a compelling portrait of the multiple scopic subject positions women may enjoy, subject positions in conversation with Clarissa Dalloway's predecessors in the novel tradition that extend from the polarities of sexual and domestic desire, subject positions that have either been dismissed or ignored by so many post-Freudian theorists of vision.

On a sunny June morning in the aftermath of World War I, Clarissa Dalloway begins her day by setting out on a buoyant walk down Bond Street in order to purchase flowers for a Westminster party that shall be attended by politicians (including the prime minister), old friends, and relatives. From the very moment Clarissa embarks on her shopping excursion, we are reminded of Benjamin's *flâneur*. Like the *flâneur*, Clarissa identifies herself as a quintessential metropolitan figure as she navigates the London metropolis with agile eyes that notice every vehicle, human figure, and window display.[2] As an upper-middle-class woman who lives and thrives in the city, she is obviously not a *flâneur*; however, as Deborah Epstein Nord has shown, Clarissa does resemble a genuine *flâneuse*.[3] Unlike the streetwalkers of the East End, Clarissa is empowered by her social class and she is the possessor of eyes accustomed to observe whatever they chance across in the course of a morning's meandering through the city streets:

> Bond Street fascinated her; Bond Street early in the morning in the season; its flags flying; its shops; no splash; no glitter; one roll of tweed in the shop where her father had bought his suits for fifty years; a few pearls; salmon on an iceblock.
>
> "That is all," she said, looking at the fishmonger's. "That is all," she repeated, pausing for a moment at the window of a glove shop where, before the War, you could buy almost perfect gloves.[4]

Clarissa's commodifying eyes flit freely around Bond Street, at times looking at her fellow citizens, at other moments, as above, penetrating critically into shop windows to contrast the commercial scarcity of the postwar present with the abundance of the prewar past. Vision, memory, and desire commingle in her consciousness to create a disjunction between what was and what is.

Yet simultaneous with her viewing of a Dutch painting on display in a Bond Street shop window, Clarissa feels herself being obscured by phenomena over which she has no control:

> But often now this body she wore (she stopped to look at a Dutch picture), this body with all its capacities, seemed nothing—nothing at all. She had the oddest sense of being herself invisible; unseen, unknown; there being no more marrying, no more having of children now, but only this astonishing and rather

> solemn progress with the rest of them, up Bond Street, this being Mrs. Dalloway; not even Clarissa any more; this being Mrs. Richard Dalloway. (14)

Clarissa has reached a point in life when her eyes are most empowered to look beyond herself into the city streets; she feels herself to be an attractive woman gradually fading with age, unnoticed and unappreciated by passersby, unsought after by sexually curious male spectators. Woolf's account of the invisibility Clarissa experiences goes far toward distinguishing the *flâneuse* from the *flâneur*. Even in advancing years, the *flâneur* remains a wholly visible metropolitan spectator, for after marriage his identity is hardly obliterated, as the *flâneuse*'s is, by taking a spouse. By contrast to Clarissa, Richard Dalloway, the Conservative minister of Parliament, the public figure, the orator in the House of Commons, remains in middle age the respected object of the public's gaze, while his wife, removed from the youthful dramas of courtship, marriage, and early motherhood, increasingly recedes from public importance.[5] In this sense, Clarissa's interlude of self-reflection before a Dutch painting is wholly appropriate, for her original identity as Clarissa Parry has largely been contained by her principally domestic role as Mrs. Richard Dalloway. Like many representations of women in seventeenth-century Dutch paintings, she frequently finds herself enclosed within a domestic space, performing the duties of wife and mother, if not, in her specific case, servant.

Consistent with Clarissa's sense of invisibility on Bond Street, of having been made an extension of her husband, she is also viewed by her former love, Peter Walsh, as having had to capitulate to Richard Dalloway's conservatism. On seeing Clarissa again for the first time in years, Walsh laments to himself what has become of the former Clarissa Parry, who in her youth had been a political radical:

> In all this there was a great deal of Dalloway, of course; a great deal of the public-spirited, British Empire, tariff-reform, governing-class spirit, which had grown on her, as it tends to do. With twice his wits, she had to see things through his eyes—one of the tragedies of married life. (116)

Walsh's criticism of the conservative views embraced by the Dalloways reminds us of the Victorian woman question debates and suffragette agitations explored in the third chapter of this book. In Peter's eyes it is a tragedy that Clarissa has traded her radical vision for the opportunity to become a political hostess and throw parties, effectively, for the Tories.

Are we disappointed with Clarissa for seeing, as Peter believes, with her husband's eyes? Do we desire that she discard a political vision that has compelled her, according to Peter, to abandon her former radicalism?

Perhaps. Our estimate of Clarissa, tainted above by Peter's overly critical view must, however, necessarily be altered when we consider how she, in fact, regards *herself* and her public/private role as "Mrs. Dalloway." Having returned home from a morning walk, Clarissa stares into a mirror, first studying her face and then moving on to a more stringent self-examination:

> How many million times she had seen her face and always with the same imperceptible contraction! She pursed her lips when she looked in the glass. It was to give her face point. That was her self—pointed; dartlike; definite. That was her self when some effort, some call on her to be her self, drew the parts together, she alone knew how different, how incompatible and composed so for the world only into one centre, one diamond, one woman who sat in her drawing-room and made a meeting point, a radiancy no doubt in some dull lives, a refuge for the lonely to come to, perhaps. (54–55)

With the mirror as her reflective medium of self-constitution, Clarissa composes a total personality out of her disparate parts. One of those parts may in fact see, as Peter thinks, with Richard's eyes, but Clarissa alone knows for which aspect of herself and to what extent this is true. In this scene, Clarissa distinguishes herself from Hetty Sorrel, another mirror gazer from sixty-five years earlier. Hetty peers into any self-reflective surface with either a narcissistic gaze or, fulfilling a quasi-Freudian paradigm of "feminine" vision, with an exhibitionistic performance. Hetty is most happy to imagine herself as the desired visual object of Arthur Donnithorne. Clarissa, quite differently, shuns both narcissism and exhibitionism to adopt a far more profound critical vision with which she retains for herself the power to constitute all of her personality's many aspects into a complex and interwoven visual subjectivity.

One of the most important aspects of Clarissa Dalloway's subjectivity is the frankly sexual gaze, expressive of Sapphist desire, that she earlier reserves for Sally Seton. In a flashback, Clarissa considers the passion she once felt for Sally when, like Clarissa Harlowe and Anna Howe before them, they were unmarried young women:

> But all that evening she could not take her eyes off Sally. It was an extraordinary beauty of the kind she most admired, dark, large-eyed, with that quality which, since she hadn't got it herself, she always envied—a sort of abandonment, as if she could say anything, do anything; a quality much commoner in foreigners than Englishwomen. (48)

Clarissa Parry and Sally Seton's explicitly lesbian desire for one another is not narratively spaced off by Woolf as Clarissa Harlowe and Anna

Howe's desire is by Richardson. Quite the contrary, for in Mrs. Dalloway Woolf places the eroticism of the two women in the middle of her narrative for all to see:

> She and Sally fell a little behind. Then came the most exquisite moment of her whole life passing a stone urn with flowers on it. Sally stopped; picked a flower; kissed her on the lips. The whole world might have turned upside down! The others disappeared; there she was alone with Sally. (52)

For Woolf, who rarely writes of carnal passion, this scene is tantamount to a sexual climax between women. More important, in terms of the way I am employing *Mrs. Dalloway*, Clarissa's look of desire directed at Sally and the orgasmic kiss exchanged between the two young women brings us back full circle to *Clarissa*, but this time with the physical fruition of desire between women. Despite Sally and Clarissa's eventual marriages to men, scopic Sapphism—the desiring gazes of women for women—reigns here as an important phenomenon that cannot altogether be obscured by what Adrienne Rich has called "compulsory heterosexuality."[6] By recalling in her mind's eye this quasi lesbian desire from her past, Clarissa Dalloway expresses her sexual and political resistance toward a society that enforces heterosexual union. Clarissa Parry is therefore the heiress of Clarissa Harlowe's Sapphism, and it is in her long-remembered, once realized, Sapphist desire for Sally that we see one important aspect of Clarissa Dalloway's youthful detachment from conservatism, both political and cultural, that led to her escape from the relentlessly heterosexual, pen-knife wielding Peter.

As an accomplished political wife and hostess, it is no surprise that Clarissa also sees with well-trained domestic eyes once her party is underway. Clarissa's domestic vision is socially distinct from either Sarah Ellis' or Mrs. Poyser's, however. As a member of the political Westminster elite, Clarissa oversees multiple servants, and she is therefore free to focus a great deal of her attention on the social interactions of her guests, leaving the details of the party under the supervision of Lucy, her chief servant. The following sequence, narrated through the hostess' consciousness, shows Clarissa to be a careful observer, even from afar, of her party's social nuances and codes:

> For there was Professor Brierly, who lectured on Milton, talking to little Jim Hutton (who was unable even for a party like this to compass both tie and waistcoat or make his hair lie flat), and even at this distance they were quarrelling, she could see. For Professor Brierly was a very queer fish. . . . Professor Brierly (Clarissa could see) wasn't hitting it off with little Jim Hutton (who wore red socks, his black being at the laundry) about Milton. She interrupted. (258–59)

Clarissa's domestic eyes permit her to judge the "look" of a conversation, in this case the bad temper of Professor Brierly and the appalling fashion *faux pas* of Jim Hutton. As the party unfolds, the all-seeing Clarissa shows herself to be the absolute mistress of her large Westminster house, ready and willing to inject herself into an awkward conversation, to exert her considerable social powers to save the party from failure.

One of the guests Clarissa most closely observes is her spinster aunt, Helena Parry, who spent part of her youth writing a book about the orchids of Burma, a feminine literary production of the British Empire. Looking at Aunt Helena causes Clarissa to examine the old woman's one remaining good eye as she imaginatively travels with her back in time to the Indian subcontinent under Victoria's rule:

> For at the mention of India, or even Ceylon, her eyes (only one was glass) slowly deepened, became blue, beheld, not human beings—she had no tender memories, no proud illusions about Viceroys, Generals, Mutinies—it was orchids she saw, and mountain passes and herself carried on the backs of coolies in the 'sixties over solitary peaks; or descending to uproot orchids (startling blossoms, never beheld before) which she painted in water-colour; an indomitable Englishwoman. (271)

In viewing Miss Parry through Clarissa's domestic eyes we encounter the seeing-woman of empire, whose imperial eyes, like Schreiner's Lyndall before them, are empowered to look out and possess the natural and cultural objects of the non-European world. In possession of her orchid watercolors, Miss Parry returns to England with images of an Oriental flower never before beheld by the Occidental eye. Her vision, refracted through Clarissa's consciousness, is shown to have performed the ideological work of empire.[7] Now she gazes into the past to the heyday of British imperial power, imperial power unquestionably in decline after the pyrrhic victory of World War I in which Britain sacrificed a generation of young men, lost worldwide economic supremacy, and bankrupted itself. It is from this diminished point of view that Woolf suggests we should regard this particular Englishwoman's imperial vision, a vision that, from a postcolonial context, betrays the exploitation perpetrated by the British Empire and from a feminist context underlines the power of female eyes abroad when they are liberated beyond the confines of British domestic politics.

Thus it is that we may read *Mrs. Dalloway*—with its *flâneuse*, domestic, Sapphist, and imperial manifestations of sight—as a tour de force of female visuality. With Woolf, as with all the novelists we have considered, we must see how female visuality emerges from many different subject positions that simply cannot be unanchored from their specific social and cultural moorings. Each deployment of vision I have focused on here and in the preceding chapters must therefore be seen as enmeshed in much larger questions of women's participation in sexual, social, and national ideological structures.

Throughout this book, I have taken seriously Freud's admonishment, cited as the epigraph to the previous chapter, to look to literature as a means of illuminating, if not the "riddle" of femininity, at least the riddle of feminine visuality. Had he read *Mrs. Dalloway*, Freud quite probably would have been befuddled by the "riddle" that Clarissa Dalloway presents; he also, I believe, would have experienced considerable difficulty interpreting the title character's multifaceted eyes as "passive." By taking up the question of women and vision from an expansive historical perspective, we do not regard either Clarissa Dalloway's or Lily Briscoe's eyes as sphinx-like riddles. Rather, Clarissa and Lily, following my case studies of Clarissa Harlowe, Dinah Morris, and Bathsheba Everdene, represent the culmination of a significant tradition of female visuality that reaches back to the late seventeenth century and that replies to Western philosophy's problem with the subject-object split by merging the subject and object into a dynamic, fluid relationship predicted not on domination and subordination but rather on mutuality, reciprocity, and desire.

Notes

Introduction

1. John Berger, *Ways of Seeing* (London: Penguin, 1972) 46.

2. See, for instance, Laura Mulvey, *Visual and Other Pleasures* (Houndmills: Macmillan, 1986), Teresa de Lauretis, *Alice Doesn't* (Bloomington: Indiana University Press, 1982), Constance Penley, *The Future of an Illusion: Film, Feminism, and Psychoanalysis* (Minneapolis: University of Minnesota Press, 1989), E. Ann Kaplan, *Women and Film: Both Sides of the Camera* (New York: Methuen, 1989), and Jacqueline Rose, *Sexuality in the Field of Vision* (Thetford: Thetford, 1986).

3. For previous interpretations of Freud within a nineteenth-century scientific, cultural, biographical, and/or Jewish context, see Lucille B. Ritvo, *Darwin's Influence on Freud: A Tale of Two Sciences* (New Haven: Yale University Press, 1990), Frank Sulloway, *Freud: Biologist of the Mind* (London: Burnett, 1979), Hannah Decker, *Freud, Dora, and Vienna* (New York: Free Press, 1991), Peter Gay, *Freud: A Life for Our Time* (London: Dent, 1988), William McGrath, *Freud's Discovery of Psycho-analysis: The Politics of Hysteria* (Ithaca: Cornell University Press, 1986), Jerry Diller, *Freud's Jewish Identity: A Case Study in the Impact of Ethnicity* (Rutherford, NJ: Fairleigh Dickinson University Press, 1991), David Bakan, *Sigmund Freud and the Jewish Mystical Tradition* (London: Free Association, 1990), and Marthe Robert, *From Oedipus to Moses: Freud's Jewish Identity*, trans. Ralph Manheim (New York: Methuen, 1976).

4. *Olinda's Adventures: Or the Amours of a Young Lady* (1693). Augustan Reprint Society Publication Number 138 (Los Angeles: William Andrews Clark Memorial Library, University of California, 1969).

5. See Audrey Jaffe, *Vanishing Points: Dickens, Narrative and the Subject of Omniscience* (Berkeley: University of California Press, 1991), W. J. Harvey, *The Art of George Eliot* (London: Chatto and Windus, 1961), and D. A. Miller, *The Novel and the Police* (Berkeley: University of California Press, 1987).

6. Jaffe 169.

7. Bakhtin 292.

8. See Ian Hacking, *Why Does Language Matter to Philosophy?* (Cambridge: Cambridge University Press, 1975) and Richard Rorty, *Philosophy and the Mirror of Nature* (Princeton: Princeton University Press, 1979).

9. Hal Foster, *Vision and Visuality* (Seattle: Bay, 1988) ix.

10. Different as they are from one another, an overriding principle shared by thinkers such as Michel Foucault, Jean-Paul Sartre, Jacques Lacan, and Guy Debord has been what Martin Jay calls the "denigration" of vision from its former place in Western—and especially French—thought as the "noblest of the senses." See Jay's *Downcast Eyes: The Denigration of Vision in Twentieth-Century French Thought* (Berkeley: University of California Press, 1993). Jay argues against the premise put forth by Hans Jonas in his well-regarded essay, "The Nobility of Sight" in *The Phenomenon of Life: Toward a Philosophical Biology* (Chicago: University of Chicago Press, 1966) 135–56.

11. See Foucault, *Discipline and Punish* (1975), trans. Alan Sheridan (New York: Vintage, 1979), *The Birth of the Clinic: An Archaeology of Medical Perception* (1973), trans. A. M. Sheridan Smith (New York: Vintage, 1975), *History of Sexuality*, v. 1 (1976), trans. Robert Hurley (New York: Vintage, 1978), and "Vision and Power," in *Power/Knowledge: Selected Interviews & Other Writings 1972–1977*, trans. and ed. Colin Gordon (New York: Pantheon, 1980).

12. See Walter Benjamin, *Charles Baudelaire: A Lyric Poet in the Era of High Capitalism* (London: New Left Books, 1973), and Charles Baudelaire, *The Painter of Modern Life and Other Essays*, trans. and ed. Jonathan Mayne (London: Phaidon, 1964) 1–40. See also John Rignall, "Benjamin's *Flâneur* and the Problem of Realism," in *The Problems of Modernity: Adorno and Benjamin*, ed. A. E. Benjamin (London: Routledge, 1989) 14–19.

13. In *The Spectator and the City in Nineteenth-Century American Literature* (Cambridge: Cambridge University Press, 1991), Dana Brand has made an interesting case for the *flâneur*'s origin, and the modernity the *flâneur* signifies, as beginning in seventeenth-century London rather than nineteenth-century Paris.

14. See Jacques Lacan, *The Four Fundamental Concepts of Psycho-analysis* (1973), trans. Alan Sheridan, ed. Jacques-Alain Miller (New York: Vintage, 1978), and Jean-Paul Sartre, *Being and Nothingness* (1940) (New York: Washington Square, 1966). Though Lacan expresses a certain admiration for Sartre's existentialist account of the gaze, he argues that Sartre never discusses the gaze per se but only the possibility of the gaze. According to Lacan, Sartre's hypothetical subjects do not meet the gaze of their antagonists and hence do not encounter "a seen gaze, but a gaze imagined by me in the Field of the Other," 84. For an excellent account of Lacan's work in the scopic realm, see Mikkel Borch-Jacobsen, *Lacan: The Absolute Master*, trans. Douglas Brick (Stanford: Stanford University Press, 1991).

15. Lacan, *The Four Fundamental Concepts of Psycho-analysis* 75.

16. See Evelyn Fox Keller, *Reflections on Gender and Science* (New Haven: Yale University Press, 1985), and Keller's essay, written with Christine R. Grontkowski, "The Mind's Eye" in *Discovering Reality: Feminist Perspectives on Epistemology, Metaphysics, Methodology, and Philosophy of Science*, ed. Sandra Harding and Merrill B. Hintikka (Dordrecht, Holland: Reidel, 1983) 207–24.

17. Ludmila Jordanova, *Sexual Visions: Images of Gender in Science and Medicine between the Eighteenth and Twentieth Centuries* (London: Harvester, 1989).

18. See Berger, *Ways of Seeing*, Griselda Pollock, *Vision and Difference* (London: Routledge, 1988), Roszika Parker and Pollock, *Old Mistresses: Women, Art and Ideology* (London: Routledge, 1981), Lynda Nead, *The Female Nude: Art, Obscenity and Sexuality* (London: Routledge, 1992), and Joseph Kestner, *Mythology and Misogyny: The Social Discourse of Nineteenth-Century British Classical-Subject Painting* (Madison: University of Wisconsin Press, 1989).

19. de Lauretis, *Alice Doesn't* 69.

20. See *Walking the Victorian Streets: Women, Representation, and the City* (Ithaca: Cornell University Press, 1995). Like Epstein Nord, Janet Wolff has turned Baudelaire's and Benjamin's male stroller inside out by posing the question of whether the *flâneuse* was a viable historical subject position in nineteenth-century France. See Wolff's essay, "The Invisible *Flâneuse*: Women and the Literature of Modernity," in *The Problems of Modernity: Adorno and Benjamin*, ed. Andrew Benjamin (London: Routledge, 1989) 141–56.

21. This work includes, for example, Linda Williams' *Viewing Positions: Ways of Seeing Film* (New Brunswick: Rutgers University Press, 1995), Judith Mayne's *The Woman at the Keyhole: Feminism and Women's Cinema* (Bloomington: Indiana University Press, 1990), and Mary Ann Doane's *Femmes Fatales: Feminism, Film Theory, Psychoanalysis* (New York: Routledge, 1991), *The Desire to Desire: The Women's Film of the 1940s* (Bloomington: Indiana University Press, 1987), and her extremely influential essay, "Film and the Masquerade: Theorizing the Female Spectator," *Screen* 23 (1982): 74–87.

22. Sigmund Freud, *The Standard Edition of the Complete Psychological Works of Sigmund Freud*, ed. James Strachey, 24 vols. (London: Hogarth, 1953–74). All subsequent references to Freud will be from the *Standard Edition* (*SE*). For this particular note, see *Three Essays on the Theory of Sexuality*, *SE* VII, 125–245.

23. Ann Kaplan, for instance, has observed the near simultaneous appearance of psychoanalysis and film upon the world stage in her introduction to *Psychoanalysis and Cinema* (New York: Routledge, 1990).

24. For a discussion of Freud's emphasis on language rather than vision, see John Forrester, *Language and the Origins of Psychoanalysis* (New York: Columbia University Press, 1980).

25. Freud, *SE* X. Martin Jay makes a similar point, citing the physical structuring of Freud's analytic methodology as articulated in "Recommendations to Physicians Practicing Psychoanalysis," *SE* XII.

26. Freud, *SE* X.

27. Hélène Cixous, "Sorties," in *New French Feminisms*, trans. Ann Liddle (Amherst: University of Massachusetts Press, 1980) 92.

28. See Luce Irigary, *This Sex Which Is Not One*, trans. Catherine Porter with Carolyn Burke (Ithaca: Cornell University Press, 1985), and *Speculum of the Other Woman*, trans. Gillian C. Gill (Ithaca: Cornell, 1985).

29. Irigary, *This Sex Which Is Not One* 101.

30. See Tennyson's *The Princess: A Medley* (London: Moxon, 1842), Patmore's domestic epic, *The Angel in the House* (London: Parker, 1858), Ruskin's "Of Queen's Garden's" in *Sesame and Lilies* (London: Smith, Elder, 1865), and Stickney Ellis' *The Women of England* (London: Fisher, 1838), *The Daughters of England* (London: Fisher, 1842), *The Mothers of England* (London: Fisher, 1843), and *The Wives of England* (London: Fisher, 1844).

31. David Buss, *Evolutionary Psychology: The New Science of the Mind* (Boston: Allyn and Bacon, 1999). For more on Buss' scholarship, see *The Evolution of Desire: Strategies of Human Mating* (New York: Basic Books, 1994), "Sex Differences in Human Mate Preferences: Evolutionary Hypotheses Tested in Thirty-seven Cultures," *Behavioral and Brain Sciences* 12 (1989): 1–14, and, in collaboration with D. P. Schmitt, "Sexual Strategies Theory: An Evolutionary Perspective on Human Mating," *Psychological Review* 100 (1993): 204–32. To his credit, Buss has also coedited a volume with Neil Malamuth investigating the relationship between evolutionary biology and feminism, *Sex, Power, Conflict: Evolutionary and Feminist Perspectives* (New York: Oxford University Press, 1996). A popularized version of Buss' and other evolutionary psychobiologists' arguments with respect to beauty and sexual selection can be found in Nancy Etcoff's *Survival of the Prettiest: The Science of Beauty* (New York: Doubleday, 1999).

32. See *Evolutionary Psychology* 139, as well as Donald Symons' "Beauty Is in the Adaptations of the Beholder: The Evolutionary Psychology of Human Female Sexual Attractiveness," *Sexual Nature, Sexual Culture*, ed. Paul R. Abramson and Steven D. Pinkerton (Chicago: University of Chicago Press, 1995) 80–118.

33. Devendra Singh, "Adaptive Significance of Waist-to-Hip Ratio and Female Physical Attractiveness," *Journal of Personality and Social Psychology* 65 (1993): 293–307. For related scholarship by Singh, see "Female Judgment of Male Attractiveness and Desirability for Relationships: Role of Waist-to-Hip Ratio and Financial Status," *Journal of Personality and Social Psychology* 69 (1995): 1089.

34. See chapter 18 ("Of Hoggamus and Hogwash: Putting Evolutionary Psychology on the Couch") in *Woman: An Intimate Geography* (Boston: Houghton Mifflin, 1999) 322–54. For other feminist perspectives on evolution, please see Janet Hibley Hyde's, "Where Are the Gender Differences? Where Are the Gender Similarities?" in *Sex Power, Conflict: Evolutionary and Feminist Perspectives* (New York: Oxford University Press, 1996) 107–18, Elizabeth A. Lloyd's "Pre-Theoretical Assumptions in Evolutionary Explanations of Female Sexuality," *Philosophical Studies* 69 (1993): 139–53, and Kim Wallen's "The Evolution of Female Sexual Desire," in *Sexual Nature, Sexual Culture,* ed. Paul R. Abramson and Stephen D. Pinkerton (Chicago: University of Chicago Press, 1995) 57–79.

35. See Gillian Beer, *Darwin's Plots: Evolutionary Narrative in Darwin, George Eliot, and Nineteenth-Century Fiction* (London: Routledge & Kegan Paul, 1983), and George Levine, *Darwin and the Novelists: Patterns of Science in Victorian Fiction* (Cambridge: Harvard University Press, 1988).

Chapter 1
The Conduct of the Eyes

1. Collier's single-authored published works in opposition to the Restoration stage included *A Short View of the Immorality, and Profaneness of the English Stage, Together with the Sense of Antiquity upon this Argument* (London, 1698), *A Defence of the Short View of the Profaneness and Immorality of the English Stage, etc. Being a Reply to Mr. Congreve's Amendments, etc. And to the Vindication of the Author of the Relapse* (London, 1699), *A Second Defence of the Short View of the Prophaneness and Immorality of the English Stage, etc. Being a Reply to a Book, Entitled, The Ancient and Modern Stages Surveyed, etc.* (London, 1700), *A Disuasive from the Play-House; In a Letter to a Person of Quality, Occasion'd by the late Calamity of the Tempest* (London, 1703), *A Farther Vindication of the Short View of the Profaneness and Immorality of the English Stage. In which the Objections Of a late Book, Entitled, A Defence of Plays, are Consider'd* (London, 1708). *A Short View of the Immorality and Prophaneness of the English Stage By Jeremy Collier: A Critical Edition*, ed. Benjamin Hellinger (New York & London: Garland, 1987) is an excellent scholarly, facsimile edition. Of the Restoration trio I have identified, their published responses to Collier include Charles Gildon's *Phaeton: or the Fatal Divorce. A Tragedy As it is Acted at the Theatre Royal in Imitation of the Antients: With Some Reflections on a Book call'd A Short View of the Immorality and Profaneness of the English Stage* (London, 1698), Dryden's "Poetical Epistle to Peter Motteux" on his tragedy called *Beauty in Distress* (London, 1698), and Congreve's *Amendments of Mr. Collier's False and Imperfect Citations etc. From the Old Batchelour, Double Dealer, Love for Love, Mourning Bride. By the Author of Those Plays* (London, 1698). Congreve's response was by far the most

detailed, running to 109 pages. Gildon and Dryden had comparatively little to say in response to Collier. Gildon's remarks amount to three pages, and Dryden's entire epistle is only two pages long. The most extensive commentary on the antitheatrical controversy remains Sister Rose Anthony's *Jeremy Collier Stage Controversy 1698–1726* (Milwaukee: Marquette University Press, 1937), though it is extremely biased in Collier's favor.

2. Locke's most well known critics included John Sergeant in *Solid Philosophy Asserted Against the Fancies of the Ideists* (1697), Henry Lee in *Anti-Scepticism* (1702), and John Broughton in *Psychologia* (1703), and John Norris in *Theory of the Ideal or Intelligible World* (1701–04).

3. The epistemological question of philosophic and scientific truth as verifiable through visual inquiry emerged as a fundamental concern in late-seventeenth- and early-eighteenth-century England. Investigations of whether vision, for example, could reliably describe natural phenomena are a central issue in a number of works from the period, including John Locke's *Essay Concerning Human Understanding* (1690), Isaac Newton's *Opticks* (1704), Bishop Berkeley's *Toward a New Theory of Vision* (1707), and David Hume's *A Treatise on Human Nature* (1739). What becomes clear in reading scientific and philosophical literature from the period is the degree to which natural philosophers were compelled to account for how the human eye did or did not provide a faithful medium for the recording of reality.

4. Trotter's works related to this portion of my argument include *A Defence of Mr. Lock's Essay of Human Understanding, Wherein its Principles with reference to Morality, Reveal'd Religion, and the Immorality of the Soul, are Consider'd and Justify'd: In Answer to Some Remarks on that Essay* (London: Printed for Will. Turner & John Nutt, 1702) and her five plays, *Agnes de Castro* (London, 1696), *The Fatal Friendship* (London, 1698), *Love at a Loss, or Most Votes Carry It* (London, 1701), *The Unhappy Penitent* (London, 1701), and *The Revolution of Sweden* (London, 1706).

5. Wycherley, for instance, composed a prologue at Trotter's request for *Agnes de Castro*, while Congreve and Trotter shared a correspondence, with Congreve providing helpful advice solicited by Trotter for *The Revolution of Sweden*. In March of 1697, one year before the *Short View* appeared with its prolific condemnation of Congreve, Trotter composed a poetic letter for Congreve honoring *The Mourning Bride*. Writing of Congreve, Trotter extols his fame and genius and exclaims her personal admiration for the dramatist, "When can my praise begin, or admiration cease!", likens him to Alexander the Great for conquering the English stage at such an early age, and declares Congreve to be Dryden's "greatest darling son." See Congreve's *Letters and Documents*, ed. John C. Hodges (New York: Harcourt Brace, 1964) 198. In response, Congreve claimed that Trotter's letter was "the first thing, that ever happened to me, upon which I should make it my choice to be vain" (199). Unfortunately for Trotter, the printing of *The Mourning Bride* had already taken place before Congreve received the letter, and her commendatory verses were therefore not included. Six

years later, in 1703, Trotter solicited dramatic advice from Congreve, and he generously provided it. He advised her on the plotting and language of *The Revolution of Sweden*, particularly regarding the third, fourth, and fifth acts. Congreve called the design of the play "very great and noble" and "the conduct of it very artful" (212), but he worried, among other things, that Constantia's escape from the Viceroy and return to Gustavus were not credible enough and that the final act "will have many harangues in it, which are dangerous in a catastrophe, if long, and not of the last importance" (212).

6. *The Life of Mrs. Catharine Cockburn* (1751) xix. For his part, the elderly Locke was appreciative of Trotter's gesture, thanking her for it with a present of books and a letter in which he calls the book "a generosity above the strain of this groveling age" and praised Trotter for having "vanquished my adversary" with the strength and clearness of your reasoning." See volume 7 of *The Correspondence of John Locke*, ed. E. S. DeBeer (Oxford: Clarendon, 1982), 8 vols., 730–31. Locke learned of Trotter's authorship by persuading the bookseller who represented the *Defence* to divulge her name.

7. Comparatively little critical attention has been paid to Catherine Trotter. Among the most important recent works of criticism are Constance Clark, "Catherine Trotter" in *Three Augustan Women Playwrights* (New York: Lang, 1986) 35–95, Nancy Clark, "The Female Wits: Catherine Trotter, Delariviere Manley, Mary Pix," in *Women Playwrights in England: c. 1363–1750* (Lewisburg, PA: Bucknell University Press, 1980) 81–121, and Edna Steeves, introduction to volume 2 of *The Plays of Mary Pix and Catharine Trotter* (New York & London: Garland, 1982) ix–xlii. Significantly, this scholarship does little more than mention the *Defence* in passing. The spelling of Trotter's first name remains open to dispute. In Trotter's published works, the second vowel in her first name alternates between *a* and *e*; in order to achieve some measure of consistency, I have elected to use the more conventional modern spelling, Catherine.

8. See Marsden's "Female Spectatorship, Jeremy Collier and the Antitheatrical Debate," *ELH* 65 (1998): 877–98. Marsden writes, "Ironically, there is no female voice in this debate. Despite the widespread concern with the effect of theater upon women, and the emphasis on the female spectator that appears in prologues and epilogues, few women actually recorded their responses to the theater" (878). Marsden's claim is indisputable if we limit female voices to responses by spectators. But I believe it is important to include the voices of female playwrights such as Trotter within the terms of the debate that Marsden chronicles so skillfully. Interestingly, Collier never attacks any of the prominent Restoration women playwrights, electing instead to direct his broadside against the likes of Wycherly and Congreve.

9. Josiah Woodward, *Some Thoughts Concerning the Stage in a Letter to a Lady* (London: Nutt, 1704).

10. It is no surprise that Woodward echoes Collier, given that the two men anonymously coauthored yet another attack against the English stage in 1705, *A Letter to a Lady Concerning the New Play House* (London, 1706). The playhouse

in question was the Queen's Theatre in the Haymarket, designed and built in partnership with Congreve by his friend and colleague John Vanbrugh, whose *Relapse* (1696) had been fiercely attacked by Collier in *The Short View*. Like Congreve, Vanbrugh responded in print to Collier's criticisms in *A Short Vindication of the Relapse and the Provok'd Wife, from Immorality and Prophaneness, By the Author* (London, 1698). The Queen's Theatre was the first playhouse built in London in the eighteenth century, opening in April 1705. It was the venue, coincidentally, of Trotter's final play, *The Revolution of Sweden*, produced in 1706.

11. Eliza Haywood, *Fantomina: Or, Love in a Maze* (1725) in *Popular Fiction by Women 1660–1730*, ed. Paula R. Backscheider and John Richetti (Oxford: Oxford University Press, 1996).

12. For more on how actresses changed the British theater, see Elizabeth Howe, *The First English Actresses: Women and Drama , 1660–1700* (Cambridge: Cambridge University Press, 1992).

13. Trotter's source for the play was Behn's *Agnes de Castro; or, The Force of Generous Love* (London: W. Canning, 1688).

14. Delariviere Manley did not share the view that Trotter was morally beyond reproach, claiming that early on Trotter slept with a well-connected man in the theater business to advance her career as a dramatist. Manley eventually published this gossip in one of her characteristic scandal stories, thinly disguising Trotter's identity by giving her the name of Calista, a transparent reference to the Trotter character in *The Female Wits*, a well-known play produced in 1704 that satirized Manley, Trotter, and Mary Pix. Anyone familiar with *The Female Wits* would have readily made the connection. In his biography of Trotter, Thomas Birch categorically rejects any imputation that Trotter was a woman of questionable virtue.

15. Collier compares the English stage unfavorably with its classical antecedents. He praises Aeschylus, Euripides, and Seneca as enthusiastically as he attacks Congreve, Vanbrugh, and Wycherly.

16. *Olinda's Adventures: Or the Amours of a Young Lady* (1693). Augustan Reprint Society Publication Number 138 (Los Angeles: William Andrews Clark Memorial Library, University of California Press, 1969). This is a facsimile of the 1718 edition, which appeared in an epistolary collection entitled *Familiar Letters of Love, Gallantry and Several Collections*. According to Robert Adams Day's introduction, "this collection was apparently made up of the best and most popular items in [the bookseller's Samuel Briscoe's] miscellanies of the past twenty-five years" (ii). *Olinda's Adventures* originally appeared in the first volume of Briscoe's epistolary miscellany, *Letters of Love and Gallantry and Several Other Subjects. All Written by Ladies.*

17. Burnet's controversial status was mainly the result of two books he published. The first, *Telluris Theoria Sacra or Sacred Theory of the Earth* (London, 1681), contained an idiosyncratic theory of the earth's structure and was attacked by John Keill, William Whiston, and Erasmus Warren (and defended by Addison).

Shortly after being appointed clerk of the closet to William I, Burnet was removed for publishing *Archaelogiae Philosophicae: sive Doctrina antiqua de Rerum Originibus* (London, 1692), in which he argued that the Mosaic account of the fall was allegorical. An English translation of this book was published in 1729, fourteen years after Burnet's death. Burnet did not publish his letters, addressed to Trotter, in criticism of Locke. Trotter excerpted large portions of these letters for the *Defence.*

18. See *Locke, Literary Criticism, and Philosophy* (Cambridge: Cambridge University Press, 1994). Without entirely discounting the importance of tabula rasa to Locke's epistemology, Walker points out "the expression *tabula rasa* does not occur in the *Essay—rasa tabula* occurs once in "Draft A" of the *Essay* (1671), but not in the *Essay* itself" (31–32).

19. Quoted in *Locke, Literary Criticism, and Philosophy* 32.

20. See Peter Earle, *The Making of the English Middle Class: Business, Society and Family Life in London, 1660–1730* (London: Methuen, 1989), and Lawrence Stone, *The Family, Sex and Marriage in England 1500–1800* (New York: Harper, 1977).

21. Trotter's notoriety was confirmed by production of the anonymously written *Female Wits,* which made something of a sensation on the London stage in 1704 with its thinly veiled depiction of Trotter, Manley, and Mary Pix as Calista, Marsilia, and Mrs. Wellfed, respectively. In the cast of characters, Calista is described as "a lady that pretends to the learned languages, and assumes to herself the name of critic." For more on the play as well as the text of the play, see Fidelis Morgan, *Female Wits: Women Playwrights on the London Stage 1660–1720* (London: Virago, 1981).

22. See Nancy Armstrong, *Desire and Domestic Fiction: A Political History of the Novel* (Oxford: Oxford University Press, 1987) 80–81.

23. See Earle's *Making of the English Middle Class: Business, Society and Family Life in London, 1660–1730,* and Stone's, *Family, Sex and Marriage in England 1500–1800* (New York: Harper's 1977). For an account of domesticity's relationship to English culture in the late eighteenth and early nineteenth centuries, see Leonore Davidoff and Catherine Hall, *Family Fortunes: Men and Women of the English Middle Class, 1780–1850* (Chicago: University of Chicago, 1987).

24. For Locke's theory of capitalism, private property, commerce, and their relation to government, see *Two Treatises of Government* (1689, 1690), ed. Peter Laslett (Cambridge: Cambridge University Press, 1960).

25. The full quote from Wilkes' text reads "[T]he very Name of *Virgin* imports a critical Niceness with respect to Virtue, Innocence, Modesty, and decent Behaviour: Every improper Curiosity defiles the Character: She that listens with Pleasure to wanton Discourse, defiles her Ears; she that speaks it defiles her Tongue, and immodest Glances pollute the Eyes" (84).

26. Wilkes 81.

27. Lady Pennington, *An Unfortunate Mother's Advice to her Daughters in The Young Lady's Pocket Library, or Parental Monitor* (Dublin: John Archer, 1790) 68.

28. Samuel Richardson, *Pamela* (London: Penguin, 1980) 103. All subsequent citations to volume 1 will appear parenthetically by page number.

29. Samuel Richardson, *Pamela Volume Two* (1742) (London: Dent and Sons, 1942) 134. All subsequent citations will refer to this edition and be cited parenthetically by page number.

30. David Hume, *A Treatise of Human Nature* (Oxford: Oxford University Press, 1928).

31. Francis Bacon, *New Atlantis and The Great Instauration,* ed. Jerry Weinberger (Wheeling, IL: Harlan Davidson, 1989) 10.

32. Samuel Richardson, *Clarissa* (1747–48) (London: Penguin, 1985). All subsequent citations will be cited parenthetically by page number.

33. Daniel Defoe, *Moll Flanders* (1722) (London: Penguin, 1978) 76–77.

34. John Cleland, *Memoirs of a Woman of Pleasure* (1748–49) (Oxford: Oxford University Press, 1985) 31–32.

35. Cleland 44.

36. For more on the "fair triumvirate of wits" see Dale Spender, *Mothers of the Novel: 100 Good Women Writers before Jane Austen* (London: Pandora, 1986), Ros Ballaster, *Seductive Forms: Women's Amatory Fiction from 1684 to 1740* (Oxford: Oxford University Press, 1992), and Toni O'Shaugnessy Bowers, "Sex, Lies, and Invisibility: Amatory Fiction from the Restoration to Mid-Century," in *The Columbia History of the British Novel*, ed. John Richetti (New York: Columbia University Press, 1994).

37. Ballaster 32. All subsequent notes will be cited parenthetically by page number.

38. See Ann Barr Snitow, "Mass Market Romance: Pornography for Women Is Different" in *Desire: The Politics of Sexuality*, ed. Ann Barr Snitow, Christine Stansell, and Sharon Thompson (London: Methuen, 1984) 258–75. O'Shaugnessy Bowers does not wholly discount the possibility of ideological subversion in amatory fiction: "This is not to say that the many representations of women's desire offered in these texts have no subversive power. On the contrary, no appraisal of the sexual force of amatory fiction can afford to leave out its tremendous potential for subversion. Merely by assuming a position as subject (both the central subject of the narrative and the possessor of active sexual subjectivity), even if that position is ironized, amatory fiction's desiring women threaten traditional male prerogatives based on female subjugation and objectification, and provide space for readers to imagine something new" (58).

39. Aphra Behn, *Love Letters Between a Nobleman and His Sister* (1684–87) (London: Virago, 1987).

40. Likewise, Manley, who followed Behn in the female tradition of Restoration drama and fiction, also regularly depicts women as scopo-sexual subjects rather than objects. In one representative sequence from her episodic fictional prose narrative, *The New Atalantis* (1709) in *The Novels of Delariviere Manley*, ed. Patricia Koster (Gainesville: Scholars' Facsimiles & Reprints, 1971), Manley paints the inaugural sexual relations between the Duchess and Germanicus almost entirely through the eyes of the Duchess: "[T]he Dutchess softly enter'd that *little Chamber of Repose*, the Weather violently hot the *Umbrelloes* were let down from behind the Windows, the Sashes open, and the Jessimine that cover'd 'em blewe in with a gentle Fragrancy . . . and to compleat the Scene, the young *Germanicus* in a dress and posture not very decent to describe; it was he that was newly risen from the Bath, and in a lose [sic] Gown of *Carnation Taffety*, stain'd with *Indian Figures*, his beautiful long, flowing Hair, for then 'twas the Custom to wear their own tied back with a Ribbon of the same Colour, he had thrown himself upon the Bed, pretending to Sleep, with nothing on but his Shirt and Night-Gown, which he had so indecently dispos'd that slumbering as he appear'd, *his whole Person stood confess'd to the Eyes of the Amorous Dutchess*, his Limbs were exactly form'd, his Skin shiningly white, and the Pleasure the Ladies [sic] graceful entrance gave him, diffus'd Joy and Desire throughout all his Form . . . ; the Dutchess, who had about her all those *Desires*, she expected to employ in the Embraces of the Count, was so blinded by 'em, that at first she did not perceive the Mistake, *so that giving her Eyes, time to wander over Beauties so inviting*, and which encreased her Flame; with an amorous Sigh, she gently threw herself on the Bed close to the desiring Youth" 305–06. Manley's vivid rendering of the Duchess' sexually charged gaze calls to mind scenes of female spectatorship and voyeurism in Behn, Defoe, and Cleland. Although the Duchess is, as O'Shaugnessy Bowers attests, duped into loving Germanicus, Manley makes clear the Duchess is only *temporarily* blinded to whom her lover actually is and "awak'd from her amorous Lethargy . . . open'd her languishing Eyes, and seeing his charming Face, which she had often admir'd, and perhaps secretly Sigh'd for once more bestow'd upon *Germanicus*, what she before in her own Opinion had bestow'd upon the Count" (307). The Duchess' depictions suggest the quite different scopo-sexual possibilities available to representations of women during the Restoration as opposed to the post-Richardsonian eighteenth century. O'Shaugnessy Bowers contends that the "Duchess eyes Germanicus with precisely the sort of appropriating, lascivious gaze that men normally use on women in amatory fiction. But her looking becomes an unconscious parody of the controlling, sexual gaze of male characters rather than a challenge to it" (55).

41. For the classic scholarly argument making the case for Richardson as an originator of the English novel, see Ian Watt, *The Rise of the Novel* (Berkeley: University of California Press, 1967). O'Shaugnessy Bowers articulates the standard critical view of the amatory fictions of Behn and Manley, still operative as late as 1994: "However interesting these texts may be as part of the Augustan cultural landscape, most critics still feel that they are simply not good literature; their present value seems to be mainly that of rather embarrassing curiosities, 'justly

neglected' (as John Richetti puts it) except by 'the most thorough of specialists or dedicated of graduate students" (69). Richetti's criticisms of amatory fiction's artistic value, which appears in *Popular Fiction before Richardson: Narrative Patterns 1700–1739* (Oxford: Oxford University Press, 1992), is forcefully challenged by Ros Ballaster in *Seductive Forms.*

42. *The Female Spectator* (London: Gardner, 1744–46) appeared monthly from April 1744 to May 1746 and by 1771 had reached its seventh edition, testifying to its enduring popularity among Englishwomen in the quarter century after its final publication. For more on Haywood's periodical see Kathryn Shevelow, *Women and Print Culture: The Construction of Femininity in the Early Periodical* (London: Routledge, 1989). All subsequent references will be cited parenthetically by page number.

43. In Greek mythology Io was one of Zeus' many mortal lovers. In order to protect her from the jealous Hera, Zeus transformed Io into a heifer. Hera, in turn, ordered the one-hundred-eyed Argus to stand guard over Io to prevent Zeus from carrying out his sexual designs on her. Indeed, judging from the first number of *The Female Spectator*, the periodical went a long way toward forming the premise of Haywood's *Invisible Spy* (1749), in which the male narrator makes himself privy to domestic scenes through the use of a magical belt inherited from the "ancient Magi of the Chaldeans" with the power to render its wearer invisible. Eliza Haywood, *The Invisible Spy* (1749) (London: Gardner, 1749) 2.

44. *The Female Spectator* 8.

45. Another important factor in Trueworth's break with Betsy is that Miss Flora deceives Trueworth into believing that Betsy has given birth out of wedlock and pays a working woman to raise the child.

46. According to Paula Backsheider and John Richetti, Haywood's *Love in Excess* (1719) was "one of the four best-selling books of the first half of the eighteenth century; only Defoe's *Robinson Crusoe* (1719), Swift's *Gulliver's Travels* (1726), and Richardson's *Pamela* (1740) equaled it. Haywood, Aubin, and Defoe absolutely dominated prose fiction in the decade of the 1720s." See Backsheider and Richetti's introduction to *Popular Fiction by Women 1660–1730* x.

47. Mrs. Delville fears a marriage between her favorite Cecilia and her son because the union would literally extinguish the Delville name. The terms of Cecilia's inheritance require her husband to drop his own surname and adopt Cecilia's.

48. Mrs. Delville's surveillance of Cecilia and young Delville parallels the supervision that Cecilia is placed under early in the novel at the Monckton residence where Mr. Monckton's wife, the irascible and jealous Lady Margaret, had regarded Cecilia with "watchful suspicion"; my point in underlining the parallels between Mrs. Delville and Lady Margaret, such vastly dissimilar matriarchal figures, is to emphasize the fundamental ideological function that novelistic representations of eighteenth-century women played in visually regulating both the domestic organization of the home and the social and sexual conduct of the

home's inhabitants and visitors. In the Harrel household, Cecilia attempts to operate as its disciplining female eye—and her proclivity to do so is a mark of her maturity and fitness as an eventual matriarchal head herself—while in the Delville and Monckton households she herself becomes the object of their eyes. What Burney makes clear throughout *Cecilia* is the normalizing roles women play in overseeing their homes.

49. Watt 297.

50. Frances Burney, *Evelina* (1778) (Oxford: Oxford University Press, 1982). All subsequent references will be cited parenthetically by page number.

51. *The History of Sir Charles Grandison* (1753–54), 3 vols., ed. Joselyn Harris (London: Oxford University Press, 1972).

52. Shortly after the auction of Lord Belgrade's estate, Burney again emphasizes how badly misdirected Miss Larolles' eyes are. On this occasion Miss Larolles focuses her eyes on the fashion choices of other women and is quick to castigate what she regards as outrageous ensembles and accessories. "'But whereabouts is Mrs. Mears? O, I see her now; I'm sure there's no mistaking her; I could know her by that old red gown half a mile off. Did you ever see such a frightful thing in your life? And it's never off her back. I believe she sleeps in it. I am sure I have seen her in nothing else all winter. It quite tires one's eye. She's a monstrous shocking dresser'" (44).

53. At the first party Cecilia attends, she becomes "the object of [Sir Robert's] attention, though neither with the look of admiration due to her beauty, nor yet with that of curiosity excited by her novelty, but with the scrutinizing observation of a man on the point of making a bargain, who views with fault-seeking eyes the property he means to cheapen" (34).

54. Edgeworth writes, "Mrs. Stanhope did not find Belinda such a docile pupil as her other nieces, for she had been educated chiefly in the country; she had early been inspired with a taste for domestic pleasures; she was fond of reading, and disposed to conduct herself with prudence and integrity. Her character, however, was yet to be developed by circumstances" (7).

55. For all her self-reproach, Belinda still seems justified in recoiling from many of the domestic scenes to which Lady Delacour subjects her, including violent quarrels with her husband and chambermaid and, most graphically, the spectacle of Lady Delacour's own "diseased" body. Having returned home from the same party in which the actions and motivations of Mrs. Stanhope were revealed to her through the eyes of a bachelor, Belinda is horror-stricken to discover the true appearance of Lady Delacour undisguised by layers of face paint and elegant dress. The "cancer" that Lady Delacour reveals to Belinda turns out to be only a serious bruise, intentionally exacerbated to fatten an unethical doctor's pocket. The ideological function of Lady Delacour's "hideous spectacle" is more important than the bruise itself. Lady Delacour's injury, incurred in a dual in which she and her opponent disguise themselves as men, seems intended by Edgeworth to highlight the domestically injurious spectacles that initially come to define the

Delacour household and that are symbolically marked on the body of the female head of that household. In Foucauldian vocabulary, the Delacour home is marked by a scopic economy of punishment rather than discipline.

56. Mr. Vincent observes of Belinda's drawing: "'What a charming woman! and what a charming family!' said Mr. Vincent as he looked at the drawing, 'and how much more interesting is this picture of domestic happiness, than all the pictures of shepherds and shepherdesses, and gods and goddesses, that ever were drawn!'" (236).

57. Lady Anne is a direct rival of Lady Delacour in terms of competition for Belinda and Helena's affections and an implicit rival of Lady Delacour because she has married Lord Percival, who had formerly been Lady Delacour's suitor.

58. Jane Austen, *Emma* (1816) (London: Penguin, 1966) 67, 68. All subsequent references will be cited parenthetically by page number.

59. Jane Austen, *Pride and Prejudice* (1813) (London: Penguin, 1966) 70. All subsequent references will be cited parenthetically by page number.

60. For a more detailed discussion of an "emergent" ideology, see Raymond Williams' discussion of ideology in *Marxism and Literature* (Oxford: Oxford University Press, 1977) 55–74.

61. Emma Donoghue, *Passions between Women: British Lesbian Culture 1668–1801* (New York: HarperCollins, 1993), and Lisa Moore, *Dangerous Intimacies: Toward a Sapphic History of the British Novel* (Durham, NC: Duke University Press, 1997).

62. See Luce Irigary, *Speculum of the Other Woman* (1974), trans. Gillian C. Gill (Ithaca: Cornell University Press, 1985).

63. For more on the historical phenomena of representing dead women in European painting and literature in the eighteenth and nineteenth centuries, see Elizabeth Bronfen's *Over Her Dead Body: Death, Femininity and the Aesthetic* (New York: Routledge, 1992).

64. For a good discussion of the female romantic friendship tradition, see Lillian Faderman, *Surpassing the Love of Men: Romantic Friendship and Love between Women from the Renaissance to the Present* (New York: William Morrow, 1981).

65. Phyllis R. Klotman, "Sin and Sublimation in the Novels of Samuel Richardson," *College Language Association Journal* 20 (1976): 365–73. Klotman writes of *Clarissa*'s narration, "The development of Richardson's epistolary style is evident in his addition of different letter writers to show varied points of view. This is a real advancement over the technique of *Pamela*." Also see *The Rise of the Novel*.

66. Teresa de Lauretis, *Technologies of Gender* (Bloomington: Indiana University Press, 1987) 25.

67. Laura Mulvey, "Visual Pleasure and Narrative Cinema," *Screen* 16 (1975): 6–18. Though Mulvey's critique specifically applies to film, it is also useful for considering narrative literature.

68. Randolph Trumbach, "London's Sapphists: From Three Sexes to Four Genders in the Making of Modern Culture," *Body Guards: The Cultural Politics of Gender Ambiguity*, ed. Julia Epstein and Kristina Straub (New York: Routledge, 1991) 112–41.

69. Michel Foucault, *History of Sexuality* v. 1. (1976), trans. Robert Hurley (New York: Vintage, 1980).

70. Terry Castle, *The Apparitional Lesbian: Female Sexuality and Modern Culture* (New York: Columbia University Press, 1993) 34.

71. Teresa de Lauretis, "Film and the Visible." Paper delivered at University of Washington Comparative Literature Colloquium, 1990. De Lauretis' justification for theorizing this dialectic is based on her analysis of the film *Desert Hearts*, where "heterosexuality as sexual behavior remains off-screen and is diegetically cast off in a quick Reno divorce, but heterosexuality as institution is still actively present in the specular expectations set up by the genre" (24). Here de Lauretis' use of the space-off is the reverse of mine in that she employs the space-off to demonstrate how hegemonic desire is eliminated from the screen yet remains present in this explicitly lesbian film. I am attempting, rather, to demonstrate how nonhegemonic desire is spaced-off in Richardson's otherwise heterosexual novel.

72. Jacques Lacan, *The Four Fundamental Concepts of Psychoanalysis* (1973), trans. Alan Sheridan (New York: Norton, 1981) 75.

73. See Freud, "Medusa's Head" *SE* XVIII. My characterization of these women as Medusa figures is derived from Beth Newman's article, "'The Situation of the Looker-On': Gender, Narration and Gaze in *Wuthering Heights*," *PMLA* 105 (1990): 1029–41. Newman considers how Freud, de Lauretis, and Cixous read the myth of the Medusa. For Freud, the Medusa elicits the fear of castration; de Lauretis concentrates on the Medusa's disempowering Evil Eye; Cixous centers on what would be seen if the Medusa's gaze was actually met, its laugh. A conflation of Freud and de Lauretis' version of the Medusa is closest to what I am depicting here.

74. See Lacan, "What Is a Picture?" in *The Four Fundamental Concepts of Psychoanalysis*.

75. Terry Eagleton, *The Rape of Clarissa* (Oxford: Blackwell, 1982) 54.

76. Richardson 636.

77. Sigmund Freud, *Dora: An Analysis of a Case of Hysteria*, *SE* VII. In *Clarissa's Ciphers: Meaning and Disruption in Richardson's Clarissa* (Palo Alto: Stanford University Press, 1987), Castle argues from a Lacanian position that Clarissa represents, for Lovelace, the phallus, which explicates the libertine's insatiable desire to possess Clarissa.

78. Armstrong makes a similar connection between Richardson and Freud. However, she draws a parallel between the seductions of Pamela and Dora rather than Clarissa and Dora. In this regard, Armstrong's analysis of Pamela's and Dora's "No's!" does not adequately contend with what I regard to be the lesbian implications of both Clarissa's and Dora's narratives.

Chapter 2
Ocular Reproduction, Sexual Difference, and Romantic Vision

1. All citations of *Zoonomia; or, The Laws of Organic Life* (New York: AMS Press, 1974, reprt.) are taken from volume 1, published in 1794. The second volume of *Zoonomia* appeared in 1796. Subsequent citations will appear parenthetically by page number.

2. The well-known arguments in favor of the importance of Wordsworth to the intellectual and artistic development of his sister Dorothy need not be rehearsed again here, but it is common knowledge in English literary history that the poet was also quite influential to Mary Shelley and George Eliot. The friend of William Godwin, and once deeply admired by Percy Shelley for his early poetry, Wordsworth was clearly a prominent artistic figure in Mary Shelley's early consciousness, and it is certainly no coincidence that in *Frankenstein* she quotes at length from "Tintern Abbey" to articulate the yawning divide that separates Henry Clerval and Victor Frankenstein, a divide predicated in large part on the fact that their eyes construct two very different visions of the world. Frankenstein's penetrating vision betrays a scientific voyeurism troped as masculine as against Clerval's feminine eyes. Though Eliot did not, like Shelley, ever meet Wordsworth, his artistic influence on her is indisputable, especially when we consider how *Adam Bede*, even more than *Frankenstein*, rests largely on the poetic pillar of *Lyrical Ballads* as the aesthetic model for its version of realism. As Stephen Gill has argued in *Wordsworth and the Victorians* (Oxford: Clarendon, 1996), Eliot's affection for Wordsworth was consonant with the way that the poet's popularity skyrocketed in the Victorian Age. Never genuinely popular in the Romantic Period, Wordsworth was the most revered poet of the Victorian Age, and it probably has a great deal to do with the preeminence of Wordsworthian aesthetics within its pages that *Adam Bede* (what Gill calls "Wordsworth at full length") was an instant bestseller in England. Two other Eliot novels, *The Mill on the Floss* (1860) and *Silas Marner* (1863), also clearly owe a great deal to Wordsworth.

3. See Southey's review of *Lyrical Ballads* in *The Critical Review* 24 (1798): 197–204, Keats' letter to John H. Reynolds on May 3, 1818, in *The Letters of John Keats*, ed. M. B. Forman, 2 vols. (Oxford: Oxford University Press, 1931), and Coleridge's well-known account of the composition of *Lyrical Ballads* in *Biographia Literaria* (New York: Leavitt, Lord, 1834). Although critical of much of the rest of *Lyrical Ballads*, particularly the prosaic subject

matter of many of its poems, Southey singles out "Tintern Abbey" as by far the most successful of the collection's experiments; Keats, comparing "human life to a large Mansion of Many Apartments, two of which I can only describe, the doors of the rest being as yet shut upon me," credits Wordsworth with reaching the innermost sanctum "whereby this Chamber of Maiden Thought becomes gradually darken'd and at the same time on all sides of it many doors are set open—but all dark—all leading to dark passages. We see not the balance of good and evil. We are in a Mist. We are now in that state—We feel the 'burden of the Mystery'—To this point was Wordsworth come, as far as I can conceive when he wrote 'Tintern Abbey' and it seems to me that his Genius is explorative of those dark passages" (155–56); Coleridge alludes to"Tintern Abbey" (which has often been taken by romantic scholars as a reply to the philosophical questions posed in "Frost at Midnight") in his observation that near the completion of *Lyrical Ballads* "Mr. Wordsworth added two or three poems written in his own character in the impassioned, lofty, and sustained diction, which is characteristic of his genius" (175). For prominent twentieth-century praise of "Tintern Abbey," see M. H. Abrams' *Natural Supernaturalism: Tradition and Revolution in Romantic Literature* (New York: Norton, 1971), Harold Bloom's *The Visionary Company: A Reading of English Romantic Poetry* (Ithaca: Cornell University Press, 1961), and Stephen's Gill's *Wordsworth: A Life* (Oxford: Clarendon, 1989). Abrams calls Wordsworth "preeminently a poet of the revelatory and luminous Moment. . . . In some few instances the revelation occurs when the visible scene, present or recollected, is entirely obliterated" (as in "Tintern Abbey") (387); Bloom identifies "Tintern Abbey" as "a miniature of the long poem Wordsworth never quite wrote" (131), a conversation poem about "the nature of a poet's imagination and that imagination's relation to external Nature"; as such, the poem stands out as the "father of Shelley's 'Mont Blanc' and Keats's 'sleep and Poetry'" (132); finally, Gill calls the poem "the climax to Wordsworth's first great creative period and a prefiguring of the future poems which seem most quintessentially 'Wordsworthian'" (152).

4. Jean-Joseph Goux, *Symbolic Economies: After Freud and Marx*, trans. Jennifer Curtis Gage (Ithaca: Cornell University Press, 1991).

5. In his anatomical research on the reproductive functions of hen and deer, Harvey appeared to find that male semen could not be found in the uterus after intercourse, which seemed to prove that males had little to do with procreation. For more on Harvey's findings see Eve Keller's "Making Up for Losses: The Workings of Gender in William Harvey's *De generatione animalium*" in *Women's Studies: An Interdisciplinary Journal* 27 (1998): 131–62. For more on the preformationists and differences between their conclusions about reproduction and sexual identity, see Londa Schiebinger, *The Mind Has No Sex? Women in the Origins of Modern Science* (Cambridge: Harvard University Press, 1989). As Schiebinger writes, "Preformationists believed that a fully formed organism exists in miniature in the egg or sperm, in contrast with the epigenesists, who believed that a fetus gradually develops from a simple to a complex organism" (179). Preformationists were split

into two camps, the ovists, who regarded women as the definitive factor in determining sex, and the animalculists or spermatists, who argued for male dominance in sexual reproduction.

6. See Aristotle, *Generations of Animals: The Complete Works of Aristotle*, trans. A. Platt, ed. J. Barnes (Princeton: Princeton University Press, 1984), and Galen, *On the Usefulness of the Parts of the Body*, trans. Margaret May (Ithaca: Cornell University Press, 1968).

7. For more on Darwin's identification with Jacobinism, see Desmond King-Hele's *Doctor of Revolution* (London: Faber and Faber, 1977), and Maureen McNeil's *Under the Banner of Science: Erasmus Darwin and His Age* (Manchester: Manchester University Press, 1987). The most notorious attack against Darwin was a satirical poem, "The Loves of the Triangles"; composed collaboratively by George Canning (under-secretary for foreign affairs in William Pitt's government), Hookham Frere, and George Ellis, the poem lampooned part 2 of Darwin's *Botanic Garden: The Loves of the Plants* and appeared in *The Anti-Jacobin* in three parts from April 16 to May 7, 1798. Canning and his collaborators recognized that Darwin removed God as the primary mover in nature and, as such, posed a serious threat to established religion and a conservative political and social order. As King-Hele observes, this publication was but one insult endured by Darwin in and around 1798 that led to his relative decline in popularity. The others were Thomas Brown's critical *Observations on the Zoonomia of Erasmus Darwin* (Edinburgh, 1797) and the publication of Wordsworth and Coleridge's *Lyrical Ballads*. Brown was a mere eighteen-year-old medical student at Edinburgh who in his polemical book rejected Darwin's materialism, theory of evolution, and division of the sensorium into four parts; as for Wordsworth and Coleridge, Wordsworth apparently targeted Darwin's literary reputation in the original Advertisement to *Lyrical Ballads* when he defends the volume's poetic language of common men against "readers accustomed to the gaudiness and inane phraseology of many modern writers." Despite Wordsworth's explicit distancing of *Lyrical Ballads* from Darwin's poetry, King-Hele emphasizes that "*Zoonomia* . . . throws its shadow over 'Tintern Abbey' giving Wordsworth the central idea of uniting animal pleasure in nature . . . with tranquil recollection of images of natural objects. . . . Darwin's general theme is that 'our ideas are animal motions of the organs of sense.' Wordsworth seizes on this mechanistic idea and transforms it into an organic vision by linking images of nature with both bodily sensations . . . and mental insights" (267). King-Hele's remarks on *Zoonomia* and "Tintern Abbey" share affinities with my argument, but the question of gender and sexual difference does not figure in his criticism.

8. Erasmus Darwin was a prolific patriarch. He fathered three sons, Erasmus, Robert, and Charles from his first marriage to Mary Howard, as well as, after her death, two illegitimate daughters, Susan and Mary Parker. His second wife, Elizabeth Pole, gave birth to four sons, Edward, Francis, Henry, and John, and three daughters, Violetta, Emma, and Harriot.

9. See Homans' *Bearing the Word: Language and Female Experience in Nineteenth Century Women's Writing* (Chicago: University of Chicago Press, 1986), and Mellor's *Mary Shelley: Her Life, Her Fiction, Her Monsters* (London: Routledge, 1989). For Homans, this is a fantasy principally of linguistic meaning that requires the death or absence of the mother and "the quest for substitutes for her, substitutes that transfer her power to something that men's minds can more readily control" (4). She argues that male poets such as Wordsworth attempt to equal in their writing the absolute material presence of presymbolic mirror-stage relations to the mother and to nature, paradoxically, through symbolic signification. They dream, in other words, of a symbolic language of presence that can transcend material-maternal reality. For Mellor, meanwhile, it is a fantasy of "[t]he Romantic attempt to marry opposites, to unite the mortal and the immortal in a transcendental dialectic, to create the human form divine" (79) and she sees this as the central mission of Blake, Coleridge, Wordsworth, and, of course, Percy Shelley.

10. Faced with the landowner's overreaching narrative of male privilege, one is tempted to reread this case history and turn the ridiculous story on its head by giving it a more plausible materialist explanation. Instead of regarding the landowner's wife as an utterly passive figure sentenced to give birth to a child who bore no resemblance either to herself or her husband, a case can be made that she was far more active than her husband imagined her to be. Perhaps this woman, similar to her husband, possessed sexually roving eyes and, like him, acted on her desires, eventually giving birth not to the child of his imagination, but to the daughter of the "inferior tenant." In this scenario, it would not be surprising if the tenant resembled his own daughter, the object of the landowner's sexual desire, and this genetic resemblance would therefore explain to late twentieth-century readers, at least, how the landowner's legal (but not biological) child might wrongly have appeared to be the offspring of his lusty visual imagination when that child was, in fact, the tenant's daughter's half-sister. Indeed, such a contrarian reading of this particular procreative act seems to have weighed heavily on the landowner's mind; Darwin's account of the story in fact suggests that the landowner, in need of quelling Darwin's skepticism about the biological facts of the birth ("he assured me that he believed it was his own imagination"), was insecure over the patrimony of his legal daughter because the girl resembled neither him nor his wife. The landowner's conclusion, that the daughter must be his paterially conceived progeny, may testify not to the (pro)creative powers of the male visual imagination but to the blinding qualities of the masculine ego.

11. Samuel Taylor Coleridge, *Collected Letters* (London: Oxford University Press 1956) 1:177.

12. *A Plan for the Conduct of Female Education* (London: Drewry, 1797). Of the volume's legacy, King-Hele writes in *The Essential Writings of Erasmus Darwin* (London: Macgibbon and Kee, 1968) that the "book has earned a distinctive place in the history of girls' education in England. Darwin was totally

opposed to the idea that girls were meant to be weak and empty-headed, and he went a long way towards modern ideas on sexual equality" (235).

13. For more on critiques of Dorothy as a mirror image of William in "Tintern Abbey" see Judith Page's *Wordsworth and the Cultivation of Women* (Berkeley: University of California Press, 1994), Robert Essick's "Gender Transgression and the Two Wordsworths in 'Tintern Abbey,'" *Texas Studies in Literature and Language* 36 (1994): 291–305, Theresa Kelley's *Wordsworth's Revisionary Aesthetics* (Cambridge: Cambridge University Press, 1988), and Daniel Watkins' *Sexual Power in British Romantic Poetry* (Gainesville: University Press of Florida, 1996). Page captures the ethos of this argument: "In 'Tintern Abbey' the beloved sister silently serves as a mirror in which the poet can gaze into his past and hope for his future" (46).

14. See Ernest De Selincourt, ed., *The Letters of William and Dorothy Wordsworth 1787–1805* (Oxford: Clarendon, 1967) 198. Subsequent citations will appear parenthetically and by page number.

15. Mary Moorman's *William Wordsworth: A Biography*, 2 vols. (London: Oxford University Press, 1968) is characteristic of this view. She mentions *Zoonomia* only twice, on both occasions with specific reference to "Goody Blake and Harry Gill." More recently, Stephen Gill ignores Darwin altogether, never mentioning him (as Richard Matlak notes) in his own full-length biography, *William Wordsworth: A Life*.

16. For instance, in "Wordsworth and 'Natural Science': The Poetry of 1798," *The Journal of English and Germanic Philology* 77 (1978): 232–46, Averill claims the poet's early associationist and pantheistic tendencies derived in large measure from eighteenth-century England's preeminent physician, and he postulates that the case study approach employed throughout *Zoonomia* is reproduced in Wordsworth's poetry. He argues this poetry frequently describes, as Darwin's science does, people at the margins (or beyond) of normal mental excitation. In "Wordsworth's Reading of *Zoonomia* in Early Spring," *The Wordsworth Circle* 21 (1990): 76–81, Matlak sees Darwin's influence on Wordsworth as even more extensive than Averill, arguing that the organization of *Lyrical Ballads*, discretely split between "poems of healthy and degenerate states of being," matches the division found in *Zoonomia*'s two thick volumes. In *Wordsworth and the Enlightenment: Nature, Man, and Society in the Experimental Poetry* (New Haven: Yale University Press, 1989), Alan Bewell has paradoxically challenged, echoed, and amplified Averill's and Matlak's discussion in his argument that "it is probably an exaggeration to say . . . Wordsworth drew from *Zoonomia* the associationist theory of perception" but implicitly agreeing in claiming that Darwin's version of the case history provided Wordsworth with a "mode of writing that could be adapted to poetic as well as philosophical argument" (146). William Galperin's *Return of the Visible in British Romanticism* (Baltimore: Johns Hopkins University Press, 1993) also discusses Wordsworth's ambivalent relationship to science and does so with particular emphasis in the

cultural register of visibility, but Galperin focuses principally on the 1802 preface to the third edition of *Lyrical Ballads* as well as *The Prelude.*

17. Kelley distinguishes between Wordsworth's representation of the revolutionary sublime and the "sense sublime," both identified with masculinity as opposed to "'those beauteous forms' the speaker hopes to remember or have Dorothy Wordsworth remember" (57).

18. I am using W. J. B. Owen's edition of the first edition of *Lyrical Ballads* (London: Oxford University Press, 1969); subsequent citations will appear parenthetically by line number.

19. If Wordsworth is in fact revising Darwin by suggesting the female optical imagination can effect sexual generation, we must not overlook the fact that he also seems to suggest that female imaginations may only be potent enough to play a decisive role in molding children when that imagination is shaped, like this particular mother's, by madness.

20. J. R. Watson, "A Note on the Date in the Title of 'Tintern Abbey,'" *The Wordsworth Circle* 10 (1979): 379–80.

21. Kenneth Johnston, "The Politics of 'Tintern Abbey,'" *The Wordsworth Circle* 14 (1983): 6–14.

22. William Wordsworth, *The Prelude*, ed. M. H. Abrams, Johnathan Wordsworth, and Stephen Gill (New York: Norton, 1979). The cited lines are drawn from the 1805 version of the poem.

23. Bloom 130.

24. John Barrell, "The Uses of Dorothy: 'The Language of the Sense' in 'Tintern Abbey,'" in *Poetry, Language, and Politics* (New York: St. Martin's, 1988) 137–67.

25. Critical reception of "Thoughts on my sick-bed" has generated very different readings. Agreeing that the poem is indeed a reply to "Tintern Abbey," Dorothy Levin and Margaret Homans on one side and James Soderholm on the other have initiated an interpretive polemic, with Levin calling the poem "an ambiguous dialogue with the poems of William's great decade, celebrating the old interdependence while shaping the words to fit her own struggle," Homans arguing that "writing out of love for William [Dorothy] takes on the persona he designs for her and adopts a 'hidden life' that is his, not hers, and therefore one that is as mystifying to her as it is to us" and Soderholm, who vehemently disagrees with these complementary feminist readings, concluding that "it seems wrongheaded to read her final lines as either a declaration of independence from her brother's work or an infirm capitulation to it" (320). Rather than arbitrate the differences among this trio of critics, I intend instead to consider more fully the visual meaning of "Thoughts on my sick-bed" relative to "Tintern Abbey" and to explore in somewhat more specific detail the intertextuality between Dorothy's poem and other immediately relevant poems in William's oeuvre, particularly "A slumber

did my spirit seal" and "I wandered lonely as a cloud," readings that place me in closer sympathy with Levin and Homans rather than Soderholm.

26. D. Wordsworth citation.

27. Mellor 95. I should point out that Darwin was also an inventor who, as a founding member along with Josiah Wedgewood of the Lunar Society of Birmingham, was a lifelong apologist for technological innovation, which can certainly be regarded as the manipulation of nature despite the fact that it was not part of his work in natural philosophy

28. See Baillie's *Introductory Discourse in British Literature: 1780–1830*, ed. Anne Mellor and Richard Matlak (San Diego: Harcourt Brace, 1996) 439–58.

29. Baillie 441. Subsequent references will appear parenthetically by page number.

30. Mary Shelley, *Frankenstein*, ed. Maurice Hindle (London: Penguin). This is the 1831 rather than 1818 edition. Subequent references will appear parenthetically by page number.

31. Sarah Stickney Ellis, *The Daughters of England* (London: Fisher, 1842) 1, and *The Women of England* (London: Fisher, 1838). Ellis's other advice books include *The Mothers of England* (London: Fisher, 1843) and *The Wives of England* (London: Fisher, 1844). Ellis wrote and published thirty-four books in her lifetime, with one title, *The Brewer's Son* (1881), appearing posthumously. All subsequent citations of *Daughters* will appear parenthetically by page number. When Ellis died in 1872, she all but disappeared from English cultural dialogue. As founding editor of *The Dictionary of National Biography*, first published in 1882, Leslie Stephen did much to contribute to Mrs. Ellis' status as a minor figure in English letters. Regardless of the description of Sarah's work by the *DNB*'s contributor as attesting to "the variety of her accomplishments and her great literary activity," Stephen subsumed Sarah within the entry of William Ellis, her missionary husband. Subsequent twentieth-century accounts of Ellis have been no more generous than *DNB*'s. Three leading feminist critics of nineteenth-century literature—Sandra Gilbert, Susan Gubar, and Elaine Showalter—variously dismiss Ellis for what they consider to be her extreme conservatism with regard to "women's mission." In *The Madwoman in the Attic* (New Haven: Yale University Press, 1984), Gilbert and Gubar describe Ellis as "that indefatigable writer of conduct books for Victorian girls" (344). Showalter, in *A Literature of Their Own* (Princeton: Princeton University Press, 1977), at least complicates the status of Mrs. Ellis to nineteenth-century letters: "Mrs. Ellis felt the binding force of the minority experience for women strongly enough to hint, in the prefaces to her widely read treatises on English womanhood, that her female audience would both read the message between her lines and refrain from betraying what they deciphered" (16).

32. Ellis 109. All subsequent references to *The Daughters of England* will be cited parenthetically by page number.

33. That women artists would be limited to what the Victorians called the "homely" sphere of art makes historical sense, for the virtually all-male British academy had, by the late eighteenth century, banned women from learning to draw nudes. The Royal Academy decision effectively excluded women from painting in the high heroic style favored by Victorian classical-subject painters such as William Etty, G. F. Watts, and Frederic Leighton and also prevented them from acquiring aesthetic eyes that focused upon the nude human figure. This exclusion from seeing nudes made it difficult for women artists to paint anything but domestic subjects and, occasionally, landscapes.

34. Over the years *Adam Bede* represents, the Methodist Church forbade women from public preaching, and in this respect Eliot's novel is true to history. Seth Bede resents Dinah's public silence but she quietly agrees with Adam that ending her preaching days is for the best.

35. Perhaps at this point we should remind ourselves that Eliot's self-conscious models for narrative vision in *Adam Bede*—the Dutch School of realist painting and John Ruskin's visual theories—also viewed the world through male eyes, albeit eyes that often focused on domestic subjects, which they desired to normalize monologically as pictorial "truth."

Chapter 3
The Descent of Sexual Selection

1. *Charles Darwin, Thomas Henry Huxley, Autobiographies*, ed. Gavin de Beer (London: Oxford University Press) 26–27.

2. A sampling of the most important scholarship tracing the intellectual connections between Erasmus and Charles Darwin include Desmond King-Hele, *Doctor of Revolution* and *The Essential Writings of Erasmus Darwin*, Roy Porter, "Erasmus Darwin: Doctor of Evolution?" in *History, Humanity & Evolution: Essays for John C. Greene*, ed. James R. Moore (Cambridge: Cambridge University Press, 1989) 39–69, Michael T. Ghiselin, "Two Darwins: History versus Criticism," *Journal of the History of Biology* 9 (1976): 121–32, Ralph Colp Jr. "The Relationship of Charles Darwin to the Ideas of His Grandfather, Dr. Erasmus Darwin," *Biography: An Interdisciplinary Quarterly* 9 (1986): 1–24.

3. Ghiseline calls the claim that Erasmus Darwin anticipated Charles Darwin's theory of sexual selection a "myth," but he is referring to fanciful interpretations of a passage from *Zoonomia* far afield from my argument about the power of the male visual imagination to determine procreative outcomes. The passage in questions reads: "The final cause of this contest among the males seems to be, that the strongest and most active animal should propagate the species, which should thence become improved" (503). Erasmus Darwin is here exploring something akin to what Charles called "the law of battle" rather than the visual, discriminating regime of sexual selection.

4. For a full-length critical account of Darwin's influence on fiction in an American context, see Bert Bender's *Descent of Love: Darwin and the Theory of Sexual Selection in American Fiction, 1871–1926* (Philadelphia: University of Pennsylvania Press, 1996). Bender's book does for Darwin and American literature what Gillian Beer's, George Levine's, and Sally Shuttleworth's scholarship has done for Darwin and British literature.

5. For an account of how Darwin's theory was steeped in the values of Victorian culture, see Rosemary Jann, "Darwin and the Anthropologists: Sexual Selection and Its Discontents," *Victorian Studies* 37 (1994): 287–306. To understand how Victorian biologists addressed female sexuality and its relationship to politics and culture, see "Science Corrupted: Victorian Biologists Consider 'The Woman Question' in *Journal of the History of Biology* 11 (1978): 1–55; Linda Marie Fedigan, "The Changing Role of Women in Models of Human Evolution," *Annual Review of Anthropology* 15 (1986): 25–66. To recognize how contemporary scientists reinscribe Darwin's historically constituted representation of gender and sexuality, see David Buss and Devendra Singh and Natalie Angier's response to their work. For a more general account of how Victorian science was imbricated with Victorian values, see Alan Rauch's excellent book, *Useful Knowledge: The Victorians, Morality, and the March of Intellect* (Durham: Duke University Press, 2001).

6. Charles Darwin, *The Descent of Man, and Selection in Relation to Sex* (Princeton: Princeton University Press, 1981). This edition is a facsimile of the first edition from 1871. All quotations appear parenthetically by page number, indicating either the first or second volume.

7. *More Letters of Charles Darwin: A Record of his Work in a Series of Hitherto Unpublished Letters*, ed. Francis Darwin and A. C. Seward (New York: Appleton, 1903) 2:75.

8. As Michael Ghiseline notes, "In *The Origin of Species* [Darwin] . . . insists that sexual combat is a purposeless, even harmful, result of evolution being caused by reproductive competition between members of the same species" (127).

9. *More Letters of Charles Darwin* 2:63.

10. For a wonderful critique of Darwin's theory of the aesthetic dimension of male and female sexual choice and that theory's relationship to the Victorian novel, see Ruth Bernard Yeazell's *Fictions of Modesty: Women and Courtship in the English Novel* (Chicago: University of Chicago Press, 1996). In particular, see the chapter, "Modesty and Female Choice" 219–28.

11. See especially Gould's "American Polygeny and Craniometry before Darwin: Blacks and Indians as Separate, Inferior Species," in *The Mismeasure of Man* (New York: Norton, 1993) 30–72.

12. John Stuart Mill, *The Subjection of Women* (New York: Appleton, 1869).

13. Gamble's feminism first manifested itself in 1869 in her support of the suffrage movement for American women. In 1870 she joined a Michigan state

suffrage organization, in which she held an executive position. She went on to a career in journalism and wrote articles in support of women's suffrage in several leading national newspapers, including the *St. Paul Pioneer Press*, the *Minneapolis Tribune*, the *Detroit Free Press*, the *Saginaw Courier*, the *New York Sun*, and the *New York Evening Post*. Gamble eventually became disillusioned with the suffrage movement, concluding that suffrage alone could not cure the ills suffered by women. She eventually researched the underlying causes of the disparities between the sexes. In this capacity she wrote three books, *The Evolution of Woman* (1894), *Theosophy, or Religion Old and New* (1895), and *The God Idea of the Ancients* (1897). For more on Gamble, see Rosemary Jann's "Revising the Descent of Woman," in *Natural Eloquence: Women Reinscribe Science*, ed. Barbara T. Gates and Ann B. Shteir (Madison: University of Wisconsin Press, 1997) 147–63.

14. See Antoinette Brown Blackwell's *The Sexes throughout Nature* (New York: Putnam's, 1875).

15. For the classic account of the controversy Darwin's theories stirred see William Irvine's *Angels, Apes and Victorians: The Story of Darwin, Huxley and Evolution* (New York: McGraw-Hill, 1955), as well as Adrian Desmond and James Moore's magisterial biography, *Darwin* (London: Joseph, 1991). For more on Victorian scientific culture and its relationship to Victorian popular culture, see Gillian Beer, "Forging the Missing Link: Interdisciplinary Stories," inaugural lecture at Cambridge University, November 18, 1991.

16. By far the best and most comprehensive study of *Punch*'s influence in the nineteenth century is Richard Altick's recent *Punch: The Lively Youth of a British Institution, 1841–1851* (Columbus: Ohio State University Press, 1997). Although Altick only concentrates on the first decade of *Punch*'s existence, his account of the periodical's early years is illustrative of the impact it had on Victorian life. As Altick writes, "Never in the history of English journalism had a new periodical, least of all a threepenny comic paper, been so much talked about. To judge from the number of references to it in the private letters and memoirs of the 1840s, as well as the evidence we have already noticed, *Punch* had become a household word within a year or two of its founding, beginning in the middle class and soon reaching the pinnacle of society, royalty itself" (17). *Punch*'s popularity proceeded unabated through the Victorian years.

17. Janet Murray's introduction to the section on "fallen" Victorian women in *Strong Minded Women and Other Lost Voices from Nineteenth-Century England* (Hammondsworth, Middlesex: Penguin, 1984) explains how the gaze of prostitutes was encoded into contemporary illustrations: "The gulf between their bold and exposed demeanor and that of 'respectable' women, privileged and poor, is apparent in contemporary illustrations in which a prostitute is immediately recognizable by her direct gaze or uncovered head" (388).

18. My analysis of Humphry's conception of women walking in public spaces concurs with Deborah Epstein Nord's thesis about the *flâneuse* being a problematic sexual figure in the nineteenth-century European metropolis. In her

chapter on Flora Tristan's *Promenades dans Londres* (1840, 1842) in *Walking the Victorian Streets*, Epstein Nord observes, "When, as in the case of Tristan, the ostensibly respectable woman assumes the role of urban spectator, she pushes the boundaries of those spaces of femininity which she can navigate with equanimity. Trespassing into those spaces of masculinity in which the male artist holds sway and in which she finds no conceivable niche, she is unwittingly thrust into the position of whore" (118).

19. For a good account of how Victorian and Edwardian women won the right to compete in sports, see Kathleen E. McCrone's *Sport and the Physical Emancipation of English Women 1870–1914* (London: Routledge, 1988). McCrone discusses the advent of women's sports at Oxbridge, which *Punch* explores in its illustrations.

20. For Leighton's extended statement of his aesthetic indebtedness to classicism, see his collected presidential addresses to the Royal Academy, published just after his death, *Lord Leighton's Addresses* (London: Kegan Paul, 1896).

21. Burne-Jones completed five paintings in the Perseus-Medusa series, including *The Call of Perseus* (1877), *The Arming of Perseus* (1877), *The Finding of Medusa* (1882), *The Death of Medusa* (1882), *The Baleful Head* (1886–87), and *Perseus and the Graiae* (1892). The series was commissioned for the future Tory prime minister, Arthur Balfour, another interesting connection between classical-subject painting and conservative politics.

22. Joseph Kestner, *Mythology and Misogyny: The Social Discourse of Nineteenth-Century British Classical-Subject Painting* (Madison: University of Wisconsin Press, 1988).

23. Kestner 14. Nina Auerbach, *Woman and the Demon: The Life of a Victorian Myth* (Cambridge: Harvard University Press, 1982).

24. Susan Casteras, in *Images of Victorian Womanhood in English Art* (Rutherford, NJ: Fairleigh Dickinson University Press, 1987), also explores the cultural implications of the proliferation of sleeping representations of women in the period.

25. Leighton wrote, "Now I want you to ask Mrs. Mary something for me—there is at this moment a movement in contemplation in which many well known women take an active interest. . . . which opposes itself to the attempt to obtain the *suffrage* for women—thereby drawing them out of the natural sphere in which they exercise such enormous and beneficial influence" (148). The appeal had already been signed by the likes of Beatrix Potter, Mrs. Leslie Stephen (Virginia Woolf's mother), Mrs. Poynter, Mrs. Alma-Tadema, and Mrs. Matthew Arnold. Kestner 147.

26. Mary Poovey, *Uneven Developments: The Ideological Work of Gender in Mid-Victorian England* (Chicago: University of Chicago Press, 1988).

27. See Rita Tulberg-McWilliams, "Women and Degrees at Cambridge University, 1862–67," in *A Widening Sphere: Changing Roles of Victorian Women*, ed. Martha Vicinius (Bloomington: Indiana University Press, 1977) 117–45.

28. Alumnae of Girton and Newnham were awarded "certificates of degrees," which amounted to pieces of paper with no official title of degree. Tulberg-McWilliams 117.

29. Tulberg-McWilliams 141.

30. Tulberg-McWilliams writes, "The defeat was interpreted for students as having fine character-forming properties, but the women's leaders were privately shocked at the crude antifeminism the campaign had revealed, particularly in its final stages" (143).

31. Tulberg-McWilliams 143.

32. For a full discussion of Mary Richardson's act of artistic violence, see Lynda Nead's *The Female Nude: Art, Obscenity and Sexuality* (London: Routledge, 1992).

33. Richardson wrote in a letter published in the *Times* on the day after her arrest, "I have tried to destroy the picture of the most beautiful woman in mythological history as a protest against the Government for destroying Mrs. Pankhurst, who is the most beautiful character in modern history" (quoted in Kestner 9). Both Leighton and Moore, in good classical-subject fashion, painted their own conventional versions of Venus in the 1860s and 1870s.

34. *The Story of an African Farm* (London: Penguin, 1995) 66. All subsequent citations appear parenthetically by page number.

35. Writing to Havelock Ellis in 1884, Schreiner asked a favor: "Please find out for me whether the picture of the horned beetle is in Darwin's "Descent of man" [sic]or "Variations of Plants&c." I make Rebekah [of *From Man to Man*] say in "Descent of Man." See *My Other Self: The Letters of Olive Schreiner and Havelock Ellis, 1884–1920* (New York: Lang, 1992) 229.

36. For the most authoritative exploration of these themes in Schreiner, see Carolyn Burdett's excellent *Olive Schreiner and the Progress of Feminism: Evolution, Gender, Empire* (London: Palgrave, 2001) 1–85, as well as Ruth First and Ann Scott's standard biography, *Olive Schreiner* (New Brunswick: Rutgers University Press, 1990) 82–107.

37. For more on the relationship between feminism and racism in *The Story of an African Farm*, see Laura Chrisman, "Empire, 'Race' and Feminism at the fin de siécle: The Work of George Egerton and Olive Schreiner," in *Cultural Politics at the Fin de Siécle,* ed. Sally Ledger and Scott McCracken (Cambridge: Cambridge University Press, 1995) 45–65, Cherry Clayton, "Women Writers and the Law of the Father: Race and Gender in the Fiction of Olive Schreiner, Pauline Smith and Sarah Gertrude Millin," *English Academy Review* 7 (1990): 99–117, and "Olive Schreiner and Katherine Mansfield: Artistic Transformations and the Outcast Figure by Two Colonial Women Writers," in *Short Fiction in the New Literatures in English* (Nice: Faculty des Lettres & Sciences Humaines, 1989) 31–39.

38. Nancy Paxton sees a strong influence of George Eliot on Schreiner's conception of Darwinism and its negative impact on women. See "*The Story of an*

African Farm and the Dynamics of Woman-to-Woman Influence," *Texas Studies in Literature and Language*, 30 (1988): 562–82.

39. For more on Lyndall's relationship to power and Schreiner's representation of female power, see "Power, Agency, Desire: Olive Schreiner and the Pre-Modern Narrative Moment," *Narrative* 4 (1996): 124–41, and Gerald Monsman's "Olive Schreiner: Literature and the Politics of Power," *Texas Studies in Literature and Language* 30 (1988): 583–610.

40. For a good account of the number of independent women farmers in Victorian Britain see Pamela Horn's *Victorian Countrywomen* (Oxford: Blackwell, 1991). Horn documents that in 1901, of 224,000 farmers in England and Wales, fewer than 22,000 were women, most of whom were widows. As for large female landowners, in 1875, at approximately the period of *Far from the Madding Crowd*'s publication, fewer than 100 of the 1,644 individuals holding at least 3,000 acres were women.

41. Thomas Hardy, *Far from the Madding Crowd* (1873) (London: Penguin, 1978) 53. All subsequent citations will be cited parenthetically by page number.

42. Although Gabriel's initial three encounters with Bathsheba increasingly resonate with his sexual desire for her, Hardy here emphasizes Bathsheba's own sexuality; in her "glide" Bathsheba mimes a coital position, an observation further augmented by her apparent disregard for Victorian conventions of decorum exemplified in her Godiva-like lack of a riding habit and side saddle. When Bathsheba later discovers that Gabriel has witnessed what she mistakenly believed to be a private performance, her reaction corresponds to that of someone caught in a sexual indiscretion as "she appeared to feel that Gabriel's espial had made her an indecorous woman without her own connivance" (69).

43. J. Hillis Miller, *Thomas Hardy: Distance and Desire* (Cambridge: Harvard University Press, 1970). Miller is one of many critics to have approached Hardy's fiction from the point of view of the male voyeur, a pervasive figure in Hardy's Wessex. Miller points to Gabriel Oak, *The Hand of Ethelberta*'s Christopher Julian, *The Woodlanders'* Dr. Fitzpiers and Giles Winterborne, and *The Return of the Native*'s Diggory Venn as characteristic Hardy figures in this regard.

44. For Marx's account of surplus value, see *Capital*, vol. 1, trans. Ben Fowkes (New York: Vintage, 1977). For Goux's critique of surplus value see 155–58 of *Symbolic Economies*.

45. George Wotton, *Thomas Hardy: Towards a Materialist Criticism* (Totowa, NJ: Barnes and Noble, 1985) 172.

46. Eustacia Vye and Sue Bridehead are the female protagonists of *The Return of the Native* (1876) and *Jude the Obscure* (1895), respectively.

47. For Marx on the fetishization of the commodity see *Capital*, vol. 1.

48. For a full account of Goux's critique of the general equivalent, see 9–63 and 88–111 of *Symbolic Economies*.

49. Richard Carpenter, "The Mirror and the Sword: Imagery in *Far from the Madding Crowd*," *Nineteenth Century Fiction* 18 (1964): 331–45. Another good essay that takes up more directly than Carpenter's the question of gaze and gender in the novel is Judith Wittenberg's "Angles of Vision and Questions of Gender in *Far from the Madding Crowd*" in *The Centennial Review* 30 (1986): 25–40.

50. Facility with foreign languages is a signifier of social superiority for Clym in *The Return of the Native*, Grace in *The Woodlanders*, Angel in *Tess of the D'Urbervilles*, and, more ironically, Jude in *Jude the Obscure*, whose knowledge of Latin and Greek as a working-class man in Christminster marks him as a social contradiction.

51. Rosemarie Morgan has pointed to Troy's financial impotence as evidence that the novel is set *after* passage of the Married Women's Property Act of 1870, which protected the property a woman possessed prior to her marriage and thus would have granted Bathsheba legal sanction to protect her wealth from the improvident Troy. But Hardy, who sets nearly all of his novels at indistinct dates, provides some minor internal evidence that suggests that the novel's dateline in fact *predates* 1870, raising the following crucial question: how has Bathsheba remained financially in control of her marriage? Near the beginning of chapter 42, Hardy offers a brief etymology that, though linguistically instructive, suggests that Bathsheba's economic predominance over Troy continues despite the lack of any binding law: "Travellers—for the variety tourist had hardly developed into a distinct series at this date" (342). Apparently, when the novel was written and published in 1873, "tourist" had entered the Dorcester/Wessex lexicon, but had not yet done so at the time of *Far from the Madding Crowd*'s action. Assuming that "tourist" did not reach remote Dorcester during the three-year gap between the novel's publication and passage of the Married Women's Property Act, one could justify the significant inference that despite the assistance of parliamentary legislation, Bathsheba has remained in control of her wealth, even though English marital law prior to 1870 made women economically subservient to their husbands. Surprisingly, Hardy never accounts for the unorthodox economic relations between Troy and Bathsheba in any manifest way. In her appendix to *Women and Sexuality in the Novels of Thomas Hardy* (London: Routledge, 1988), Morgan investigates the internal dating of *Far from* on the basis of the Married Women's Property Act. She does not, however, use the etymology of "traveller" and "tourist" to secure her argument.

Chapter 4
Sigmund Freud, Virginia Woolf, and the Modernist Female Spectator

1. Freud, *SE* XI 284.

2. Freud, *SE* XI 285.

3. For more on the influence of Darwin on Freud, please see Lucille Ritvo, *Darwin's Influence on Freud: A Tale of Two Sciences* (New Haven: Yale

University Press, 1990), Frank Sulloway, *Freud, Biologist of the Mind: Beyond the Psychoanalytic Legend* (New York: Basic Books, 1979), Peter Gay, *Freud: A Life for Our Time* (New York: Norton, 1988), C. R. Badcock, *PsychoDarwinism: The New Synthesis of Darwin & Freud* (London: Flamingo, 1995), Adam Phillips, *Darwin's Worms* (New York: Basic Books, 2000).

4. The novel also, of course, describes a day in the life of the young English World War I veteran, Septimus Smith, who functions as a kind of shadow or parallel character to Clarissa Dalloway.

5. For more on Freud and the Bloomsbury circle see *Bloomsbury/Freud: The Letters of James and Alix Strachey 1924–25*, ed. Perry Meisel and Walter Kendrick (London: Chatto & Windus, 1986).

6. For a discussion of Woolf's relationship to psychoanalysis see Abel's *Virginia Woolf and the Fictions of Psychoanalysis* (Chicago: University of Chicago Press, 1989) 1–29. For psychoanalytic readings of Woolf's novels, see both Abel and Makiko Minow-Pinkney's *Virginia Woolf and the Problem of the Subject* (Brighton: Harvester, 1987).

7. See Strachey's *Eminent Victorians: Cardinal Manning, Florence Nightingale, Dr. Arnold, General Gordon* (1918) (Hammondsworth: Penguin, 1971), and *Elizabeth and Essex* (New York: Harcourt, Brace, 1928).

8. Quentin Bell, *Virginia Woolf: A Biography* (London: Hogarth, 1972), 2:19. Leonard Woolf was presumably familiar with the fundamental tenets of psychoanalysis, if not the theory of scopophilia/exhibitionism.

9. *A Change of Perspective: The Letters of Virginia Woolf, 1923–28*, ed. Nigel Nicolson (London: Hogarth, 1977) 134–35.

10. *The Sickle Side of the Moon: The Letters of Virginia Woolf, 1932–35*, ed. Nigel Nicholson (London: Hogarth, 1979) 36.

11. Woolf integrated some of Freud's insights into her essay "A Sketch of the Past" (1939), in *Moments of Being: Unpublished Autobiographical Writings*, ed. Jeanne Schulkind (London: Chatto &Windus, for Sussex University Press, 1976).

12. Freud, *SE* VII 156.

13. Freud's opening salvo on the gendered meanings of sado-masochism laid the groundwork for several later influential papers, including, among others, "Instincts and Their Vicissitudes," "A Child is Being Beaten," and "The Economic Problem in Masochism," not to mention perhaps his most provocative and controversial monograph, *Beyond the Pleasure Principle*, which I explore later in this chapter.

14. Freud, *SE* VII 152.

15. Freud, *SE* XVIII.

16. Freud, *SE* VII 159.

17. *To the Lighthouse* (San Diego: Harcourt Brace, 1981) 23. All subsequent references will appear parenthetically by page number. Ann Banfield ex-

plores the philosophical meanings of the kitchen table and other domestic objects in her excellent study, *The Phantom Table: Woolf, Fry, Russell and the Epistemology of Modernism* (Cambridge: Cambridge University Press, 2000). Banfield's investigation of how Woolf employs everyday objects to represent philosophical problems reaches back to the British empiricist tradition of the eighteenth century but focuses on the successors to that tradition, especially Bertrand Russell and G. E. Moore.

18. See, for instance, Berkeley's *A Treatise concerning the Principles of Human Knowledge* (1710) and *Three Dialogues between Hylas and Philonous* (1713) in *The Works of George Berkeley, Bishop of Cloyne*, 9 vols., ed. A. A. Luce (Edinburgh: Edinburgh University Press, 1949). Berkeley attempted to resolve the difficulty of the double existence by posing that the world continued to exist apart from human perception because the world was always subject to the perception of God.

19. For another interpretation of the importance of the visible in Woolf's narrative epistemology, see Emily Dalgarno's *Virginia Woolf and the Visible World* (Cambridge: Cambridge University Press, 2001). Dalgarno considers the visible in relation to Woolf's reading of classical philosophy, particularly the *Symposium* and the *Phaedrus*, which consider what we can know of the visible and invisible worlds; she also investigates how techno-scientific advances, such as progress in the technology of the camera, compelled Woolf to revisit her understanding of visual tropes.

20. Russell was duly impressed with the impregnability of Hume's skepticism. Writing in *A History of Western Philosophy* (New York: Simon & Schuster, 1972), he gives Hume his due: "David Hume (1711–76) is one of the most important among philosophers, because he developed to its logical conclusion the empirical philosophy of Locke and Berkeley, and by making it self-consistent made it incredible. He represents, in a certain sense, a dead end: in his direction, it is impossible to go further. To refute him has been, ever since he wrote, a favourite pastime among metaphysicians. For my part, I find none of their refutations convincing; nevertheless, I cannot but hope that something less sceptical than Hume's system may be discoverable" (659). For his part, Mr. Ramsay never finds a less skeptical system to overcome Hume.

21. Elsewhere in the chapter "Of Scepticism with Regard to the Senses," Hume employs the trope of his chamber to make his case against empirical reasoning. Hume writes, "When I return to my chamber after an hour's absence, I find not my fire in the same situation, in which I left it: But then I am accustom'd in other instances to see a like alteration produc'd in a like time, whether I am present or absent, near or remote. This coherence, therefore, in their changes is one of the characteristics of external objects, as well as their constancy" (195); or again, "The paper on which I write at present, is beyond my hand. The table is beyond the paper. The walls of the chamber beyond the table. And in casting my eye towards the window, I perceive a great extent of fields and buildings beyond my chamber. From all this it may be infer'd, that no other faculty is requir'd,

beside the senses, to convince us of the external existence of body" (190–91). In both of these passages, Hume relies on the closed, domestic space of the chamber to give his argument a personal, materialist specificity that it would otherwise lack were any other kind of space employed.

22. See Gillian Beer, "Hume, Stephen, and Elegy in *To the Lighthouse*," in *The Uncommon Ground: Essays on Virginia Woolf* (Edinburgh: Edinburgh University Press, 1996) 29–47.

23. See Stephen's *History of English Thought in the Eighteenth Century* (New York: Harbinger, 1962) 36. Later in the same chapter, Stephen rehearses charges against Hume's skepticism by taking up subject matter that would become the preoccupations of his daughter in *To the Lighthouse*: "Yet it is a plain fact of consciousness that we think of a table or a house as somehow existing independently of our perception of it" (39).

24. See Hinton, *The Perverse Gaze of Sympathy: Sado-Masochistic Sentiments from Clarissa to Rescue 911* (Albany: State University of New York Press, 1999). See Adam Smith, *The Theory of Moral Sentiments* (1759), ed. Knud Haakonssen (Cambridge: Cambridge University Press, 2002).

25. Hinton 54.

26. For an extensive treatment of the relationship between Virginia Woolf and Vanessa Bell, see Diane Filby Gillespie, *The Sisters' Arts: The Writing and Painting of Virginia Woolf and Vanessa Bell* (Syracuse: Syracuse University Press, 1988).

27. Auerbach's discussion of *To the Lighthouse*'s narrative technique sets the critical standard. See "The Brown Stocking," in *Mimesis: The Representation of Reality in Western Literature* (New York: Doubleday, 1957) 463–88.

28. For more on same-sex desire in the novel, see Ruth Vanita's "Bringing Buried Things to Light: Homoerotic Alliances in *To the Lighthouse*," in *Virginia Woolf: Lesbian Readings*, ed. Eileen Barrett and Patricia Cramer (New York: New York University Press, 1997) 165–79, and Lisa Weil's "Entering a Lesbian Field of Vision: *To the Lighthouse* and *Between the Acts*" 241–58 of the same volume. Applying the conceptual framework of Marilyn Frye on vision and lesbianism to the novel, Weil asserts, "As Lily moves from her marginal role in 'The Window' to 'The Lighthouse,' where she becomes the novel's central perceiver, the reader's perceptions are increasingly drawn into her field of vision. Along with Lily, the reader begins to see like a lesbian" (242).

29. Berkeley was preoccupied with the question of vision and distance for virtually his entire career. He returned to the subject on at least three occasions, in *An Essay towards a New Theory of Vision* (1709), *Alciphron: or the Minute Philosopher* (1732), and *The Theory of Vision Vindicated and Explained* (1733).

Conclusion

1. Of Woolf's interest in reading *Clarissa* (and other texts) while she composed *Mrs. Dalloway*, Quentin Bell writes, "[S]he was contemplating what she supposed must be the eightieth systematic beginning of *The Common Reader* and was modestly proposing to read *Clarissa* as well as *The Pilgrim's Progress*, the *Medea* and Plato" (105).

2. For Epstein Nord's discussion of Clarissa Dalloway as a *flâneuse*, see *Walking the Victorian Streets: Women, Representation, and the City* (Ithaca: Cornell University Press, 1995).

3. Epstein Nord includes a wonderful discussion of Woolf's *Pargiters*, in which Woolf articulates the utter impossibility of a woman walking alone in certain morally questionable sections of Victorian London and retaining her respectability. See *Walking the Victorian Streets* 244–48.

4. Virginia Woolf, *Mrs. Dalloway* (1925) (New York: Harcourt Brace Jovanovich, 1953) 15. All citations will appear parenthetically by page number. Woolf herself was fond of walking through London's streets, and her delight in this activity is demonstrated in her essay "Street Haunting: A London Adventure," in *Collected Essays*, 4 vols. (London: Hogarth, 1966–67) 4:155–66. "Street Haunting" shows Woolf to have been something of a *flâneuse* herself.

5. In *Virginia Woolf and London: The Sexual Politics of the City* (Chapel Hill: University of North Carolina Press, 1985) 91–121, Susan Squier explores the effect of the urban landscape on the consciousnesses of the novel's three primary characters, Clarissa, Peter Walsh, and Septimus Smith. Squier's interpretation of the novel in terms of its representation of London is outstanding.

6. See Rich's "Compulsory Heterosexuality and Lesbian Existence," Abel and Abel, 139–68.

7. Mary Louise Pratt, *Imperial Eyes: Travel Writing and Transculturation* (New York: Routledge, 1992). Pratt and others have, in my view, focused too narrowly on the seeing man of empire, underestimating the power of the seeing woman in the formation and perpetuation of British imperialism. In *Discourses of Difference: An Analysis of Women's Travel Writing and Colonialism* (London: Routledge, 1991), Sara Mills concurs, arguing that "[m]ost studies which consider women and imperialism consist of descriptions of 'native' and British women as objects of the male gaze or male protection within colonial texts" (16).

Bibliography

Primary Sources

Austen, Jane. *Pride and Prejudice* (1813). Ed. Tony Tanner. London: Penguin, 1966.

———. *Emma* (1816). Ed. Ronald Blythe. London: Penguin, 1966.

Bacon, Francis. *New Atlantis and the Great Instauration*. Ed. Jerry Weinberger. Wheeling, IL: Harlan Davidson, 1989.

Behn, Aphra. *Love Letters between a Nobleman and His Sister* (1684–87). London: Virago, 1987.

Berkeley, George. *The Works of George Berkeley, Bishop of Cloyne*. 9 vols. Ed. A. A. Luce. Edinburgh: Edinburgh University Press, 1949.

Birch, Thomas. "The Life of Mrs. Cockburn." *The Works of Mrs. Catharine Cockburn, Theological, Moral, Dramatic, and Poetical, Several of them now first printed, Revised and published, With an Account of the Life of the Author*. London: Knapton, 1751: I: i–xlviii.

Bold, Samuel. *The Life of Mrs. Catharine Cockburn*. London, 1751.

Broughton, John. *Psychologia*. London, 1703.

Brown, Thomas. *Observations on the Zoonomia of Erasmus Darwin*. Edinburgh, 1797.

Brown Blackwell, Antoinette. *The Sexes throughout Nature*. New York: Putnam's, 1875.

Browning, Robert. *The Poems of Robert Browning*. Ed. John Woolford and Daniel Karlin. London: Longman, 1991.

Burnet, Thomas. *Telluris Theoria Sacra or Sacred Theory of the Earth*. London, 1681.

———. *Archaelogiae Philosophicae: Sive Doctrina antiqua de Rerum Originibus*. London, 1692.

Burney, Fanny. *Evelina* (1778). Ed. Edward A. Bloom. Oxford: Oxford University Press, 1982.

———. *Cecilia* (1782). Ed. Peter Sabor and Margaret Anne Doody. Oxford: Oxford University Press, 1988.

Canning, George, Hookham Frere, and George Ellis. "The Loves of the Triangles," *The Anti-Jacobin*. 1798.

Cleland, John. *Memoirs of a Woman of Pleasure* (1748–49). Oxford: Oxford University Press, 1985.

Coleridge, Samuel Taylor. *Biographia Literaria*. New York: Leavitt, Lord, 1834.

———. *Collected Letters*. 6 vols. Ed. Earl Leslie Griggs. Oxford: Clarendon, 1956.

———, and William Wordsworth. *Lyrical Ballads*. (1798) Ed. W. J. B. Owen. London: Oxford University Press, 1969.

Collier, Jeremy. *A Short View of the Immorality, and Profaneness of the English Stage, Together with the Sense of Antiquity upon this Argument*. London, 1698.

———. *A Defence of the Short View of the Profaneness and Immorality of the English Stage, etc. Being a Reply to Mr. Congreve's Amendments, etc. And to the Vindication of the Author of the Relapse*. London, 1699.

———. *A Second Defence of the Short View of the Prophaneness and Immorality of the English Stage, etc. Being a Reply to a Book, Entitled, The Ancient and Modern Stages Surveyed*. London, 1700.

———. *A Disuasive from the Play-House; In A Letter to a Person of Quality, Occasion'd By the late Calamity of the Tempest*. London, 1703.

———. *A Farther Vindication of the Short View of the Profaneness and Immorality of the English Stage. In which the Objections Of a late Book, Entitled,* A Defence of Plays, *are Consider'd*. London, 1708.

Congreve, William. *Amendments of Mr. Collier's False and Imperfect Citations etc. From the Old Batchelour, Double Dealer, Love for Love, Mourning Bride. By the Author of those Plays*. London, 1698.

———. *Letters and Documents*. Ed. John C. Hodges. New York: Harcourt Brace, 1964.

———. *The Complete Plays of William Congreve*. Ed. Herbert Davis. Chicago: University of Chicago Press, 1967.

Darwin, Charles. *The Origin of Species* (1859). Harmondsworth: Pelican, 1968.

———. *The Descent of Man, and Selection in Relation to Sex* (1871). Princeton: Princeton University Press, 1981.

———. *The Expression of the Emotions in Man and Animals* (1872). Chicago: University of Chicago Press, 1965.

———, and Thomas Henry Huxley. *Charles Darwin, Thomas Henry Huxley, Autobiographies*. Ed. Gavin de Beer. London: Oxford University Press, 1974.

———. *More Letters of Charles Darwin: A Record of his Work in a Series of Hitherto Unpublished Letters*. Ed. Francis Darwin and A. C. Seward. New York: Appleton, 1903.

Darwin, Erasmus. *Zoonomia; or, The Laws of Organic Life*. 2 vols. New York: AMS Press, 1974, reprt.

———. *A Plan for the Conduct of Female Education*. London: Drewry, 1797.

———. *The Essential Writings of Erasmus Darwin*. Ed. Desmond King-Hele. London: Macgibbon & Kee, 1968.

Defoe, Daniel. *Moll Flanders* (1722). London: Penguin, 1978.

Dryden, John. "Poetical Epistle to Peter Motteux on his Tragedy Called *Beauty in Distress*." London, 1698.

Edgeworth, Maria. *Belinda* (1801). Oxford: Oxford University Press, 1994.

Eliot, George. *Adam Bede* (1859). New York: Signet, 1963.

———. *The Essays of George Eliot*. Ed. Thomas Pinney. London: Routledge, 1963.

———. *Selections from George Eliot's Letters*. Ed. Gordon Haight. New Haven: Yale University Press, 1985.

———. *George Eliot: Selected Essays, Poems and Other Writings*. Ed. A. S. Byatt and Nicholas Warren. London: Penguin, 1990.

Ellis, Sarah Stickney. *The Women of England*. London: Fisher, 1838.

———. *The Daughters of England*. London: Fisher, 1842.

———. *The Mothers of England*. London: Fisher, 1843.

———. *The Wives of England*. London: Fisher, 1844.

Freud, Sigmund. *The Standard Edition of the Complete Psychological Works of Sigmund Freud*. 24 vols. Ed. James Strachey. London: Hogarth, 1953–74.

Galen. *On the Usefulness of the Parts of the Body*. Trans. Margaret May. Ithaca: Cornell University Press, 1968.

Gamble, Eliza. *The Evolution of Woman*. New York: Putnam's, 1894.

Gildon, Charles. *The Plays of Charles Gildon*. Ed. Paula R. Backscheider. New York: Garland, 1979.

Hardy, Thomas. *Far from the Madding Crowd* (1873). Ed. Ronald Blythe. Middlesex: Penguin, 1978.

Haywood, Eliza. *Fantomina: Or, Love in a Maze* (1725). *Popular Fiction by Women 1660–1730*. Ed. Paula R. Backscheider and John Richetti. Oxford: Oxford University Press, 1996.

———. *The Female Spectator*. London: Gardner, 1744–46.

———. *The Invisible Spy*. London: Gardner, 1749.

———. *Miss Betsy Thoughtless* (1751). London: Pandora, 1986.

Hume, David. *A Treatise on Human Nature* (1739). Ed. L. A. Selby-Bigge. Oxford: Oxford University Press, 1928.

Keats, John. *The Letters of John Keats.* 2 vols. Ed. M. B. Forman. Oxford: Oxford University Press, 1931.

Lee, Henry. *Anti-Scepticism.* London, 1702.

Leighton, Frederic. *Lord Leighton's Addresses.* London: Kegan Paul, 1896.

Locke, John. *The Correspondence of John Locke.* 8 vols. Ed. E. S. DeBeer. Oxford: Clarendon, 1982.

Locke, John. *An Essay Concerning Human Understanding* (1690). Ed. P. H. Nidditch. Oxford: Oxford University Press, 1975.

———. *Two Treatises of Government* (1689 and 1690). Cambridge: Cambridge University Press, 1960.

Manley, Delariviere. *The Novels of Mary Delariviere Manley.* 2 vols. Ed. Patricia Koster. Gainesville: Scholars' Facsimiles & Reprints, 1971.

Mill, John Stuart. *The Subjection of Women.* New York: Appleton, 1869.

Newton, Isaac. *Opticks: Or, a Treatise of the Reflexions, Refractions, Inflexions and Colours of Light* (1704). New York: Dover, 1952.

Norris, John. *Theory of the Ideal or Intelligible World.* London, 1701–04.

Patmore, Coventry. *The Angel in the House.* London: Parker, 1858.

Punch. London: Punch, 1841–1993.

Richardson, Samuel. *Pamela* (1740). Ed. Peter Sabor. London: Penguin, 1980.

———. *Pamela Volume Two* (1742). London: Dent and Sons, 1942.

———. *Clarissa* (1747–48). London: Penguin, 1985.

———. *The History of Sir Charles Grandison* (1753–54). 3 vols. Ed. Joselyn Harris. London: Oxford University Press, 1972.

Rossetti, Christina. *The Poetical Works of Christina Georgina Rossetti.* London: Macmillan, 1914.

Ruskin, John. *Sesame and Lilies: Two Lectures Delivered at Manchester in 1864.* London: Smith, Elder, 1865.

Schreiner, Olive. *The Story of an African Farm* (1883). London: Penguin, 1995.

———, and Havelock Ellis. *My Other Self: The Letters of Olive Schreiner and Havelock Ellis, 1884–1920.* Ed. Claire Yaffa Draznin. New York: Peter Lang, 1992.

Sergeant, John. *Solid Philosophy Asserted Against the Fancies of the Ideists.* London, 1697.

Shelley, Mary. *Frankenstein, or, the Modern Prometheus* (1818). Ed. Maurice Hindle. London: Penguin, 1992.

Smith, Adam. *The Theory of Moral Sentiments* (1759). Ed. Knud Haakonssen. Cambridge: Cambridge University Press, 2002.

Southey, Robert. "Review of *Lyrical Ballads*." *The Critical Review* 24 (1798): 197–204.

Stephen, Leslie. *History of English Thought in the Eighteenth Century* (1876). 2 vols. New York: Harcourt Brace, 1962.

———. *George Eliot*. London: Macmillan, 1902.

———, and Sidney Lee, eds. *The Dictionary of National Biography*. 22 vols. London: Oxford University Press, 1967–68.

Strachey, Lytton. *Eminent Victorians: Cardinal Manning, Florence Nightingale, Dr. Arnold, General Gordon* (1918). Hammondsworth: Penguin, 1971.

———. *Elizabeth and Essex: A Tragic History*. New York: Harcourt, Brace, 1928.

Tennyson, Alfred. *The Princess*. London: Moxon, 1847.

Trotter, Catherine. *Agnes de Castro, A Tragedy*. London: Printed for H. Rhodes, R. Parker & S. Briscoe, 1696.

———. *Fatal Friendship: A Tragedy*. London: Printed for Francis Saunders, 1698.

———. *Love at a Loss, or, Most Votes Carry It: A Comedy*. London: Printed for William Turner, 1701.

———. *The Unhappy Penitent: A Tragedy*. London: Printed for William Turner & John Nutt, 1701.

———. *A Defence of Mr. Lock's Essay of Human Understanding, Wherein its Principles with reference to Morality, Reveal'd Religion, and the Immorality of the Soul, are Consider'd and Justify'd: In Answer to Some Remarks on that Essay*. London: Printed for Will. Turner & John Nutt, 1702.

———. *The Revolution of Sweden: A Tragedy*. London: Printed for James Knapton & George Strahan, 1706.

———. *The Works of Mrs. Catharine Cockburn, Theological, Moral, Dramatic, and Poetical, Several of them now first printed, Revised and published, With an Account of the Life of the Author*. London: Printed for J & P Knapton, 1751.

———. *Olinda's Adventures: Or the Amours of a Young Lady* (1693). Augustan Reprint Society Publication Publication Number 138. Los Angeles: William Andrews Clark Memorial Library, University of California: 1969.

Vanbrugh, John. *The Complete Works of Sir John Vanbrugh*. Ed. Bonamy Dobrée and Geoffrey Webb. 4 vols. London: Nonesuch, 1927–28.

Wilkes, Wetenhall. *A Letter of Genteel and Moral Advice to a Young Lady.* London: Cooper, 1744.

Woodward, Josiah. *Some Thoughts Concerning the Stage in a Letter to a Lady.* London: Nutt, 1704.

———, and Jeremy Collier. *A Letter to a Lady Concerning the New Play House.* London, 1706.

Woolf, Virginia. *Mrs. Dalloway* (1925). New York: Harcourt Brace Jovanovich, 1953.

———. *To the Lighthouse* (1927). San Diego: Harcourt Brace, 1981.

———. *Collected Essays.* 4 vols. London: Hogarth, 1966–67.

———. *Moments of Being: Unpublished Autobiographical Writings.* Ed. Jeanne Schulkind. London: Chatto & Windus, for Sussex University Press, 1976.

———. *The Letters of Virginia Woolf.* 5 vols. Ed. Nigel Nicolson. London: Hogarth, 1977.

Wordsworth, Dorothy. *Journals: The Alfoxden Journal, 1798; The Grasmere Journal 1800–1803.* Ed. Helen Darbishire. London: Oxford University Press, 1958.

Wordsworth, William. *The Prelude.* Ed. M. H. Abrams, Johnathan Wordsworth, and Stephen Gill. New York: Norton, 1979.

Wordsworth, William, and Dorothy Wordsworth. *The Letters of William and Dorothy Wordsworth 1787–1805.* Ed. Ernest De Selincourt. Oxford: Clarendon, 1967.

The Young Lady's Pocket Library, or Parental Monitor. Dublin: Archer, 1790.

Secondary Sources

Abel, Elizabeth. *Virginia Woolf and the Fictions of Psychoanalysis.* Chicago: University of Chicago Press, 1984.

Abrams, M. H. *Natural Supernaturalism: Tradition and Revolution in Romantic Literature.* New York: Norton, 1971.

Altick, Richard. *Punch: The Lively Youth of a British Institution, 1841–1851.* Columbus: Ohio State University Press, 1997.

Annan, Noel. *Leslie Stephen: The Godless Victorian.* London: Weidenfeld & Nicolson, 1984.

Anthony, Sister Rose. *The Jeremy Collier Stage Controversy 1698–1726.* Milwaukee: Marquette University Press, 1937.

Aristotle. *The Complete Works of Aristotle.* Trans. A. Platt. Ed. J. Barnes. Princeton: Princeton University Press, 1984.

Armstrong, Nancy. *Desire and Domestic Fiction: A Political History of the Novel*. Oxford: Oxford University Press, 1987.

———. "The Rise of Feminine Authority in the Novel." *Why the Novel Matters: A Postmodern Perplex*. Ed. Mark Spilka and Caroline McCracken-Flesher. Bloomington: Indiana University Press, 1990: 94–112.

———, and Leonard Tennenhouse, eds. *The Ideology of Conduct: Essays on Literature and the History of Sexuality*. New York: Methuen, 1987.

Auerbach, Eric. *Mimesis: The Representation of Reality in Western Literature*. Trans. Willard Trask. New York: Doubleday, 1957.

Auerbach, Nina. *Woman and the Demon: The Life of a Victorian Myth*. Cambridge: Harvard University Press, 1982.

Averill, James. "Wordsworth and 'Natural Science': The Poetry of 1798." *The Journal of English and Germanic Philology* 77 (1978): 232–46.

Badcock, C. R. *PsychoDarwinism: The New Synthesis of Darwin and Freud*. London: Flamingo, 1995.

Bakan, David. *Sigmund Freud and the Jewish Mystical Tradition*. London: Free Association, 1990.

Bakhtin, M. M. *The Dialogic Imagination*. Trans. Caryl Emerson and Michael Holquist. Ed. Michael Holquist. Austin: University of Texas Press, 1981.

Ballaster, Ros. *Seductive Forms: Women's Amatory Fiction from 1684 to 1740*. Oxford: Oxford University Press, 1992.

Banfield, Ann. *The Phantom Table: Woolf, Fry, Russell and the Epistemology of Modernism*. Cambridge: Cambridge University Press, 2000.

Barrell, John. "The Uses of Dorothy: 'The Language of the Sense' in 'Tintern Abbey.'" *Poetry, Language, and Politics*. New York: St. Martin's, 1988: 137–67.

Barrett, Eileen, and Patricia Cramer, eds. *Virginia Woolf: Lesbian Readings*. New York: New York University Press, 1997.

Baudelaire, Charles. *The Painter of Modern Life and Other Essays*. Trans. and ed. Jonathan Mayne. London: Phaidon, 1964.

Beer, Gillian. *Darwin's Plots: Evolutionary Narrative in Darwin, George Eliot and Nineteenth-Century Fiction*. London: Routledge, 1983.

———. *George Eliot*. Brighton: Harvester, 1986.

———. "Forging the Missing Link: Interdisciplinary Stories." Inaugural Lecture at Cambridge University, November 18, 1991.

———. *Virginia Woolf: The Common Ground*. Edinburgh: Edinburgh University Press, 1996.

Bell, Quentin. *Virginia Woolf: A Biography*. 2 vols. London: Hogarth, 1972.

Bender, Bert. *The Descent of Love: Darwin and the Theory of Sexual Selection in American Fiction, 1871–1926*. Philadelphia: University of Pennsylvania Press, 1996.

Benjamin, Walter. *Charles Baudelaire: A Lyric Poet in the Era of High Capitalism*. London: New Left Books, 1973.

Berger, John. *Ways of Seeing*. London: Penguin, 1972.

Bewell, Alan. *Wordsworth and the Enlightenment: Nature, Man, and Society in the Experimental Poetry*. New Haven: Yale University Press, 1989.

Blake, Kathleen. *Love and the Woman Question in Victorian Literature*. Totowa, NJ: Barnes & Noble, 1983.

Bloom, Harold. *The Visionary Company: A Reading of English Romantic Poetry*. Ithaca: Cornell University Press, 1961.

Borch-Jacobsen, Mikkel. *Lacan: The Absolute Master*. Trans. Douglas Brick. Stanford: Stanford University Press, 1991.

Boumella, Penny. *Thomas Hardy and Women*. Totowa, NJ: Barnes & Noble, 1982.

Bowers, Toni O'Shaugnessy. "Sex, Lies, and Invisibility: Amatory Fiction from the Restoration to Mid-Century." *The Columbia History of the British Novel*. Ed. John Richetti. New York: Columbia University Press, 1994: 50–72.

Brand, Dana. *The Spectator and the City in Nineteenth-Century American Literature*. Cambridge: Cambridge University Press, 1991.

Bronfen, Elizabeth. *Over Her Dead Body: Death, Femininity and the Aesthetic*. New York: Routledge, 1992.

Burdett, Carolyn. *Olive Schreiner and the Progress of Feminism: Evolution, Gender, Empire*. London: Palgrave, 2001.

Burroughs, Catherine B. "English Romantic Women Writers and Theatre Theory: Joanna Baillie's Prefaces to the Plays on the Passions." *Re-Visioning Romanticism: British Women Writers, 1776–1837*. Philadelphia: University of Pennsylvania Press, 1994: 274–99.

Buss, David. "Love Acts: The Evolutionary Biology of Love." *The Psychology of Love*. Ed. Robert J. Sternberg and Michael L. Barnes. New Haven: Yale University Press, 1988: 101–18.

———. "Sex Differences In Human Mate Preferences: Evolutionary Hypotheses Tested in Thirty-seven Cultures." *Behavioral and Brain Sciences* 12 (1989): 1–14.

———. *The Evolution of Desire: Strategies of Human Mating*. New York: Basic Books, 1994.

———. *Evolutionary Psychology: The New Science of the Mind*. New York: Allyn & Bacon, 1998.

———, and Neil M. Malamuth, eds. *Sex, Power, Conflict: Evolutionary and Feminist Perspectives*. New York: Oxford University Press, 1996.

———, and D. P. Schmitt. "Sexual Strategies Theory: An Evolutionary Perspective on Human Mating." *Psychological Review* 100 (1993): 204–32.

Carlisle, Janet. *The Sense of an Audience*. Athens: University of Georgia Press, 1981.

Carpenter, Richard. "The Mirror and the Sword: Imagery in *Far from the Madding Crowd*." *Nineteenth Century Fiction* 18 (1964): 331–45.

Casey, Janet Gallignani. "Power, Agency, Desire: Olive Schreiner and the Pre-Modern Narrative Moment." *Narrative* 4 (1996): 124–41.

Casteras, Susan. *Images of Victorian Womanhood in English Art*. Rutherford, NJ: Fairleigh Dickinson University Press, 1987.

Castle, Terry. *Clarissa's Ciphers: Meaning and Disruption in Richardson's Clarissa*. Palo Alto: Stanford University Press, 1987.

Chodorow, Nancy. *The Reproduction of Mothering: Psychoanalysis and the Sociology of* Gender. Berkeley: University of California Press, 1978.

———. *Feminism and Psychoanalytic Theory*. New Haven: Yale University Press, 1989.

———. *Femininities, Masculinities, Sexualities: Freud and Beyond*. Lexington: University Press of Kentucky, 1994.

Chrisman, Laura. "Empire, 'Race' and Feminism at the Fin de Siècle: The Work of George Egerton and Olive Schreiner." *Cultural Politics at the Fin de Siècle*. Ed. Sally Ledger and Scott McCracken. Cambridge: Cambridge University Press, 1995.

Cixous, Hélène. "Sorties." *New French Feminisms*. Trans. Ann Liddle. New York: Schoeken, 1981: 90–98.

———. "The Laugh of the Medusa." *New French Feminisms*. Trans. Keith Cohen and Paula Cohen. New York: Schoeken, 1981: 245–64.

Clark, Constance. "Catherine Trotter." *Three Augustan Women Playwrights*. New York: Lang, 1986: 35–95.

Clark, Nancy. "The Female Wits: Catherine Trotter, Delariviere Manley, Mary Pix." *Women Playwrights in England: c. 1363–1750*. Lewisburg, PA: Bucknell University Press, 1980: 81–121.

Clayton, Cherry. "Olive Schreiner and Katherine Mansfield: Artistic Transformations and the Outcast Figure by Two Colonial Women Writers." *Short Fiction in the New Literatures in English*. Nice: Faculté des Lettres & Sciences Humaines, 1989: 31–39.

———. "Women Writers and the Law of the Father: Race and Gender in the Fiction of Olive Schreiner, Pauline Smith and Sarah Gertrude Millin." *English Academy Review* 7 (1990): 99–117.

Colp, Ralph, Jr. "The Relationship of Charles Darwin to the Ideas of his Grandfather, Dr. Erasmus Darwin." *Biography: An Interdisciplinary Quarterly*, 9 (1986): 1–24.

Dalgarno, Emily. *Virginia Woolf and the Visible World*. Cambridge: Cambridge University Press, 2001.

Davidoff, Leonard, and Catherine Hall. *Family Fortunes: Men and Women of the English Middle Class, 1780–1950*. Chicago: University of Chicago Press, 1987.

Davis, Lennard J. *Factual Fictions: Origins of the English Novel*. New York: Columbia University Press, 1983.

———. *Resisting Novels: Ideology and Fiction*. New York: Methuen, 1987.

Decker, Hannah. *Freud, Dora, and Vienna*. New York: Free Press, 1991.

De Lauretis, Teresa. *Alice Doesn't*. Bloomington: Indiana University Press, 1982.

———. *Technologies of Gender*. Bloomington: Indiana University Press, 1987.

———. "Film and the Visible." Paper delivered at University of Washington Comparative Literature Colloquium, 1990.

Desmond, Adrian, and James Moore. *Darwin*. London: Michael Joseph, 1991.

Diller, Jerry. *Freud's Jewish Identity: A Case Study in the Impact of Ethnicity*. Rutherford, NJ: Fairleigh Dickinson University Press, 1991.

Doane, Mary Ann. "Film and the Masquerade: Theorising the Female Spectator." *Screen* 23 (1982): 74–87.

———. *The Desire to Desire: The Women's Film of the 1940s*. Bloomington: Indiana University Press, 1987.

———. *Femmes Fatales: Feminism, Film Theory, Psychoanalysis*. New York: Routledge, 1991.

Eagleton, Terry. *The Rape of Clarissa*. Oxford: Blackwell, 1982.

Earle, Peter. *The Making of the English Middle Class: Business, Society and Family Life in London, 1660–1730*. London: Methuen, 1989.

Essick, Robert. "Gender Transgression and the Two Wordsworths in 'Tintern Abbey.'" *Texas Studies in Literature and Language* 36 (1994): 291–305.

Etcoff, Nancy. *Survival of the Prettiest: The Science of Beauty*. New York: Doubleday, 1999.

Faderman, Lillian. *Surpassing the Love of Men: Romantic Friendship and Love between Women from the Renaissance to the Present*. New York: Morrow, 1981.

Fedigan, Linda Marie. "The Changing Role of Women in Models of Human Evolution." *Annual Review of Anthropology* 15 (1986): 25–66.

First, Ruth, and Ann Scott. *Olive Schreiner*. New Brunswick: Rutgers University Press, 1980.

Flint, Kate. *The Victorians and the Visual Imagination*. Cambridge: Cambridge University Press, 2000.

Forrester, John. *Language and the Origins of Psychoanalysis*. New York: Columbia University Press, 1980.

Foster, Hal. *Vision and Visuality*. Seattle: Bay, 1988.

Foucault, Michel. *The Birth of the Clinic: An Archaeology of Medical Perception*. Trans. A. M. Sheridan Smith. New York: Vintage, 1975.

———. *History of Sexuality*, vol. 1. Trans. Robert Hurley. New York: Vintage, 1978.

———. *Discipline and Punish: The Birth of the Prison*. Trans. Alan Sheridan. New York: Vintage, 1979.

———. *Power/Knowledge: Selected Interviews and Other Writings 1972–1977*. Trans. and ed. Colin Gordon. New York: Pantheon, 1980.

Frye, Marilyn. "To See and Be Seen: The Politics of Reality." *The Politics of Reality: Essays in Feminist Theory*. Trumansburg, NY: Crossing, 1983: 152–74.

Galperin, William. *The Return of the Visible in British Romanticism*. Baltimore: Johns Hopkins University Press, 1993.

Gamman, Lorraine, and Margaret Marshment, eds. *The Female Gaze: Women as Viewers of Popular Culture*. London: Women's, 1988.

Gates, Barbara, and Ann B. Shteir. *Natural Eloquence: Women Reinscribe Science*. Madison: University of Wisconsin Press, 1997.

Gay, Peter. *Freud: A Life for our Time*. London: Dent, 1988.

Ghiselin, Michael T. "Two Darwins: History versus Criticism." *Journal of the History of Biology* 9 (1976): 121–32.

Gilbert, Sandra, and Susan Gubar. *The Madwoman in the Attic: The Woman Writer and the Nineteenth-Century Literary Imagination*. New Haven: Yale University Press, 1979.

Gill, Stephen. *Wordsworth: A Life*. Oxford: Clarendon, 1989.

———. *Wordsworth and the Victorians*. Oxford: Clarendon, 1998.

Gillespie, Diane Filby. *The Sisters' Arts: The Writing and Painting of Virginia Woolf and Vanessa Bell*. Syracuse: Syracuse University Press, 1988.

Gittings, Robert. *Young Thomas Hardy*. Harmondsworth: Penguin, 1978.

———. *The Older Hardy*. Harmondsworth: Penguin, 1980.

Gould, Stephen Jay. "American Polygeny and Craniometry before Darwin: Blacks and Indians as Separate, Inferior Species." *The Mismeasure of Man*. New York: Norton, 1993: 30–72.

Goux, Jean-Joseph. *Symbolic Economies: After Marx and Freud*. Trans. Jennifer Curtiss Gage. Ithaca: Cornell University Press, 1990.

Grontkowski, Christine R., and Evelyn Fox Keller. "The Mind's Eye." *Discovering Reality: Feminist Perspectives on Epistemology, Metaphysics, Methodology, and Philosophy of Science*. Ed. Sandra Harding and Merrill B. Hintikka. Dordrecht, Holland: Reidel, 1983: 207–24.

Grundy, Joan. *Hardy and the Sister Arts*. London: Macmillan, 1979.

Hacking, Ian. *Why Does Language Matter to Philosophy?* Cambridge: Cambridge University Press, 1975.

Haight, Gordon. *George Eliot: A Biography*. Oxford: Oxford University Press, 1968.

Harrison, Brian. *Separate Spheres: The Opposition to Women's Suffrage in Britain*. London: Helm, 1978.

Harvey, W. J. *The Art of George Eliot*. London: Chatto & Windus, 1961.

Hellinger, Benjamin, ed. *A Short View of the Immorality and Prophaneness of the English Stage by Jeremy Collier: A Critical Edition*. New York & London: Garland, 1987.

Hinton, Laura. *The Perverse Gaze of Sympathy: Sado-Masochistic Sentiments from Clarissa to Rescue 911*. Albany: State University of New York Press, 1999.

Homans, Margaret. *Bearing the Word: Language and Female Experience in Nineteenth-Century Women's Writing*. Chicago: University of Chicago Press, 1991.

Horn, Pamela. *Victorian Countrywomen*. Oxford: Blackwell, 1991.

Howe, Elizabeth. *The First English Actresses: Women and Drama, 1660–1700*. Cambridge: Cambridge University Press, 1992.

Huet, Marie Hélène. *The Monstrous Imagination*. Cambridge: Harvard University Press, 1993.

Hyde, Janet Shibley. "Where Are the Gender Differences? Where Are the Gender Similarities?" *Sex Power, Conflict: Evolutionary and Feminist Perspectives*. Ed. David Buss and Neil M. Malamuth. New York: Oxford University Press, 1996: 107–18.

Irigary, Luce. *This Sex Which Is Not One*. Trans. Catherine Porter with Carolyn Burke. Ithaca: Cornell University Press, 1985.

———. *Speculum of the Other Woman*. Trans. Gillian C. Gill. Ithaca: Cornell University Press, 1985.

Irvine, William. *Angels, Apes and Victorians: The Story of Darwin, Huxley and Evolution*. New York: McGraw-Hill, 1955.

Jaffe, Audrey. *Vanishing Points: Dickens, Narrative, and the Subject of Omniscience*. Berkeley: University of California Press, 1991.

Jann, Rosemary. "Darwin and the Anthropologists: Sexual Selection and Its Discontents." *Victorian Studies* 37 (1994): 287–306.

Jay, Martin. *Downcast Eyes: The Denigration of Vision in Twentieth-Century French Thought*. Berkeley: University of California Press, 1993.

Johnston, Kenneth. "The Politics of 'Tintern Abbey.'" *The Wordsworth Circle* 14 (1983): 6–14.

Jonas, Hans. "The Nobility of Sight." *The Phenomenon of Life: Toward a Philosophical Biology*. Chicago: University of Chicago Press, 1966: 135–56.

Jordanova, Ludmila. *Sexual Visions: Images of Gender in Science and Medicine between the Eighteenth and Twentieth Centuries*. London: Harvester, 1989.

Kaplan, E. Ann. *Women and Film: Both Sides of the Camera*. New York: Methuen, 1989.

———. *Psychoanalysis and Cinema*. New York: Routledge, 1990.

Keller, Eve. "Making Up for Losses: The Workings of Gender in William Harvey's *De generatione animalium*." *Women's Studies: An Interdisciplinary Journal* 27 (1998): 131–62.

Keller, Evelyn Fox. *Reflections on Gender and Science*. New Haven: Yale University Press, 1985.

Kelley, Theresa. *Wordsworth's Revisionary Aesthetics*. Cambridge: Cambridge University Press, 1988.

Kestner, Joseph. *Mythology and Misogyny: The Social Discourse of Nineteenth-Century British Classical-Subject Painting*. Madison: University of Wisconsin Press, 1988.

King-Hele, Desmond. *Doctor of Revolution*. London: Faber & Faber, 1977.

Klotman, Phyllis R. Klotman. "Sin and Sublimation in the Novels of Samuel Richardson." *College Language Association Journal* 20 (1976): 365–73.

Lacan, Jacques. *Écrits: A Selection*. Trans. Alan Sheridan. London, Tavistock, 1977.

———. *The Four Fundamental Concepts of Psycho-analysis*. Trans. Alan Sheridan. New York: Norton, 1977.

Levine, George. *Darwin and the Novelists: Patterns of Science in Victorian Fiction*. Cambridge: Harvard University Press, 1988.

Lloyd, Elizabeth A. "Pre-Theoretical Assumptions in Evolutionary Explanations of Female Sexuality." *Philosophical Studies* 69 (1993): 139–53.

Marks, Elaine, and Isabelle de Courtivron, eds. *New French Feminisms*. New York: Schoeken, 1981.

Marsden, Jean. "Female Spectatorship, Jeremy Collier and the Antitheatrical Debate." *ELH* 65 (1998): 877–98.

Marsh, Jan. *The Pre-Raphaelite Sisterhood*. London: Quartet, 1985.

———. *Pre-Raphaelite Women: Images of Femininity in Pre-Raphaelite Art*. London: Weidenfeld & Nicolson, 1987.

———, and Pamela Gerrish Nunn. *Women Artists and the Pre-Raphaelite Movement*. London: Virago, 1989.

Marx, Karl. *Capital,* vol 1. Trans. Ben Fowkes. New York: Vintage, 1977.

Matlak, Richard. "Wordsworth's Reading of *Zoonomia* in Early Spring." *The Wordsworth Circle* 21 (1990): 76–81.

Mayne, Judith. *The Woman at the Keyhole: Feminism and Women's Cinema*. Bloomington: Indiana University Press, 1990.

McCrone, Kathleen E. *Sport and the Physical Emancipation of English Women 1870–1914*. London: Routledge, 1988.

McGrath, William. *Freud's Discovery of Psycho-analysis: The Politics of Hysteria*. Ithaca: Cornell University Press, 1986.

McKeon, Michael. *The Origins of the English Novel 1600–1740*. Baltimore: Johns Hopkins University Press, 1987.

McNeil, Maureen. *Under the Banner of Science: Erasmus Darwin and His Age*. Manchester: Manchester University Press, 1987.

Meisel, Perry, and Walter Kendrick, eds. *Bloomsbury/Freud: The Letters of James and Alix Strachey 1924–25*. London: Chatto & Windus, 1986.

Mellor, Anne. *Mary Shelley: Her Life, Her Fiction, Her Monsters*. London: Routledge, 1989.

———, and Richard Matlak, eds. *British Literature 1780–1830*. San Diego: Harcourt Brace, 1996.

Miller, D. A. *The Novel and the Police*. Berkeley: University of California Press, 1987.

Miller, J. Hillis. *Thomas Hardy: Distance and Desire*. Cambridge: Harvard University Press, 1970.

Millgate, Michael. *Thomas Hardy: A Biography*. Oxford: Oxford University Press, 1982.

Mills, Sara. *Discourses of Difference: An Analysis of Women's Travel Writing and Colonialism*. London: Routledge, 1991.

Minow-Pinkney, Makiko. *Virginia Woolf and the Problem of the Subject*. Brighton: Harvester, 1987.

Monsman, Gerald. "Olive Schreiner: Literature and the Politics of Power." *Texas Studies in Literature and Language* 30 (1988): 583–610.

Moorman, Mary. *William Wordsworth: A Biography*. 2 vols. London: Oxford University Press, 1968.

Morgan, Fidelis. *The Female Wits: Women Playwrights on the London Stage 1660–1720*. London: Virago, 1981.

Morgan, Rosemarie. *Women and Sexuality in the Novels of Thomas Hardy*. London: Routledge, 1988.

Mosedale, Susan. "Science Corrupted: Victorian Biologists Consider 'The Woman Question.'" *Journal of the History of Biology* 11 (1978): 1–55.

Mulvey, Laura. "Visual Pleasure and Narrative Cinema." Screen 16 (1975): 6–18.

———. *Visual and Other Pleasures*. Houndmills: Macmillan, 1989.

Murray, Janet. *Strong Minded Women and Other Lost Voices from Nineteenth-Century England*. Hammondsworth, Middlesex: Penguin, 1984.

Nead, Lynda. *Myths of Sexuality: Representations of Women in Victorian England*. Oxford: Blackwell, 1988.

———. *The Female Nude: Art, Obscenity and Sexuality*. London: Routledge, 1992.

Newman, Beth. "'The Situation of the Looker-On': Gender, Narration and Gaze in *Wuthering Heights*." *PMLA* 105 (1990): 1029–41.

Nord, Deborah Epstein. *Walking the Victorian Streets: Women, Representation, and the City*. Ithaca: Cornell University Press, 1995.

Ogden, Daryl. "Bathsheba's Visual Estate: Female Spectatorship in *Far from the Madding Crowd*." *The Journal of Narrative Technique* 23 (1993): 1–16.

———. "Double Visions: Sarah Stickney Ellis, George Eliot and the Politics of Domesticity." *Women's Studies: An Interdisciplinary Journal* 25 (1996) 585–602.

———. "Richardson's Narrative Space-Off: Freud, Vision, and the (Heterosexual) Problem of Reading *Clarissa*." *Literature and Psychology* 42 (1996): 37–52.

O'Shaugnessy Bowers, Toni. "Sex, Lies, and Invisibility: Amatory Fiction from the Restoration to Mid-Century." *The Columbia History of the British Novel*. Ed. John Richetti. New York: Columbia University Press, 1994: 50–72.

Page, Judith. *Wordsworth and the Cultivation of Women*. Berkeley: University of California Press, 1994.

Parker, Roszika, and Griselda Pollock. *Old Mistresses: Women, Art and Ideology*. London: Routledge, 1981.

Paxton, Nancy. "*The Story of an African Farm* and the Dynamics of Woman-to-Woman Influence." *Texas Studies in Literature and Language* 30 (1988): 562–82.

Penley, Constance. *The Future of an Illusion: Film, Feminism and Psychoanalysis*. Minneapolis: University of Minnesota Press, 1989.

Phillips, Adam. *Darwin's Worms*. New York: Basic Books, 2000.

Pollock, Griselda. *Vision and Difference*. London: Routledge, 1988.

Poovey, Mary. *Uneven Developments: The Ideological Work of Gender in Mid-Victorian England*. Chicago: University of Chicago Press, 1988.

Porter, Roy. "Erasmus Darwin: Doctor of Evolution?" *History, Humanity, and Evolution: Essays for John C. Greene*. Ed. James R. Moore. Cambridge: Cambridge University Press, 1989: 39–69.

Pratt, Mary Louise. *Imperial Eyes: Travel Writing and Transculturation*. New York: Routledge, 1992.

Praz, Mario. *The Hero in Eclipse in Victorian Fiction*. Trans. Angus Davidson. Oxford: Oxford University Press, 1956.

Rauch, Alan. *Useful Knowledge: The Victorians, Morality, and the March of Intellect*. Durham: Duke University Press, 2001.

Rich, Adrienne. "Compulsory Heterosexuality and Lesbian Existence." Abel and Abel: 139–68.

Richetti, John. *Popular Fiction before Richardson: Narrative Patterns 1700–1739*. Oxford: Oxford University Press, 1992.

Rignall, John. "Benjamin's *Flâneur* and the Problem of Realism." *The Problems of Modernity: Adorno and Benjamin*. Ed. A. E. Benjamin. London: Routledge, 1989: 14–19.

Ritvo, Lucille B. *Darwin's Influence on Freud: A Tale of Two Sciences*. New Haven: Yale University Press, 1990.

Robert, Marthe. *From Oedipus to Moses: Freud's Jewish Identity*. Trans. Ralph Manheim. New York: Methuen, 1976.

Rorty, Richard. *Philosophy and the Mirror of Nature*. Princeton: Princeton University Press, 1979.

Rose, Jacqueline. *Sexuality in the Field of Vision*. Thetford: Thetford, 1986.

Rose, Phyllis. *Woman of Letters: A Life of Virginia Woolf*. London: Routledge, 1978.

Russell, Bertrand. *A History of Western Philosophy*. New York: Simon & Schuster, 1972.

Sartre, Jean-Paul. *Being and Nothingness*. New York: Washington Square, 1966.

Schiebinger, Londa. *The Mind Has No Sex? Women in the Origins of Modern Science*. Cambridge: Harvard University Press, 1989.

Shevelow, Kathryn. *Women and Print Culture: The Construction of Femininity in the Early Periodical*. London: Routledge, 1989.

Showalter, Elaine. *A Literature of Their Own: British Women Novelists from Bronte to Lessing*. Princeton: Princeton University Press, 1977.

Shuttleworth, Sally. *George Eliot and Nineteenth-Century Science: The Make-Believe of a Beginning*. Cambridge: Cambridge University Press, 1984.

Singh, Devandra. "Adaptive Significance of Female Physical Attractiveness: Role of Waist-to-Hip Ratio." *Journal of Personality and Social Psychology* 65 (1993): 293–307.

———. "Female Judgment of Male Attractiveness and Desirability for Relationships: Role of Waist-to-Hip Ratio and Financial Status." *Journal of Personality and Social Psychology* 69 (1995): 1089.

———, and R. K. Young. "Body Weight, Waist-to-Hip Ratio, Breasts, and Hips: Role in Judgments of Female Attractiveness and Desirability for Relationships." *Ethology and Sociobiology* 16 (1995): 483–507.

Snitow, Ann Barr. "Mass Market Romance: Pornography for Women is Different." *Desire: The Politics of Sexuality*. Ed. Ann Barr Snitow, Christine Stansell, and Sharon Thompson. London: Methuen, 1984: 258–75.

Spender, Dale. *Mothers of the Novel*. Pandora: London, 1986.

Squier, Susan M. *Virginia Woolf and London: The Sexual Politics of the City*. Chapel Hill: University of North Carolina Press, 1985.

Steeves, Edna, ed. *The Plays of Mary Pix and Catharine Trotter*. 2 vols. New York: Garland, 1982.

Stone, Lawrence. *The Family, Sex and Marriage in England 1500–1800*. New York: Harper, 1977.

Strachey, Lytton. *Elizabeth and Essex: A Tragic History*. New York: Harcourt Brace, 1928.

———. *Eminent Victorians: Cardinal Manning, Florence Nightingale, Dr. Arnold, General Gordon*. Harmondsworth: Penguin, 1971.

Sulloway, Frank. *Freud: Biologist of the Mind*. London: Burnett, 1979.

Symons, Donald. "Beauty Is in the Adaptations of the Beholder: The Evolutionary Psychology of Human Female Sexual Attractiveness." *Sexual Nature, Sexual Culture*. Ed. Paul R. Abramson and Steven D. Pinkerton. Chicago: University of Chicago Press, 1995: 80–118.

Tickner, Lisa. *The Spectacle of Women: Imagery of the Suffrage Campaign 1907–14*. London: Chatto & Windus, 1987.

Trumbach, Randolph. "London's Sapphists: From Three Sexes to Four Genders in the Making of Modern Culture." *Body Guards: The Cultural Politics of Gender Ambiguity*. Ed. Julia Epstein and Kristina Straub. New York: Routledge, 1991: 112–41.

Tulberg-McWilliams, Rita. "Women and Degrees at Cambridge University, 1862–67." *A Widening Sphere: Changing Roles of Victorian Women*. Ed. Martha Vicinius. Bloomington: Indiana University Press, 1977: 117–45.

Uglow, Jennifer. *George Eliot*. New York: Virago/Pantheon, 1987.

Walker, William. *Locke, Literary Criticism, and Philosophy*. Cambridge: Cambridge University Press, 1994.

Wallen, Kim. "The Evolution of Female Sexual Desire." *Sexual Nature, Sexual Culture*. Ed. Paul R. Abramson and Steven D. Pinkerton. Chicago: University of Chicago Press, 1995: 57–79.

Watkins, Daniel. *Sexual Power in British Romantic Poetry*. Gainesville: University Press of Florida, 1996.

Watt, Ian. *The Rise of the Novel*. Berkeley: University of California Press, 1967.

Watson, J. R. "A Note on the Date in the Title of "'Tintern Abbey.'" *The Wordsworth Circle* 10 (1979): 379–80.

Weber, Samuel. *The Legend of Freud*. Minneapolis: University of Minnesota Press, 1980.

Williams, Linda. *Viewing Positions: Ways of Seeing Film*. New Brunswick: Rutgers University Press, 1995.

Williams, Raymond. *Marxism and Literature*. Oxford: Oxford University Press, 1977.

Witemeyer, Hugh. *George Eliot and the Visual Arts*. New Haven: Yale University Press, 1979.

Wittenberg, Judith. "Angles of Vision and Questions of Gender in *Far from the Madding Crowd*." *The Centennial Review* 30 (1986): 25–40.

Wolff, Janet. "The Invisible *Flâneuse*: Women and the Literature of Modernity." *The Problems of Modernity: Adorno and Benjamin*. Ed. Andrew Benjamin. London: Routledge, 1989: 141–56.

Wotton, George. *Thomas Hardy: Towards a Materialist Criticism*. Totowa, NJ: Barnes & Noble, 1985.

Yeazell, Ruth Bernard. *Fictions of Modesty: Women and Courtship in the English Novel*. Chicago: University of Chicago Press, 1991.

Index

Page numbers in italics refer to figures.